The Problems with Teamwork, and How to Solve Them

This book offers practical, evidence-based solutions to help professionals implement and support effective teamwork. Lantz, Ulber and Friedrich draw on their considerable professional experience to present common problems in team-based organizations, what empirical research tells us the causes are and which solutions are more effective in overcoming team-based obstacles.

In *The Problems with Teamwork, and How to Solve Them*, nine common problems are identified, ranging from lack of leadership and adaptability to conflict and cohesiveness, accompanied by clear instructions on how to approach and resolve the individual issues. Detailed case studies are presented throughout the book, demonstrating how theory can be applied to real-life situations to produce optimal results for both the team and the larger organization. By combining theory and practice, and using state-of-the-art research, the book constructs a cognitive map for identifying problem causes and effects, and step-by-step instructions on how to solve the problems.

This is essential reading for anyone working in team-based organizations, as well as students and academics in related areas such as organizational psychology and organizational behaviour.

Annika Lantz is a professor of psychology at the University of Stockholm, Sweden. Her main research interests are team development, leadership and innovation processes. She also works as a consultant for Fritz Change AB and has worked as a psychotherapist and supervisor in private practice.

Daniela Ulber is a professor at HAW Hamburg University, Germany. Her research focuses on organizational development, management and coaching as well as systemic and solution-orientated consulting in organizations.

Peter Friedrich, Dr., is a senior consultant at Fritz Change AB, Sweden, with expertise in organizational development, action research and cross-cultural studies of innovation processes. He has an academic background in industrial engineering, and is a former researcher at the Swedish National Institute of Occupational Health and Safety and the Wiesbaden Business School.

"Lantz, Ulber and Friedrich have achieved a rare integration of deep scientific research and extensive experience with work teams grappling with tough problems. They provide a cogent and powerful guide for how to create teams that fulfil the potential of humans working cooperatively together in small, skilled collectives to meet the challenges they face. This book is not some superficial appeal to vague notions of positivity in working together but rather a rich source of knowledge about how to ensure we work effectively together in teams in ways that make the best use of our human emotional and cognitive capacities to perform at the highest levels. It is a gift for both researchers and practitioners."

—*Michael West, Lancaster University, UK*

The Problems with Teamwork, and How to Solve Them

Annika Lantz, Daniela Ulber and Peter Friedrich

LONDON AND NEW YORK

First published 2020
by Routledge
2 Park Square, Milton Park, Abingdon, Oxon, OX14 4RN

and by Routledge
52 Vanderbilt Avenue, New York, NY 10017

Routledge is an imprint of the Taylor & Francis Group, an informa business

© 2020 Taylor & Francis

The right of Annika Lantz, Daniela Ulber and Peter Friedrich to be identified as authors of this work has been asserted by them in accordance with sections 77 and 78 of the Copyright, Designs and Patents Act 1988.

All rights reserved. No part of this book may be reprinted or reproduced or utilised in any form or by any electronic, mechanical, or other means, now known or hereafter invented, including photocopying and recording, or in any information storage or retrieval system, without permission in writing from the publishers.

Trademark notice: Product or corporate names may be trademarks or registered trademarks, and are used only for identification and explanation without intent to infringe.

Library of Congress Cataloging-in-Publication Data
A catalog record for this book has been requested

ISBN: 978-0-367-17286-2 (hbk)
ISBN: 978-0-367-17288-6 (pbk)
ISBN: 978-0-429-05602-4 (ebk)

Typeset in Gill Sans
by Apex CoVantage, LLC

 Printed in the United Kingdom by Henry Ling Limited

Contents

List of figures and tables		vii
Case study		ix
Acknowledgements		xi
1	Why work in teams, and for what are teams effective?	1
2	The problem with problem-solving	30
3	We have teams but little teamwork	48
4	Team composition: "We have a team, but team members do not benefit from each other"	77
5	The team does not carry out the tasks in a coordinated manner	107
6	The team does not cooperate adequately due to conflicts and a lack of a positive and amicable climate	137
7	The problem with lack of adaptability	163
8	The teams do not perform well because of a lack of good leadership	189
9	Teamwork and team learning do not result in organizational learning	217
10	Requirement specification of systematic team interventions	251
11	Effective teams over time	278
Index		299

Figures and tables

Figures

1.1	The performance chain	14
1.2	A model of team effectiveness	20
2.1	The problem-solving circle	45
3.1	Mindmap about causes of problems with little teamwork	54
4.1	Mindmap about causes of problems with team composition	80
5.1	Mindmap about main causes of a lack of coordinated performance	110
6.1	Mindmap about reasons why teams do not cooperate adequately due to interpersonal issues	140
7.1	Model for the team adaptation process	169
7.2	Mindmap about causes for team's lack of adaptation	170
8.1	Mindmap about why leadership causes ineffective teamwork	193
8.2	Team leadership tasks in transition and action phase	196
9.1	An example of multilevel learning processes	223
9.2	An example of OL – platforms for communication and cooperation in and between teams and support functions in a production system	225
9.3	Mindmap about causes for inefficient embeddedness of OL in TL	228
10.1	The book's key concepts for describing team effectiveness put in the IMOI model	257
11.1	Examples of the role of interventions for teamwork development	290

Tables

1.1	Results from survey on positive outcomes of teamwork for the individual, team and the organization, according to managers, team members working in production teams, consultants, researchers and students working in project teams	7
1.2	Relative performance as a function of group size	15
1.3	The most common problems in teams according to managers, team members in production teams, consultants, researchers and students working in project teams	22
3.1	Interventions in different domains for a suitable work design	70
3.2	An example of how interventions are mutually dependent	72
4.1	Variables for the assessment of team members	81
4.2	Personality facets related to teamwork	82

4.3	Questions for the identification of solutions for problems with team composition	94
4.4	Domains for designing measures for team composition	95
5.1	Domains in which solutions to enhance coordinated performance in the action phase can be found	124
6.1	Domains for designing measures for team climate and conflict management	153
7.1	Domains for solutions to a problem with adaptation	181
8.1	Domains for designing measures for team leadership	208
9.1	Questions for diagnosing the embeddedness of OL into TL	238
9.2	Domains for developing teamwork for OL	239
10.1	A description of team interventions, aim, target dimensions and timing of intervention	261
10.2	An example of a CMO configuration	269
11.1	Examples of behavioural markers for the selection and monitoring of TDIs	293

Case study

Chapter 2 *The way a problem is addressed hinders the implementation of a solution*

Chapter 3 *Low task inter-dependence and goal un-clarity within teams lead to lack of teamwork*

Chapter 4 *Team composition and the associated little willingness to work together contribute to poor results*

Chapter 5 *Team processes inhibit team members combining and making the best use of their emotional and cognitive capacities to perform at the highest levels*

Chapter 6 *Conflict between team members leads to a hostile atmosphere and suboptimal stakeholder satisfaction*

Chapter 7 *Team members are reluctant to change habitual routines and adapt to new management strategy*

Chapter 8 *A lack of strong and considerate leadership depletes team morale and reduces efficiency*

Chapter 9 *Organizational Learning Strategy does not make use of company-wide teamwork*

Acknowledgements

Special thanks to the many teams and managers who worked with us and gave us the opportunity to give examples of what teamwork in real life is about. Our thanks to Richard Martin for so carefully reading most of the book and helping us overcome our difficulties with the English language. For some chapters, Leonie Stüdemann was a helpful proofreader and gave support in managing the references. We also thank Margarete Imhof, Nancy-Meyer-Adams, Nancy and David Caple who offered useful suggestions for improvements, too. Thanks also to Jasmine Low who inspired our thinking about team facilitation processes and tools. Lastly, to Sara Henrysson Eidvall who gave us valuable feedback after reviewing the book.

Chapter 1

Why work in teams, and for what are teams effective?

It is often said: "The whole is more than the sum of its parts." But does teamwork create outcomes for the organization, the team and the employees that are greater than what the individuals by themselves accomplish? This is a central issue as this book is based on the assumption that investing in teams is worthwhile. The book's general aim is that the reader should learn more about how to implement and support effective teamwork. We first describe the motives for working in teams and the outcomes of teamwork. Second, the concept of team effectiveness is discussed to distinguish between more effective and less effective teams. No two teams are alike, and teamwork is a dynamic process of social interactions that occur in an organizational context. We present a model of effective teamwork that takes into account the context. We have identified nine core problems with teamwork. The model is used throughout the book to understand, and find solutions to these common problems in teamwork.

1 Why work in teams?

1.1 The social brain and our social nature

Throughout evolution people have lived and worked in families and groups. Doing things together, whether it is hunting, building shelter or bringing up children, has been shown to be more rewarding and effective than doing things in isolation. Maslow (1943) identified our basic love and esteem needs as motivational forces. In the well-known pyramid of needs, Maslow put physiological and safety needs, such as physical shelter and food at the base. Higher up the pyramid, social and esteem needs are found. These are not essential for survival. Maslow put self-actualization on the top. The prominent psychologist and neuroscientist Liebermann argues that this is wrong. "Our biology is built to thirst for connection because it is linked to our most basic survival needs" Lieberman (2013, p. 43). He explains how three major adaptations in the brain lead us to be connected to the social world, to take advantage of social connections and to form and work in groups. Throughout evolutionary steps mammals evolved to feel social pains and pleasures, and our well-being is linked to the desire to be socially connected. Primates have developed the ability to mindread, and this capacity allows us to interact strategically and anticipate the needs of others. This is one component of what some call emotional intelligence. Neural adaptations throughout evolutionary history have allowed us to be influenced by others and be socialized by those around us, and harmonizing is essential for group interaction.

1.2 Working more effectively

Many organizations structure their work around teams based on the belief that teamwork can be beneficial to organizational effectiveness. *Why is that so?* We summarize the many motives for implementing teamwork into three main categories:

Working harder. Group dynamics can result in employees naturally working harder, stimulated and motivated by working together towards a common goal. Seeing and monitoring what others do motivates many to show the better sides of themselves. It is important to note that there may be a negative outcome to peer pressure. Working tightly together may result in team members watching each other closely and exerting strong pressure to achieve high levels of team performance.

Working more smartly. Salas, Burke, and Cannon-Bowers (2000) argue that teamwork may also lead employees to work more efficiently. In traditional working systems, production problems can often only be solved by functional specialists, whereas self-managing teams are capable of solving problems as soon as they occur, thus reducing interruptions to the production process. Teams can take on more complex tasks than individuals. Team members combine different and complementary competences and skills, support one another, provide backup behaviour, monitor work progress and balance individual's workload. Team members can monitor and assess the situation and scan the environment to identify cues indicating that they need to adapt work routines (Goodwin, Blacksmith, & Coats, 2018). West (2012) advocates that quality management is increased, and innovations and changes are eased – as team members have different points of views, experiences, knowledge and skills; so they challenge and discuss decisions, proposals and processes from these perspectives and can find new approaches and procedures.

Organizational change and development. In the last decades, environments have become more turbulent and dynamic. There is increasing global competition and increasing demands for individualized and specialized products and services. This means that organizations require flexibility to adapt to novel demands. A team structure is a good answer to such requirements, as teams can be connected and involved when needed. For example, different teams can communicate about good practice and can cooperate to meet special demands. Furthermore, teams may identify imminent changes in the external surrounding, and adapt to proactively ensure that these changes are met. Teamwork simplifies organizational structure and reduces the need for coordination. Decentralizing decision-making to teams can reduce the number of supervisors and middle managers. A flatter hierarchy has positive implications for faster reactions to external changes, to the implementation of organizational strategies and to intra-organizational coordination. A team-based organization can lead to improvements of efficiency (e.g. lower costs and process times). Many lean-based organizations are based on the idea that "teamwork is the pillar for process innovation" (Netland & Aspelund, 2013).

2 Many groupings are called teams – the outcomes depend on if it is a team or not

In some cases, loosely connected employees are called a team even though team members hardly communicate while working. If the question "do you work as a team?" is asked in workplaces, the answer would often be yes despite work tasks being carried out individually, possibly coordinated, but team members are not dependent upon each other for doing their jobs. In such cases, it is often the aggregation of individual tasks that is meant by "being a team," or that there is a positive climate and people help each other. It is important to distinguish work teams from other groupings, as loose groupings of individuals with little need to interact do not develop interaction patterns that enable the group to accomplish the positive outcomes described earlier.

2.1 A team definition

In the literature, most researchers rely on a definition of a team in line with how Kozlowski and Bell (2013) define a work group:

> Groups are composed of two or more individuals, share one or more common goals, exist to perform organizationally relevant tasks, exhibit task interdependencies, interact socially, maintain and manage boundaries, and are embedded in an organizational context that sets boundaries, constrains the team, and influences exchanges with other units in the broader entity.
>
> (p. 415)

The general team definition gives guidance in what a team is, but others have tried to characterize the team interaction, in order to distinguish between all those groupings that are called teams, and those that work as teams. West and Lyubovnikova (2012) identified four characteristics that distinguish teams from "pseudo-teams." These "pseudo-teams" are groups whose members mainly carry out their work individually. Teams are characterized by a specific way of interacting:

Reflexivity: Teams discuss, reflect upon and evaluate their ongoing work and cooperation. They review their performance systematically, while pseudo-teams' communication is rather restricted to e.g. the sharing of information for coordination of individual tasks. Teams *reflect* on habitual routines, such as how to coordinate work, and how these habitual routines might impede effectiveness and satisfaction – an opportunity to develop a shared understanding of the tasks and how to perform.

Task interdependence: Tasks vary a lot in how closely team members need to work together to fulfil the task, as will be shown in Chapter 3. Task interdependence is the degree to which members of the team are mutually dependent on the others. High task interdependence means that the main task requires that the team members work in close collaboration to fulfil subtasks that are coordinated and aligned with overall goals. Task interdependence puts demand on collective regulation processes, and a shared understanding about what to do and how. Low interdependence puts higher demand on coordination mechanisms as team members have little to do with one another, and less of a shared understanding of how to carry out the work.

Shared objectives: In pseudo-teams there is a lack of a shared understanding of what the goal is, and what the team should strive for. A team has a shared understanding of a common goal that *regulates* what different team members do and how.

Boundedness: In a team, members (more or less) identify with their specific team. Pseudo-teams are permeable to a degree that creates uncertainty about who the team players are, and the cohesion is low. If team members do not have a sense of belonging to the team, they will be less motivated to contribute to the team and invest less in creating relationships with the others. Teams may be geographically dispersed and, in an emergency, teams can form quickly and comprise team members who do not know each other, but still share a sense of boundedness at that specific time. Furthermore, team members may work in different teams, which may affect the sense of belonging. With fluid boundaries and multiple memberships, team members are bounded in varying degrees to different teams. Bonding to several teams, and to several people, forming special relationships with each may be possible.

2.2. No two teams are the same

Some consultants sell products off the shelves, such as interventions, that are marketed as enhancing team effectiveness in *any* team. The rationale would be that all teams somehow are the same, and the context does not matter. But we all know that teams are not created equal. Salas, Reyes, and McDaniel (2018) write, "[T]here are countless factors that affect the makeup of the team and subsequently influence the team's interactions" (p. 595). Teams differ in a number of aspects that impact interaction and outcomes. This cannot be stressed enough, as it has vast consequences for how to solve problems in teamwork and the design of interventions. Teams differ in many ways: temporal stability, life span, virtuality, team composition, skill differentiation, task interdependence and the decision-making process. *Each team is uniquely composed to serve a specific purpose within a specific context.* It is not possible to address problems with teamwork by making a list of all sorts of different teams, describing each teams' prerequisites and challenges. Instead we should look into what is known about the transportable mechanisms that make smooth teamwork possible.

> *To summarize:* It is not enough for employees grouped together to be called a team. No two teams are alike. Team members are interdependent and engage in both work task, and interpersonal related processes.

3 What is teamwork?

Teamwork is the means by which the team carries out the task by doing it together. *Individual task work* is the component of team member performance that does not demand interdependent interactions with other team members, while *teamwork* is defined as the interdependent component of performance by the team members. "Teamwork is about cooperative actions that facilitate dealing with task objectives and realizing coordinated, adapted performance" (Haar, Segers, & Jehn, 2013, p. 2).[1] It is a description of all kinds of team processes that stem from the individuals' interrelated thoughts, feelings and actions that are needed for them to function as a team. These psychosocial processes are combined to "facilitate coordinated, adaptive performance and task objectives resulting in value-added outcomes" (Salas, Sims, & Burke, 2005, p. 562). *Key aspects are coordination and adaptation.* The team needs to carry out the task in a coordinated manner, and the team needs to change its habitual routines to adapt to changes and new demands.

3.1 Teamwork is to engage in interpersonal and task-work processes

Team members are interdependent and hence must integrate, synthesize, share information, coordinate, cooperate and reflect on results and work processes, both throughout and after a performance episode to accomplish and evaluate their task and the results. Doing so, they engage in both task-work processes and interpersonal processes. Task work is obviously what the team is doing with its tasks, tools, machines, systems, etc. to accomplish a result. By interpersonal is meant those interpersonal processes that are salient over time, such as building trust, confidence and a friendly atmosphere, or managing conflicts. A sense of trust – or the lack of it – will impact not only on how the team cooperates and on team performance, but also on team learning and team adaptation. Chapter 6 explores this in greater detail.

3.2 Processes generate emergent states

Teams develop routinized patterns of interaction. Over time, teams tend to form patterns in how they think, feel and act. Over time, processes become *emergent states*: habitual ways of thinking, relatively stable affective states and typical patterns of behaviour. Over time these emergent states/phenomena change: as team members and leaders encounter and adapt to new situations and integrate new information, they will think, feel and behave differently. An emergent state is a process that one measures or observes at a specific moment, and it may be a more or less stable characteristic of the team process. Kozlowski and Ilgen (2006, p. 81) describe these as *indicative of the nature and quality of the processes*: "[E]mergent states, and routinized behaviour patterns are the echoes of repeated process interactions." Emergent states have been shaped by processes in the past, regulate the present processes and form future processes. DeChurch and Mesmer-Magnus (2010) *define team processes as the nature of team interaction,* whereas *emergent states enable and regulate effective teamwork.* Processes are most often divided into behavioural, affective and cognitive processes, as well as emergent states.

3.3 Effective teams shift between action and transition phase

Depending on what problem researchers have been interested in, they have categorized team processes in different ways to suit the problem at hand. Some researchers have found it fruitful to distinguish between what is happening when the team is in an action phase and when it is in a transition phase. Building on Marks, Mathieu, and Zaccaro (2001) work, Maynard, Kennedy, and Sommer (2015, p. 655) describe what team members do during action phases: "Members address task accomplishment, monitoring progress and systems, coordinating with team members, as well as monitoring and backing up teammates."

During a transition phase, there are specific team processes that enable the team to change habitual routines and adapt to new demands. Transition phases occur when a team moves from one performance to another, and use this phase for critical reflection on the previous work experience in order to bring meaningful change about. Team members engage in mission analysis, planning, goal clarification and specification, and form strategies for the future (Marks et al., 2001; Maynard et al., 2015). Adaptation processes in the transition phase are described in Chapter 7.

Making the distinction between action phase and transition phase is to split a work process into activities and thinking about the work process. These two processes may follow one another sequentially, or they may run in parallel. Researchers such as Konradt, Otte, Schippers, and Steenfatt (2016) argue that reflexivity is a process that takes place during both transition and action phases of teamwork.

> *To summarize:* Team processes inhibit or enable team members to combine their behaviours and capabilities to reach their end result. Core characteristics of effective teamwork are smooth coordination and adaptation. Depending on the issue at hand, researchers have different ways of categorizing and understanding team processes. One example is the distinction between action and transition phase, another is to split teamwork into task-work performance and interpersonal relations. Over time, team processes become emergent states, and these are more or less stable characteristics of processes. Emergent states tell us about the nature and quality of those processes, and also guide future processes.

4 Outcomes of teamwork

It is often said: "The whole is more than the sum of its parts." As individuals differing in knowledge, skills, qualifications, experiences, personal traits and other individual factors come together, they complement each other, and make use of these capabilities. But is the whole more than the sum of its parts? Does teamwork create outcomes for the organization, the team and the employees that are greater than what the individuals by themselves accomplish?

4.1 What are the outcomes of teamwork according to those who know a lot about it?

Before writing this book, we made an explorative study and asked about 15 managers, 25 experienced team members, 25 experienced consultants and psychologists, 30 researchers, and 40 students working in project teams: "What are the positive outcomes of teamwork according to your knowledge and experience?" The informants identified a range of positive outcomes of well-functioning teamwork. These were clustered into themes, and the results are shown in Table 1.1.

The results could be structured into three groupings of positive outcomes. When teamwork works well it is beneficial for the individual, the team and the organization. The different groups of informants had somewhat different focus, but all described

Table 1.1 Results from survey on positive outcomes of teamwork for the individual, team and the organization, according to managers, team members working in production teams, consultants, researchers and students working in project teams

Outcome	Managers	Team members working in production teams	Consultants	Researchers	Students working in project teams
For the organization	Productivity	A more effective work	Synergies 1+1=3	Necessary for complex problem-solving	Enables complex problem-solving
	Efficiency	Higher individual performance	New ideas through different perspectives	Continuity	Easier to carry out boring and frustrating tasks
	Flatter hierarchy	Fast and smooth work flow	Complementing competencies for better results	Backup behaviour and mutual support	Different perspectives lead to better results
	A more simple organizational structure	Adaptations of work flow to everyday events	Change and development of work routines	Better transfer of individual knowledge to business processes	The work gets more structured
	Adaptability through change and development	Unexpected events are better dealt with	Commitment	Productivity	More efficient work
	Low turnover	Different competencies for problem-solving	Team can easily evaluate their performance	Learning on all levels	Possible to take on larger and more complex projects
	Reduction in costs for competence-development	Newcomers learn rapidly	New perspectives on how to learn from each other	Shared leadership	Faster (productivity)
		Flexibility	Feedback	Better work environment: Health, well-being and reduced stress	Team members are more motivated and do more
		Stable processes	Reflexivity and learning		
		Rapid response to new demands and changes	More effective problem-solving		
		All understand the work assignments in the same way	Mutual performance monitoring		
For the team	Cohesion	No statements	Transparency in individual task work and teamwork	Reflexivity	Team learns to better handle future setbacks
	Motivation to take on more challenging tasks in the future		Develop shared leadership	Collective learning is an outcome in itself	Cohesion that enables future projects
	When good results the team gains belief in efficacy		Mutual learning	After a performance cycle the team has a history that is an input to future performance	
	Mutual learning			Team viability	

(Continued)

Table 1.1 (Continued)

Outcome	Managers	Team members working in production teams	Consultants	Researchers	Students working in project teams
For team members	More fun to go to work A sense of being needed and important An essential part of good working conditions Life-long learning	Personal development Competence-development Mutual understanding between different groups functions A more varied work Reduced workload Does not need to know or learn everything Less stress A sense of being needed More meaningful work	Not having to know everything Fun and stimulating to be with others A sense of being important to others and for work Meaningfulness A sense of belonging Solidarity Increased understanding of own work role and its importance for others Learning Participation Creativity Helping each other and support	A sense of being needed Understanding of how the workflow is part of the bigger system Belonging Learning Personal development Reduced workload	Inspiration and motivation Energy to complete boring tasks Learning from others Solidarity Participation in decisions Cannot procrastinate Reduced workload Training in teamwork for future work in real life Belonging Self-reflection and insights in who I am Less psychological strain as one is not alone Fun New perspectives on the task

similar dimensions and listed hundreds of positive reasons to work in teams. Most stated the positive outcomes for the individual, such as learning and job satisfaction, and all informants noted the outcomes for the organization. Not as many described outcomes for the team. Let's discover if empirical research supports our informants' positive description of teamwork.

4.2 Does empirical research support the professionals' experience?

Researchers have studied different aspects of teamwork and related these to different outcomes, such as innovation, productivity, team learning, and job satisfaction. This is one way to find out if teamwork brings about positive outcomes. Research shows how different aspects of the team's functioning affect outcomes, e.g. how team cohesion affects the team's performance. If many studies report consistent findings, it is possible to draw the conclusion that there is a positive relationship between different aspects of team interaction and outcomes. We learn what the key triggers for certain outcomes are, and this is useful information for enhancing team effectiveness. Another more difficult option is to compare teamwork with other ways of working to see if there is a difference in outcomes. This is to answer the question if teamwork is better than other ways of working. Researchers have done both, but the latter kind of studies are rare, as it takes a much more complicated research design.

What then are the outcomes of teamwork according to empirical research? The outcomes of teamwork can be gauged in many ways, but as teams have different tasks in different organizations, it is impossible to study and report on all contextually driven outcomes of teamwork. In a restaurant, the chef and the staff in the kitchen jointly produce something that is a very different result from a team within elderly care.

Mathieu and Gilson (2012) make a distinction between two fairly general forms of criteria for team outcomes, namely tangible outcomes (e.g. reduction of costs) and team members' reactions (e.g. job satisfaction). The distinction is not clear-cut, but by tangible it is meant that the outcome can be measured by objective or external measures. Other constituencies of team functioning, such as customer satisfaction (e.g. Kirkman, Rosen, Tesluk, & Gibson, 2006), organizational safety (e.g. Smith-Jentsch, Mathieu, & Kraiger, 2005) and conservation (also known as green practices) (Kim, Kim, Han, Jackson, & Ployhart, 2017; Kozlowski, & Bell, 2013), have been featured (but far less often) and are also important outcomes or by-products of team activities.

4.2.1 What does teamwork mean for the individual?

In work psychology the principle of "social and societal embeddedness" in terms of communication and interaction is seen as an important criterion for humane work (Ulich & Weber, 1996; Volpert, 1992). The origins of team effectiveness research is often traced to the Hawthorne studies conducted at the Western Electric Company during the 1920s and 1930s (see e.g. Salas et al., 2008). The Hawthorne Works commissioned a study to see if workers became more productive in higher or lower levels of light. The workers' productivity seemed to improve when changes in lighting were made, no matter for good or for worse, and slumped when the study ended. The results were interpreted as productivity was raised as a result of the motivational effect on the workers by being grouped in experimental and control groups, and of the interest being shown in them from the researchers.

There are abundant empirical findings showing positive effects of work-related social support on mental health and on quality of working life in general (de Lange, Taris, Kompier, Houtman, & Bongers, 2003; Stansfeld & Candy, 2006; Taris & Kompier, 2014). But social needs can be met in different ways, and exchange of social support exists in most workplaces, team-based or not. Does teamwork impact individuals' work-related attitudes, competence, well-being, personal growth and their contribution to the completion of overall goals? Decades of research show at the individual level of analysis, members' performance measured with criteria such as productivity (e.g. O'Reilly & Roberts, 1977), contributions to the team (e.g. Price, Harrison, & Gavin, 2006), helping behaviours (e.g. Gonzalez-Mulé, DeGeest, McCormick, Seong, & Brown, 2014) and reduction of absence (e.g. Duff, Podolsky, Biron, & Chan, 2014; Mathieu & Kohler, 1990) are examples of tangible outcomes.

Reaction criteria, such as work-related attitudes, have been a commonly studied output of teamwork in research. Work attitudes, such as job satisfaction (e.g. Pritchard, Jones, Roth, Stuebing, & Ekeberg, 1988; Rasmussen & Jeppesen, 2006; Van der Vegt, Emans, & Van de Vliert, 2001), turnover intentions (e.g. Chen, Sharma, Edinger, Shapiro, & Farh, 2011) and reduced symptoms of depression (e.g. Parker, 2003) are examples of reaction criteria. Many studies have been conducted in health care where well-functioning cooperation is essential for good care, e.g. Kristensen et al. (2015) showed that teamwork impacted nurses' perceptions of their general quality of work. Fay, Shipton, West, & Patterson (2014) have consistently shown how teamwork in combination with HR-practices affect attitudinal outcomes in health care.

In many studies both kinds of outcomes have been targeted. In line with previous research, mutual support in teams promotes job satisfaction, health and reduces stress and burnout rates (van Dick & Haslam, 2012). For partly autonomous work groups Ulich and Weber (1996) reported the following positive tangible effects for individuals: enhancement of skills and qualification and reaction criteria outcomes as high intrinsic motivation. Work motivation is "a psychological process that influences how personal effort and resources are allocated to actions pertaining to work, including the direction, intensity, and persistence of these actions" (Kanfer, Chen, & Pritchard, 2008, p. 5). Intrinsic motivation is the self-desire to do something, to seek out challenges and to gain competence. It is driven by interest in the task itself, rather than being driven by external pressures or rewards (extrinsic motivation). Bacon and Blyton (2003) showed in a longitudinal study that teamwork has a positive impact on employees' perception of skills development, which supports previous findings. Delarue, Van Hootegem, Procter, and Burridge (2008) showed that the large-scale use of teamwork correlates with lower levels of absenteeism, whereas a study by Glassop (2002) found that firms with teams had lower levels of employee turnover. In a meta-analysis Richter, Dawson, and West (2011) found that staff who work in teams report higher levels of commitment and involvement (reaction criteria), and also show lower stress levels than those who do not work in teams (tangible outcomes). Correlation, r, is a measure of the strength, and shows a positive or negative direction, of the linear relationship between two variables. The factor r varies between -1 to $+1$, where 1 is the strongest relationship. In a meta-analysis, results from several studies are combined, and the results are more valid than those of a single study. It is possible to calculate the average correlation (r) corrected for the measurement error. The sign for the corrected correlation is rho = ρ.

These results have been repeated over and over.

To *summarize:* The informants' descriptions of how well-functioning teamwork affects the individual in a positive way are well supported by empirical research. Research has shown that important outcomes are tangible outcomes such as helping behaviour and reduction of absence, and reactions e.g. job satisfaction and reduction in turnover intentions.

4.2.2 Outcomes for the team

Members' collective emergent states (a pattern in how the team thinks, feels and behaves) have been featured as reactive outcomes for the team itself. When discussing reactive outcomes we are faced with the question of the chicken or the egg. Some concepts are the result of experiences of teamwork over time but can also be said to be a state characterizing the team interaction. On the team level, team efficacy is well recognized in the literature as a reactive output of well-functioning teamwork, but it is also an emergent state in the team interaction. Team efficacy is analogous to self-efficacy but on a collective level (Gully, Incalcaterra, Joshi, & Beaubien, 2002). Self-efficacy is defined as a personal judgement of how well one can execute courses of action required to deal with prospective situations (Bandura, 1982). Self- and team efficacy is related to confidence. Stajkovic (2006) conceptualizes self-efficacy as one manifest variable of core confidence, which comprises hope, self-efficacy, optimism and resilience. Confidence is one's (or the team's) belief in the ability to handle job demands for any given domain of related activities. Without such confidence the team will not take on more challenging tasks, or leave its comfort zone in that domain. It is the result of previous experiences of successfully accomplishing different tasks through teamwork. Team efficacy is hence hypothesized to influence what the team does (goal setting), persistence when meeting obstacles and in overcoming hindrances, and in how much effort it will exert, i.e. team efficacy will impact behaviour. A meta-analysis of Gully et al. (2002) supports these assumptions. They found a significant correlation of $\rho = .41$ between team efficacy and team performance outcomes.

Some researchers including Sy, Côté, and Saavedra (2005) regard affective tone to be an outcome of teamwork. It can also be argued that it is what characterizes the team interaction. Another example is cohesion which is regarded by some as an outcome of teamwork (e.g. Greene & Schriesheim, 1980; Gully, Devine, & Whitney, 2012). It is also a concept used for describing the forces that bring the team together and a feature of team interaction. It describes the team members' commitment to the team, "the resultant of all the forces acting on the members to remain in the group" (Festinger, 1950, p. 254). The results of a meta-analyses by Beal, Cohen, Burke, and McLendon (2003) revealed stronger correlations between cohesion and performance when performance was defined as behaviour (as opposed to outcome). Mathieu, Kukenberger, D'Innocenzo, and Reilly (2015) also conducted a meta-analytic study to examine how cohesion and performance criteria are related. They found that cohesion and performance criteria were reciprocally and positively related over time. What comes first – the chicken or the egg? The "cohesion impacts performance" relationship was significantly higher than the "performance impacts cohesion" relationship. Further, over time the "cohesion impacts performance" relationship became stronger, while the "performance impacts cohesion" was the same over time. Moreover, team learning is part of team interaction and can be considered also as an outcome, at least at a specific time-point. This is because when team members share their expertise and get into a mutual learning process they create knowledge (West, 2012). Knowledge can be regarded as an outcome, but will impact a future performance episode.

The constructs presented here can be regarded as both descriptions of team interaction and outcomes of interaction. There is growing agreement that team viability is an outcome of teamwork. Team viability is defined as the "team's capacity for the sustainability and growth required for success in future performance episodes" (Bell & Marentette, 2011, p. 279). Maybe some readers have experienced and can recognize the feeling of relief after completing a project in a team that does not function well. "Now it is done, and never again will I work in this team." Or "Next time I will do it on my own." Team viability is the opposite: What can we take on together as a team next, that is even more challenging? Team viability has shown to be supported on the team level by team processes such as cohesion, coordination, good ways of communication and problem-solving (e.g. Druskat & Wolff, 1999; Kozlowski & Bell, 2013). Team proactivity is linked to team viability and has shown to be an important outcome of team interaction and is linked to organizational change and development (Barker, 1993; Lantz Friedrich, Sjöberg, & Friedrich, 2016). Crant (2000) compared four constructs of proactive behaviour. These included: proactive personality, personal initiative, extra-role behaviour and taking charge. It was concluded that they overlap conceptually and capture an individual's propensity to engage in proactive behaviour. The construct can be adapted to team level and be defined as: "[T]eam proactivity entails voluntary and constructive efforts, by a team, to effect functional organizational change with respect to how work is executed within the contexts of the jobs, work units, or organizations" (Lantz, 2011, p. 77). It is to go beyond the routine task work, take the initiative to change and carry out developmental activities, i.e. to be part of innovation processes. A recent literature review showed that both individual and team proactive behaviour is increased by good leadership, favourable team and organizational climates, support from the organization and high quality interactions between team members (Cai, Parker, Chen & Lam, 2019). Especially team learning impacts the team's propensity to go beyond the stipulated task, and proactively engage in change and developmental activities (Lantz, Friedrich, &., 2016).

> *To summarize:* Empirical research has shown that teamwork results in outcomes on a team level, and some of these outcomes such as cohesion and team learning can be regarded as both descriptions of team interaction and outcomes of interaction. Team viability is an outcome of teamwork.

4.2.3 Outcomes for the organization

In a review of empirical research on the links between teamwork and outcomes, Delarue et al. (2008) found that the many studies on this topic had investigated a wide range of performance indicators. To systemize previous findings on these results, Delarue et al. (2008) distinguished between operational outcomes for the organization and financial outcomes. The former would include productivity (e.g. the number of hours to assemble a transmission), the quality of the product or service, innovation and customer satisfaction and flexibility. The financial outcomes include the value-added per employee and return on capital employed and profitability.

In the analysis of team interaction, various antecedents have been associated with tangible outcomes such as productivity (e.g. McEwan, Ruissen, Eys, Zumbo, &

Beauchamp, 2017; Pepinsky, Pepinsky, Minor, & Robin, 1959); efficiency (e.g. Shuffler, Pavlas, & Salas, 2012; Wiest, Porter, & Ghiselli, 1961); work quality (e.g. Maier & Hoffman, 1961); retention (e.g. Hausknecht & Trevor, 2010); proactive behaviour (Cai, Parker, Chen & Lam, 2019), creative outcomes (e.g. Cohen, Whitmyre, & Funk, 1960); and innovation processes (e.g. Lantz Friedrich et al., 2016). The references show that organizational performance outcomes have been studied for many years, and extensive research supports the assumption that teamwork shows a positive impact on organizational performance outcomes and financial outcomes (e.g. Delarue et al., 2008; Richter et al., 2011).

> *To summarize*: Empirical research has shown that teamwork positively impacts organizational outcomes such as productivity, efficiency, work quality and innovation processes.

4.3 Outcomes on different levels are interlinked

The reaction criteria outcomes for the individuals are important. They impact the employees' behaviour that in turn impacts outcomes for the team and organization. Motivated and satisfied team members contribute more to the team process than those who are not, as we will see in Chapter 3. Further, the work-related attitudinal outcomes affect other outcomes for the team and the organization. In a meta-analysis Whitman, Van Rooy, and Viswesvaran (2010) found that the relationship between job satisfaction and performance is significant (ρ = .34). Specifically, significant relationships were found between job satisfaction and productivity, customer satisfaction organizational citizenship behaviours (OCB) and withdrawal (reversed relationship). Organizational citizenship behaviour (OCB) is a concept describing the employees' willingness to take on tasks and responsibilities that go beyond the pre-described work task. Organ (1988) defines OCB as "individual behavior that is discretionary, not directly or explicitly recognized by the formal reward system, and that in the aggregate promotes the effective functioning of the organization" (p. 4). Organ's definition of OCB includes three critical aspects that are central to this construct: First, OCBs are thought of as discretionary behaviours, which are not part of the job description, and are performed by the employee as a result of personal choice. Second, OCBs go above and beyond the enforceable requirements of the job description. Finally, OCBs contribute positively to overall organizational effectiveness. It is a behaviour characterized by persistence of enthusiasm, supporting and giving assistance to others, rule and prescribed procedure following, and openly defending the organizations objectives (Borman & Motowidlo, 1993). Supporting others could affect the team's functioning and the outcome for the team itself.

In a review of teamwork and organizational performance Delarue et al. (2008) come to the conclusion that "changes in work organization (the introduction of teams) can have a direct impact on employee behavior (e.g. less absenteeism) and, subsequently, on operational performance (higher productivity), which, in turn, can contribute to higher levels of financial performance (higher profits)" (p. 131). This is called a "performance chain" (see Figure 1.1). We can conclude that over time, outcomes for the individual will impact what the individual does, and this in turn will impact outcomes for the team itself, and the organization. The outcomes on different levels are interlinked in a performance chain.

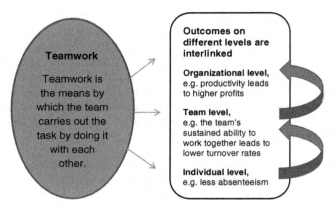

Figure 1.1 The performance chain

Teamwork can of course result in outcomes on one level only, or several, and a performance chain may occur or not.

4.4 Outcomes depend on the organizational context

We have shown that there is extensive research showing that teamwork has a positive impact on the performance chain, but *positive effects of teamwork cannot be generalized over all organizational contexts*. A meta-analysis of 61 studies by Richter et al. (2011) showed that teamworking in general has significant, but only small or moderate effects on organizational performance and personal attitudes (such as satisfaction, commitment and aspects of well-being). The extent of the relationship with effectiveness criteria depends on the organizational context. For instance, if accompanying human resource management measures are implemented and in what sector an organization is situated. Delarue et al. (2008) came to the same conclusion. Out of 21 studies, 18 showed a positive relationship between the implementation of teamwork and performance outcomes. The review showed that teamworking had positive impact on attitude, behaviours, organizational performance and financial outcomes. In line with Richter et al.'s findings their results showed that when teamwork is combined with structural change, performance can be further enhanced.

4.5 The negative sides of teamwork

Most people have an experience of teamwork and many have felt the joy of accomplishing things together, and getting good and rewarding results. Sometimes teamwork functions very well, but teamwork is not always efficient or rewarding. The first article on teamwork was published more than 100 years ago and highlighted a social phenomenon well known by most team workers. Maximilien Ringelmann (1913), a French agricultural engineer, researched the relative performance as a function of group size. In a most famous experiment he studied how much force people use at rope-pulling. People pulling together as a team exerted less effort than individuals. The more people pulling, the less force was applied individually (the social loafing effect).

WHY WORK IN TEAMS?

The phenomenon social loafing has been studied for more than a hundred years, and most scholars refer to Ringelmann as the first researcher who documented the effect. Kravitz and Martin (1986) took great effort in finding the original works, and since this is one of the most referred to experiments within social psychology, it might be interesting to see some of Ringelmann's results (see Table 1.2). Details of the task the workers carried out in the experiment are not mentioned by Ringelmann, but by co-workers who later wrote that it was rope-pulling.

Table 1.2 Relative performance as a function of group size

Number of workers	Furnished per worker	Work usable in practice
1	1.00	1.00
2	0.93	1.86
3	0.85	2.55
4	0.77	3.08
5	0.70	3.50
6	0.63	3.78
7	0.56	3.92
8	0.49	3.92

Note: This table is a translation and copy of the table given on page 9 of Ringelmann (1913).

Searching these early works, Kravitz and Martin (1986) found that Ringelmann explicitly stated that similar performance decrements had been observed in draft animals. Humans are social animals indeed.

Not only social loafing decreases team effectiveness. Experimental research has shown that decision-making in teams, for example, may be less effective than individual decision-making (Ladbury & Hinsz, 2009). This may be more problematic as the joint decision may be less accurate than if the most competent person would take the decision. Doing things together can be more rewarding than doing things individually, but social interaction is complex, sometimes complicated, and most experienced team workers have also seen the challenges presented by teamwork.

As researchers within the field we find *a tendency to romanticize teamwork* both among researchers themselves and in organizations (and not to talk about many consultants). Investing in a team-based organization needs to have a sound rationale for doing so. It also needs clear and explicit expectations of specified outcomes. The rationale must be in line with how teamwork is implemented, designed and supported. The work-organizational solution needs to be in alignment with other organizational features.

To summarize: Outcomes are found on individual, team and organizational levels, and the effects of teamwork on outcomes are moderate. Many aspects of how an organization is structured and other processes within an organization affect the outcomes as well. Negative outcomes of teamwork have been found as well. Nevertheless, there is substantial support for us to say yes, teamwork is more effective than other work forms, but it depends on a) the context and b) the team interaction.

5 What are performance, team effectiveness and efficiency?

We discussed performance and touched upon team effectiveness earlier. As the word performance has different meanings, and performance, effectiveness and efficiency are related, it is important to define the different concepts in this context.

Performance is what people do. Salas et al. (2008) stress that performance is a process, arising as team members engage in managing their individual- and team level task work together with interpersonal processes. Performance ultimately depends upon the objectives of the particular organization. Kozlowski and Ilgen (2006) state that what teams strive to *do* in order to achieve a goal, resolve task demands and coordinate activities is their performance. Different results from the team depend on how the team does things to achieve outcomes. Productivity is the assessment of this behaviour to achieve the different performance criteria. We will go into depth in the coming chapters to describe performance in different aspects. Here it is enough to say that performance is behaviour; it is what people do, and the result of this behaviour can be evaluated by different performance criteria related to the outcome, as shown earlier.

What then is team effectiveness? A dictionary defines effective as "adequate to accomplish a purpose; producing the intended or expected result." A team is effective when it accomplishes what it is supposed to do within given prerequisites. The key here is that what it is "supposed to do" is not always so obvious. A team is interlinked to other teams and specialists, and exists in a workflow that will put external demands on the team. *Team effectiveness is the result of dynamic team processes, which depends on a broader system context that drives team task demands* (Kozlowski & Ilgen, 2006). Each organization has an overall goal, key values and a culture that set the rules for how things should be done. Task demands are always determined by the surrounding organizational system. Sometimes they may be contradictory or vague, and different stakeholders, such as customers and labour unions, may have different priorities. Salas, Rosen, Burke, and Goodwin (2009) describe the team's ability to adapt its performance processes in response to changes in the external demands from the surrounding system as a first core characteristic of teamwork.

> Team performance accounts for the outcomes of the team's actions regardless of how the team may have accomplished the task. Conversely, team effectiveness takes a more holistic perspective in considering not only whether the team performed (e.g., completed the team task) but also how the team interacted (i.e., team processes, teamwork) to achieve the team outcome.
>
> (Salas et al., 2005, p. 557)

Kozlowski and Ilgen (2006) describe the essence of team effectiveness pragmatically: "When team-processes are aligned with environmentally driven task demands, the team is effective: when they are not, the team is not" (p. 78). That is, when the performance is in line with others' expectations of what the team should accomplish, the team is effective. The team is effective when the team's cognitive, motivational/ affective and behavioural resources are appropriately aligned with task demands (DeChurch & Mesmer-Magnus, 2010). As said, performance criteria are always contextually determined, as teams' tasks differ. What is effective in one context may be counterproductive in another.

Efficiency is to accomplish a task or a job with the minimum expenditure of time, effort and resources.

> *To summarize:* So far we have identified two core aspects of teamwork: the task work – and the social interaction that influence how the work is carried out. These are the core processes, and it cannot be stressed enough. To adapt the team's performance processes and to enhance the effectiveness, the team needs to reflect upon, identify and alter habitual routines that impede effectiveness in these two core aspects of teamwork. This ensures that their performance and the outcome are achieved in line with stakeholders' expectations.

6 A model to describe effective teamwork

Team effectiveness has been studied in different cultures and contexts and from a wide range of perspectives. The research is vast. More than 50 years ago, McGrath (1964) proposed a descriptive Input-Process-Outcome (IPO) model for studying team phenomena. Inputs form and shape team processes, and are found on three levels: Team members are individuals and differ in many respects e.g. competencies, attitudes and personality (individual level). On a team level, we find team design: team composition, the nature of the task or problem that is the focus and main input to team processes and work design. The task is obviously the most important input. On an organizational level aspects such as support to the teams, leadership, organizational structure such as hierarchy, how different teams and functions are integrated, organizational culture, etc. will impact team interaction. Inputs describe antecedents in the context and situation that enable and constrain team members' interactions (processes). In line with e.g. Kozlowski and Bell (2003) and many others we classify team processes according to whether they are cognitive, affective/motivational or behavioural in nature. Contextual and situational inputs are dealt with by making use of and coordinating these cognitive, affective and behavioural resources through team member interaction. These processes drive and impact the outcomes.

The static IPO model has been interpreted causally, and although contemporary perspectives on team effectiveness often use the basic logic in the IPO, and we do too, we *stress the dynamic process* that underlies it. Researchers over the years have criticized the simplicity of the IPO. For instance Ilgen, Hollenbeck, Johnson, and Jundt (2005) proposed an Input-Mediator-Outcome-Input (IMOI model), rather than the IPO model. The IMOI model describes team performance and development as a cycle of relations between inputs, mediators, outcomes and (second) inputs.

Major research reviews have shown that team processes not only impact, but drive outcomes of teamwork. There is solid and growing evidence that team processes *mediate* (M) the relation between input factors and outcomes, and P in process is instead called M as mediator. This means that the relationship between A and B goes through a factor C (mediating factor). An example: How difficult the task is and the demand on problem-solving (A) impacts how much the team partakes in change and developmental activities (B), through learning processes (C).

> Theoretically one can distinguish between roots to a problem, what causes a problem and what impacts a problem. A factor is considered a root cause if its removal prevents the final undesirable outcome from recurring, whereas a causal factor is one that directly affects an event's outcome, but is not a root cause. Impacting factors can influence for example the strength of a relationship between A and B (moderating factor) or the relationship between A and B goes through a factor C (mediating factor).

The IMOI-researchers emphasize the importance of interactions between different elements. One example: Team cognition, such as thinking about how things can be done more productively, together with the feelings of mutual trust and amicability and the behaviours required to carrying out the tasks such as coordinating and communicating, are interlinked. Collective regulation encompasses all that team members do to direct their efforts toward the goal (Johnson, Smith, Wallace, Hill, & Baron, 2015). Team members have knowledge about how to perform and accomplish the task to reach the end result, and this knowledge regulates activities when team members communicate about work, i.e. cognitive processes and behaviour are inter-related. Emotions, such as the degree of openness and trust, will affect how team members can share thoughts and build knowledge. Further, some phenomena exist on different levels, and this implies that there might be an interaction between levels. A few examples: Adaptation is a multi-level phenomenon; it exists on an individual level, team level and organizational level, and hence there might be interaction effects between these levels that impact the adaptation outcome. Another example: Individuals learn and teams learn, and how an individual learns impacts the teams' learning. These levels are inter-related, and to draw conclusions about how team learning affects an outcome, one should consider the interaction effect between individual and team learning, as well as the unique impact of the individual's and the team's learning on the outcome.

Teamwork develops over time through episodic and/or cyclical processes. Most often different cognitive, affective and behavioural processes are studied in relation to team performance effectiveness, and researchers assess these at a specific time (or longitudinally over several lagged time-points). Although the processes are dynamic, what one can measure is in that moment a state. Over time teams develop relatively stable patterns in how they think, perform their task, feel and how they relate. Processes yield emergent states. Kozlowski and Bell (2013) characterize emergent states as dynamic, interactive, multilevel, process oriented and temporal in nature. Team phenomena and constructs, e.g. team trust, are not static, but emerge upwards from individuals to the team level, and the emergence is not linear, e.g. it is not as if a low level of trust in the beginning automatically will develop into complete trust over time. The emergence is maybe episodic or cyclical. Episodic means that it develops through a series of separate events that might occur occasionally or at irregular intervals. Cyclical means the development goes through cycles occurring repeatedly. Some phenomena may need more time to evolve than others. Maybe it goes more rapidly to form a state of amicable climate rather than a state of collective efficacy. A team may be engaged in team learning processes for a period of time, then there is a time for making use of that learning, or there is nothing that triggers learning, and the learning activities are paused. Perhaps learning is needed again, and maybe how the team learns is due to past experiences.

Feedback loops exist during the developmental processes. The second input, the *I* in the IMO*I*, is what was learned over time or during a performance cycle. The lessons learned about how and why contextual factors and processes resulted in certain outcomes, or why they did not. These lessons learned can be fed back, and if so the *I* will impact future performances. The second input creates a feedback loop and might bring change about in the inputs that will feed another performance cycle for the team, but it might also give input to change the team processes and the emergent states. The notion of cyclical causal feedback is essential for understanding how teams develop. The second *I* needs to be made use of, and it can be used in an ongoing developmental process part of daily work, or be used when forming a systematic team intervention. We will come back to how teams develop in Chapters 10 and 11. An example: During a performance cycle a team learned to be self-managing and this resulted in higher collective efficacy and team viability. This output might be fed back and result in the team having more autonomy, more leeway in forming their work and different leadership style (work design and leadership as contextual input factors).

Mathieu, Maynard, Rapp, and Gilson (2008) capture the general framework of previous extensive research on team effectiveness in a model that is presented in Figure 1.2. The model serves our purposes for addressing how inputs, processes and outcomes are inter-related in a multi-level context. It serves our purposes as two teams are not the same but still can be described by certain characteristics that are transportable. These can be used irrespective of team and task when analyzing what impedes team effectiveness. Some will be more important than others for a specific team. As a consequence, we do not use typologies such as project teams, production teams, academic teams, etc. These teams are not the same, although they can be grouped into a category in one respect. Each team has a set of certain characteristics, and we cover a wide range of such characteristics that can be used to describe a specific team. It is noted that each characteristic, and the mix, will differ between teams. Using examples of different teams, such as senior management teams or virtual teams, we will highlight how different teams and their specific mix of team design features will impact that team's specific interactions and challenges. We will use the IMOI model to guide us through this book, see Figure 1.2.

Figure 1.2 shows that individual members who comprise the team as a collective entity also provide a context that influences individual team members. Linkages across multiple levels (team members, team context and organizational context) are key resources or demands that necessitate aligned team processes in order for the team to be effective. Contemporary perspectives on team effectiveness regard teams as part of a multilevel system. They put emphasis on the dynamic nature of teamwork.

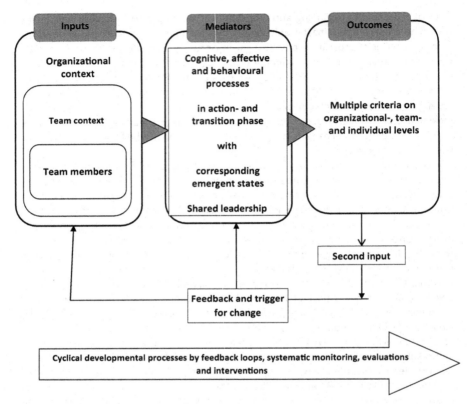

Figure 1.2 A model of team effectiveness
Source: (Mathieu et al., 2008)

They view team processes as emergent phenomena that develop over time in specific contexts. In summary, the evidence over many years of research (e.g. Lacerenza et al., 2018; Lepine et al., 2008; Mathieu et al., 2017) has made it clear that a) different team processes are linked with one another over time, b) the different processes are each associated with important team outcomes, and c) different mechanisms can be employed to enhance such processes.

7 The aim and the outline of the book

In this book we have a normative perspective on what is effective teamwork. It is to perform routine task work, and to go beyond the stipulated work and engage in non-routine work to implement meaningful change to meet changing demands in the environment, and improve the environment. Outcomes of such performance are found on an individual, team and organizational level. This requires adaptation to new circumstances or demands by altering routines and how the work is carried out to balance performance and novel demands. One characteristic of an effective

WHY WORK IN TEAMS?

team is team adaptation – see the definition of team effectiveness. It is individual and team learning that engages teams in the development of organizational structures and processes. These enhance the overall organization performance, i.e. to give input to others so they can learn from and make use of what is learned within the team.

The book's general aim is that the reader should learn more about how to implement and support effective teamwork, and how to solve problems in teams. It raises the reader's understanding of the complex systemic interactions among elements on different levels in the context and processes that develop over time. Such an understanding should help the reader to assess the value of more simplistic models of how teams are described. This includes the popular stage models in which all teams (no matter what the task or makeup of the team) are described as to go through certain phases during a life-span. By understanding the elements and the interactions in the IMOI model, the reader can describe a specific team and understand what needs to be addressed to support that specific team. The book combines practice and theory. The starting point is problems/challenges that we encounter in most workplaces. Instead of writing a text-book explaining theory, and hoping that the reader will apply what is relevant for a specific problem, we got inspired by the approach: "We have a problem regarding teamwork in real life – how can theory help us solve it?" To select core obstacles for effective teamwork, we first conducted a literature review on what are the most commonly reported problems with teamwork. A next step was to analyze answers in our survey (discussed earlier): "What are the most common challenges with teamwork?" The answers were clustered into descriptions of core problems. In this way we identified a range of issues that all those who work in, or support teamwork, might need to cope with, and deal with in order to make teamwork more worthwhile. *The book is structured around these core problems.*

7.1 The most common problems with teamwork according to the informants in our study

In Table 1.3 we summarize the problems that were identified as important problems to cope with in order to enhance effectiveness according to the informants in our study. They could be grouped regarding organizational/situational factors impacting team interaction; teamwork as task work, social processes, together with the lack of outputs for the organization, and problems with interventions.

We have structured the book around the problems in Table 1.3. Two chapters are focused on contextual and situational aspects that affect teamwork, and the importance of, and problems in setting the stage for teamwork (Chapter 3 on work design, and Chapter 4 on team composition). Leadership is both a contextual aspect that impacts teamwork, and it is a process. In Chapter 8 leadership is described by how it can support teamwork. Four chapters are focusing on team processes and outcomes of teamwork. These include the problems in handling routine-task performance (Chapter 5); handling interpersonal relations and conflicts that impede effectiveness (Chapter 6); lack of learning and adaptation (Chapter 7); and lack of team input to organizational learning (Chapter 9). In Chapter 10 the focus is on interventions and we address the problem that so many efforts to enhance team effectiveness fail and we describe what is known about evidence-based solutions and team development in general. In Chapter 11 it is shown how different concepts and solutions discussed

Table 1.3 The most common problems in teams according to managers, team members in production teams, consultants, researchers and students working in project teams. Bold letters indicate the largest category of descriptions for respective group of respondents.

	Input (Contextual/situational aspects)			Processes			Output	Interventions
	Category 1: Work design	Category 2: Team composition	Category 3: Leadership	Category 4: Coordination	Category 5: Climate and conflicts	Category 6: Adaptation	Category 7: Organizational learning	Category 8: Interventions
Managers	(1) It is not clear nor for team or team leaders what the team members should do together or accomplish as a team	(2) We have the employees we have, and difficult to know how to compose optimal teams	(3) Team leaders have problems being both a work-mate and a leader	**(4) Difficulties in coordination due to inadequate communication**	(5) Managers compete rather than cooperate in top management teams	(6) We want proactive and self-managerial teams but the teams are reactive and dependant	We have set goals for change and development but we focus on daily productivity	We support teams in real trouble, but mainly we rely on them developing themselves, and they don't. Too little time spent on evaluation, and planning for developing future performance
Team members working in production teams	(1) We are organized in teams, but carry out our work tasks individually	(2) One does not like each other on a personal level	(3) Someone takes on leadership tasks, and it is not always the right person	**(4) Different opinions on how to carry out tasks**	(5) Conflicts are not openly discussed or dealt with	(6) We are more than busy doing what needs to be done. We know what should be done, but no time and energy for that, so we do as we have always done	No statements	No statements
Consultants	(1) Teamwork is implemented without clarity about what for, and tasks are standardized or unsuitable for teamwork	(2) The team cannot make use of and benefit from different perspectives and competences	**(3) Lack of clear leadership and diffusion of work roles between team leaders and team members**	(4) Communication problems, misunderstandings and too little communication about how to work together	(5) Conflicts due to lack of clarity of goals and work roles	(6) The team is stagnant and works the way it always has	Much talk about teams' contribution to change and development, but learning is not a priority and there are rarely platforms for exchange between teams and different professional groups	Often more far-reaching interventions are needed that involve organizational issues and leadership, but most clients want a quick fix and that we work only with the team

Researchers	**(1) Pseudo-teams instead of real teams** (2) Lack of teamwork competence causes conflicts and this is much more important than personality (3) Far too often a misunderstanding of self-managerial teams: all teams need leadership	(4) Lack of shared understanding of work, goals, and teamwork and difficult to balance workloads (5) Conflict management is always a challenge, and task and personal conflicts go together which makes it even more difficult (6) Collective learning is based on systematic reflection and that is what most often is lacking	Teamwork rarely impacts changes in the surrounding system as most teams lack knowledge of what others do and how they can contribute. Lack of transparency is a major problem.	We know a great deal about the effects of interventions, but very little about what makes them work
Students working in project teams	(1) We are grouped in teams for the only reason that it reduces the professors' workload. The task can be carried out individually and we receive individual grades (2) Very often differences in motivation, investment in teamwork and competence. Some prefer to work by their own. (3) Someone takes on being the team leader without discussion or agreement	(4) Difficult to carry out the project when no consensus of how to work and what to achieve, and some do more and some do less **(5) Conflicts and misunderstandings due to personal differences and slackers always create trouble** (6) No statements	No statements	We don't get help to solve conflicts and it is difficult for us to handle problems in the team by our own – sometimes it affects learning a lot

WHY WORK IN TEAMS?

in the book are interlinked, and fit into the IMOI model from a time perspective. In this chapter we discuss the problem with reactive interventions rather than formative proactive interventions.

To implement successful teamwork and overcome barriers that hinder successful implementation requires competence in problem-solving and implementation processes. A common error in managing issues/problems with teamwork is to jump to interventions before a thorough analysis of what causes the problem has been carried out. It is the causes that are hindrances that should be eliminated, and not the symptoms. Most often there are several causes to a problem. Throughout the book we describe and follow the rationale in the "problem-solving circle." This will be explained in Chapter 2. An observation from practice is that often the *way problems are tackled in the workplace, is a problem in itself.* The attempts made to solve an issue/problem may be unsuccessful, due to lack of understanding of the basic elements in the problem-solving process, and this problem might be the most common problem of all.

Note

1   Task work refers to the actions needed to carry out a specific duty that contributes to the overall goal. Teamwork, on the other hand, deals with the interdependent interactions between members of a team while they work toward a specific goal (Salas et al., 2005).

Bibliography

Bacon, N., & Blyton, P. (2003). The impact of teamwork on skills: Employee perceptions of who gains and who loses. *Human Resource Management Journal, 13*(2), 13–29. https://doi.org/10.1111/j.1748-8583.2003.tb00088.x

Bandura, A. (1982). Self-efficacy mechanism in human agency. *American Psychologist, 37*, 122–147.

Barker, J. R. (1993). Tightening the iron cage: Concertive control in self-managing teams. *Administrative Science Quarterly, 38*(3), 408. https://doi.org/10.2307/2393374

Beal, D. J., Cohen, R. R., Burke, M. J., & McLendon, C. L. (2003). Cohesion and performance in groups: A meta-analytic clarification of construct relations. *Journal of Applied Psychology, 88*(6), 989–1004. https://doi.org/10.1037/0021-9010.88.6.989

Bell, S. T., & Marentette, B. J. (2011). Team viability for long-term and ongoing organizational teams. *Organizational Psychology Review, 1*(4), 275–292. https://doi.org/10.1177/2041386611405876

Borman, W. C., & Motowidlo, S. J. (1993). Expanding the criterion domain to include elements of contextual performance. In N. Schmitt & W. C. Borman (Eds.), *Personnel selection in organizations* (pp. 71–98). San Francisco: Jossey-Bass.

Cai, Z., Parker, S. K., Chen, Z., & Lam, W. (2019). How does the social context fuel the proactive fire? A multilevel review and theoretical synthesis. *Journal of Organizational Behavior, 40*(2), 209–230. https://doi.org/10.1002/job.2347

Chen, G., Sharma, P. N., Edinger, S. K., Shapiro, D. L., & Farh, J.-L. (2011). Motivating and demotivating forces in teams: Cross-level influences of empowering leadership and relationship conflict. *Journal of Applied Psychology, 96*(3), 541–557. https://doi.org/10.1037/a0021886

Cohen, D., Whitmyre, J. W., & Funk, W. H. (1960). Effect of group cohesiveness and training upon creative thinking. *Journal of Applied Psychology, 44*(5), 319–322. https://doi.org/10.1037/h0041655

WHY WORK IN TEAMS? | 25

Crant, J. M. (2000). Proactive behavior in organizations. *Journal of Management, 26*(3), 435–462. https://doi.org/10.1177/014920630002600304

DeChurch, L. A., & Mesmer-Magnus, J. R. (2010). The cognitive underpinnings of effective teamwork: A meta-analysis. *Journal of Applied Psychology, 95*(1), 32–53. https://doi.org/10.1037/a0017328

de Lange, A. H., Taris, T. W., Kompier, M. A. J., Houtman, I. L. D., & Bongers, P. M. (2003). 'The very best of the millennium': Longitudinal research and the demand-control-(support) model. *Journal of Occupational Health Psychology, 8*(4), 282–305. https://doi.org/10.1037/1076-8998.8.4.282

Delarue, A., Van Hootegem, G., Procter, S., & Burridge, M. (2008). Teamworking and organizational performance: A review of survey-based research. *International Journal of Management Reviews, 10*(2), 127–148. http://10.0.4.87/j.1468-2370.2007.00227.x

Druskat, V. U., & Wolff, S. B. (1999). Effects and timing of developmental peer appraisals in self-managing work groups. *Journal of Applied Psychology*. US: American Psychological Association. https://doi.org/10.1037/0021-9010.84.1.58

Duff, A. J., Podolsky, M., Biron, M., & Chan, C. C. A. (2014). The interactive effect of team and manager absence on employee absence: A multilevel field study. *Journal of Occupational and Organizational Psychology, 88*(1), 61–79. https://doi.org/10.1111/joop.12078

Fay, D., Shipton, H., West, M. A., & Patterson, M. (2014). Teamwork and organizational innovation: The moderating role of the HRM context. *Creativity and Innovation Management, 24*(2), 261–277. https://doi.org/10.1111/caim.12100

Festinger, L. (1950). Informal social communication. *Psychological Review*. US: American Psychological Association. https://doi.org/10.1037/h0056932

Glassop, L. I. (2002). The organizational benefits of teams. *Human Relations: HUM RELAT, 55*. https://doi.org/10.1177/0018726702055002184

Gonzalez-Mulé, E., DeGeest, D. S., McCormick, B. W., Seong, J. Y., & Brown, K. G. (2014). Can we get some cooperation around here? The mediating role of group norms on the relationship between team personality and individual helping behaviors. *Journal of Applied Psychology, 99*(5), 988–999. https://doi.org/10.1037/a0037278

Goodwin, G. F., Blacksmith, N., & Coats, M. R. (2018). The science of teams in the military: Contributions from over 60 years of research. *American Psychologist, 73*(4), 322–333. https://doi.org/10.1037/amp0000259

Greene, C. N., & Schriesheim, C. A. (1980). Leader-group interactions: A longitudinal field investigation. *Journal of Applied Psychology, 65*(1), 50–59. https://doi.org/10.1037/0021-9010.65.1.50

Gully, S. M., Devine, D. J., & Whitney, D. J. (2012). A meta-analysis of cohesion and performance. *Small Group Research, 43*(6), 702–725. https://doi.org/10.1177/1046496412468069

Gully, S. M., Incalcaterra, K. A., Joshi, A., & Beaubien, J. M. (2002). A meta-analysis of team-efficacy, potency, and performance: Interdependence and level of analysis as moderators of observed relationships. *Journal of Applied Psychology, 87*(5), 819–832. https://doi.org/10.1037/0021-9010.87.5.819

Haar, S. R., Segers, M., & Jehn, K. (2013). Towards a contextualized model of team learning processes and outcomes. *Educational Research Review, 10*. https://doi.org/10.1016/j.edurev.2013.04.001

Hausknecht, J. P., & Trevor, C. O. (2010). Collective turnover at the group, unit, and organizational levels: Evidence, issues, and implications. *Journal of Management, 37*(1), 352–388. https://doi.org/10.1177/0149206310383910

Ilgen, D. R., Hollenbeck, J. R., Johnson, M., & Jundt, D. (2005). Teams in organizations: From input-process-output models to IMOI models. *Annual Review of Psychology, 56*(1), 517–543. https://doi.org/10.1146/annurev.psych.56.091103.070250

Johnson, P., Smith, M., Wallace, C., Hill, A., & Baron, R. (2015). A review of multilevel regulatory focus in organizations. *Journal of Management, 41*(5), 1501–1529. https://doi.org/10.1177/0149206315575552

Kanfer, R., Chen, G., & Pritchard, R. D. (2008). The three C's of work motivation: Content, context, and change. In R. Kanfer, G. Chen, & R. D. Pritchard (Eds.), *Work motivation: Past, present, and future* (pp. 1–16). New York: Routledge.

Kim, A., Kim, Y., Han, K., Jackson, S. E., & Ployhart, R. E. (2017). Multilevel influences on voluntary workplace green behavior: Individual differences, leader behavior, and coworker advocacy. *Journal of Management, 43*(5), 1335–1358. https://doi.org/10.1177/0149206314547386

Kirkman, B. L., Rosen, B., Tesluk, P. E., & Gibson, C. B. (2006). Enhancing the transfer of computer-assisted training proficiency in geographically distributed teams. *Journal of Applied Psychology, 91*(3), 706–716. https://doi.org/10.1037/0021-9010.91.3.706

Konradt, U., Otte, K.-P., Schippers, M. C., & Steenfatt, C. (2016). Reflexivity in teams: A review and new perspectives. *The Journal of Psychology, 150*(2), 153–174. https://doi.org/10.1080/00223980.2015.1050977

Kozlowski, S. W. J., & Bell, B. S. (2003). Work groups and teams in organizations. In W. C. Borman, D. R. Ilgen, & R. J. Klimoski (Eds.), *Handbook of psychology (vol. 12): Industrial and organizational psychology* (pp. 333–375). New York: Wiley.

Kozlowski, S. W. J., & Bell, B. S. (2013). Work groups and teams in organizations. In *Handbook of psychology: Industrial and organizational psychology* (Vol. 12, 2nd ed., pp. 412–469). Hoboken, NJ: John Wiley & Sons Inc.

Kozlowski, S. W. J., & Ilgen, D. (2006). Enhancing the effectiveness of work groups and teams. *Psychological Science in the Public Interest, 7*(3), 77–124. https://doi.org/10.1111/j.1529-1006.2006.00030.x

Kravitz, D., & Martin, B. (1986). Ringelmann rediscovered: The original article. *Journal of Personality and Social Psychology, 50*, 936–941. https://doi.org/10.1037/0022-3514.50.5.936

Kristensen, S., Hammer, A., Bartels, P., Suñol, R., Groene, O., Thompson, C. A., Wagner, C. (2015). Quality management and perceptions of teamwork and safety climate in European hospitals. *International Journal for Quality in Health Care, 27*(6), 499–506. http://dx.doi.org/10.1093/intqhc/mzv079

Lacerenza, C. N., Marlow, S. L., Tannenbaum, S. I., & Salas, E. (2018). Team development interventions: Evidence-based approaches for improving teamwork. *American Psychologist, 73*(4), 517–531. https://doi.org/10.1037/amp0000295

Ladbury, J. L., & Hinsz, V. B. (2009). Individual expectations for group decision processes: Evidence for overestimation of majority influence. *Group Dynamics: Theory, Research, and Practice, 13*(4), 235–254. https://doi.org/10.1037/a0015424

Lantz, A. (2011). Teamwork on the line can pay off down the line. *Journal of Workplace Learning, 23*(2), 75–96. https://doi.org/10.1108/13665621111108765

Lantz Friedrich, A., Sjöberg, A., & Friedrich, P. (2016). Leaned teamwork fattens workplace innovation: The relationship between task complexity, team learning and team proactivity. *European Journal of Work and Organizational Psychology, 25*(4), 561–569. https://doi.org/10.1080/1359432X.2016.1183649

Lepine, J. A., Piccolo, R., Jackson, C., Mathieu, J., & Methot, J. (2008). A meta-analysis of teamwork processes: Tests of a multidimensional model and relationships with team effectiveness criteria. *Personnel Psychology, 61*. https://doi.org/10.1111/j.1744-6570.2008.00114.x

Lieberman, M. D. (2013). *Social: Why our brains are wired to connect*. New York, NY: Crown Publishers and Random House.

Maier, N. R. F., & Hoffman, L. R. (1961). Organization and creative problem solving. *Journal of Applied Psychology, 45*(4), 277–280. https://doi.org/10.1037/h0041850

Marks, M. A., Mathieu, J. E., & Zaccaro, S. J. (2001). A temporally based framework and taxonomy of team processes. *Academy of Management Review, 26*(3), 356–376. https://doi.org/10.5465/amr.2001.4845785

Maslow, A. H. (1943). A theory of human motivation. *Psychological Review, 50*(4), 370–396. https://doi.org/10.1037/h0054346

WHY WORK IN TEAMS?

| 27

Mathieu, J. E., & Gilson, L. L. (2012). *Criteria issues and team effectiveness* (S. W. J. Kozlowski, Ed.). Oxford: Oxford University Press. https://doi.org/10.1093/oxfor chb/9780199928286.013.0027

Mathieu, J. E., Hollenbeck, J. R., van Knippenberg, D., & Ilgen, D. R. (2017). A century of work teams in the Journal of Applied Psychology. *Journal of Applied Psychology, 102*(3), 452–467. https://doi.org/10.1037/apl0000128

Mathieu, J. E., & Kohler, S. S. (1990). A cross-level examination of group absence influences on individual absence. *Journal of Applied Psychology, 75*(2), 217–220. https://doi. org/10.1037/0021-9010.75.2.217

Mathieu, J. E., Kukenberger, M. R., D'Innocenzo, L., & Reilly, G. (2015). Modeling reciprocal team cohesion: Performance relationships, as impacted by shared leadership and members' competence. *Journal of Applied Psychology, 100*(3), 713–734. https://doi.org/10.1037/a0038898

Mathieu, J. E., Maynard, M. T., Rapp, T., & Gilson, L. (2008). Team effectiveness 1997–2007: A review of recent advancements and a glimpse into the future. *Journal of Management, 34*(3), 410–476. https://doi.org/10.1177/0149206308316061

Maynard, M. T., Kennedy, D. M., & Sommer, S. A. (2015). Team adaptation: A fifteen-year synthesis (1998–2013) and framework for how this literature needs to "adapt" going forward. *European Journal of Work and Organizational Psychology, 24*(5), 652–677. https://doi.org/10.1080/1359432X.2014.1001376

McEwan, D., Ruissen, G. R., Eys, M. A., Zumbo, B. D., & Beauchamp, M. R. (2017). The effectiveness of teamwork training on teamwork behaviors and team performance: A systematic review and meta-analysis of controlled interventions. *PLoS One, 12*(1), e0169604. https://doi.org/10.1371/journal.pone.0169604

McGrath, J. E. (1964). *Social psychology: A brief introduction.* New York: Holt, Rinehart and Winston.

Netland, T. H., & Aspelund, A. (2013). Company-specific production systems and competitive advantage: A resource-based view on the Volvo production system. *International Journal of Operations & Production Management, 33*(11/12), 1511–1531. https://doi.org/10.1108/IJOPM-07-2010-0171

O'Reilly, C. A., & Roberts, K. H. (1977). Task group structure, communication, and effectiveness in three organizations. *Journal of Applied Psychology, 62*(6), 674–681. https://doi. org/10.1037/0021-9010.62.6.674

Organ, D. W. (1988). *Organizational citizenship behavior: The good soldier syndrome.* Lexington, MA: Lexington Books and D. C. Heath and Com.

Parker, S. K. (2003). Longitudinal effects of lean production on employee outcomes and the mediating role of work characteristics. *Journal of Applied Psychology, 88*(4), 620–634. https://doi.org/10.1037/0021-9010.88.4.620

Pepinsky, H. B., Pepinsky, P. N., Minor, F. J., & Robin, S. S. (1959). Team productivity and contradiction of management policy commitments. *Journal of Applied Psychology, 43*(4), 264–268. https://doi.org/10.1037/h0040646

Price, K. H., Harrison, D. A., & Gavin, J. H. (2006). Withholding inputs in team contexts: Member composition, interaction processes, evaluation structure, and social loafing. *Journal of Applied Psychology, 91*(6), 1375–1384. https://doi.org/10.1037/0021-9010.91.6.1375

Pritchard, R. D., Jones, S. D., Roth, P. L., Stuebing, K. K., & Ekeberg, S. K. (1988). Journal of applied psychology monograph: Effects of group feedback, goal setting, and incentives on organizational productivity. *Journal of Applied Psychology, 73*(2), 337–358. Retrieved from https://ezp.sub.su.se/login?url=http://search.ebscohost.com/login.aspx?direct=true&db=buh&AN=5111758&site=ehost-live&scope=site

Rasmussen, T. H., & Jeppesen, H. J. (2006). Teamwork and associated psychological factors: A review. *Work & Stress, 20*(2), 105–128. Retrieved from http://10.0.4.56/02678370600920262

Richter, A. W., Dawson, J. F., & West, M. A. (2011). The effectiveness of teams in organizations: A meta-analysis. *The International Journal of Human Resource Management, 22*(13), 2749–2769. https://doi.org/10.1080/09585192.2011.573971

Ringelmann, M. (1913). Recherches sur les moteurs animés: Travail de l'homme [Research on animate sources of power: The work of man]. *Annales de l'Institut National Agronomique, 12*(2nd series), 1–40. Retrieved from http://gallica.bnf.fr/ark:/12148/bpt6k54409695.image. f14.langEN

Salas, E., Burke, C. S., & Cannon-Bowers, J. A. (2000). Teamwork: Emerging principles. *International Journal of Management Reviews, 2*(4), 339–356. https://doi.org/10.1111/1468-2370.00046

Salas, E., Cooke, N. J., & Rosen, M. A. (2008). On teams, teamwork, and team performance: Discoveries and developments. *Human Factors, 50*(3), 540–547. https://doi.org/10.1518/001872008X288457

Salas, E., Reyes, D. L., & McDaniel, S. H. (2018). The science of teamwork: Progress, reflections, and the road ahead. *American Psychologist, 73*(4), 593–600. https://doi.org/10.1037/amp0000334

Salas, E., Rosen, M. A., Burke, C. S., & Goodwin, G. F. (2009). The wisdom of collectives in organizations: An update of the teamwork competencies. In *Team effectiveness in complex organizations: Cross-disciplinary perspectives and approaches* (pp. 39–79). New York, NY: Routledge and Taylor & Francis Group.

Salas, E., Sims, D. E., & Burke, C. S. (2005). Is there a "Big Five" in teamwork? *Small Group Research, 36*(5), 555–599. https://doi.org/10.1177/1046496405277134

Shuffler, M., Pavlas, D., & Salas, E. (2012). Teams in the military: A review and emerging challenges. In J. H. Laurence & M. D. Matthews (Eds.), *The Oxford handbook of military psychology* (pp. 282–310). New York, NY: Oxford University Press. https://doi.org/10.1093/oxfordhb/9780195399325.013.0106

Smith-Jentsch, K. A., Mathieu, J. E., & Kraiger, K. (2005). Investigating linear and interactive effects of shared mental models on safety and efficiency in a field setting. *Journal of Applied Psychology, 90*(3), 523–535. https://doi.org/10.1037/0021-9010.90.3.523

Stansfeld, S., & Candy, B. (2006). Psychosocial work environment and mental health: A meta-analytic review. *Scandinavian Journal of Work, Environment & Health, 32*(6), 443–462. Retrieved from www.jstor.org.ezp.sub.su.se/stable/40967597

Stajkovic, A. (2006). Development of a core confidence-higher order construct. *The Journal of Applied Psychology, 91*(6), 1208–1224. https://doi.org/10.1037/0021-9010.91.6.1208

Sy, T., Côté, S., & Saavedra, R. (2005). The contagious leader: Impact of the leader's mood on the mood of group members, group affective tone, and group processes. *The Journal of Applied Psychology, 90*, 295–305.

Taris, T. W., & Kompier, M. A. J. (2014). Cause and effect: Optimizing the designs of longitudinal studies in occupational health psychology. *Work & Stress, 28*(1), 1–8. https://doi.org/10.1080/02678373.2014.878494

Ulich, E., & Weber, W. G. (1996). Dimensions, criteria and evaluation of work group autonomy. In M. West (Ed.), *Handbook of work group psychology* (pp. 247–282). Chichester, UK: Wiley.

Van der Vegt, G. S., Emans, B. J. M., & Van de Vliert, E. (2001). Patterns of interdepence in work teams: A two-level investigation of the relationship with job and team satisfaction. *Personnel Psychology, 54*(1), 51–69. https://doi.org/10.1111/j.1744-6570.2001.tb00085.x

van Dick, R., & Haslam, S. A. (2012). Stress and well-being in the workplace: Support for key propositions from the social identity approach. In J. Jetten, C. Haslam, & S. A. Haslam (Eds.), *The social cure: Identity, health and well-being.* (pp. 175–194). New York, NY, US: Psychology Press.

Volpert, W. (1992). Work design for human development. In R. Keil-Slawik, C. Floyd, H. Züllighoven, & R. Budde (Eds.), *Software development and reality construction* (pp. 336–348). Berlin: Springer-Verlag.

West, M. (2012). *Effective teamwork: Practical lessons from organizational research* (3rd ed.). Oxford: Blackwell.

West, M., & Lyubovnikova, J. (2012). Real teams or pseudo teams? The changing landscape needs a better map. *Industrial and Organizational Psychology, 5*(1), 25–28. https://doi.org/10.1111/j.1754-9434.2011.01397.x

Whitman, D. S., Van Rooy, D. L., & Viswesvaran, C. (2010). Satisfaction, citizenship behaviors, and performance in work units: A meta-analysis of collective construct relations. *Personnel Psychology, 63*(1), 41–81. https://doi.org/10.1111/j.1744-6570.2009.01162.x

Wiest, W. M., Porter, L. W., & Ghiselli, E. E. (1961). Relationship between individual proficiency and team performance and efficiency. *Journal of Applied Psychology, 45*(6), 435–440. https://doi.org/10.1037/h0046225

Chapter 2

The problem with problem-solving

In this chapter we present a general methodology suitable for dealing with problems which arise when using teamwork. This methodology ensures that a problem is tackled efficiently and that the interventions chosen target the core problems and bring about functional change. Ill-managed problem-solving can be both de-motivating and unproductive. Based on empirical research, the chapter shows the steps from problem to solution; from a thorough description of the current situation from different perspectives that results in consensus about the core problem, an analysis of its causes, to forming the intervention and evaluating the results. We will use this methodology throughout the book and apply it to specific problems in each chapter. This chapter provides the reader with a tool to avoid the very way in which a problem is tackled becoming in itself a major obstacle to bringing about effective and meaningful change.

In this book we address a range of problems which impact the team's performance and effectiveness. The starting point for solving problems with teamwork is a thorough analysis of the current situation and an awareness that something needs to be done to change it for the better. In an organization, the gap between "this is how it is" and "this is how we want it" needs to be frankly acknowledged by those concerned, and the discrepancy needs to be substantial enough to provide the motivation to actually do something. D'Zurilla and Nezu (1988) defined problem-solving as a: "[C]ognitive – affective – behavioral process through which an individual (or group) attempts to identify, discover, or invent effective means of coping with problems encountered in everyday living." With a well-defined problem it is simple to set specific goals and so form well-defined solution paths from which clear solutions can be expected. Many workplaces are characterized by several ongoing different change-and-developmental activities: sometimes so many it is difficult to manage them all and they seem unending. Ill-managed problem-solving can over time be de-motivating for those who are once again involved in changing habitual routines. They can also be non-productive if the original cause of the problem remains unchanged. Hence knowing about, and making use of good practice in evidence-based problem-solving lies at the heart of organizational and team development.

To show the importance of a methodology for solving practical problems in the workplace, we first present a case. We have chosen an authentic and complicated case as it illustrates a) a common problem with problem-solving and b) a common problem when implementing teamwork.

CASE: THE WAY A PROBLEM IS ADDRESSED HINDERS THE IMPLEMENTATION OF A SOLUTION

The case: The head of a national authority with branches throughout the country gathered the managers of all local offices to a conference and presented the new organizational strategy: the implementation of teamwork in all offices. The current situation was described: the public's expectations of levels of service and new services; the need to speed up decision-making (productivity) and efficiency. The need for change and to work more effectively was explained in several ways. After the overall goal had been stated, a guest consultant gave a workshop to prepare the managers for implementing teamwork in their departments.

This is how the consultant described what happened during the conference.

> After my introduction to what teamwork is about, I asked them individually to reflect upon why one should work in teams, and list the advantages of teamwork over work by individuals. I asked them to be concrete in describing the raison d'etre for teamwork. We used an app to present their answers on the screen so all could see the other managers' answers.
>
> We reflected on what was shown on the screen. At first everyone agreed on the many good reasons for introducing teamwork. But then someone observed that the statements were a mixture of descriptions of efficiency losses due to a lack of cooperation and of goals for what the new teams should strive for. Someone else noted that managers focused on different expected outcomes, and that these were often very vague, e.g. "teamwork is more rewarding." Another jokingly counted statements about job satisfaction and social needs, and drew the conclusion that this seemed to be more important than getting the work done. It ended up in a heated discussion on whether and why teamwork should be implemented, and whether the expected outcomes were actually different from what could be achieved by an aggregate of individual work. The more they discussed, the clearer it became that the managers had no difficulty in formulating what did not function well in the current work situation. But sometimes they could not clearly describe how teamwork would make it better, nor what the expected outcomes of teamwork should be. Some found no problems at all that could be solved by teamwork: rather they were problems of a lack of resources and difficulty in recruiting competent staff. A few were quite content with the current situation and referred to excellent productivity figures. Others, however, regarded doing things in a team as always better, yet were vague in describing why this was so. At the end of this session the only agreement was that there was no consensus among the managers on: a) what the problems in the current situation were, b) why work in teams, c) what the teams should achieve, d) what should they say to their employees.

There are many interesting problems in this case: e.g. different perceptions on problems in the current work situation, on outcomes of teamwork, even the why and wherefore of teamwork. These are important issues, and if they are not resolved there is a risk of organizing employees in groupings which lack direction and structure. The case illustrates a common problem with the implementation of teamwork that has to do with the problem-solving process: Top management had an idea of a solution and took a decision without a thorough analysis of what the problem was, or of what different factors might plausibly have contributed to the problem. *We need to know what creates or causes a problem before we can decide how it can be solved.* This is common sense, but in everyday discussions about problems at work, we often think of solutions without an in-depth analysis of why these problems occur. That is in contrast to what we expect from a physician: When we seek help for a medical problem, we expect to get a diagnosis first, and then a cure for the cause of the symptoms. In the case just cited, at the outset teamwork is pronounced to be the cure – but to what problem? We will use this case to see how the consultant tried to use the problem-solving circle to compensate for the initial inadequacies of the problem-solving process.

> *To summarize*: Lack of success in solving problems with teamwork is often due to problems with the problem-solving itself. Good practice in how to solve problems will ensure quality and effectiveness in the process of solving team problems.

1 The problem-solving process

Problem-solving strategies are the steps that one would use to find the problem that is hindering the attainment of one's goal. Many refer to the "problem-solving cycle" as formulated by Bransford and Stein (1984). In this cycle one can recognize the problem, define it, develop a strategy to fix it by identifying its causes, consider the resources available, eliminate or alter those causes, monitor progress and evaluate the solution for accuracy. The reason it is called a cycle is that once it is completed, a further problem frequently arises.

Recognizing the problem is one thing, but *who should be involved in the problem-solving process*? This will impact the whole process, from deciding what the problem is, to the evaluation of how successfully it was solved. Those who take part in the problem-solving will have different contributions and perspectives, and need to build a shared meaning of what the problem is, what causes the problem and how it best can be solved.

> ## MAKING USE OF DIVERGENT AND CONVERGENT PROCESSES FOR BUILDING SHARED MEANING AND TAKING DECISIONS
>
> The process of building shared meaning is closely related to team learning (Decuyper, Dochy, & Van den Bossche, 2010 and Chapter 7). All who take part in the process share divergent opinions and perspectives. Conflicts arise and the differences must be overcome and converged into a collectively shared understanding of the problem and what to do. Tools to facilitate the process of building

THE PROBLEM WITH PROBLEM-SOLVING | 33

> shared meaning can be classified into two main types: *divergent* and *convergent*. Divergent tools are mainly brainstorming techniques used to generate many ideas, whereas convergent tools facilitate decision-making and are used to categorize ideas, to shortlist and/or to prioritize. There are many facilitation tools in the literature (Schumann, 2005) and more can easily be found on the internet.

Further, is there competence in the organization to *manage the process* – from problem identification, to formulating interventions, to solve the problem, to evaluating results (for example HR specialists or managers)? Or should external expertise be brought in? Research shows that facilitation is a determining factor for successful deliberate discussion (Kuhar, Krmelj, & Petrič, 2019).

1.1 Step 1. Describe the current situation

Depending on the workplace, on resources, as well as on how major the problem is, it must be decided who should be involved in identifying hindrances to effective teamwork and to doing something about it. Naturally there is no single correct answer, but the decision has implications for the interventions. *An analysis of the current situation in order to identify the need for change depends largely on whether the stakeholders' viewpoints are considered.* Relying solely on expertise from external consultants or from managers has the disadvantage of reducing the number of divergent perspectives. For example, the production manager, the manager for technical support, the head of logistics, unions and employees might all have different perceptions of how the production is running and how the production flow could become more effective. Those who are closest to the problem probably know a lot about the current situation, what needs to be addressed first, and have ideas or knowledge about what is creating and contributing to the problem. This would imply that regarding problems with teamwork, the team members should be involved from the start. Making use of divergent perspectives *gives a fuller picture of the current situation*, and more motives for change and what should be aimed at.

To design or redesign work and work organization is related to organizational strategy and structure. It involves taking decisions that affect different functions, groupings and teams. Therefore, the manager in charge for those functions who are affected, or involved, and who is also in charge for the integration of different functions' work and results, needs to be part of the process and supporting it. If not – it is not possible to change the work design or work organization.

There are clear advantages in involving those affected by the problem in the problem-solving process. As we will see later, collective problem-solving based on heterogeneous perspectives and competences has advantages, but it is time-consuming and depends on those who take on the task. It is advisable to look for a) those who are intellectually curious and know about work and its organization, b) those who are dependent on the outcome of the team's work and c) those who impact the problem. These are the stakeholders.

Research shows that participation in the whole intervention by those who are the object of the intervention, including the preceding steps such as finding out what the problem is about, raises motivation and the later willingness to change ways of working. Participation increases acceptance for change and reduces uncertainty and resistance (Hasson, Tafvelin, & von Thiele Schwarz, 2013). Employee involvement in change leads to changes that are permanent and long-lasting in organizations (Nielsen, Randall, Holten, & González, 2010). Understanding why something needs to be done is essential for motivation and engagement.

Carrying out a stakeholder analysis means a) identifying the stakeholders – who they are; b) asking their perceptions of the current situation; and c) finding out their expectations of the team, department, organization or other unit that is being analyzed. Such a procedure provides a description of "where we are today" and "where do we want to be" from all those who are dependent on the outcome of the team's work.

THE WAY A PROBLEM IS ADDRESSED HINDERS THE IMPLEMENTATION OF A SOLUTION CONT.

In this case, teamwork was chosen as a solution by top management, without prior analysis of the current situation. The consultant raised this problem, and suggested that a more fruitful way of taking the process of implementing teamwork further would be to step back and make use of the problem-solving circle for implementing teamwork. The top management agreed, and the consultant was asked to re-start the process.

The first step in the problem-solving circle is to bring in the stakeholders to describe the current situation. To describe the current situation, the consultant met managers, the HR specialist, union representatives and representatives of employees from different backgrounds and functions from local offices. A very broad topic was introduced like "What is it like to work in a local office?" The consultant relied on a simple and structured divergent process method to find as many different viewpoints as possible and to ensure that all were active in the discussion. Participants were divided into subgroups according to function, and they individually wrote descriptions on Post-it Notes. These were collected and presented on a whiteboard. The necessary clustering in higher order categories of the great number of answers was done by the different subgroups gathering around the whiteboard and putting those statements they thought described a similar thing into one category, and giving the category a name, e.g. "leadership."

To summarize: The first step in the problem-solving circle is to describe the current situation to identify the needs for change. Research about problem-solving and interventions suggests that unlike interventions implemented top-down, participation by employees and team members in the entire process from identifying needs for change to planning the intervention will enhance motivation, make sense to those involved and have a better chance of permanent and functional change. The process of carrying out a solid problem-solving circle often benefits from being facilitated and managed.

1.2 Step 2. Identify the core problem(s)

It is often difficult to distinguish between a symptom, a problem and what causes the problem. One example is "lack of motivation." Is it a symptom of poor work conditions? Or is it a cause, for example, of poor performance? The cause could be seen as the problem, and the symptom is indeed a problem in itself. Ultimately one needs to identify one or more important problems that one decides to work on. Our advice is to avoid splitting hairs, as all symptoms, problems and causes of problems are interlinked.

There are different ways to go about identifying core problems. One is to *cluster similar symptoms that are related to an underlying problem* into a more general descriptive category and give this cluster a name. E.g. "Sometimes when I have a headache I decide not to go to work, but maybe I could have," "I often feel moody on Sunday evenings when I start thinking about work tomorrow," "I don't feel very appreciated by my boss," "I don't think it is so much fun anymore doing more than I have to," and "I wouldn't say that I am content with my work tasks: I have been doing the same thing for years." In this case such a cluster could be "job satisfaction." In most cases a description of the situation will result in a range of problems or challenges. These problems can usually also be grouped into higher order categories. Several statements will describe a similar thing.

> ## THE WAY A PROBLEM IS ADDRESSED HINDERS THE IMPLEMENTATION OF A SOLUTION CONT.
>
> The next step was to identify the core problems in the current situation according to the stakeholders and find consensus regarding core problems. The consultant ran a new workshop and applied a convergent process method to get consensus. Dimensions (clusters of statements) describing things that were working well were excluded in a joint discussion. The rest of the dimensions were clustered into a grid where different themes were first judged on a 1–5 scale by each individual in terms of a) importance for efficiency, b) the possibility to change it and c) the cost and resource involved in changing it (scale reversed). This meant, for example, that an important problem like lack of technical support (mean: 5) got a low score as it was deemed not possible to change (mean: 1.2), and costing too much (mean: 1.8). The mean sum of these ratings for each dimension was the basis for identifying the core problems and their order of priority. The core problems were described in broad categories (with subcategories) such as 1) recruitment and training, 2) leadership, 3) work organization and 4) systems for feedback and controlling results. In this case there was a delicate situation due to the consequences of the initial problem: Top management had decided on implementing teamwork, without prior analysis of the situation. By using the problem-solving circle, step 1 and step 2 suggested that the work organization was one of the prioritized problems. It was decided that this problem should be tackled.

To summarize: There might be different problems with a team's work, different stakeholders have different views, and not everything can be tackled at the same time, or even at all. Symptoms of a problem can be clustered to identify a core problem. If there are disparate problems, one simply has to come up with a decision based on what has highest priority. At some point there needs to be a decision on what is believed to be the core problems – or on one issue that one decides to work on.

1.3 Step 3. Cause analysis

In this book we propose a cause analysis as an important step in the problem-solving process, and more specifically *to use theory* to examine different plausible causes to different problems with teamwork. A scientific theory is a well-substantiated explanation of some aspect, (e.g. team effectiveness) based on a body of facts that have been repeatedly confirmed through empirical research. Such fact-supported theories are not "guesses" but reliable accounts of the phenomenon under study. Interventions formed where theory and practice meet increase the benefit of the implementation (Nylén, 2017).

Teams are embedded in a complex context. Factors on individual, group and organizational level interact (see the IMOI model in Chapter 1). All these factors (and the interaction between them) can be roots of the problem, directly cause the problem or impact the problem. Theory provides us with possible explanations to a problem, as it provides knowledge about what are generally the main factors that impact the problem. Sometimes theory also tells what the main predictors (explaining factors) to a problem are. Within a specific workplace there are probably other factors as well, and the theoretical model might be more or less suitable to describe a unique problem. Theory gives guidance to what to investigate, but when solving problems with teamwork there must be a readiness to take other contextually determined factors into account. Theory and a description of the situation from divergent perspectives make it possible to form a local theory of what causes a specific problem with teamwork. *This theoretical framework can be used to describe and assess the status of a specific team: to diagnose the team.* A diagnosis is an investigation or analysis of the cause or nature of a condition, situation or problem. If we know about different factors that may affect the problem, it is possible to identify the most influential ones. In an ideal world this would imply that we investigate empirically in the specific workplace what causes the problem by examining those factors that theory tells are the most important. This can be done by a systemized data collection in line with the principles of research methodology, collecting data from a few focus groups or interviews with those concerned, as was done in the present case. Doing something is a lot better than doing nothing. Theory provides us with work hypotheses, and we can explore these one by one. By so doing, the intervention will be based on a local theory on what the main causes of the problem at hand are. In each chapter we present a mind-map of plausible causes of the problem addressed, and each mind-map is an example of a theoretical analysis of plausible causes of a problem. In each chapter we describe how such a theory-based cause analysis, a diagnosis of the team, can be carried out.

With problems in teams it is difficult to distinguish between whether a factor causes a problem or whether it impacts a problem. Correspondingly in the book we sometimes write "there is a causal relationship between X and Y" when such empirical evidence exists; we write "impact," "is related to" or "influence, etc." when the relationship between factors is more complicated. When we refer to cases, we write that a work hypothesis could be, or a possible explanation could

THE PROBLEM WITH PROBLEM-SOLVING | 37

be that X is caused by something, meaning that we propose a certain explanation to a problem. By "cause" in cause analysis we mean "the producer of an effect." We then use the word "cause" in its everyday meaning and not its statistical meaning. We do not know if the work hypothesis is correct until this has been empirically examined.

1.3.1 Avoid simplistic explanations
The most important thing is that simplistic explanations of a problem should always be avoided. Lack of success in different interventions is too often due to an inadequate analysis of the current situation and the "causes" of its challenges. It is easier to make a systematic mapping of a problem's different plausible causes or impacting factors if one has a theoretically based model of which contextual aspects impact such a problem. In the example given earlier – lack of work satisfaction – it is easy through brainstorming to come up with many different reasons for such an attitude towards work. It can be the task itself, the work organization, colleagues and social relationships, pay, leadership, one's own knowledge, skills and interests, etc. Theory would contribute more.

THE WAY A PROBLEM IS ADDRESSED HINDERS THE IMPLEMENTATION OF A SOLUTION CONT.

The consultant facilitated a new discussion among stakeholders aiming at identifying plausible causes of problems in the current *work organization* within local branches of the national authority. Again, the same procedure was used: first a divergent process to ensure as many different perspectives as possible. The theme was introduced as "What causes the problems in how we organize work?" The participants were asked to brainstorm around four questions: Is the problem caused by the organization? By the physical environment? By the work design? By how people interact and work together? The statements were clustered into themes on a whiteboard, and resulted in 12 dimensions of problems related to work organization that impeded effectiveness, e.g. seasonal peaks in workload, autonomy that not everyone could handle responsibly, coordination, lack of cooperation, little knowledge of others' expertise and ways of working, different work routines, sometimes a competitive climate, unproductive meetings and lack of mutual support. A conclusion of the workshop was that there were problems in the work organization that should be addressed, and that one important cause of problems in the work organization was a lack of cooperative work.

1.3.2 Mental barriers that impede problem-solving
Theory and models help us to avoid certain common errors in the initial phase in the problem-solving process, but there are also other barriers that impede our ability to

correctly analyze and solve problems (Pretz, Naples, & Sternberg, 2003). Some of these are:

- One's own limited competence or mental set determining the causes of the problem. Mental set represents rigidity in how an individual behaves or believes in a certain way due to prior experience. E.g. "I am a specialist in teamwork and the problem in the organization is that they have no team-based organization."
- One reason explains the full effect. The problem is explained by one factor, often the first that springs to mind.
- Confirmation bias, which is the tendency to search for, interpret, favour and recall information in a way that confirms one's pre-existing beliefs or hypotheses.
- Unnecessary constraints, which is when a person trying to solve the problem subconsciously places boundaries on the task at hand and constructs mental blocks to solving a problem which reduces the capability to be innovative. Group-think, or taking on the mindset of the other team members, can be an unnecessary constraint while trying to solve problems.
- The problem is not explained – instead a solution to the problem is found, and the solution determines what the problem is.
- Unrealistic belief in experts. E.g. when a solution that is said to be useful is sold in by a consultant. "You have people who need to collaborate in your organization – team building will enhance the team's effectiveness – and we have an excellent team-building program that can help you."
- Misguided motivation. The motive is not to solve the fundamental problem and bring about essential change, but to show that one has done something.

THE WAY A PROBLEM IS ADDRESSED HINDERS THE IMPLEMENTATION OF A SOLUTION CONT.

Coming back to the initial problem in the case: There the top management was *perhaps* impeded by a cognitive barrier when the decision to implement teamwork was taken without prior cause analysis that involved those concerned. The top management had a problem with efficiency. And the solution to the problem, teamwork, was presented as a cause: We have a problem with a lack of cooperation – and the solution is to cooperate more in teams.

To summarize: Empirical research provides knowledge about plausible causes of the problem. These can be used as hypotheses when investigating a problem within a specific workplace, and be the foundation for a diagnosis of the team's status. The cause analysis as well as the general problem-solving might be hindered by cognitive barriers, and being aware of those helps keep an open mind when examining a problem and its causes.

1.4 Step 4. Select target dimensions and set goals

A cause analysis and a diagnosis of a specific team's functioning will most often result in a description of many factors that impact or create the problem. Some will be of greater importance than others, as research has shown that different factors impact the problem more or less and what is most important differs also between contexts. Not all of these factors might be open to change, e.g. laws and regulations, or the problem in a team might stem from a different part of the organization. Answering the question "Do we have the mandate to change the cause of the problem?" will help choose meaningful aspects/dimensions for an intervention. In an existing team such target dimensions can be e.g. communication or performance monitoring. In this case no teamwork yet existed and the question was "What factors cause problems in the current work organization?"

THE WAY A PROBLEM IS ADDRESSED HINDERS THE IMPLEMENTATION OF A SOLUTION CONT.

In the following convergent process participants were asked to grade each aspect/cause of problems in the work organization on a 1–5 scale according to the staff's influence on this phenomenon. Those with a mean value above 4 turned out to be work division (unbalanced and considered unfair), coordination (e.g. things fall between two stools), little knowledge of others' expertise and ways of working (e.g. having different work routines makes it difficult to help out or take over others' assignments), lack of social support and transfer of knowledge (e.g. those newly recruited were left to themselves and given little feedback), information exchange and monitoring of one another's work progress, and goal un-clarity. Analyzing the potential for change would ideally have involved an analysis of factors that impede effectiveness and outcomes that can be influenced within the organization at other hierarchical levels and different functions, but this was not done in this case.

The idea is not to waste time and energy discussing issues that cannot be influenced. Problems that can only be handled by others might be forwarded to the decision-maker in charge.

The discrepancy between the current and a future situation helps in formulating goals for how target dimensions should be changed. Goal-setting theory (Locke & Latham, 2002) has tremendous empirical support and can be used for formulating goals that impact behaviour through motivation. More specific and ambitious goals lead to greater performance improvement than easy or general goals, such as "do your best." As long as the person accepts the goal, has the ability to attain it and does not have conflicting goals, there is a positive linear relationship between goal difficulty and task performance. Sometimes there is a risk of setting goals for activities that are easily measured, rather than setting goals for those things that matter. The essential thing is that goals should be set for the target dimensions: How should these be changed and how can this change be observed or measured?

> ### THE WAY A PROBLEM IS ADDRESSED HINDERS
> ### THE IMPLEMENTATION OF A SOLUTION CONT.
>
> In this case the head of the authority had explained that there was a need to speed up decision-making (productivity). The managers of local offices were advised by the consultant to involve employees and set explicit and measurable goals for productivity for the coming year, and to continuously follow up on these results. Such goals were e.g. "within six months, the time between an incoming task to a communicated decision should be less than one month." This is a goal for the expected outcome, and not a goal for developing a team. It was too early for setting such goals, as the proposed means – teamwork – was so far only discussed.

To summarize: Theory provides a framework for selecting target dimensions, the main causes to a specific problem in a specific context. To analyze the possibility to change different identified causes to a problem makes it easier to prioritize what to work on. Goals impact behaviour through motivation, and specific and ambitious goals affect performance more than easy or general goals.

1.5 Step 5. Identify solutions

A problem can usually be solved in different ways, and a suggestion is to explore many so there is a wide range of possible solutions that can be compared in the selection process. *First* one needs to decide if the causes lie in the physical environment (e.g. communication problems might be due to an open-space office design), the organization (e.g. leadership structure), in the personnel (e.g. a member might lack essential teamwork skills) or in the team. Often factors in different domains interact and impact a problem in one domain. The chapters of this book present what we have found to be useful solutions for specific causes of problems with teamwork, and in Chapter 10 we go in depth into interventions. We stress that such solutions often need to be accompanied with solutions within other domains, although these are not covered in the book.

> ### THE WAY A PROBLEM IS ADDRESSED HINDERS
> ### THE IMPLEMENTATION OF A SOLUTION CONT.
>
> Ideally the problems in the *work organization* (not the overall problem with efficiency) would have been targeted by exploring different ways of organizing work before implementing a specific kind of teamwork. A few examples of important questions in this case: Should all types of tasks be handled in the local offices or some at a central level? (For example, decisions that involve regulations.) Should different types of tasks be handled by different

THE PROBLEM WITH PROBLEM-SOLVING | 41

> groups of employees, or should one group handle all types of tasks? Should support functions be in separate functions or should they be integrated in cross-functional groups? This is an issue at an organizational level and not a team level. In this case there were no such discussions and the decisions taken affect what the teams should do and set the frame for the interaction.

A solution is the means for solving the problem. Sometimes there are solutions for solving problems with teamwork or for developing teams that have proved to be useful and that can be found in the literature or on the market, and sometimes one has to be creative and rely on experience of what might work. Solutions for solving a problem with teamwork or for developing team effectiveness are often called team development interventions (TDIs). It is useful to have different criteria for the comparison of different solutions. *A main criterion is if empirical research has shown that the solution works.* There are plenty of popular products for team development on the market although they are useless in the sense that they do not impact team performance at all. Another important criterion is if the solution is likely to bring about a visible change within the time frame. To see a result is motivating and gives momentum to the development. The solution needs to be realistic and evidence-based; it needs support and decisions from management; it needs resources; and it needs to be accepted by those involved. Most often several solutions are needed.

THE WAY A PROBLEM IS ADDRESSED HINDERS THE IMPLEMENTATION OF A SOLUTION CONT.

In this case, the top management and local managers had an internal meeting and decided that teamwork should be implemented. The rationale was that the top management had come to this conclusion, and managers and representatives from local offices had identified that a core problem with the work organization was lack of cooperation. Different managers decided on different types of teamwork, e.g. virtual teamwork and different team structures.

> *To summarize:* There are often numerous solutions to a specific problem with teamwork, and it is worthwhile searching the literature and the market for those that are evidence-based. These solutions for solving problems with teamwork or enhancing team effectiveness are often called team development interventions. Choosing a solution involves setting up criteria so that different solutions can be compared, and one important criterion is whether previous research has shown that the solution enhances team performance.

1.6 Step 6. Plan the intervention

Needless to say, the forming of an intervention depends on the problem, the context, the resources, project management, etc. Research about interventions in general provides a few guidelines. Interventions at the workplace level can be divided into primary, secondary and tertiary. Sometimes this means that the interventions are targeted towards the individual (primary), the group/team (secondary) or the organization (tertiary). But sometimes the same terminology is used to describe when they are used (Kelloway, Hurrell & Day, 2008). Then primary interventions aim to prevent an incident before it ever occurs. Secondary interventions aim to reduce the impact of an incident that has already occurred. This is done by detecting and dealing with the effects as soon as possible to halt or slow the progress. Tertiary preventions aim to soften the impact of an ongoing problem that has lasting effects. This is done by helping people to manage the problem and its consequences in a better way. Primary efforts identify different obstacles at work and eliminate them, thereby changing individuals' experiences of the work environment and work. Of course, it is generally advisable to choose primary interventions when possible.

THE WAY A PROBLEM IS ADDRESSED HINDERS THE IMPLEMENTATION OF A SOLUTION CONT.

In this case, the consultant tried to compensate for errors made when deciding on teamwork without carrying out the steps in the problem-solving circle. This was done by introducing the problem-solving circle at this later stage and by introducing a bottom-up process based on participation by those concerned. It can be regarded as a secondary type of intervention.

Organizationally oriented interventions (sometimes also called tertiary) e.g. to reduce fluctuations in workload, versus individual-oriented (primary), e.g. teaching individuals to cope with stress, have shown to have both an effect on the well-being of individuals and an organizational benefit. It is generally advisable to choose interventions aimed at changing organizational structures and processes rather than interventions directed towards the individual (Lamontagne, Keegel, Ouie, Ostry, & Landsbergis, 2007). It may very well be that a problem in a team is related to a specific individual's personality, but better to form an intervention for handling diversity in the group than try to change the individual. There will always be the issue about individual differences, and we are the way we are. Nonetheless, sometimes an individual might be too different to fit in and interventions to handle this are needed, e.g. individual competence-development. A full-scale intervention should be preceded by a feasibility study. That involves proactively identifying obstacles that will impact the intervention, and removing them.

What, then, should be learned from carrying out an intervention? There will be future problems to be solved, and raising the organization's competence in managing problem-solving is essential. A suggestion is to set goals in line with Latham and

THE PROBLEM WITH PROBLEM-SOLVING | 43

Locke's findings that also describe learning outcomes from the change process itself: it is to build competence in effective problem-solving and organizational development, and these are ongoing processes in most workplaces.

> ## THE WAY A PROBLEM IS ADDRESSED HINDERS THE IMPLEMENTATION OF A SOLUTION CONT.
>
> Four months later a local manager asked the consultant for further help in implementing teamwork (see Chapter 3). It was decided that a goal was that the team leaders should learn structured methods for team facilitation, so that in the long run the organization would become more independent of consultants.

To summarize: An intervention is both the content of the solution and how it is implemented. Research about interventions shows that it may well be worth first carrying out a feasibility study to identify and remove obstacles that will impact the implementation of solutions. Setting goals for what should be learned from carrying out the problem-solving circle might seem very ambitious, but practical experience tells, and the case in this chapter confirms, that it is essential. Organizations often need to enhance competence in problem-solving, and teams need methods for tackling the problems which occur in any team.

1.7 Step 7. Implement the intervention

It is beyond the scope of this book to include intervention theory and project management. The result of an intervention depends both on the quality of the solution (this will be discussed in Chapter 10) and the quality of the implementation process itself, which here we leave aside. Both aspects differ for each and every change-and-developmental project, including team development initiatives. We refer to other literature regarding the implementation process. Timing will also affect the result. Is the intervention carried out when the problem first occurs, when it has shown to be persistent, or when it affects team-performance outcomes?

In each chapter we describe different problems in teams and what research has found to be effective solutions for solving these problems. E.g. Chapter 7 discusses that one solution for enhancing team learning is team debriefs. It is to look back, to look forward and to reflect upon habitual routines or how critical situations were handled. Debriefs can be done in different ways depending on the situation. There is such an abundance of tools and methods that no book can cover them all, and how to do it depends on the context. We will give examples in the following chapters and some general advice in Chapter 10. But we will discuss what the causes may be, where the causes are to be found and what kind of interventions can be used. As we pointed out earlier, the foundation for forming an adequate team intervention to enhance teamwork is the decision whether the causes lie in the physical environment, the organization, the individuals or within the team domain. This is a crossroad, and success lies in choosing the right path.

THE WAY A PROBLEM IS ADDRESSED HINDERS THE IMPLEMENTATION OF A SOLUTION CONT.

Ideally the team implementation in all offices would have been planned before organizing the workforce into teams, but this did not happen. General advice from the consultant to the top management and to the local managers was to form a plan for the implementation in collaboration with the teams. It was recommended to first set the stage for teamwork regarding basic prerequisites in work design and team composition (see Chapters 3 and 4), second to support team leadership with training and tools for team facilitation and coaching and third to supervise and coach team leaders over the initial six months.

To summarize: The end result of implementing a solution depends on how valid the solution is, and how well the intervention was planned and carried through. It is advisable to learn about project management and intervention theory, but that is beyond the scope of this book.

1.8 Step 8. Evaluate

To increase the quality of the evaluation of effects, different methods and multiple measurements from different sources may be used. Research methodology shows good practice and helps to set up a design that makes it possible to conclude if the intervention has worked or not. It is advisable to evaluate both the process and the results, and also the learning outcomes. Process evaluation takes place during the intervention, and it is formative: using what is leaned to make the ongoing work more effective. Evaluating the results is done by comparing goals and what was achieved. The complexity of the evaluation will depend on how profound the changes aimed at were, and how extensive the solving-problem process was. In a larger intervention it might be worthwhile to use an external expert for the evaluation.

THE WAY A PROBLEM IS ADDRESSED HINDERS THE IMPLEMENTATION OF A SOLUTION CONT.

In this case, the local managers were advised by the consultant to involve employees and help set explicit and measurable goals, e.g. productivity (discussed earlier). These results should be evaluated, but also the work process

> that impacts to what extent the goals were achieved. Work progress could e.g. be evaluated by the teams during a weekly meeting to identify hindrances in habitual routines that impede goal fulfilment.

To summarize: Evaluation means evaluating both the process and the results.

1.9 Step 9. End the intervention

Many employees are wary of all change activities, and it is not unusual that one project develops into another. An intervention follows the logic of any activity: Goal setting – Planning – Activity – Control of Result – Feedback. Once this sequence is completed, this intervention is finished. A recommendation is to highlight the end, perhaps by including some sort of official or festive conclusion to the intervention. *In many cases new problems have by now arisen, and another problem-solving circle starts.* The IMOI model allows for outcomes in one performance episode to alter inputs in a subsequent performance episode, the second I creates a feedback loop, and in that sense team development is without end. In Figure 2.1 the problem-solving circle is shown.

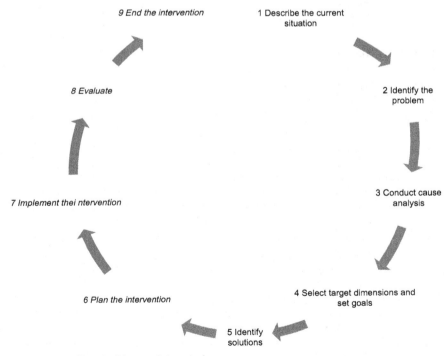

Figure 2.1 The problem-solving circle

Based on empirical research, we show the steps from problem to solution. A thorough description of the current situation from different perspectives (1) results in consensus about the core problem (2). A theory-based analysis of what causes a specific problem provides the foundation for an assessment of how the team functions in aspects relevant to the problem. This structured approach makes it possible to carry out a diagnosis of the team's functioning (3), to decide what needs to be changed, to determine the potential for change and select target dimensions for the intervention and to set goals (4), and identify solutions and what should be targeted (physical environment, the organization, individuals or the teamwork). There are solutions, such as team development interventions, that research has shown to be useful for bringing change about in the target dimensions and developing team effectiveness (5). Thereafter it is about forming the intervention by choosing solution(s), tools and methods depending on the context and the situation (6) and carrying out what was planned (7). An intervention is a process that needs to be monitored and supported and the results need to be continuously evaluated during and after implementation (8). Although there is an end to an intervention (9), new problems or possibilities arise, and what was learned during an intervention or performance cycle gives input to further development.

> *To summarize:* The problem-solving circle is a method for systematically solving problems with teamwork, and the end result depends on the content and result of each step in the problem-solving circle. Steps 1–4 in the problem-solving circle form the content of an intervention, and steps 5–9 bring change about.

Bibliography

Bransford, J. D., & Stein, B. S. (1984). *The ideal problem solver: A guide for improving thinking, learning, and creativity.* New York: Freeman.

Decuyper, S., Dochy, F., & Van den Bossche, P. (2010). Grasping the dynamic complexity of team learning: An integrative model for effective team learning in organisations. *Educational Research Review, 5.* https://doi.org/10.1016/j.edurev.2010.02.002

D'Zurilla, T. J., & Nezu, A. M. (1988). On problems, problem solving, blue Devils, and snow: A reply to Krauskopf and Heppner (1988). *The Counseling Psychologist, 16*(4), 671–675. https://doi.org/10.1177/0011000088164009

Hasson, H., Tafvelin, S., & von Thiele Schwarz, U. (2013). Comparing employees and managers' perceptions of organizational learning, health, and work performance. *Advances in Developing Human Resources, 15*(2), 163–176. https://doi.org/http://dx.doi.org/10.1177/1523422313475996

Kelloway, E. K., Hurrell, J. J. Jr., & Day, A. (2008). Workplace interventions for occupational stress. In K. Naswall, J. Hellgren, & M. Sverke (Eds.), *The Individual in the Changing Working Life* (pp. 419–441). Cambridge: Cambridge University Press. https://doi.org/10.1017/CBO9780511490064.020

Kuhar, M., Krmelj, M., & Petrič, G. (2019). The impact of facilitation on the quality of deliberation and attitude change. *Small Group Research, 50*(5), 623–653. https://doi.org/10.1177/1046496419861439

LaMontagne, A., Keegel, T., Louie, A., Ostry, A., & Landsbergis, P. (2007). A systematic review of the job-stress intervention evaluation literature, 1990–2005. *International Journal of*

Occupational and Environmental Health, 13, 268–280. https://doi.org/10.1179/oeh.2007.13.3.268

Locke, E.A., & Latham, G. P. (2002). Building a practically useful theory of goal setting and task motivation: A 35-year odyssey. *American Psychologist, 57*(9), 705–717. https://doi.org/10.1037/0003-066X.57.9.705

Nielsen, K., Randall, R., Holten, A. L., & González, E. R. (2010). Conducting organizational-level occupational health interventions: What works? *Work and Stress, 24*(3), 234–259. https://doi.org/10.1080/02678373.2010.515393

Nylén, E. C. (2017). Psykosocial arbetsmiljö i välfärdssektorn. Krav i arbetet, resurser i arbetet och personliga resurser samt betydelsen av organiserade arbetsmiljöinsatser. [Psychosocial work environment in the welfare sector: Job demands, job resources, and personal resources and the importance of organized occupational health interventions]. Doctoral dissertation. Stockholm: Stockholms University.

Pretz, J. E., Naples, A. J., & Sternberg, R. J. (2003). Recognizing, Defining, and Representing Problems. In J. E. Davidson & R. J. Sternberg (Eds.), *The Psychology of Problem Solving* (pp. 3–30). Cambridge: Cambridge University Press.

Schumann, S. (Ed.). (2005). *The IAF handbook of group facilitation: Best practices from the leading organization in facilitation.* San Francisco: Jossey-Bass.

Chapter 3

We have teams but little teamwork

The task determines the primary focus of team activities. Confusion about reasons to work in a team and what to accomplish might be due to lack of collective regulation of work, a suitable work design and collective challenging goals. The chapter describes how collective regulation of work is the basis for building a shared perception of work. It is fundamental that a team's work is designed in such a way that it is actually suitable for teamwork. Our contribution lies in showing how different work-design features, and the alignment of a set of interrelated features, affect individual team members, team performance and performance outcomes. The chapter covers a range of task performance and knowledge characteristics that affect individual motivation and attitudes and team performance. Work design and goals go hand in hand, and from our normative perspective this means that one should set the stage so that the team can be effective in carrying out both routine and non-routine tasks.

In this chapter we focus on what needs to be in place before teams can perform effectively. The starting point is a common problem: Employees are organized in teams, but they do not work as a team (step 2 in the problem-solving circle: The core problem has been identified).

To implement teamwork is to change the structure in the organization, and strategy and structure are closely related. If an organizational strategy says, "Teamwork is a pillar for innovation," such a strategy – if meant seriously – has implications for how the work is structured and designed. The work should then be designed in such a way that it supports learning and creative processes in the team. Although simple to agree on, it is a prescription often violated in practice. Sometimes teams have little autonomy and tasks are standardized, yet they are still expected to have a rich exchange and be involved in innovation processes. Sometimes the strategy is very vague; teamwork has been implemented, but why and what should be accomplished is not obvious to all.

1 What is work design?

A typical definition of a job is "an aggregation of tasks assigned to a worker" (Wong & Campion, 1991). *In teams, the task is a main input, as it determines the primary focus of team activities* (Kozlowski & Ilgen, 2006). The content and the design of the work determine how team members work together and what KSAs (Knowledge, Skills, and Abilities) are necessary for carrying out the task through teamwork. Work design is a wide concept as it acknowledges both the job, and the link between the job and the broader environment. Morgeson and Humphrey (2008) defined it as "the study, creation, and modification of the composition, content, structure, and environment within which jobs and roles are enacted" (p. 47). Such a definition allows both for work to be redefined and for work design to be considered at the team level (Parker, Morgeson, & Johns, 2017).

Further, they advocate that the main approach in research during the last hundred years has been to ask: "[H]ow does work design affect an expanded array of outcomes?" (p. 415). Instead, they propose that one should ask "[W]hat is the role of work design in achieving important outcomes?" (p. 415). It might be worthwhile to focus *on a set of work characteristics*, and the consequences of those organizing choices for important team-performance outcomes (Parker, Knight, & Ohly, 2017).

We have two points:

1. Teamwork is a means to an end result. Designing the team's work presupposes a shared understanding among stakeholders of what the end result should be.
2. Work design is to orchestrate different interrelated aspects of work design simultaneously and in alignment with overall organizational structure and processes.

1.1 Work design is formed from different directions

Factors that influence *how* work is designed are, according to Parker, Van den Broeck, and Holman (2017), a combination of external, organizational and local influences. Think of how safety legislation differs between countries, how the work differs in a hospital to a film studio and how the history of a firm influences how things are done. These factors affect a) the leader's formal decision-making about work design, and b) employees' informal decision-making through their KSAs, motivation and opportunities. Work design is formed from these two different directions. As an example of b), Li, Fay, Frese, Harms, and Gao (2014) showed that work design predicts the development of a more proactive personality, which in turn has lagged beneficial effects on work design characteristics. Wu, Griffin, and Parker (2015) showed that autonomy predicts the development of more internal loci of control, which then predicts later autonomy.

> *To summarize:* Work design is the content of, *and* organization of, individual or team tasks, activities, relationships and responsibilities. *How* work is designed is a key feature of work design. It is formed in a cultural and historical context, and from different directions, and might be redesigned over time by both managers and teams. When designing and redesigning work, it is not only a matter of identifying the prominent characteristics that fit with the task and the team's way of working; *the process of designing work* is perhaps equally important if one is to set the stage for effective teamwork. Different aspects of work design are interrelated and should be in alignment.

1.2 Work design and important outcomes of work

The different ways work can be designed, and its consequences for work performance and for workers, has been a topic for research since Taylor's studies of more than a century ago on time-motion to increase labour productivity (Taylor, 1911). Some of his ideas, such as standardization of tasks and specialization, are features of work design in many modern workplaces. The perspectives on work design have come to include motivation, work-related attitudes such as job satisfaction, health and work performance outcomes in many more aspects than productivity.

Thousands of studies, many reviews and meta-analyses have been conducted, and study after study have shown that work design affects a range of individual, team and organizational outcomes (e.g. Fried & Ferris, 1986; Hackman & Oldham, 1980; Humphrey, Nahrgang, & Morgeson, 2007; Parker, et al., 2017; Stewart, 2006). Work design affects individual and team routine-task performance and non-routine-task performance, and adaptability – the degree employees cope well with the ongoing change and challenges in organizations (e.g. Griffin, Neal, & Parker, 2007). Later in this chapter we will go into detail and describe how different features of work affect the individual and the team.

A meta-analysis of 250 studies and 217,081 participants showed that nine work characteristics explain, on average, 34% of the variance in worker attitudes and behaviour (Humphrey et al., 2007). Recent reviews (Parker, 2017; Sverke, Falkenberg, Kecklund, Magnusson-Hanson & Lindfors, 2016) confirm the results.

1.2.1 The impact of work design on work roles and job crafting

Employees do not only execute assigned static tasks, but they also engage in emergent, social and sometimes self-initiated activities; they can enact flexible work roles that involve going beyond the stipulated work (Hacker, 2001; Parker, et al., 2017). Ilgen and Hollenbeck (1992) argued that, whereas jobs focus on established and objective task elements, roles are broader and include emergent and self-initiated elements. Role breadth describes how many different roles an employee takes. For example team members may take on roles as e.g. being the team's spokesperson or team leader, or taking responsibility for ensuring that safety regulations are followed, reporting results, taking minutes or organizing social activities. Some roles may be asked for, and some may be self-initiated.

More recently the concept of job crafting has been used to describe the process by which employees cognitively and behaviourally shape their roles to enhance their sense of giving work meaning and making it more motivating. Job crafting (seeking resources and challenges and decreasing demands) positively affects work engagement, task performance as well as career satisfaction (Dubbelt, Demerouti & Rispens, 2019). Most research has regarded work design as an independent variable and employee behaviour as the dependent variable. (The dependent variable represents the output or outcome whose variation is being studied, e.g. employee behaviour, and the independent variable, e.g. complexity, represents inputs or causes of the variation e.g. in employee behaviour.) Job crafting suggests that the relationship is reciprocal. But the work characteristics, such as autonomy and complexity, impact whether employees go beyond the stipulated task, and that in turn predicts job performance (Hacker, 2001; Parker, et al., 2017).

In a large longitudinal study Kohn and Schooler (1982) investigated how task complexity affects intellectual flexibility over long periods of time and gave evidence "that the relationship between occupational conditions and psychological functioning is reciprocal: people's occupational conditions both affect

> and are affected by their psychological functioning" (p. 47). They showed that task complexity at work positively impacts intellectual flexibility (measured by different estimations of intelligence). Personality has importance in determining who enters what type of jobs and how they perform those jobs, but *work characteristics directly affect adult personality, which in turn will impact the employees' future work situation.*

To summarize: Work design affects individual and team performance, and team performance outcomes. Although some individuals on their own initiative go beyond the stipulated work and redesign work, research shows that this also depends on the work design.

After this introduction to what work design is, we now address how problems in teamwork can be explained by inadequate work design.

2 Step 1. Describe the current situation

We continue with the problem-solving circle and with the case presented in Chapter 2 as it illustrates some fundamental team-design issues.

CASE: LOW TASK INTERDEPENDENCE AND GOAL UN-CLARITY WITHIN TEAMS LEAD TO LACK OF TEAMWORK

In the example in Chapter 2 the consultant's sessions to support the implementation of teamwork were described.

Four months later, the consultant was contacted by the manager of one of the local offices who asked for advice on how to tackle the negativistic discussions among staff about the implementation of teamwork. Staff were now organized in ten teams of eight to ten members. The teams consisted of three different professions (a technical expert, an engineer responsible for gathering decision-relevant data and an assistant responsible for administrative tasks). All worked on different tasks in parallel and in different constellations of these three functions. The technical expert was in charge of one task and responsible for the first sequence in the task flow. The team leader was responsible for leading a weekly team meeting to prioritize incoming tasks, division of work/tasks, monitoring the workflow, following up results and deviations, and reporting deviations to a manager. The manager had stressed at a meeting that "it is not about working harder, but smarter" and was now pressed to clarify what that meant. Minutes from a meeting, led by the consultant, with some important stakeholders such as the manager, HR representative, team leaders and a few team members revealed:

According to the manager, through teamwork the teams should work more effectively, learn from one another so that all could do a better job, and become more motivated. "They are responsible for a range of tasks and are autonomous in deciding how to do them."

HR stressed the employees should make use of the possibilities inherent in teamwork, and "the teams need to find their own answers."

Team members described that they did not need to interact when carrying out individual tasks. What should they be "teaming" about? "We have always been supportive and helped each other – what else should we do?" What should they learn from each other since they did different things?

Team leaders candidly questioned why their knowledge on how to organize their own work was not asked for. Some teams tried to be self-managing and had meetings (in their opinion too many) to manage task flow, task division and coordination. In other teams the team leader took on these tasks, a strategy those teams found practical and effective. Team leaders felt pressed to come up with answers to the questions about how to work in teams. What should the team accomplish that was different from what they had done before? They asked the manager for direction on how to organize the teamwork.

In sum: The participants gave a very rich description of the current situation and found many challenges.

2.2 Step 2. Identify the core problem

The next step in the problem-solving process is to identify important problems in a situation, and we illustrate this with the case.

CASE: LOW TASK INTERDEPENDENCE AND GOAL UN-CLARITY WITHIN TEAMS LEAD TO LACK OF TEAMWORK CONT.

Although there is a team structure, members do not work as a team. The consultant asked participants to individually write down what they considered the problems in the work organization, and in a joint discussion the different descriptions were clustered into themes on a whiteboard: Tasks are carried out individually; individual contributions are pooled; lack of shared understanding of how to work; teams work in different ways; lack of directive leadership; insufficient resources; unclear work roles; unrealistic goals; etc.

There are several problems in the case on an organizational level, such as strategy, goals, leadership and organizational support, and there is also a problem with the work design on the team level (see inputs in IMOI model in Chapter 1).

3 Step 3. Cause analysis

Before exploring other possible explanations, we recommend a tentative exploration of whether the problem illustrated in the case, "we have teams but not teamwork," can be explained by:

a   No consensus on the expected outcome of teamwork
b   Basic prerequisites in work design are not in place
c   Lack of alignment of work design characteristics

The mindmap in Figure 3.1 shows main features of work design that impact team effectiveness. First order branches show possible explanations to the problem. Second and third order branches show aspects of work design that theory tells are important for effective teamwork, and the lack of these can be causes of the problem "We have teams, but little teamwork". It can be used as a practical tool as it provides the reader with an overview of aspects that can be explored one by one to find out if these three theoretical explanations cause such a problem in a specific work-place. In the following text we follow this rationale. In section 3 later in this chapter, we give advice in how such a diagnosis of the work design can be carried out.

3.1 No consensus on the expected outcome of teamwork

How can the confusion in the case of "Why work in teams and what to accomplish" be theoretically explained? It may be due to a) team members' individual regulation of work activities, b) lack of collective regulation of work and/or c) no goal that demands collaboration.

3.1.1 Individual regulation of activities

According to activity theory (Hacker, 2001) all work activities are goal-directed, and in a workplace this would most often be to produce a product or a service. Work activities that are aimed at overall goals therefore require an internal representation of what the result should be (Hacker, 2003). What am I to accomplish? What am I striving for? An action proceeds from a goal, to the planning of activities, execution, control of results, and feedback on results and performance. The goal is motivational and drives the action. The *understanding* of this sequence will regulate the activities. A task that only consists of execution will affect performance as it limits the possibility to intrinsic regulation, and as a consequence the task needs to be externally regulated, e.g. by written prescriptions of procedures. Second, an action is regulated by cognition. "I do this because of (something)." This something is the motive, and the motive determines the objective. Individual tasks are regulated in an internal, iterative and reciprocal process of handling motive, goal and activity (Hacker, 2003).

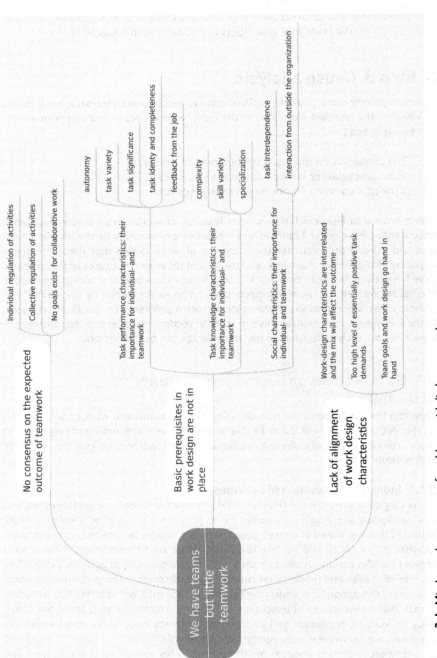

Figure 3.1 Mindmap about causes of problems with little teamwork

Work activities are hence idiosyncratically defined since people differ in e.g. motives, aspirations, knowledge and experiences. An example: Cleaning the house can be done in different ways and with different results. Some tidy up to make the house spotless, and some tidy up to get the task over and done with.

A task or activity can be redefined. If it is accepted as first presented, the stipulated task will be performed. The propensity to go beyond the stipulated task and a pre-defined result presupposes that the individual has somehow redefined what the expected result should be. Hacker (2001, 2003) underlines the importance of a redefinition process to explain why some take the initiative to go beyond routine task work and implement meaningful change, while some do not.

CASE: LOW TASK INTERDEPENDENCE AND GOAL UN-CLARITY WITHIN TEAMS LEAD TO LACK OF TEAMWORK CONT.

One work hypothesis is that the process of finding a motive and setting goals for teamwork is impeded by individuals interpreting the work idiosyncratically. The team members' understanding of their individual work will affect how they understand what the team should accomplish. The consultant arranged a workshop for team members in which the broad question was put: "Why do we go to work?" The aim was to invite all to share their way of thinking about the chain *motives – goal – work activities* in an amicable atmosphere, and to give everyone a moment to reflect upon the implications of their attitudes in relation to performance, learning opportunities and job satisfaction.

3.1.2 Collective regulation of activities

Collective behaviour is regulated by recognizing different perceptions of the motive – goal – work activities chain, reflection on these differences, communication on them and *converging different views* to a shared understanding (Tschan, 2000). Such a communication is the basis for the process of building a shared perception of work. In a team, individual members need to regulate their individual activities in alignment with others, and the shared understanding – a consensus in the team on important matters – is the foundation for individual and collective regulation processes.

CASE: LOW TASK INTERDEPENDENCE AND GOAL UN-CLARITY WITHIN TEAMS LEAD TO LACK OF TEAMWORK CONT.

The consultant summarized different perceptions of motives and goals on the whiteboard as a start to a converging process. Making the differences transparent is a big step forward in the process of bringing about consensus.

Setting goals is part of organizational strategy, and team goals should be in alignment with this and with external expectations. Clear, realistic and concrete goals steer, motivate, energize behaviour and increase persistence (Locke & Latham, 2002). If one does not know what activities are aimed for, one cannot evaluate if they are effective. Effective teams collectively regulate team activities so that these are aligned with others' expectations on team performance and team outcomes. This implies that stakeholders have a clear idea of what the team is to accomplish and how results should be evaluated. This is not always the case, and it impedes the team's regulation of activities. We address two important issues here. What should the team do? What are the expected outcomes of teamwork? *Goals might blend both types of result (e.g. completed tasks in the earlier case), and aspects of goals that refer to changes in behaviour or thinking (e.g. commitment)* for routine-task performance, non-routine-task performance and interpersonal relations.

CASE: LOW TASK INTERDEPENDENCE AND GOAL UN-CLARITY WITHIN TEAMS LEAD TO LACK OF TEAMWORK CONT.

The team members found it difficult to describe what the end results should be. The reflective discussion described earlier was followed up by a brainstorming session on goals on the individual, team and organizational levels. A distinction was made between tangible results and changes in behaviour. The team leaders were encouraged to follow up the results in team meetings to set specific team goals for each team.

Clarity in what to strive for makes it easier to see how the team can accomplish it.

3.1.3 No goals exist for collaborative work

It might be the case that there are no goals for collective work, but only goals for the sum of the results of individual tasks. An example: Assembling parts of a transmission can be done by workers who individually assemble different subparts, and another worker puts these together. One could say that together they have a goal to produce the transmission, but the individual tasks are not regulated by that goal.

CASE: LOW TASK INTERDEPENDENCE AND GOAL UN-CLARITY WITHIN TEAMS LEAD TO LACK OF TEAMWORK CONT.

The stipulated task was not carried out through teamwork, and no goal existed for collective work. The teams may find goals for teamwork through a

> redefinition process of work, and expand work to include non-routine perfor-
> mance. This would resemble job crafting and result in expanded work roles.

To summarize: Goals can be interpreted differently as individuals have different motives, experiences and abilities, which impact how the goal is understood. Hence what they do will differ, and while individual activities are regulated by an internal process of handling the *motive – goal – activity* chain, a team's activities are regulated by communication, shared understanding and decisions about these issues. Goals are more than results, and include a blend of both results and aspects of goals that refer to changes in behaviour or thinking. Goals steer, motivate and energize behaviour and impact persistence. *If no goal exists for collaborative work, then teamwork is obsolete.*

The expected outcomes determine what set and mix of work-design features support the performance to attain that goal.

3.2 Basic prerequisites in work design are not in place

Bell (2004) conducted a meta-analysis on the relationship between work-design features and team effectiveness, and concluded that this area had been insufficiently studied, and remained substantially behind individual-level work-design research. After searching for further and later research, we share these conclusions. The reason might be that researchers have relied on the vast literature based on the individual as the unit of analysis. If it is important for the individual, it is important for groups of individuals. *Hence we describe how work design impacts both the individual and the team.*

The work situation values different types of individual behaviour such as performance, adaptability and proactivity (Griffin et al., 2007). In a model, Morgeson and Humphrey (2008) clustered features of work design into 1) *motivational*, 2) *social* and 3) *contextual characteristics*. Motivational characteristics are both those that describe how the task is accomplished, and the kinds of knowledge, skills and ability demands that are placed on the individual or the team. Social characteristics reflect the extent that work facilitates contacts and relationships to others. Contextual aspects refer to the physical and environmental context. These involve e.g. ergonomics, physical demands, work conditions such as health hazards, noise, temperature, etc. and equipment use (technology, etc.). As research is scarce on how contextual features of work design affect *team* performance, we leave these out. In Chapter 1 we gave many examples of the importance of the social context (support from the organization, leadership etc.) for team performance, e.g. its importance for individual and team proactivity (Cai, Parker, Chen & Lam, 2019).

3.2.1 Task performance characteristics: their importance for individual- and teamwork

We describe a number of essential characteristics for a motivating and healthy task.

3.2.1.1 Autonomy

Autonomy includes three interrelated aspects centred on degrees of freedom in a) work scheduling, b) decision-making and c) work methods (Morgeson & Humphrey, 2006). Others such as Hacker (2001) also include degrees of freedom in goal formation.

> ## CASE: LOW TASK INTERDEPENDENCE AND GOAL UN-CLARITY WITHIN TEAMS LEAD TO LACK OF TEAMWORK CONT.
>
> How is autonomy measured? Typical statements in a survey to measure autonomy would be e.g. a) "The job allows me to take my own decisions about how to schedule my work," b) "The job gives me a chance to use my personal initiative or judgement in carrying out the work" or c) "The job allows me to decide on my own how to go about doing my job" (Morgeson & Campion, 2003). Typical points to study a team's autonomy would be, "The job allows the team to decide how to proceed." Such questions are often answered on a scale. The mean value of all team members' mean values will be the team's perception of autonomy. In this case the manager said, "They are responsible for a range of tasks and are autonomous in deciding how to do them." But are they? The autonomy was restricted as the tasks were to be carried out sequentially, and one person was responsible for the task flow. A work hypothesis is that the lack of teamwork can be explained by too little autonomy.

Teamwork requires autonomy (West, 2012). Why is that so? Without autonomy to decide e.g. how to work, to coordinate the team's work or implement changes, the teams cannot be self-managing. Greater autonomy increases the scope for using intellectual skills and creates potential for learning and redefining work (Hacker, 2001).

The research on the impact of autonomy on *individual* work is vast, and following are just a *few examples* of the many findings. Autonomy is linked to individual intrinsic motivation and attitudes such as job satisfaction and commitment (Hackman & Oldham, 1980). It is positively related to job involvement and negatively to absenteeism and anti-social behaviour. Autonomy promotes role breadth (Morgeson, Delaney-Klinger, & Hemingway, 2005; Humphrey et al., 2007) and role breadth self-efficacy (Parker, 1999), which enhances job performance (Grant & Parker, 2009), and is negatively correlated with role ambiguity and role conflict (Humphrey et al., 2007). Autonomy is decisive for the development of personal initiative and proactivity (Frese, Garst, & Fay, 2007; Marinova, et al., 2015; Tornau & Frese, 2013). Further, it is related to performance outcomes (Humphrey et al., 2007) and innovation (Hammond, Neff, Farr, Schwall, & Zhao, 2011).

Autonomy is positively correlated with team performance outcomes, mainly studied as the team's effectiveness in the performance of routine tasks (Li, Li, & Wang, 2009). In a meta-analysis Stewart (2006) found correlations varying between $\rho = .26$ to $\rho = .36$ (depending on task) and performance outcomes such as productivity.

Humphrey et al. (2007) did not find such high correlations, but autonomy was the only motivational characteristic that was related to objective ratings of performance. Autonomy impacts innovation processes in teams (West, Hirst, Richter, & Shipton, 2004). The results presented by Rashkovits and Drach-Zahavy (2017) indicate that team autonomy positively affects team innovation through team learning. It is no surprise that team autonomy positively impacts team members' engagement (Malinowska, Tokarz, & Wardzichowska, 2018) and job satisfaction (Humphrey et al., 2007). An engaged employee approaches the task with a sense of self-investment and energy. Engagement and workaholism can be depicted as the healthy or the pathological form of heavy work investment, and have some overlapping features (Di Stefano & Gaudino, 2019). Autonomy predicts engagement, but can it predict also workaholism? A recent study found no such relationship (Malinowska, Tokarz, & Wardzichowska, 2018).

3.2.1.2 Task variety

Task variety refers to the degree to which the job requires employees to perform a wider or narrower range of tasks. It triggers intrinsic motivation, as one can make better use of one's potential (Hackman & Oldham, 1980). Meta-analytic findings by Humphrey et al. (2007) have demonstrated that task variety is positively related to subjective ratings of *individual* performance.

Bell (2004) found in a meta-analysis that task variety positively and moderately impacts *team* routine-task performance. It is also related to perceptions of overload. Findings on task variety are mixed, and one reason might be that it depends on the tasks, but it does impact team members' job satisfaction (Bell, 2004).

3.2.1.3 Task significance

Task significance is the degree to which a job influences the lives of others, inside or outside the organization. Such jobs are deemed to be more meaningful than others. In an experimental study participants performed better, were more dedicated and showed more conscientiousness after taking part in an intervention to raise awareness of significance (Grant, 2008). In meta-analyses task significance has shown a moderate impact on individuals' job satisfaction, organizational commitment, performance and subjective (but not objective) performance outcomes. It is fairly strongly related to engagement (Christian, Garza, & Slaughter, 2011) and to a sense of overload (but not to stress) (Humphrey et al., 2007).

Task significance positively and moderately impacts *team* routine-task performance (Bell, 2004).

CASE: LOW TASK INTERDEPENDENCE AND GOAL UN-CLARITY WITHIN TEAMS LEAD TO LACK OF TEAMWORK CONT.

The case: What would the team members' answers be to statements like "The job involves doing a number of different things" or "The job requires the

> performing of a wide range of *different* tasks"? Probably the mean value would have been high for doing different things, and low for performing different tasks.

3.2.1.4 Task identity and completeness

Task identity and *completeness* are two words for the same thing, meaning performing a task from the beginning to the end: setting goals, planning, implementing, evaluating and getting feedback (Hacker, 2001). Seeing the results of what was aimed at, and how the planning worked for the execution, provides insights into how the task can be carried out differently. Compared to other work characteristics, the size of the meta-analytic effects (Humphrey et al., 2007) of the relationship between completeness and attitudinal outcomes is relatively smaller in magnitude, but it has an impact on e.g. organizational commitment, and on subjective performance evaluations. There are studies showing that completeness is also related to externally rated performance outcomes (Hacker, 2001; Richter, Hemman, & Pohlandt, 1999). Further it is related to lower absenteeism and less role conflict, experience of stress, burnout and exhaustion (Humphrey et al., 2007).

Completeness positively and moderately impacts *team* routine-task performance and job satisfaction (Bell, 2004; Li et al., 2009). Completeness positively impacts team-learning processes, which in turn impact the team's proactivity and non-routine work performance (Lantz, 2011).

3.2.1.5 Feedback from the job

Feedback from the job reflects whether the job provides clear and direct information about both the work process and the result. This provides insights into what could be done differently, and is a trigger to reflectiveness and discussions about work. Feedback from the job has shown to have numerous outcomes. It strongly affects *individual* intrinsic motivation and job satisfaction, and is negatively related to role ambiguity and role conflict, as well as to various well-being outcomes such as anxiety and stress (Nahrgang, Morgeson, & Hofmann, 2011). It is related to subjective reports of performance (Nahrgang et al., 2011).

Feedback from the job has a positive albeit moderate impact on *team* routine-task performance and team members' job satisfaction (Bell, 2004).

CASE: LOW TASK INTERDEPENDENCE AND GOAL UN-CLARITY WITHIN TEAMS LEAD TO LACK OF TEAMWORK CONT.

In this case, some team leaders planned and coordinated work, and followed up the results. The team members executed the tasks in a sequential order.

> We are not certain, but these teams reported that the team struggled to find a consensus about goals, and a work hypothesis could be that this might be due to the limited autonomy and completeness.

To summarize: Motivational task design characteristics are autonomy, variety, significance, task identity or completeness, and feedback from the job. All are important for a range of attitudinal and behavioural outcomes both for individual employees and teams. Autonomy stands out as it is clearly related to both routine and non-routine performance.

3.2.2 Task knowledge characteristics: their importance for individual- and teamwork

Task knowledge characteristics decide the scope for learning and making use of an individual's and the team's cognitive abilities.

3.2.2.1 Complexity

Complexity is about how difficult the task is. It depends on the demand on cognition in problem-solving, the coordination due to the degree of mutual dependency and the change of tasks over time.

Task complexity stimulates learning and adaptation (Wood, 1986). Employees who master complex tasks that make use of their potential will be intrinsically motivated, be engaged, and see opportunities for and invest in implementing change (Frese et al., 2007). Routine tasks that put little demand on cognition can be accomplished without collective regulation, while complex tasks will typically stimulate team discussions about work-related problems. The higher the demand on cognition, information processing and collaborative problem-solving, the more important team learning becomes, and the more possible it is to build team efficacy (the team's belief in its potential) in mastering challenging tasks.

The meta-analytic results of Humphrey et al. (2007) showed that higher complexity is related to *individuals'* higher subjective performance ratings. A range of studies have also found a relation to external measures of performance (Hacker, 2003). Meta-analytic findings have shown positive relations between task complexity, job satisfaction and job involvement (Humphrey et al., 2007), as well as for work engagement (Christian, Garza, & Slaughter, 2011). Complexity impacts individual proactivity (Frese et al., 2007). Complexity is related to higher levels of learning at work (Hacker, 2001), but also to perceptions of overload (Humphrey et al., 2007). Task routinization is negatively related to behaviour such as altruism, courtesy, conscientiousness and civic virtue (Podsakoff, MacKenzie, Paine, & Bachrach, 2000).

Complexity has been shown to strongly impact team learning processes, which in turn affect a team's participation in innovation processes (e.g. Lantz Friedrich, Sjöberg, & Friedrich, 2016; West et al., 2004). Bell (2004) however could not find that ratings of team task difficulty or complexity were related to team routine-task performance.

> **CASE: LOW TASK INTERDEPENDENCE AND GOAL UN-CLARITY WITHIN TEAMS LEAD TO LACK OF TEAMWORK CONT.**
>
> We have no information about task complexity in this case, but a hypothesis is that although it is complex, the demands vary for different team members, consequently impacting the demand on collective learning. Task complexity can be measured subjectively by a team member, e.g. by responding to a range of statements such as "The job involves dealing with problems that I have not met before," "The job requires me to monitor a great deal of information" or "The tasks on the job are simple and uncomplicated (reverse scored) (Morgeson & Campion, 2003). People differ in intellectual ability and experience, and what is difficult for some is less complex for others. Further, there might be a tendency to overrate the complexity as it may be disturbing to perceive or present one's job as simple and routine. Some researchers use expert-task analysis of complexity instead. Each task (or subtask) can be evaluated on a scale measuring demand on cognition. The scale's lowest point describes a task that requires only sensory motor regulation. At the other end of the scale, the task puts very high demands on problem-solving capacity (Hacker, 2003).

3.2.2.2 Skill variety

Skill variety is the extent to which an individual uses a variety of skills and abilities when performing the job. Meta-analytic results have demonstrated that skill variety does keep employees motivated, involved and satisfied, but it has not been shown to impact other behavioural, cognitive and well-being outcomes. Skill variety does, however, relate positively to self-rated performance in one meta-analysis (Humphrey et al., 2007).

Little is known about how skill variety affects *team* performance or team outcomes.

3.2.2.3 Specialization

Specialization is how specialized and deep the knowledge and skills need to be to complete a job. Although there is only limited research, Morgeson and Humphrey (2008) find reason to believe that specialization may be positively related to both job satisfaction and efficiency.

> *To summarize:* Motivational knowledge characteristics are complexity, skill variety and specialization. Although there are fewer studies of knowledge characteristics than of task characteristics, there is enough evidence to say that the knowledge characteristics, especially complexity, have a substantial impact on motivation, work-related attitudes, learning performance and performance outcomes.

3.2.3 Social characteristics: their importance for individual- and teamwork

In work design, social support and feedback from others are two main features of the social characteristics of work. Both have impact on the individual's motivation, well-being and performance (Nahrgang et al., 2011). Exchange of support and feedback are intra-team processes, and we leave these aspects aside, although we do discuss them as team processes in later chapters. Here it is enough to state that both aspects impact job satisfaction (Humphrey et al., 2007).

> Feedback is related to subjective performance, and the less there is of social support and feedback, the more of role ambiguity, role conflict, anxiety and overload. Social support is an important antecedent to proactive behaviour (Parker, Williams, & Turner, 2006), as is confirmed by meta-analytic results (Tornau & Frese, 2013). Feedback also predicts additional role behaviour, such as altruism, courtesy, conscientiousness and civic virtue (Podsakoff et al., 2000). They are certainly important for the design of individual work and a good reason for investing in teamwork.

3.2.3.1 Task interdependence

Task interdependence is one aspect of task complexity, but it is also a social characteristic. A low level of task interdependence exists in a pooled form – team members make different contributions to the outcome but do not interact with each other. Team members can also be connected sequentially, so that the chronological sequence of team members' actions is fixed. In teams with reciprocal task interdependence, single team members interact with another team member one-to-one, and back and forth. Being more or less dependent on how others perform their task will impact the interpersonal processes such as how much the team needs to communicate, coordinate and cooperate. It also impacts affective processes, e.g. being the last person in a sequential dependency chain and realizing that others have not fully delivered, might create tensions.

Interdependence is positively related to individual job satisfaction, well-being and subjectively rated performance. Further, it is negatively related to turnover intentions (Nahrgang et al., 2011). Humphrey et al. (2007) reported that it also impacts organizational commitment. Task interdependence necessitates higher levels of implicit coordination (Rico, Sánchez-Manzanares, Gil, & Gibson, 2008), and it is not surprising that workers often perceive higher levels of overload in high interdependence situations (Humphrey et al., 2007).

Stewart's (2006) and Bell's (2004) meta-analyses showed that ratings of both task- and outcome interdependency are positively related to *team* performance. There are substantial differences in how different aspects of interdependency impact performance: goal interdependence and task performance ($\rho = .22$), reward interdependence and task performance ($\rho = 0.19$), and mixed goal and reward (ρ = .59) (Bell, 2004). De Dreu (2006) showed that goal interdependence is related to better learning, information sharing and team effectiveness. Task interdependence requires more communication between team members, and tacit job knowledge is often transferred (Berman, Down, & Hill, 2002). In a review Rico, de la Hera, and Tabernero (2011) found that it impacts team trust, helping behaviour, communication, conflict (reversed) and flexibility. The psychological reason may be that the more one is dependent on others, the more important it is to invest in building good relations.

> ### CASE: LOW TASK INTERDEPENDENCE AND GOAL UN-CLARITY WITHIN TEAMS LEAD TO LACK OF TEAMWORK CONT.
>
> The team members expressed their concerns about the interdependence as "What should we be teaming about?" A work hypothesis is that the dependencies are too weak to trigger teamwork. With pooled or sequential team interdependence, it can be questioned if it is meaningful to implement teamwork when the stipulated task is not redefined.

3.2.3.2 Interaction from outside the organization

Does the task put require interaction with stakeholders outside the organization? It can be that contacts with suppliers, customers, etc. may stimulate team processes and the building of a shared understanding of goals. Little is known about how interaction with stakeholders impacts individual employees, but tentative results show that it is related to job satisfaction (Humphrey et al., 2007). Empirical research on cross-boundary collaboration from a motivational perspective is limited.

> *To summarize:* Social characteristics are social support, feedback from others, task interdependence and interaction with others outside the organization. Social support and feedback from others impact both individual and team performance and outcomes. Task interdependence, and specifically combinations of result, reward and goal interdependence, strongly and positively affects team processes and team performance outcomes.

3.2.3.3 Summary: what are the most important work-design predictors of effective teamwork?

We compared findings from different meta-analyses and studied how much variance different factors explained in outcomes. Looking into those that have the strongest correlations (Fried & Ferris, 1986; Humphrey et al., 2007; Nahrgang et al., 2011; Parker, Morgeson et al., 2017) to *individual* intrinsic motivation, and work related attitudes (job satisfaction in general, organizational commitment and job engagement), *and* performance (objective and subjectively rated), we find:

- Autonomy
- Complexity
- Feedback from the job
- Task identity/completeness
- Task interdependence

It should be noted that other work characteristics are important for attitudinal and behavioural outcomes as well, *but we include only those that also impact performance*. Further, social support and feedback from others are not included, as explained earlier. Meta-studies show that complexity shows a stronger relation to performance than autonomy. When it comes to impact on stress and overload, autonomy, task identity, feedback and interdependence all impact negatively, i.e. these factors *reduce* stress and overload, but the explained variance is not large. Complexity does have a substantial impact on overload.

Based on the meta-analyses by Bell (2004) and Stewart (2006) we used the same procedure to find the most important work-design predictors for teams as for individuals. We chose those work-design features that have shown substantial impact on team members' attitudes, team performance and team-performance outcomes, and those that impact on individuals' attitudes and performance as well (discussed earlier). Key work-design characteristics for teamwork are:

- Complexity: Tasks put demand on team cognition and team learning.
- Autonomy: Teams can decide how to carry out the work, redefine goals, redesign work and take decisions on these issues.
- Interdependence: Team members need to interact in many different ways to accomplish the task.
- Variety: A chain of interrelated tasks puts demand on a wide range of KSAs.
- Completeness: The team is responsible for a job from beginning to end – from goal formation, to planning, execution, control of results and feedback.

All other work-design features will contribute more or less to team members' attitudes, satisfaction and other positive behavioural outcomes.

3.3 Lack of alignment of work design characteristics

A job is perceived as a whole set of inter-related different characteristics that need to be aligned within, with other features of the organization and the expectations on the team's result for achieving positive outcomes at multiple levels in the organization (Tafvelin, Stenling, Lundmark & Westerberg (2019).

3.3.1 Work-design characteristics are interrelated, and the mix will affect the outcome

We advocated that when designing work a set of interrelated characteristics should be taken into account simultaneously. This is because *negative mixes should be avoided*, e.g. high complexity and little autonomy. Work design needs to be aligned with other organizational features, e.g. remuneration system and leadership structure, as the larger context in which jobs are embedded can either shape or countervail what was intended with the job design (Johns, 2010).

CASE: LOW TASK INTERDEPENDENCE AND GOAL UN-CLARITY WITHIN TEAMS LEAD TO LACK OF TEAMWORK CONT.

In this case there might be a risk of creating a disturbing mix of low autonomy, low interdependence and significant task complexity. A work hypothesis could be that lack of alignment of work design characteristics causes the teams' problems. Some professions are caught in a seemingly never-changing negative mix of work-design features. E.g. medical staff or others within health care most often have complex tasks, high skill variety, task variety and tasks with a very high significance. These features are not infrequently combined with low completeness and little autonomy. This has been known for many years, and despite research showing how teamwork and good HR practices impact outcomes, including patient mortality (see Woods & West, 2014), decision-makers often prefer to ignore it.

Different characteristics are interrelated, and the positive effects of one depend on another characteristic being in place (e.g. Humphrey et al., 2007). We give a few examples of such relations. Complexity and autonomy are related, as complex tasks can most often be solved in different ways, which requires autonomy in decision-taking, and having autonomy but no complexity leaves the team with freedom to decide only on matters that are of little importance (Frese et al., 2007). Langfred (2005) claims that positive effects of autonomy are only found in teams with high interdependence, as high autonomy puts demands on coordination and synchronizing team members' activities towards a joint goal. In a study of production teams in industry, Lantz Friedrich et al. (2016) showed that teams that took on non-stipulated additional tasks (increased task variety) showed more learning processes and were rated by managers as being more engaged in process innovation than those who did not. Why was that so? Additional tasks were higher in complexity.

3.3.2 Too high level of essentially positive task demands

Task characteristics are also designed so that employees can adapt to rapid changes, to enhance proactivity and to make employees enlarge work roles to make use of potential future opportunities (Griffin et al., 2007). It involves learning, competence-development, perhaps personal growth and a sense of mastery and self-efficacy. This might also be a strain because one has to plan actions and invest time and effort in the proactive behaviour, and these hours might not be part of the regulated work time (Podsakoff, Podsakoff, MacKenzie, Maynes, & Spoelma, 2014).

Johns (2010) put the heretical question of whether jobs can be too rich in work-design characteristics. He argued that this might be the case, e.g. highly complex jobs with high levels of autonomy and interdependence may be a burden, and the opposite of what was intended. Johns proposes that the effect of all features taken together is what matters. Further, some features have a paradoxical double-edged quality: "The same autonomy that leads some academics to produce scientific break-throughs enables other to produce crackpot ideas in the name of academic freedom" (p. 361).

3.3.3 Team goals and work design go hand in hand

We have shown that work-design features impact similar, but also different, things. E.g. task variety is more important to attitudinal outcomes than to performance. Complexity does not seem to impact routine-task performance, but it impacts team learning and non-routine performance. The starting point for work design is the expected outcome.

> *To summarize:* Work design should be assessed and evaluated as a set of interrelated characteristics, and with regard to the team goals.

3.4 To carry out an analysis of team goals and work design in a workplace

An analysis or diagnosis of the existing work design precedes the planning of an intervention to change the preconditions for the team's work. Teamwork is the means by which the team carries out the task by doing it together. These "doings" are restricted by what it takes to carry out the task, if it takes a team to do it and the work design. In this chapter the problem was "We have a team but little teamwork." In a workplace with a similar problem, work design would probably explain at least part of the problem. There are other theoretically plausible explanations as well, (see the whole IMOI model), and probably also specific contextual features that contribute to the problem. We made an informed choice, and to tackle the problem in a workplace the advice would be to investigate a) team goals and b) the work design.

3.4.1 The problem is due to unclear team goals

There are at least three questions about team goals that need to be answered before features of work design can be altered or implemented: strategy, stakeholders' expectations of results, existing team goals and the alignment between these. To the best of our knowledge there is no validated method for carrying out such an analysis. We give some advice on how it could be done.

3.4.1.1 What is the organizational strategy for using a team-based organization?

Find out:

- If there is a written or communicated organizational strategy that describes for what reasons, and how, teams should contribute to overall organizational outcomes.
- Is the strategy communicated well enough to ensure a shared understanding among stakeholders and individual team members of what the teams should achieve?

- If the strategy is clear and directional, or if it is general and gives leeway for interpretation. The latter would indicate a possibility to redefine goals.

3.4.1.2 What are different stakeholders' expectations of team performance and team-performance outcomes?

- Identify divergent perspectives on expected end results among stakeholders, decision takers and team representatives, and ensure that all parties understand the line of reasoning behind different viewpoints.
- Cluster different perspectives/ideas. Facilitation tools for divergent and convergent processes might be useful.

3.4.1.3 What are the team's goals?

- Converge different perspectives on team goals.
- Do the team goals refer to both routine- and non-routine-task performance? Specify different goals in relation to routine and non-routine performance.

3.4.1.4 Alignment between strategy, stakeholders' expectations and team goals

- Is there alignment between the general organizational strategy, stakeholders' expectations and team goals?

3.4.1.5 Is there a need for organizational decisions on team goals?

What were the results of this examination of team goals? Decisions on altering or adding goals might be needed, and this is a possible target area for an intervention on the organizational level (see Table 3.1). In Chapter 5 we will describe the important team process of building a shared meaning of goals, and how this process influences performance. This presupposes that such goals exist.

3.4.2 The problem is due to the work design

General advice: Choose from and list those aspects of work design (see mindmap) that theoretically could impact the expected results. Looking into the specific context (the workplace) there might also be other features of the work design that are important. Add these to the list. These features together form a "local" theory – a model for what to "diagnose" in a specific workplace.

3.4.2.1 "Diagnosis" of features of work design that impact teamwork in a workplace

The listed work-design features are the basis for the "diagnosis." It can be done in various ways, and there are several instruments for evaluating the work design, e.g. the "Work Design Questionnaire (WDQ) by Morgeson & Humphrey (2006). There are a number of different tools used in research and practice, and as long they have been found to be reliable and valid, and cover a range of work-design elements, any of these can be used. There are methods based on observations of work, such as REBA (Richter et al., 1999), TBS (see Frese & Zapf, 1994 for a short English summary) and Vera (see Frese & Zapf, 1994 for a short English summary), but these detailed analyses can only be carried out by experts in work psychology. Some are not for public use, but the WDQ is easily found. Some aspects of work design are also covered in inventories mainly developed to describe team performance, see Chapter 5. Instruments like the WDQ can be used as a survey, adapted to an interview guide or used as a basis for a discussion in a focus group. Such data collection is only descriptive, and the analysis can only result in showing weaknesses and strengths in the specific workplace. Depending on what the chosen instrument measures and how many different aspects are covered, there will be a broader or more limited scope for design decisions. Our perspective is that when designing work, the focus should be on a whole set of work-design dimensions and on *how these together* make effective performance possible.

4 Step 4. Select target dimensions and set goals

What are the results regarding work design prerequisites for teamwork? We give some advice on how to choose dimensions for an intervention.

- What kind of task-related dependencies exist between team members (pooled, sequential, reciprocal, goals and results, etc.)? Is it meaningful to talk about teamwork?
- Are key dimensions of work design that impact both routine and non-routine performance examined?
- If dimensions of work design are altered, what are the consequences for other teams and functions in the workflow?
- Prioritize and select those dimensions that seem most meaningful with regard to their impact on team effectiveness.

Can the prioritized team goals and work-design characteristics be changed? In Chapter 2 we underlined the importance of analyzing the potential for change. E.g. one cause of a problem could be task significance which can rarely be changed, but employees' perception of the task's significance may be altered. Or it might be possible to change something, but this would take many years. *After such an analysis, the dimensions that should be targeted in the intervention can be chosen.*

The process of designing or redesigning work starts with the discrepancy between "This is where we are when it comes to goals and work design" and "This is where we wish to be." It is too complicated to discuss goal setting for the change in team goals, so we leave that aside. However, some decisions about team goals might need to be taken.

We focus instead on setting goals for the change in the selected dimensions of work design. For example, the diagnosis in a workplace showed that each member carried out two similar tasks with several subtasks, and task variety was deemed to be low. The team goal was that each member should carry out a minimum of four tasks with several subtasks, and that these should be of different kinds (e.g. administrative tasks as well as assembly tasks). Although in most organizations it is not possible to fully use goal-setting theory (see Chapter 2) and the often used S.M.A.R.T. principle for goal setting (specific, measurable, attainable, realistic and time-framed), it is important to review goal formulations so that one can follow up the results. Avoid everything abstract or general such as "learning," and instead specify *what* should be learned.

5 Step 5. Identify solutions

Setting new or altered goals for teamwork and changing the work design involves the organization and the team. In order to identify possible solutions to the problem, *the next step is to select the level for interventions appropriate for dimension(s) chosen in step 4.* Decisions on team goals, on what work-design characteristic to change and what the change should be, are decisions on the organizational level. Implementing goals and work design by giving direction and initiating structure for how to work is both part of the leaders' tasks and also an organizational issue. Teams *may* be involved in forming work-design features and in redesigning work, and work design are prerequisites for work on the team level. In Table 3.1 it is shown that designing work might involve interventions in different domains.

Table 3.1 shows that interventions to design work most often involve organizational decisions as well as interventions on a team level to alter those aspects of work design that impede team performance. In order to change the selected dimensions (e.g. task variety) other related aspects might need to be changed as well. Before choosing a solution – how to bring change about in the selected dimension – it is important to find out if other solutions are also needed. It might be that changing one aspect of work design presupposes that other aspects are in place. For example: Increasing autonomy might only be possible if the leadership structure is changed, if systems to follow up results to balance autonomy and control are put in place, and the teams are coached to make use of the increased autonomy. Or task

Table 3.1 Interventions in different domains for a suitable work design

Choose domain(s) for solutions(s) to enhance work design			
Prerequisites in the physical environment for enhancing work design:	Prerequisites on organizational level for enhancing work design:	Solutions on team level for enhancing work design by changes in:	Prerequisites on individual level to enhance work design:
• Solutions can be needed to ensure possibilities for communication, to enhance ergonomics, etc.	• Production technology • Production processes • Organizational structure • Leadership • Decisions on team goals and task • Decisions on work design	• Task performance characteristics • Task knowledge characteristics • Social characteristics	• KSAs

WE HAVE TEAMS BUT LITTLE TEAMWORK

variety can only be addressed if team members are trained to carry out these new tasks. There are *several types of solutions*, and although even only one change, e.g. in task complexity, is what is wished for, this might require a combination of solutions. Table 3.2 shows how a bundled solution might look like if one is to increase task variety.

Choosing the dimensions which are most important for reaching the goal (e.g. an increase in task variety) can be done by identifying related dimensions that a) hinder or b) support the change in the chosen main dimension.

What the solution should be, i.e. how to change the chosen dimension (e.g. task variety), depends on the actual workplace. There are no general solutions for redesigning work as features of work design are highly dependent on the context. Later chapters will give examples of solutions to different problems, see also Chapter 10.

In this case it was decided that task interdependence first had to be changed in order to solve the problem ("We have teams but little teamwork"). The solution was to establish reciprocal dependencies with regard to results. This would also involve other solutions. The team goal needed to be changed to include results for non-routine tasks and for changes in behaviour as well as tangible results. (Completing the stipulated task was done solely by pooling individuals' tasks to an end result.) The teams were given the task to identify such goals. In one team they decided to enhance productivity by including the following goals: a) to jointly identify best practice in the different functions' specific task and reduce non-value-adding activities with regard to the end result, b) once a month to carry out an analysis of the workflow of one task that was successfully completed ahead of scheduled time and c) identify criteria for how the decision should be communicated to the client, regarding both content and form, to reduce the number of complaints. All functions contributed to the workflow and the content of what was communicated. These added goals imply further changes, e.g. in work roles, leadership and individual KSAs.

6 Step 6. Plan the intervention

To form and plan the intervention (what to do and how to do it) is about selecting tools and methods for changing the selected dimensions, and deciding the steps in the change process. (In following chapters it will be possible to give examples of different methods and tools, but not here within the topic of work design.) The plan of the intervention naturally depends on the chosen solution, tools and methods and cannot be discussed in general terms. In Chapter 2 we highlighted some important issues for a successful implementation process, such as the importance of participation and involvement of team members.

Table 3.2 An example of how interventions are mutually dependent

Environmental domain	Organizational domain	Individual domain	Team domain				
			Teamwork design	Team training	Team coaching	Team leadership	Team performance monitoring
e.g. changing the physical environment so that team members can communicate while performing added tasks	e.g. functions close to the team need to delegate tasks to the team	e.g. *learning a computer system*	*increased variety*	training in rotation, how to monitor and follow up added tasks	e.g. supporting reluctant members to take on new and challenging tasks	e.g. explaining why task variety enhances team effectiveness and explaining the added value for the individual, team and the organization	e.g. developing the system for reporting results to include the results of added tasks

7 Step 7. Implement the intervention

The next step is to carry out the intervention. It also involves monitoring and supporting the process and adapting methods and tools where alterations are needed, see Chapter 10.

8 Step 8. Evaluate

To ensure quality, the process should be evaluated during the process. If so, the evaluation is formative and gives input to how the original plan can be changed. In many cases the evaluation of the results is a step that tends to be forgotten. Too many interventions are carried out without knowing whether the original problem was solved, see Chapters 10 and 11.

9 Step 9. End the intervention

It is rewarding to see the end results of efforts. Ending the intervention helps to keep track of the many change and developmental projects in an organization.

In following chapters we refrain from descriptions of steps 4, 6, 7, 8 and 9 in the problem-solving circle as these depend on the context.

Bibliography

Bell, S. T. (2004). *Setting the stage for effective teams: A meta-analysis of team design variables and team effectiveness*. Doctoral dissertation. College Station: Texas A&M University.

Berman, S. L., Down, J., & Hill, C. W. L. (2002). Tacit knowledge as source of competitive advantage in the national basketball association. *Academy of Management Journal, 45*(1), 13–31. https://doi.org/10.2307/3069282

Cai, Z., Parker, S. K., Chen, Z., & Lam, W. (2019). How does the social context fuel the proactive fire? A multilevel review and theoretical synthesis. *Journal of Organizational Behavior, 40*(2), 209–230. https://doi.org/10.1002/job.2347

Christian, M. S., Garza, A., & Slaughter, J. (2011). Work engagement: A quantitative review and test of its relations with task and contextual performance. *Personnel Psychology, 64*. https://doi.org/10.1111/j.1744-6570.2010.01203.x

De Dreu, C. K. W. (2006). When too little or too much hurts: Evidence for a curvilinear relationship between task conflict and innovation in teams. *Journal of Management, 32*(1), 83–107. https://doi.org/10.1177/0149206305277795

Di Stefano, G., & Gaudino, M. (2019). Workaholism and work engagement: How are they similar? How are they different? A systematic review and meta-analysis. *European Journal of Work and Organizational Psychology, 28*(3), 329–347. https://doi.org/10.1080/1359432X.2019.1590337

Dubbelt, L., Demerouti, E., & Rispens, S. (2019). The value of job crafting for work engagement, task performance, and career satisfaction: Longitudinal and quasi-experimental evidence. *European Journal of Work and Organizational Psychology, 28*(3), 300–314. https://doi.org/10.1080/1359432X.2019.1576632

Frese, M., Garst, H., & Fay, D. (2007). Making things happen: Reciprocal relationships between work characteristics and personal initiative in a four-wave longitudinal structural equation model. *Journal of Applied Psychology, 92*(4), 1084–1102. https://doi.org/10.1037/0021-9010.92.4.1084

Frese, M., & Zapf, D. (1994). Action as the core of work psychology: A German approach. *Handbook of Industrial and Organizational Psychology, 4*. In H. C. Triandis, M. D. Dunnette, & L. Hough (Eds.), *Handbook of industrial and organizational psychology* (Vol. 4, pp. 271–340). Palo Alto, California: Consulting Psychologists Press.

Fried, Y., & Ferris, G. R. (1986). The dimensionality of job characteristics: Some neglected issues. *Journal of Applied Psychology, 71*(3), 419–426. https://doi.org/10.1037/0021-9010.71.3.419

Grant, A. M. (2008). The significance of task significance: Job performance effects, relational mechanisms, and boundary conditions. *Journal of Applied Psychology, 93*(1), 108–124. https://doi.org/10.1037/0021-9010.93.1.108

Grant, A. M., & Parker, S. K. (2009). 7 redesigning work design theories: The rise of relational and proactive perspectives. *The Academy of Management Annals, 3*(1), 317–375. https://doi.org/10.1080/19416520903047327

Griffin, M. A., Neal, A., & Parker, S. K. (2007). A new model of work role performance: Positive behavior in uncertain and interdependent contexts. *Academy of Management Journal, 50*(2), 327–347. https://doi.org/10.5465/amj.2007.24634438

Hacker, W. (2001). Activity theory. In N. J. Baltes & P. B. Smelser (Eds.), *International encyclopedia of the social and behavioural sciences* (pp. 58–62). Amsterdam, Netherlands: Elsevier.

Hacker, W. (2003). Action regulation theory: A practical tool for the design of modern work processes? *European Journal of Work and Organizational Psychology, 12*(2), 105–130. https://doi.org/10.1080/13594320344000075

Hackman, J. R., & Oldham, G. R. (1980). *Work redesign*. Reading, MA: Addison-Wesley.

Hammond, M. M., Neff, N. L., Farr, J. L., Schwall, A. R., & Zhao, X. (2011). Predictors of individual-level innovation at work: A meta-analysis. *Psychology of Aesthetics, Creativity, and the Arts, 5*(1), 90–105. https://doi.org/10.1037/a0018556

Humphrey, S. E., Nahrgang, J. D., & Morgeson, F. P. (2007). Integrating motivational, social, and contextual work design features: A meta-analytic summary and theoretical extension of the work design literature. *Journal of Applied Psychology, 92*(5), 1332–1356. https://doi.org/10.1037/0021-9010.92.5.1332

Ilgen, D. R., & Hollenbeck, J. R. (1992). The structure of work: Job design and roles. In M. D. Dunnette & L. M. Hough (Eds.), *Handbook of industrial and organizational psychology* (2nd ed., Vol. 2, pp. 165–207). Palo Alto, CA: Consulting Psychologists Press.

Johns, G. (2010). Some unintended consequences of job design. *Journal of Organizational Behavior, 31*(2–3), 361–369. https://doi.org/10.1002/job.669

Kohn, M. L., & Schooler, C. (1982). Job conditions and personality: A longitudinal assessment of their reciprocal effects. *American Journal of Sociology, 87*(6), 1257–1286. Retrieved from www.jstor.org/stable/2779361

Kozlowski, S., & Ilgen, D. (2006). Enhancing the effectiveness of work groups and teams. *Psychological Science in the Public Interest, 7*(3), 77–124. https://doi.org/10.1111/j.1529-1006.2006.00030.x

Langfred, C. W. (2005). Autonomy and performance in teams: The multilevel moderating effect of task interdependence. *Journal of Management, 31*(4), 513–529. https://doi.org/10.1177/0149206304272190

Lantz, A. (2011). Teamwork on the line can pay off down the line. *Journal of Workplace Learning, 23*(2), 75–96. https://doi.org/10.1108/13665621111108765

Lantz Friedrich, A., Sjöberg, A., & Friedrich, P. (2016). Leaned teamwork fattens workplace innovation: The relationship between task complexity, team learning and team proactivity. *European Journal of Work and Organizational Psychology, 25*(4), 561–569. https://doi.org/10.1080/1359432X.2016.1183649

Li, F., Li, Y., & Wang, E. (2009). Task characteristics and team performance: The mediating effect of team member satisfaction. *Social Behavior and Personality: An International Journal, 37*(10), 1373–1382. https://doi.org/10.2224/sbp.2009.37.10.1373

Li, W., Fay, D., Frese, M., Harms, P. D., & Gao, X. Y. (2014). Reciprocal relationship between proactive personality and work characteristics: A latent change score approach. *Journal of Applied Psychology, 99*(5), 948–965. https://doi.org/10.1037/a0036169

Locke, E. A., & Latham, G. P. (2002). Building a practically useful theory of goal setting and task motivation: A 35-year odyssey. *American Psychologist, 57*(9), 705–717. https://doi.org/10.1037/0003-066X.57.9.705

Malinowska, D., Tokarz, A., & Wardzichowska, A. (2018). Job autonomy in relation to work engagement and workaholism: Mediation of autonomous and controlled work motivation. *International Journal of Occupational Medicine and Environmental Health, 31*(4), 445–458. https://doi.org/10.13075/ijomeh.1896.01197

Marinova, S. V., Peng, C., Lorinkova, N., Van Dyne, L., & Chiaburu, D. (2015). Change-oriented behavior: A meta-analysis of individual and job design predictors. *Journal of Vocational Behavior, 88*, 104–120. https://doi.org/10.1016/j.jvb.2015.02.006

Morgeson, F. P., & Campion, M. A. (2003). Work design. In *Handbook of psychology: Industrial and organizational psychology* (Vol. 12, pp. 423–452). Hoboken, NJ: John Wiley & Sons Inc.

Morgeson, F. P., Delaney-Klinger, K., & Hemingway, M. A. (2005). The importance of job autonomy, cognitive ability, and job-related skill for predicting role breadth and job performance. *Journal of Applied Psychology, 90*(2), 399–406. https://doi.org/10.1037/0021-9010.90.2.399

Morgeson, F. P., & Humphrey, S. E. (2006). The Work Design Questionnaire (WDQ): Developing and validating a comprehensive measure for assessing job design and the nature of work. *Journal of Applied Psychology, 91*(6), 1321–1339. https://doi.org/10.1037/0021-9010.91.6.1321

Morgeson, F. P., & Humphrey, S. E. (2008). Job and team design: Toward a more integrative conceptualization of work design. In *Research in personnel and human resources management* (Vol. 27, pp. 39–91). https://doi.org/10.1016/S0742-7301(08)27002-7

Nahrgang, J. D., Morgeson, F. P., & Hofmann, D. A. (2011). Safety at work: A meta-analytic investigation of the link between job demands, job resources, burnout, engagement, and safety outcomes. *Journal of Applied Psychology, 96*(1), 71–94. https://doi.org/10.1037/a0021484

Parker, S. (1999). Enhancing role breadth self-efficacy: The roles of job enrichment and other organizational interventions. *The Journal of Applied Psychology, 83*. https://doi.org/10.1037//0021-9010.83.6.835

Parker, S. K., Knight, C., & Ohly, S. (2017). *The changing face of work design research: Past, present and future directions*. In A. Wilkinson, N. Bacon, S. Snell, & D. Lepak (Eds.), *In SAGE Handbook of Human Resource Management* (pp. 402–420). London: Sage.

Parker, S. K., Morgeson, F. P., & Johns, G. (2017). One hundred years of work design research: Looking back and looking forward. *Journal of Applied Psychology, 102*(3), 403–420. https://doi.org/10.1037/apl0000106

Parker, S. K., Van den Broeck, A., & Holman, D. (2017). Work design influences: A synthesis of multilevel factors that affect the design of jobs. *Academy of Management Annals, 11*(1), 267–308. https://doi.org/10.5465/annals.2014.0054

Parker, S. K., Williams, H. M., & Turner, N. (2006). Modeling the antecedents of proactive behavior at work. *Journal of Applied Psychology, 91*(3), 636–652. https://doi.org/10.1037/0021-9010.91.3.636

Podsakoff, N. P., Podsakoff, P. M., MacKenzie, S. B., Maynes, T. D., & Spoelma, T. M. (2014). Consequences of unit-level organizational citizenship behaviors: A review and recommendations for future research. *Journal of Organizational Behavior, 35*(S1), S87–S119. https://doi.org/10.1002/job.1911

Podsakoff, P. M., MacKenzie, S., Paine, J. B., & Bachrach, D. (2000). Organizational citizenship behaviors: A critical review of the theoretical and empirical literature and suggestions for future research. *Journal of Management, 26.* https://doi.org/10.1177/014920630002600306

Rashkovits, S., & Drach-Zahavy, A. (2017). The moderating role of team resources in translating nursing teams' accountability into learning and performance: A cross-sectional study. *Journal of Advanced Nursing, 73*(5), 1124–1136. https://doi.org/10.1111/jan.13200

Richter, P., Hemman, E., & Pohlandt, A. (1999). Objective task analysis and the prediction of mental workload: Results of the application of an action-oriented software tool (REBA). In M. Wiethoff & F. R. H. Zijlstra (Eds.), *New approaches for modern problems in work psychology* (pp. 67–76). Tilburg: Univeristy Press.

Rico, R., de la Hera, C. M. A., & Tabernero, C. (2011). Work team effectiveness: A review of research from the last decade (1999–2009). *Psychology in Spain, 15.* Retrieved from www.psychologyinspain.com/content/full/2011/15006.pdf

Rico, R., Sánchez-Manzanares, M., Gil, F., & Gibson, C. (2008). Team implicit coordination processes: A team knowledgebased approach. *Academy of Management Review, 33*(1), 163–184. https://doi.org/10.5465/amr.2008.27751276

Stewart, G. L. (2006). A meta-analytic review of relationships between team design features and team performance. *Journal of Management, 32*(1), 29–55. https://doi.org/10.1177/0149206305277792

Sverke, M., Falkenberg, H., Kecklund, G., Magnusson Hanson, L., & Lindfors, P. (2016). *Kvinnors och mäns arbetsvillkor: betydelsen av organisatoriska faktorer och psykosocial arbetsmiljö för arbets- och hälsorelaterade utfall* [Women's and men's working conditions: The importance of organizational factors and psychosocial work environment for work and health related outcomes]. *Kunskapssammanställning 2016:2.* Stockholm: Arbetsmiljöverket.

Tafvelin, S., Stenling, A., Lundmark, R., & Westerberg, K. (2019). Aligning job redesign with leadership training to improve supervisor support: a quasi-experimental study of the integration of HR practices. *European Journal of Work and Organizational Psychology, 28*(1), 74–84. https://doi.org/10.1080/1359432X.2018.1541887

Taylor, F. W. (1911). *The principles of scientific management.* New York, NY: Harper and Brothers.

Tornau, K., & Frese, M. (2013). Construct clean-up in proactivity research: A meta-analysis on the nomological net of work-related proactivity concepts and their incremental validities. *Applied Psychology, 62*(1), 44–96. https://doi.org/10.1111/j.1464-0597.2012.00514.x

Tschan, F. (2000). *Produktivität in Kleingruppen: Was machen produktive Gruppen anders und besser? [Productivity in small groups: What do productive groups do different and better?].* Bern: Huber Verlag.

West, M. A. (2012). *Effective teamwork: Practical lessons from organizational research* (3rd ed.). Oxford: Blackwell.

West, M. A., Hirst, G., Richter, A., & Shipton, H. (2004). Twelve steps to heaven: Successfully managing change through developing innovative teams. *European Journal of Work and Organizational Psychology, 13*(2), 269–299. https://doi.org/10.1080/13594320444000092

Wong, C., & Campion, M. A. (1991). Development and test of a task level model of motivational job design. *Journal of Applied Psychology, 76*(6), 825–837. https://doi.org/10.1037/0021-9010.76.6.825

Wood, R. E. (1986). Task complexity: Definition of the construct. *Organizational Behavior and Human Decision Processes, 37*(1), 60–82. https://doi.org/10.1016/0749-5978(86)90044-0

Woods, S. A., & West, M. A. (2014). *The psychology of work and organizations.* Andover, UK: South Western Cengage Learning.

Wu, C.-H., Griffin, M. A., & Parker, S. K. (2015). Developing agency through good work: Longitudinal effects of job autonomy and skill utilization on locus of control. *Journal of Vocational Behavior, 89,* 102–108. https://doi.org/10.1016/j.jvb.2015.05.004

Chapter 4

Team composition

"We have a team, but team members do not benefit from each other"

The composition of a team sets the stage for effective teamwork and ensures that team members can use their capabilities to carry out the teamwork. We will learn about characteristics of individual team members and qualities of the whole team that impact teamwork. Besides team members' personality (the big five personality factors), interpersonal and self-management KSAs (knowledge, skills, abilities) are crucial for team performance, among others, social skills to get along with each other and team regulation skills, such as goal setting, performance management and coordination. Depending on the team task other factors such as adaptability and cognitive ability are important as well. Moreover, team members' attitudes and motivation such as collectivism, team orientation and learning goal orientation affect the quality of teamwork.

Teams are composed of several individuals who can be more or less alike – so different kinds of diversity (task related, surface and deep-level diversity) and their impact on team performance play an important role in this chapter as well. Moreover, we have a look at the organizational context comprising factors such as team size, team structure (e.g. skill differentiation) and team task that set the frame for team composition. In the solution part of the chapter, we consider that it makes a difference, if a new team is being formed – and adequate personnel selection instruments are needed – or if there is an existing team whose composition has negative implications for the teams' work processes and interventions as individual feedback, team training and team building are appropriate.

One basic idea of teamwork is that the competencies, expertise and potentials of different individuals are not just added up but create synergies and so enhance the effectiveness of a team. Team members need to be qualified and suitable to perform their tasks, and in addition, to cooperate with their colleagues in the team. Obviously, this is not always the case, and teams do not always perform well – and one reason for this may be the characteristics of team members or their specific combination. People care about with whom they work; it is an important aspect of their perception of workplace quality.

1 Step 1. Describe the current situation

Let us start with an authentic case of a team having problems due to their composition.

CASE: TEAM COMPOSITION AND THE ASSOCIATED LITTLE WILLINGNESS TO WORK TOGETHER CONTRIBUTE TO POOR RESULTS

The team is part of a social project aiming to prepare young people, who have not graduated from the traditional school, for a craft trade. For a period of one year, 32 adolescents come to the organization every weekday from 8 AM until 4 PM to be trained and supported because of their difficult social situations. After the year, they are expected to succeed in passing exams to earn a vocational degree. The team exists since two years. Team members are two female and one male social workers and three male carpenters. The idea of the team composition was that the craftsmen have the competencies to teach the skills, and the social workers have the expertise to meet the challenges of dealing with the young people and can offer possibilities to support them.

How do stakeholders describe the situation? The promoters of the projects are dissatisfied, as the team does not achieve acceptable results: Compared to other projects, fewer young people achieve a vocational degree and there is a high dropout rate. The managers' impression is that social workers and craftsmen do not support, but impede each other, e.g. by criticizing their way of working. The students report that they sometimes do not know how to act, as different people in the team make varying and sometimes contradictory demands.

When we asked the team members about their cooperation, we heard the following statements:

All team members

- "We are too different to work with each other."
- "We cannot reach our aims properly."
- "It cannot go on like this, in this composition. We would work more effectively with new persons in the team."
- "The project promoters want us to submit complicated commercial calculations – none of us knows how to do it, and so we are estimating, but it is hard to get the funding we really need."

Social workers

- "The craftsmen have no understanding of the difficult situation of the young and are too authoritative."
- "There are a lot of misunderstandings with the craftsmen. And they talk, if at all, only with our male colleague."
- "There are also social workers with manual skills – why don't we hire one of them?"

> **Craftsmen**
>
> - "In a craft profession, punctuality, accuracy and reliability are central. The young people have to learn that, and they can only do so if we insist. The social workers put a spoke into the wheel, which is not good for the young people either."
> - "The social workers do not share with us, what management is telling them."
> - "Social workers look down on us."

Many problems in teams can arise because of who is on the team and how persons have been combined into a team – for very different reasons. Apparently, it is not enough to ensure that team members have the qualifications to perform their tasks – they also need to be able to cooperate with different people in a constructive way.

2 Step 2. Identify the core problem(s)

Obviously, the team is not performing in an optimal way, as many students do not achieve their goal – a vocational degree. The problem seems to be that the team – in spite of good qualifications of the team members – cannot make use of their capabilities. The team members do not consider themselves to work as an effective team, and they explain it for example by the diversity within the team. In reality several problems could be identified (e.g. lack of leadership, lack of shared meaning of how to work, coordination, etc.), but in this chapter we focus on team composition as one of the problems. In the next section we describe in accordance with the problem-solving cycle what can be the causes to such a problem.

3 Step 3. Cause analysis: what are the main causes of problems with team composition?

In this step, we identify possible causes of the problem derived from theory – we call them work hypotheses. Team composition can be defined as a configuration of persons in a team with regard to several individual characteristics, e.g. abilities, personality, demographic background and attitudes (Levine & Moreland, 1990; Mathieu et al., 2017). Therefore, there are two main aspects: first, characteristics of team members (the individual level), predestining them for teamwork (or not); and second, qualities of the entire team on the team level.

Wageman, Hackman, and Lehman (2005) describe the following factors of successful team composition (in the sense that team members complement each other to fulfil the team task): an adequate team size for the task accomplishment, an appropriate diversity in the team and team members with task-related as well as interpersonal skills. What does appropriate diversity mean? In section 3.2 we will learn that differences of team members do not necessarily provoke difficulties and

TEAM COMPOSITION

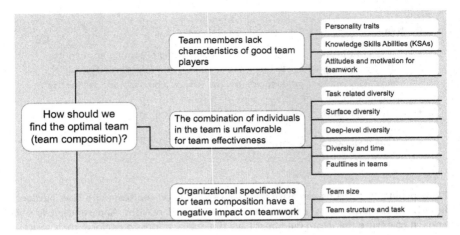

Figure 4.1 Mindmap about causes of problems with team composition

can be fruitful for the team. The authors include all levels of the IMOI model: Team size is usually determined on the organizational level, diversity is a characteristic on the team level, and individual knowledge and skills are related to the level of team members.

In this chapter, we will mainly focus on the team level and on the individual level. Additionally, as important preconditions for the team composition are determined on the organizational level, we will make some preliminary remarks on this context as well.

The following mindmap (see Figure 4.1) gives an overview over main features of team composition. First order branches include possible causes of problems and second order branches show main theoretical and evidence-based aspects related to these causes. These aspects can be explored in practice to find out how problems can be explained, and section 3.4 describes how to diagnose them.

3.1 Team members lack characteristics of good team players

In the following, we will focus on factors that are important for individuals to be good team players. These characteristics are usually desirable for all teams in general, but as dependent on the specific team task the relevance may vary from team to team.

What demands does teamwork put on team members? Working in a team includes the following dimensions of teamwork (based on Cannon-Bowers, Tannenbaum, Salas, & Volpe, 1995; Driskell, Goodwin, Salas, & O'Shea, 2006; Salas & Cannon-Bowers, 2001):

- Performance monitoring, mutual backup behaviour and feedback: Team members observe the team processes to reach the goal, support each other and give mutual feedback (see Chapter 5).

TEAM COMPOSITION

Table 4.1 Variables for the assessment of team members (based on the dimensions of Liu, Huang, & Dickson, 2017, adapted; and for interpersonal and self-management KSAs on Stevens & Campion, 1994)

A Personality	B KSAs	C Values and motivational orientations
Emotional stability	Interpersonal KSAs for:	Collectivism
Extraversion	• Conflict resolution	Preference for teamwork
Openness	• Collaborative problem-solving	Team orientation
Agreeableness	• Communication	Learning goal orientation
Conscientiousness	Self-management KSAs:	Performance goal orientation
	• Goal setting and performance management	
	• Planning and task coordination	
	Adaptability	
	Cognitive ability	

- Shared situational awareness: Teams have shared knowledge and a common view on the task, the teamwork and the external context (see Chapters 5 and 7).
- Coordination: The common task fulfilment has to be organized – regarding resources, time, responsibilities, etc. (see Chapter 5).
- Communication: Teams need to exchange information and arguments and communicate clearly (see Chapter 5).
- Interpersonal relations: Teams need an amicable team climate to be effective (see Chapter 6).
- Decision-making: In teams, well-grounded decisions have to be taken (see Chapter 5).
- Adaptability: Teams need to react flexibly to changing external environments (see Chapter 7).

Beyond this, team leadership behaviours and contributions of the team to organizational change and development are essential (see Chapters 8 and 9). What aspects matter for being an adequate team member? We categorize them into personality-based traits, specific knowledge domains, skills, abilities (KSAs) and values/motivational orientations (see Table 4.1) and describe those aspects that are of particular importance for teamwork (based on empirical research).

3.1.1 Personality

The big five model claims a set of trait dimensions regarded as the most relevant general components to describe personality (Cervone, Pervin, & John, 2005). Driskell et al. (2006) have, based on a literature research, adapted the model for teamwork and named specific facets of these personality traits that have shown to be of importance to team effectiveness (see Table 4.2).

In a meta-analysis, Bell (2007) found relationships between all personality traits and team performance (defined as the extent to which a team accomplishes its goals or mission). Agreeableness and conscientiousness have a medium-sized impact on team performance – but also the p-values of the other traits show small, but statically significant effect sizes (see box).

TEAM COMPOSITION

Table 4.2 Personality facets related to teamwork (Driskell et al., 2006)

Trait	Facets for teamwork
Extraversion (sensation seeking and the quantity and the intensity of interpersonal relationships)	• Dominance • Affiliation • Social perceptiveness • Expressivity
Openness (autonomous thinking, a willingness to examine unfamiliar ideas and an inclination to try new things)	• Flexibility regarding interpersonal situations
Agreeableness (quality of interpersonal interactions)	• Trust • Cooperation
Conscientiousness (sense of duty, persistence and self-disciplined goal-directed behaviour)	• Dependability • Dutifulness • Achievement
Emotional stability (lack of a tendency to experience negative emotions)	• Adjustment • Self-esteem

---

Relationship between field team means and personality traits:

- Emotional stability: ρ .21
- Extraversion: ρ .18
- Openness: ρ .25
- Agreeableness: ρ .34
- Conscientiousness: ρ .33

Meta-analysis (Bell, 2007): personality traits and team performance

---

Bell, Brown, Colaneri, and Outland (2018) summarize several studies about team members' traits that show a positive impact on teamwork behaviour, such as sharing information, supporting each other, cooperating and problem-solving as well.

CASE: TEAM COMPOSITION AND THE ASSOCIATED LITTLE WILLINGNESS TO WORK TOGETHER CONTRIBUTE TO POOR RESULTS CONT.

From these theoretical assumptions we could deduce a hypothesis about the cause of the problem: work hypothesis 1: The problem could be explained by team members' personal traits e.g. that they are not open enough to work with persons who have a different professional background.

What should not be forgotten is that although personality is associated with capacity for teamwork, it is not the only factor that determines it. It is therefore too short-sighted to simply attribute difficulties in teams to personality traits.

TEAM COMPOSITION

Therefore, it is important to consider those aspects that can be influenced on the basis of interventions.

3.1.2 KSAs – knowledge, skills, abilities

Traits and dispositions are hard to change as they form a part of personality. Knowledge, skills and abilities (KSAs) for teamwork can be impacted by trainings and other personnel development measures. We will describe the most important general teamwork competencies that are valid for (nearly) all work teams, or in other words generic skills, that refer to key competencies and can be used in different workplace situations (Kearns, 2001).

Stevens and Campion (1994) have – based on a literature review – developed a model that comprises two dimensions: interpersonal KSAs, needed to interact and communicate in a positive and constructive manner with other team members; and self-management KSAs, which are important for steering and managing team processes as well as individual task work.

Interpersonal KSAs are needed as team members should be able to manage conflicts in a constructive way, to solve problems together and to communicate openly and in a friendly way.

Self-management KSAs refer to qualities, such as setting goals and managing the processes to achieve them (including monitoring, evaluation and feedback). Team members need to be able to plan and coordinate their activities. Kozlowski and Ilgen (2006) explain self-regulation as an iterative process to reach difficult goals: "Behaviour directed at goal striving; feedback and self-reactions to current progress; and revision of effort investment, strategies, or goal levels to lessen the discrepancy between the goal and performance" (p. 96). Accordingly, self-regulation is a conscious personal management behaviour that involves the process of guiding one's own thoughts, behaviours and feelings to reach goals. To do so, individuals need to self-monitor their behaviour and to evaluate how this behaviour affects performance. If the desired effect is not realized, new strategies to reach the goal need to be found.

The same applies for the team level and specific team regulation skills that are included in the model by Stevens and Campion (1994):

- How to establish team goals (goal setting)?
- How to realize a common performance management or monitoring – by monitoring and evaluating team as well as individual processes and giving feedbacks on that basis? Performance monitoring means monitoring progress toward goals. Systems monitoring focuses the internal and external environments – for instance external changes of customers' requests. Team monitoring means to keep an eye on the others' work, identify mistakes and support each other with feedback and advice (Driskell, Salas, & Driskell, 2018).
- How to plan and coordinate the team's activities and tasks, distribute responsibilities and make sure that relevant information is available (see Chapter 5).

Weick and Roberts (1993) introduced a similar concept, heedful interrelating, which includes attitudes and behaviours of an individual member in order to act in close alignment with situational and team requirements. Team members pay attention to, constantly monitor and reconsider their contributions in relation to team goals. The more leeway a team has, the more self-management KSAs become relevant as team members need to regulate more team processes than in teams with rigid specifications by the management or with a highly structured work assignment.

> ### CASE: TEAM COMPOSITION AND THE ASSOCIATED LITTLE WILLINGNESS TO WORK TOGETHER CONTRIBUTE TO POOR RESULTS CONT.
>
> Work hypothesis 2: In the case description it was mentioned that team members do not support each other and that there are misunderstandings – a possible cause could be that members lack interpersonal and communicative skills. Therefore, they do not know how to solve their conflicts and problems adequately.

It should be mentioned that the model of Stevens and Campion (1994) includes a set of important KSAs, but it is not exhaustive. Research has found more factors that are important with high relevance for team performance.

The following two abilities are of high relevance for team effectiveness: cognitive ability and adaptability. Cognitive ability or intelligence is an umbrella term with several different meanings (and tests to assess it). Spearman's (1904) influential two factor theory of intelligence describes two components: The g-factor (general intelligence or general mental ability) that underlies all mental abilities of a person and specific ability factors (s-factors) which determine performance in particular task areas in addition to the g-factor. Gottfredson (1997, p. 13) gives a broader definition of intelligence, basing it on an agreement of more than 50 experts of intelligence research. They describe intelligence as a general mental capability, with elements such as abilities of reasoning, planning, problem-solving, abstract thinking, comprehending complex ideas and learning from experience. In the statement it is highlighted that intelligence is not only a narrow academic competence, but includes the ability to comprehend the surroundings, make sense and plan concrete actions. Cognitive ability has generally proven to predict job performance (Hunter & Hunter, 1984) and impacts team performance (Bell, 2007; Devine & Philips, 2001; Stewart, 2006). Schmidt and Hunter (2004) explain this correlation with the key process of knowledge acquisition. Less complex tasks require task-related knowledge only up to a certain point. After this, the job becomes routine. In complex tasks on the other hand there is more to learn and the knowledge acquisition will continuously be important for performance. Bell et al. (2018) report several studies which show that teams whose members have higher cognitive abilities are better at developing common knowledge structures e.g. about the task, the environment and resources (shared mental models, see Chapter 5).

Adaptability is the ability to adjust strategies or courses of action in response to changes inside or outside the team (Driskell et al., 2018; Salas, Sims, & Burke, 2005). In times of changing demands and environments, adaptability of teams is of high relevance. Is a team able to adjust its goals, behaviours and strategies? Adaptability does not only include the team's process of change – but also a diagnosis of the situation as a basis for a reasonable planning before a team adapts its procedures and approaches (Driskell et al., 2018). In addition, adaptability is closely linked with team learning (see Chapter 9).

3.1.3 Values and motivation for teamwork

The third category includes values and motivation that are relevant for team members. The value collectivism implicates that the team's needs are considered more important than individual needs. In the meta-analysis of Bell (2007), teams' mean collectivism has been shown to be connected to team performance outcomes ($\rho = .35$). Preference for teamwork, defined as the degree to which individuals prefer to work in a team rather than working alone has a medium-sized impact on team performance outcomes, too (Bell, 2007). Team orientation is a broader construct than collectivism and preference for teamwork, as it includes the propensity to take the behaviour and feedback of other team members into account and accept, coordinate and evaluate team processes.

Learning goal orientation is a motivational construct that is important for team effectiveness. It is linked to a person's beliefs in ability and intelligence. Vandewalle (1997) defines learning goal orientation as the "desire to develop the self by acquiring new skills, mastering new situations and improving one's competence" (p. 1000). Individuals with learning goal orientation seek feedback on past performance to evaluate current performance, focus on improving skills and acquiring knowledge, and are less concerned with making mistakes. In a meta-analysis, learning goal orientation has shown to be linked to both performance and learning (Payne, Youngcourt, & Beaubien, 2007; Porter, Webb, & Gogus, 2010). Learning goal orientation is positively related with adaptability, as well: LePine (2005) showed in an experimental study that teams with difficult goals and a high goal orientation were more likely to adapt.

For another motivational orientation, research status is more ambiguous. Performance goal orientation is defined as "seeking to demonstrate and validate the adequacy of one's competence by seeking favourable judgements and avoiding negative judgements about one's competence" (Vandewalle, 1997, p. 997). Che-Ha, Mavondo, and Mohd-Said (2014) have shown in a study with managers (not teams) that learning goal as well as performance orientations have a positive impact on market orientation, innovativeness, financial performance and marketing effectiveness. On the other hand team members with high performance orientation faced with challenging tasks and difficult goals are less likely to adapt (LePine, 2005). Christian, Christian, Pearsall, and Long (2017) report as results of their meta-analysis that learning goal orientation positively impacts team processes, but performance goal orientation does not.

As the definition of performance goal orientation includes two tendencies, sometimes a distinction is made between prove goal orientation (desire to prove competence) and avoid goal orientation (desire to avoid appearing incompetent). Payne et al. (2007) showed in a meta-analysis that the avoid goal orientation is dysfunctional – whereas prove goal orientation is often connected with learning goal orientation. These results indicate that learning and prove performance goal orientations may exist simultaneously.

Lim, Laosirihongthong, and Chan (2006) have mainly focused on motivational aspects of working in teams. From their study they draw the conclusion that team members support organizational and team learning: "(1) who are continuously improving their work skills, (2) who are motivated to learn job-relevant skills, and (3) who are willing to invest in self-improvement" (p. 54). Note that the authors do not focus on team performance but on team learning as an output – as working in a team means learning from each other.

TEAM COMPOSITION

> **CASE: TEAM COMPOSITION AND THE ASSOCIATED LITTLE WILLINGNESS TO WORK TOGETHER CONTRIBUTE TO POOR RESULTS CONT.**
>
> Transfer to our case: Some team members say that they are too different to work together – but could it also be possible that they just do not want it? Then our work hypothesis 3 would be that team members are not motivated to work in a team. They would prefer to work alone and not collectively.

To summarize: We have learned, that many individual characteristics are supposed to have an influence on the aptitude to work in a team. To be a competent team worker, more attributes are needed than task related qualifications.

In general – what do we know about team members in well-performing teams?

- They are agreeable, conscientious and open (personality).
- They are socially competent.
- They have – in case of complex tasks – a high degree of cognitive ability and are ready to adapt flexibly to external changes.
- They should really want to be part of a team – and not prefer to work individually (preference for teamwork) and be willing to support team processes and consider their teammates' behaviours and feedbacks (team orientation).
- They are collectivists – that means team goals are more important to them than individual goals (collectivism).
- They are goal-orientated and therefore willing to develop themselves, their skills and competencies based on their experiences and the organizational needs.
- The team as a whole has team regulation skills and knows how to set goals, monitor team performance, coordinate team tasks and activities and evaluate their goal attainment.

3.2 The combination of individuals in the team is unfavourable for team effectiveness

The last section was about characteristics that are desirable for all team members (although the degree of their importance depends on the team task and context). Besides such composition patterns team compilation is important as well: Compilation means that individual team members differ and that this variance is relevant, as "diverse groups have the potential to provide a broader range of individual inputs related to knowledge, information, and perspective" (Carter, Mead, Stewart, Nielsen, & Solimeo, 2019, p. 143). Individuals are different in many ways which makes diversity an important factor when describing and analyzing teams. If team members can choose new team members, they often look for similarity – of age, social status, norms and values. This can be explained with the similarity-attraction paradigm (Dickson, Resick, & Goldstein, 2008). One core idea is that teamwork is fruitful because team members learn from different perspectives complementing and inspiring each other. So, teams need heterogeneity, and it can be a problem if there is a lack of it – but to what degree heterogeneity is needed also depends on the nature of the team tasks. And we have to consider that heterogeneity can cause problems as well.

First, team members can be distinguished by their qualifications, as in some teams members contribute different knowledge and skills. Second, diversity aspects can be categorized in surface- and deep-level characteristics. The surface level includes overt attributes that can be observed or noticed after a brief contact – as gender, age, race and cultural background. Deep-level diversity refers to invisible factors – e.g. values and personality.

What we will see for all areas of diversity – and which is in contrast to the individual variables reported before – is that there are no unambiguous results and the specific team context is of great importance, as well as time (teams develop). In the following section, we first take a look at task related diversity of expertise, and then we focus on surface and deep diversity variables.

3.2.1 Task related diversity

There is broad agreement that heterogeneity of task related attributes has a positive impact on team effectiveness, because it provides a broader knowledge base. For complex and innovative team tasks more heterogeneity is needed concerning a broad knowledge base built on expertise (West, Hirst, Richter, & Shipton, 2004). Teams that tackle complex tasks and need to find innovative solutions necessitate a wide qualification, different ideas and points of views. In meta-analyses it was found that task related diversity and functional background variety diversity has a positive relationship with general team performance (Horwitz & Horwitz, 2007) and with team creativity and innovation – especially in design and product development teams (Bell & Marentette, 2011).

In a field study, Jehn, Northcraft, and Neale (1999) found positive effects in so far as diversity of qualification (caused by differing educational background, expertise and work-related experiences) correlated positively with team performance. This diversity was also connected with more task conflicts – as performance increased, these task conflicts obviously were functional and had positive effects (more about conflicts in teams in Chapter 6).

It is challenging to set up teams of individuals with diverse knowledge. If team members have differing specialized qualification they need to work across knowledge domains (Bunderson & Sutcliffe, 2002; Contu & Pecis, 2017; Majchrzak, Birnbaum, & Faraj, 2012). Most people take the norms and values within their own professions, organizations or industries for granted, sharing largely unquestioned assumptions so communication across boundaries can get difficult (Cronin & Weingart, 2007; Edmondson & Reynolds, 2016; Seidel & O'Mahony, 2014).

3.2.2 Surface diversity

How does surface diversity impact team performance? In a literature review, Mannix and Neale (2005) found that surface-level diversity (regarding race and gender) has negative effects on team effectiveness. Other studies show that the effects also depend on context variables. Schneid, Isidor, Li, and Kabst (2015), for instance, found in a meta-analysis that gender diversity has a small but significant negative relationship with team performance – that was moderated by cultural dimensions, such as gender egalitarianism and collectivism, so this negative relationship cannot be generalized to all teams. That means that in teams with team members seeing men and women as equal and being positive about collectivist values, gender diversity does not matter. Organizational context can also determine if diversity is salient or not: In an enterprise with a predominantly male workforce, gender differences can stand out more than in an organization with a balanced ratio of men and women (Bell et al., 2018).

Surface diversity is not always a problem – for example different meta-analyses show no negative effects of age diversity on team performance (Paoletti, Gilberto, Beier, & Salas, 2020; Schneid, Isidor, Steinmetz, & Kabst, 2016). So different ages do not seem to be of importance for the performance of a team. Accordingly, surface diversity does not always matter – and perhaps should not be overestimated.

3.2.3 Deep-level diversity

Deep-level diversity is harder to discover and more complex than task-related and surface-level diversity – like values, attitudes, goals and personality factors. Deep-level characteristics have a higher impact on team performance outcomes than surface-level characteristics (Bell et al., 2018).

In the study mentioned earlier by Jehn et al. (1999) value difference had a negative influence on member satisfaction, intent to remain and commitment to the group. Johns and Saks (2008) argue that deep-level diversity in attitudes, vision and goals can persist as a negative factor.

Cultural diversity has become an important factor in teams – mainly because many societies are culturally diverse and because international joint ventures are quite common. Stahl, Maznevski, Voigt, and Jonsen (2010) found in a meta-analysis both positive and negative effects of cultural diversity: There are process losses due to task conflicts and decreased social integration in the team, and gains because of more creativity and satisfaction.

How do team members perceive deep-level diversity? Mannix and Neale (2005) argue that social category differences could trigger expectations of deeper-level differences and might result in self-fulfilling prophecies. Meyer (2017) states that teams, whose members appreciate diversity, are more likely to have positive outcomes. That means that it is not so much diversity itself that hinders performance but negative attitudes towards diversity – instead of perceiving diversity as a potential.

3.2.4 Diversity and time

Kozlowski and Bell (2013) argue that team age is an important factor – in the initial phase more process losses might occur, but after a certain time of team cooperation, heterogeneous teams might achieve better results than homogeneous teams. It is assumed that diverse teams need more time to become an effective and cohesive team, because they need more time to establish common norms. After this period, surface-level diversity (for example gender, age, nationality) should not be a problem anymore. In contrast, Meyer (2017) found inconsistent results in different articles about change processes in diverse teams – sometimes, negative effects of surface-level diversity remained over time.

3.2.5 Faultlines in teams

Diversity can result in *faultlines* in a team. The team is divided in two or more relatively homogeneous subgroups varying in one or more attributes – and the more attributes split a team, the stronger is the faultline (for instance younger female economists and elder male engineers in a team). The original concept of diversity faultlines by Lau and Murnighan (1998) refers only to demographic attributes such as gender, age and race, but has been expanded to deep-level characteristics such as attitudes and personality attributes (Cunningham, 2015; Thatcher & Patel, 2011).

Faultlines can cause coalitions, conflicts (see Chapter 6), reduced job satisfaction, lower team performance and a lack of communication and information sharing between the subgroups (Bell et al., 2018; Bezrukova, Jehn, Zanutto, & Thatcher, 2009; Cunningham, 2015; Jehn & Bezrukova, 2010; Thatcher & Patel, 2011).

> **CASE: TEAM COMPOSITION AND THE ASSOCIATED LITTLE WILLINGNESS TO WORK TOGETHER CONTRIBUTE TO POOR RESULTS CONT.**
>
> For this case work hypothesis 4: The problem is caused by a faultline, based on different educational backgrounds (social workers versus craftsmen) and deep-level attributes, such as values regarding pedagogical ideas and adequate interactions with the clients. This faultline dividing the team into two subgroups causes conflicts and a lack of information and communication in the team.

> *To summarize:* It is not possible to describe the influence of team diversity in a simple way, as the effects can be positive (for example innovative ideas and great solutions for complex problems) or negative (such as misunderstandings and conflicts). And sometimes diversity does not even matter, respectively only matters when team members have a negative attitude toward diversity. One main issue is in what respect team members differ: Task related differences can have a positive impact on performance if task related conflicts are managed in a positive way. Surface-level diversity can cause problems – some studies show that they only occur in the initial phase after team composition, others see persisting negative effects. Deep-level diversity (differing values, attitudes, goals, etc.) is viewed as a factor that can have a sustaining negative influence – but again, it also depends on team members' attitudes towards diversity.

3.3 Organizational specifications for team composition have a negative impact on teamwork

As mentioned in the beginning, team composition is impacted by the organizational level. The organization gives resources, such as the number of team members, and makes demands on the team, e.g. by providing a specific structure and defining the team task.

3.3.1 Team size

It depends on the number of persons in a team, if team goals can be achieved. On the one hand there should be enough people to accomplish the task (see Wageman et al., 2005, earlier). On the other hand, too many team members are not economically sensible. Wheelan (2009) found in a study with 329 teams that teams with three to eight team members were more productive than larger teams. Bell (2004) reports several studies that show that teams consisting of too many members have negative effects on team processes, such as participation and coordination. The more persons there are in a team, the more there is a need for collective coordination of communication and regulation of team processes.

3.3.2 Team structure and task

Team composition needs to be suitable for the specific team structure and task. There are several classifications to differentiate team types. Hollenbeck, Beersma, and Schouten (2012) have extracted three main dimensions to describe different teams – we will use them to show exemplarily what demand structural conditions put to team composition, and how these are related to the definition of the team task.

1. *Skill differentiation*: The role structure of a team (how is work divided among team members?) has an impact on team composition. The team task (especially its knowledge characteristics: complexity, skill variety and specialization, see Chapter 3) determines the different expertise and specialized competencies that team members need to bring. This again sets the scope for different ways of work division: In a team with a functional work division, team members have different expertise and take over different tasks based on their dissimilar competencies. The more similar the qualifications of team members, the more interchangeable their roles can be. (Wildman et al., 2012)
2. *Authority differentiation*: What about authority and responsibility – do all team members equally participate in decision-making or are there differences? We will see later in Chapter 8 that leadership tasks can be shared within the team. For this purpose, team members with specific competencies are needed. This is another aspect for team composition. Again, these competencies are related to the team task – the more complex, autonomous and complete it is (see Chapter 3), the more responsibility can be shared in the team.
3. *Temporal stability*: It makes a difference for team composition, for how long these teams are to exist: In teams who work together on temporally limited tasks (for example project teams) team members need competencies to build a solid work relationship in a short time. In contrast, in stable teams that are part of the organizational structure and work on continual tasks, they have more time to develop together and to improve team processes, based on common experiences.

All in all, we can conclude that there are several potential theoretical causes for problems that are related to team composition – team members' characteristics, their combination in the team and the fit of composition with structural frame conditions of the team context as well. The next step is to show how to profoundly diagnose the impacts of such problems.

3.4 How to assess causes of problems with team composition

We have seen that problems caused by an inadequate team composition can be situated at the three levels of the input part in the IMOI model (individual, team,

TEAM COMPOSITION | 91

and organizational level). How can it be analyzed if a problem in a team is due to composition?

In general, open team discussions or interviews with team members can be a measure – but sometimes problems are not discovered as team members do not want to talk openly about problems they see in other team members. That's why we mainly focus on methods that can be used anonymously.

In the following, we will first focus on instruments to assess team members' KSAs (see 3.1), then we will show how to diagnose problems with the combination of individual team members (see 3.2), and finally come to the assessment of organizational specifications (see 3.3).

3.4.1 How to diagnose team members' KSAs

There are many instruments for the assessment of KSAs for teamwork that are used in personnel selection and personnel development. Some of them can be found on the internet – but it is important that these instruments meet psychometric criteria. An example is the website of the Individual and Team Performance (ITP) Lab (O'Neill, 2019, www.itpmetrics.com). It should be noted that personality tests (e.g. to diagnose the big five, see 3.1.1) should only be analyzed and interpreted by experts such as psychologists, as they assess very personal details.

One example for the assessment of competencies is the Team Work Competency Test (TWCT) by Aguado, Rico, Sánchez-Manzanares, and Salas (2014). The questionnaire comprises 36 items (published in the article) focusing on the different interpersonal and self-management KSAs established by Stevens and Campion (1999) and has shown to have adequate psychometric properties. Items are for instance "When I interact with my team mates, I ask questions to better understand what they say." And "When I disagree with others, I make an effort to focus on what we have in common instead of centring on what separates us" (p. 120). Respondents answer on a 4-point scale of frequency (1 never/almost never and 4 always/almost always). The results of the test show weaknesses and strengths related to team members' competencies in the specific workplace in a descriptive way.

The test can be used for individual team members, but it is also possible to analyze the team level. Problems on the individual as well as on the team level can be diagnosed. How can we transfer individual characteristics into team characteristics? Usually the average (the mean team value) is used, but the same mean value can stand for very different constellations: All team members could be at the identical level, or some have extremely high and others extremely low values – and this makes a great difference for teams and their cooperation. Therefore, it makes sense to look at the dispersion of the data: Are there values quite similar, or do they differ a lot? What is the team minimum, in other words, the lowest value of a team member? For example, Valcea, Hamdani, and Bradley (2019) showed in a study that one team member with low values on learning goal orientation – the weakest link – has a negative impact on team performance. And are there two subgroups? What can be a hint to a faultline in a team? That guides us to the next section about diversity in teams.

3.4.2 How to assess diversity in teams

We have learned that diversity in teams can refer to many characteristics and have positive as well as negative effects. As mentioned in the last section, differing degrees of KSAs in a team can indicate diversity – but these data do not show if diversity is regarded as fruitful or problematic for the cooperation in the team.

The Team Diagnostic Survey developed by Wageman et al. (2005, published in the article) includes a subscale about diversity in an optimal extent (neither too similar to inspire each other, nor so different that cooperation is difficult, see 3.2 about heterogeneity in teams). The scale includes the following items (to be answered on a 5-point scale from highly inaccurate 1 to highly accurate 5):

1   Members of this team are too dissimilar to work together well.
2   This team does not have a broad enough range of experiences and perspectives to accomplish its purposes.
3   This team has a nearly ideal "mix" of members – a diverse set of people who bring different perspectives and experiences to the work.

The items are quite general and can discover problems with diversity (high score in items 1 and 2, low score in item 3) in a descriptive way. In a further step, the results need to be discussed to find more specific causes, e.g. regarding the type of diversity that is problematized by the team.

3.4.3 How to diagnose team structure and task

Team structure and team task have a great impact on how teams should be composed (see 3.3). In this section the main focus is on how to describe these specifics to find out criteria for team composition of a specific team.

There are few instruments to diagnose structure and task (see Chapter 3) – we will give two examples for questionnaires about team size and task, and propose some key questions to assess the conditions team structure prescribes for team composition.

Team size

The Team Diagnostic Survey (Wageman et al., 2005, published in the article) includes a subscale about team size, as well, with the following items:

1   This team is larger than it needs to be.
2   This team has too few members for what it has to accomplish.
3   This team is just the right size to accomplish its purposes.

The results give guidance about adequacy of team size.

Team task

There are several subscales about the team task in the Work Design Questionnaire (WDQ) (Morgeson & Humphrey, 2006, see Chapter 3), such as autonomy, task variety, job complexity, problem-solving, skill variety and specialization, that are a good basis for assessing what KSAs team members need. For instance, the more autonomy a task includes the more important team regulation skills are (see 3.1.2).

Team structure

To diagnose team structure (skill differentiation, authority differentiation and temporal stability; see above, Hollenbeck et al., 2012) and derive criteria for team composition, we have formulated some key questions (see box).

Skill differentiation

Which and how many different skills are needed to complete the team tasks?

Is there a scope of skills that is usually covered by one qualification or are different educations needed? (such as law, IT, engineering, economics)

Do all team members need similar qualifications and competencies, or should they be specialized in their skills as well as in their contributions to the work process?

Is there a functional work division – team members have different expertise and take over different tasks based on their dissimilar competencies – or a divisional role structure, meaning that each team member can perform all tasks of the team?

Authority differentiation

Shall all team members equally participate in decision-making or are there differences?

Are there specific authorities and responsibilities for different team members? E.g. is there an internal team leader, or have team members different authorities? (See also Chapter 8, shared leadership.)

Temporal stability

How long will the team exist? Is it a stable team that forms a part of the organizational structure, or an ad-hoc team that is to work together for a limited amount of time, e.g. a project team?

Box: Key questions team structure

To summarize: To assess problems with team composition the individual level (bring team members appropriate KSAs for teamwork?), the team level (how is the composition?) and the organizational level (what demands are made and what resources are given to the team) are important. Team composition should fit organizational demands, and so it needs to be assessed if team members' individual KSAs and their heterogeneity are adequate and used in a good way to fulfil the team task.

4 Step 4. Select target dimensions and set goals

After the data collection the results need to be analyzed with the team and stakeholders. If there is evidence for specific causes of the problem (e.g. a lack of specific KSAs), dimensions for interventions need to be determined: Besides being related to the problem these dimensions need to be modifiable. Then specific goals need to be set, most suitable with stakeholders again to integrate their perspectives. How to reach these goals is the subject of the next section on solutions.

5 Step 5. Identify solutions

We have seen that problems with team composition are caused on two levels (that furthermore need to be in fit with the demands of team structure and task):

1. Team members do not have adequate prerequisites for teamwork. But caution – is it really a problem with recruitment of an individual that does not meet the selection criteria for the job, or can the person develop team relevant KSAs?
2. Combination of team members is not optimal: "Teams are a question of balance. What is needed is not well-balanced individuals but individuals who balance well with one another."

(Belbin, 2017, p. 73)

Above that, to solve problems with team composition – or even better – prevent them, we can act at different times in the team's lifespan:

1. A new team has to be composed or an existing team needs a new team member.
2. An existing team has problems and needs support.

Putting these two dimensions together, we have four different questions with regard to team composition. It makes a difference if we search for solutions for an existing team or if we are composing a new one. And we need different ideas for individual team members in contrast to whole teams (see Table 4.3).

The composition of a new team (question 1 and 2) is an intervention per se (DiazGranados, Shuffler, Wingate, & Salas, 2017; Shuffler, Diazgranados, Maynard, & Salas, 2018). Solutions refer to finding the right team members and combining them in a way that they can benefit from each other in performing the team task.

Furthermore, we have a look at how to handle the consequences of a miscarried team composition in existing teams (question 3 and 4). If problems exist because of an unfavourable team composition, intervention can affect the individual level (personnel development of individual team members, e.g. to develop team relevant skills)

Table 4.3 Questions for the identification of solutions for problems with team composition

	Team composition	**Existing team**
Individual level	1 How do we find the right individuals for a new team?	3 How do we support individuals in teams to develop KSAs for teamwork?
Team level	2 How do we find the right team composition for a new team?	4 How do we support teams having problems caused by their composition?

TEAM COMPOSITION | 95

Table 4.4 Domains for designing measures for team composition

Choose domain(s) for solutions(s) to enhance team composition			
Prerequisites in the physical environment	**Prerequisites on organizational level**	**Solutions on team level**	**Solutions on individual level**
Not relevant	Decision about team size	Composition of teams (question 2)	Selection of team members (question 1)
	Decision about team structure and task	Support of teams (question 4)	Support of team members (question 3)

as well as the team level (team building and team training interventions to support the cooperation of the team as a whole).

The following section on solutions is structured around these four questions. Table 4.4 shows what target domains for solutions exist.

In this section, our focus will be basically on the individual and the team domain. What about the organizational domain? We will briefly address team size, but mainly we regard the organizational level as set – and therefore as prerequisites for decisions about solutions on the team and individual level. Team and work design was the subject of the last chapter. It is an important precondition for finding the right team composition that fits these settings, but we will not discuss in this chapter again how it could be improved. All the same it is important to analyze it so the team composition can be adapted to it.

It needs to be considered that solutions in one domain sometimes need to be complemented with solutions on other domains to be effective. E.g. if the cause analysis has shown that a team member needs training in communication skills to enhance this person's capability to contribute to the team's effectiveness, this can put a demand on team leadership to ensure that this does not create an extra burden for other team members who need to carry out the work in the time of training. In addition, it might take individual coaching to motivate that person.

There are literally thousands of different methods and tools that can be used for team development. Some have been tested in research and many not, and we rely on the former. Such solutions are e.g. team training, team building, team charters, etc. and these will be explained the first time they are introduced, chapter by chapter. A main conclusion is that team development can work if it is done correctly. What matters is a) the strength of the link between plausible cause and solution, b) what methods and tools are used in the chosen solution and c) how it is done.

The four questions deduced earlier (see Table 4.3) structure the description of solutions. We will describe possible solutions, give examples for specific methods and show empirical evidence for their usefulness. Keep in mind that this is not a kind of toolbox, but examples for good practice – there are more methods to solve problems with team composition. Chapter 10 provides more information about interventions in general.

5.1 How do we find the right individuals for a new team?

Whenever new teams are composed or existing teams are recomposed the question on how to select individuals with appropriate prerequisites for teamwork arises. So we find ourselves in the complex field of personal selection methods. There are different methods to assess KSAs for teamwork, and we mention three of them:

- Situational judgement tests (SJTs) use scenarios of specific and concrete job-related situations, and test-takers have to decide how to handle these situations.
- Structured employment interviews are common measures of staff selection and social skills and personality traits as behavioural tendencies are very often part of these questionings.

(Huffcutt, Conway, Roth, & Stone, 2001)

- Assessment centres are a way to evaluate the performance of candidates on the basis of several exercises simulating work task demands (e.g. group discussions, role plays, presentations and in-tray exercises). The candidates are observed and rated by experts. The method can be used for the needs assessment of personnel development as well.

(Kuncel & Sackett, 2014; Rupp et al., 2015)

An example for a specific method is the interview format developed by Morgeson, Reider, and Campion (2005), a highly structured interview with situational questions and past behaviour questions to identify social skills, such as active listening, speaking and social perceptiveness (among others). A situational question for example is about getting more unpleasant tasks than other team members. A past behaviour question asks about situations of the old job putting good attitudes (like being pleasant to others) to the test. The authors explain in the article structure and content of the interview and give examples for a situational and a past behaviour question including rating scales to evaluate the answers with definitions, descriptions and example anchors.

What about empirical evidence for solutions to select individuals who have the prerequisites to work in a team? For SJTs Christian, Edwards, and Bradley (2010) found in a meta-analysis that they predict teamwork skills with a criterion-related validity of .38. More research has been done about the adequacy for personal selection in general (not specifically for teamwork). McDaniel, Whetzel, Schmidt, and Maurer (1994) conducted a meta-analysis about interviews and their predictive value for job performance. Structured interviews show a correlation value of p .44 and are clearly superior to unstructured interviews. The results for assessment centres are not as positive – in a meta-analysis about assessment centres Hoffman, Kennedy, LoPilato, Monahan, and Lance (2015) found only small correlations (< . 2) between the results of the exercises and the big five personality factors as well as general mental ability.

5.2 How do we find the right team composition for a new team?

There are no concrete evidence-based methods or tools. But based on research some general guidelines with regard to diversity and team size can be given.

5.2.1 Is the degree of diversity in keeping with the team-task?

There is no clear rule on what attributes of team members are needed, and how they should be distributed. But based on the studies mentioned earlier, we can assume that

TEAM COMPOSITION

| 97

- The more innovative and complex the task, the more diversity is needed.
- Surface-level diversity is easier to handle than deep-level diversity.
- A diverse team needs more time to adapt – but after this process it might work more effectively than a homogenous team.

5.2.2 How do we make sure that team size is appropriate?

Again, there is no general rule, as team size depends on the tasks range and complexity, the number of different qualifications needed and sometimes on the size and structure of the whole organization. It should be restricted to the number of persons needed to carry out the job well (Hackman, 1987; Paris, Salas, & Cannon-Bowers, 2000; Sundstrom, De Meuse, & Futrell, 1990). The size of other teams in the organization with similar scope of tasks can be a benchmark. If teams are introduced for the first time, it can be considered how long individual employees need for task fulfilment.

5.3 How do we support individuals in teams to develop KSAs for teamwork?

Single team members lacking the attributes predestinating them to be suitable team members may cause problems. Possible interventions are individual feedback and training. It needs to be mentioned that feedback and training are general ways to support team members – not only to solve problems related to team composition. We mention them in this chapter because they can make an important contribution to enhance team relevant KSAs (see 3.1).

5.3.1 Feedback

To solve such problems a first step may be to give feedback. Feedback is a specific kind of communication. The idea is that team members can change their behaviour in the team if they become aware of what is not optimal. Feedback on performance is information given by an external source regarding the quantity or quality of their past performance that allows the recipient to adjust the performance (Daniels, 2000; Prue & Fairbank, 1981), but feedback can focus social behaviour in the team as well.

Aguinis, Gottfredson, and Joo (2012) have developed research-based recommendations for a strengths-based performance feedback, e.g.

- Closely link any negative feedback to employees' knowledge and skills rather than traits
- Choose an appropriate setting
- Deliver the feedback in a considerate manner
- Provide feedback that is specific
- Ensure that feedback is accurate

The results on how performance feedback affects the individual's performance are somewhat mixed. In a review, Balcazar, Hopkins, and Suarez (1985) found that feedback had consistent effects in 41% of the studies evaluated. Kluger and DeNisi (1996) conducted a meta-analysis about feedback interventions and report that more than a third of them had negative effects on performance. The authors see a possible reason for this result in the fact that feedback shifts the attention away from the task to the individual. A review of Alvero, Bucklin, and Austin (2001) showed among other things that when feedback is combined with other procedures (e.g. training or behavioural consequences) it had consistent effects in 58% of the articles assessed.

5.3.2 Team training

If one or several team members lack relevant KSAs, team training is a possible solution. Team training is "a planned effort designed to improve team performance (...) by assisting individuals in the acquisition of new information, skills, and attitudes essential to effective performance in a team environment" (Delise, Gorman, Brooks, Rentsch, & Steele-Johnson, 2010, p. 55). Trainings are formalized and structured, and they are based on a curriculum (Lacerenza, Marlow, Tannenbaum, & Salas, 2018). They include different methods of trainings, like simulations, lectures, videos, exercises, etc.

There are several team trainings for generic teamwork skills (see 3.1.2), and some of them have been evaluated (for example Salas et al., 2008). Behavioural modelling training is a specific method aiming at the improvement of interpersonal skills. It includes observation, role-playing and feedback for modifying the behaviour (Klein, 2009). The author conducted a meta-analysis on the effects of behavioural modelling training. The results show that it is an effective form to improve interpersonal skills. Training outcomes refer to cognition (such as declarative knowledge), affects and attitudes (e.g. beliefs about the efficacy of the team and satisfaction), and skills (such as planning and coordination).

Another example for a team training is the generic teamwork skills training with a focus on competencies that are relevant for action teams (Ellis, Bell, Ployhart, Hollenbeck, & Ilgen, 2005). Action teams, for instance surgery or investigative teams, need to perform complex and time-limited tasks in challenging situations. After a team training analysis (see 3.4.1) to identify the training needs with regard to task- and team-generic competencies, a lecture format was developed, using work-related case studies about team situations with focus on the skills of planning/task coordination, collaborative problem-solving and communication (basing on the KSA-model of Stevens and Campion, discussed earlier). Trainees first needed to decide what they would do in the team situation, and then the trainer explained what adequate and inadequate responses are. The training was evaluated with a sample of students who worked in teams of four persons in a dynamic decision-making simulation. The evaluation showed positive effects on knowledge about teamwork competencies as well as on team performance in the simulation task regarding planning, task coordination, collaborative problem-solving and communication.

What about the effectiveness of team trainings in general? Delise et al. (2010) conducted a meta-analysis on the effects of team training on team outcomes. The results show that training is positively related to team effectiveness. They found effects on different kinds of training outcomes: affective outcomes (feelings that regard the team as a whole), cognitive outcomes (e.g. knowledge), task-based skill outcomes (e.g. accuracy and speed) as well as teamwork skill outcomes (e.g. conflict handling and coordination). The largest effects resulted for cognitive outcomes (Delise et al., 2010).

5.4 How do we support teams having problems caused by their composition?

Trainings – the latest mentioned solution – can be used as an intervention on the team level as well, if the whole team participates. Besides trainings focusing mainly on skill acquisition, there is another intervention on the team level called team building, which is particularly suitable when strong emotions are affecting teamwork, and team processes should be improved, e.g. because of faultlines in a team. Team-building interventions focus on problem-solving and interpersonal issues (Delise et al., 2010). Main components of team building are – besides problem-solving – goal setting, interpersonal-relationship management and role clarification (Lacerenza et al., 2018).

Team-building interventions do not only address problems that are caused by team composition. With their focus on emotions and interpersonal aspects they are suitable for problems in existing teams to handle diversity (see 3.2).

An example for an evidence based team-building intervention is the Interdisciplinary Management Tool (IMT, Nancarrow, Smith, Ariss, & Enderby, 2015; for a more detailed description see the workbook of Smith et al., 2012). The intervention has a focus on the improvement of interdisciplinary teamwork in the care sector by structured team reflection, and so it is concerned with task related diversity in teams (see 3.2.1). The team building lasts six months, and it includes several workshops and team learning sessions that are supported by a facilitator. Content of these sessions are i.e. reflection about the teamwork practices, barriers to effective working, team values, professional development, team structure, communication, leadership as well as the development and implementation of an action plan derived from these analyses.

Evaluation studies on team-building interventions (in general, not restricted to problems caused by team composition) have resulted in inconsistent findings for their effectiveness (for example Salas, Rozell, Mullen, & Driskell, 1999). Klein et al. (2009) showed in a meta-analysis of 20 team building evaluation studies that team building had the strongest effects outcomes on team processes (e.g. coordination and communication) and affects (e.g. trust). A study of Hämmelmann and van Dick (2013) for instance showed positive effects of different team-building interventions on team identification, social support and collective self-efficacy (a team's shared belief in its capabilities to reach their goals, see Bandura, 1997) – all these aspects can be impaired by negative effects of team composition, e.g. faultlines in teams. Especially role clarification and goal setting as components of team building resulted to have positive effects on team performance (Klein et al., 2009).

> *To summarize*: For problems with team composition solutions are needed that are in fit with the specific situation, with regard to team task and structure. It makes a difference if we are just composing a team or have an existing team. And it needs to be considered if the individual or the team level should be addressed.
> To match individuals to a team it is good to integrate team relevant KSAs into the job profile and assess them with valid measures, like situational judgement tests or specifically developed and validated tests for team competencies. At the stage of composition of a new team also an appropriate team size and diversity should be considered. In an existing team, different measures of personnel development can influence these factors in a positive way. Strength

based feedback is a good basis to find solutions for better cooperation. Team training (for individuals as well as for teams) and team building can be useful measures – if they are matching the specific problem of the team caused by a challenging team composition.

CASE: TEAM COMPOSITION AND THE ASSOCIATED LITTLE WILLINGNESS TO WORK TOGETHER CONTRIBUTE TO POOR RESULTS CONT.

One last time back to our case – we have now derived several work hypotheses about problem causes – what could be possible solutions? The lack of traits like openness and agreeableness, interpersonal, team- and self-management skills, motivation to work in a team as well as a negative attitude toward teamwork have been focused in work hypotheses 1, 2 and 3. But also diversity could have caused the problems, as there are different goals and values in the team (deep-level diversity) and surface-level diversity may cause a faultline between two subgroups (see work hypothesis 4).

At first, the manager of the team talked to all team members to find out more about which solutions fit the team's situation. In these conversations, it became clear that one of the social workers wanted to leave the team. She argued that she had discovered for herself that she is an individualist: She prefers to work alone, so she really can decide what to do. Therefore, she had applied for another job and would leave the organization. The manager accepted this decision and did not try to change her mind knowing that preference for teamwork and collectivism are important prerequisites for teamwork. Another social worker was found, and personal selection criteria comprised – besides good task-related qualification – experiences with teamwork, openness, conscientiousness and interpersonal skills. Human resource specialists gave support to the recruitment process.

The other team members are more optimistic. They say that there are heavy problems in the team, but on the other hand they are convinced that the diversity of the team is important for their mission – giving the young people the support they need.

The manager decided to hire a counsellor for a team building measure. This counsellor was recommended to him for working profoundly with research-based methods and evaluating his team building – not only regarding the participants' subjective satisfaction, but as well the effects on the team performance some months later.

The team building measure covered measures like strength-based mutual feedbacks of all team members, discussions of the values, the development of specific goals as well as guiding principles for interactions in the team. With the counsellor's support, the team developed a tandem solution to overcome the faultline in their team. As the team consists of six persons, they formed three diverse tandems (one social worker and one craftsman each). They also entered agreements about information flow in the team and regular team sessions.

There was a bundle of solutions on the individual level (personnel selection based on team relevant KSAs) and the team level (team building and a tandem-solution as a changed team work design).

The manager as well as the young people see that the cooperation of the team has improved. Team members are more motivated, and in case of positive developments of the adolescents, proud of the team. Is everything perfect in the team now? Of course, it is not. There are still controversies and conflicts (see Chapter 6), but they are more constructive and focus on improving their working process. Team members have learned to value that other team members take different perspectives and do not deprecate them anymore.

Bibliography

Aguado, D., Rico, R., Sánchez-Manzanares, M., & Salas, E. (2014). Teamwork Competency Test (TWCT): A step forward on measuring teamwork competencies. *Group Dynamics: Theory, Research, and Practice, 18*(2), 101–121. https://doi.org/10.1037/a0036098

Aguinis, H., Gottfredson, R. K., & Joo, H. (2012). Delivering effective performance feedback: The strengths-based approach. *Business Horizons, 55, 105–111.* https://doi.org/10.1016/j.bushor.2011.10.004

Alvero, A. M., Bucklin, B. R., & Austin, J. (2001). An objective review of the effectiveness and essential characteristics of performance feedback in organizational settings (1985–1998). *Journal of Organizational Behavior Management, 21*(1), 3–29. https://doi.org/10.1300/J075v21n01_02

Balcazar, F., Hopkins, B. L., & Suarez, Y. (1985). A critical, objective review of performance feedback. *Journal of Organizational Behavior Management, 7*(3–4), 65–89. https://doi.org/10.1300/J075v07n03_05

Bandura, A. (1997). Collective efficacy. In A. Bandura (Ed.), *Self-efficacy: The exercise of control* (pp. 477–525). New York: Freeman.

Belbin, R. M. (2017). *Team roles at work.* Amsterdam: Butterworth-Heinemann. https://doi.org/10.4324/9780080963242

Bell, S. T. (2004). Setting the stage for effective teams: A meta-analysis of team design variables and team effectiveness. Doctoral Dissertation. Texas A& M University.

Bell, S. T. (2007). Deep-level composition variables as predictors of team performance: A meta-analysis. *Journal of Applied Psychology, 92*(3), 595–615. https://doi.org/10.1037/0021-9010.92.3.595

Bell, S. T., Brown, S. G., Colaneri, A., & Outland, N. (2018). Team composition and the ABCs of teamwork. *American Psychologist, 73*(4), 349–362. https://doi.org/10.1037/amp0000305

Bell, S. T., & Marentette, B. J. (2011). Team viability for long-term and ongoing organizational teams. *Organizational Psychology Review, 1*(4), 275–292. https://doi.org/10.1177/2041386611405876

Bezrukova, K., Jehn, K. A., Zanutto, E. L., & Thatcher, S. M. B. (2009). Do workgroup faultlines help or hurt? A moderated model of faultlines, team identification, and group performance. *Organization Science, 20*(1), 35–50. https://doi.org/10.1287/orsc.1080.0379

Bunderson, J. S., & Sutcliffe, K. M. (2002). Comparing alternative conceptualizations of functional diversity in management teams: Process and performance effects. *The Academy of Management Journal, 45*(5), 875–893. https://doi.org/10.2307/3069319

Cannon-Bowers, J. A., Tannenbaum, S. I., Salas, E., & Volpe, C. E. (1995). Defining team competencies and establishing team training requirements. In R. Guzzo, E. Salas, & Associates (Eds.), *Team effectiveness and decision making in organizations* (pp. 333–380). San Francisco: Jossey-Bass.

Carter, K. M., Mead, B. A., Stewart, G. L., Nielsen, J. D., & Solimeo, S. L. (2019). Reviewing work team design characteristics across industries: Combining meta-analysis and comprehensive synthesis. *Small Group Research, 50*(1), 138–188. https://doi.org/10.1177/1046496418797431

Cervone, D., Pervin, L. A., & John, O. P. (2005). *Personality: Theory and research.* Hoboken, NJ: Wiley.

Che-Ha, N., Mavondo, F. T., & Mohd-Said, S. (2014). Performance or learning goal orientation: Implications for business performance. *Journal of Business Research, 67*(1), 2811–2820. https://doi.org/10.1016/J.JBUSRES.2012.08.002

Christian, J. S., Christian, M. S., Pearsall, M. J., & Long, E. C. (2017). Team adaptation in context: An integrated conceptual model and meta-analytic review. *Organizational Behavior and Human Decision Processes, 140*, 62–89. https://doi.org/10.1016/j.obhdp.2017.01.003

Christian, M. S., Edwards, B. D., & Bradley, J. C. (2010). Situational judgment tests: Constructs assessed and a meta-analysis of their criterion-related validities. *Personnel Psychology, 63*(1), 83–117. https://doi.org/10.1111/j.1744-6570.2009.01163.x

Contu, A., & Pecis, L. (2017). Groups and teams at work. In D. Knights & H. Willmott (Eds.), *Introducing organizational behaviour and management* (pp. 119–158). Andover, UK: Cengage Learning.

Cronin, M. A., & Weingart, L. R. (2007). Representational gaps, information processing, and conflict in functionally diverse teams. *The Academy of Management Review 32*(3), 761–773. https://doi.org/10.2307/20159333

Cunningham, Q. W. (2015). *The effects of surface-level and deep-level team faultline strength on information elaboration and effectiveness: Examining the moderating role of leader sensemaking and team prosocial motivation and the mediating role of transactive memory systems.* Doctoral Dissertation. Drexel University.

Daniels, K. (2000). Measures of five aspects of affective well-being at work. *Human Relations, 53*(2), 275–294. https://doi.org/10.1177/a010564

Delise, L. A., Allen Gorman, C., Brooks, A. M., Rentsch, J. R., & Steele-Johnson, D. (2010). The effects of team training on team outcomes: A meta-analysis. *Performance Improvement Quarterly, 22*(4), 53–80. https://doi.org/10.1002/piq.20068

Devine, D. J., & Philips, J. L. (2001). Do smarter teams do better: A meta-analysis of cognitive ability and team performance. *Small Group Research, 32*(5), 507–532. https://doi.org/10.1177/1046496401032005001

DiazGranados, D., Shuffler, M. L., Wingate, J. A., & Salas, E. (2017). Team development interventions. In E. Salas, R. Rico, & J. Passmore (Eds.), *The Wiley Blackwell Handbook of the Psychology of Team Working and Collaborative Processes* (pp. 555–586). Chichester, UK: John Wiley & Sons, Ltd. https://doi.org/doi:10.1002/9781118909997.ch24

Dickson, M. W., Resick, C. J., & Goldstein, H. W. (2008). Seeking explanations on people, not in the result of their behaviour: Twenty-plus years of the attraction-selection-attrition model. In D. B. Smith (Ed.), *LEA's organization and management series: The people make the place: Dynamic linkages between individuals and organizations* (pp. 5–36). New York, NY: Taylor & Francis Group and Lawrence Erlbaum Associates.

Driskell, J. E., Goodwin, G. F., Salas, E., & O'Shea, P. G. (2006). What makes a good team player? Personality and team effectiveness. *Group Dynamics: Theory, Research, and Practice, 10*(4), 249–271. https://doi.org/10.1037/1089-2699.10.4.249

Driskell, J. E., Salas, E., & Driskell, T. (2018). Foundations of teamwork and collaboration. *American Psychologist, 73*(4), 334–348. https://doi.org/10.1037/amp0000241

Edmondson, A. C., & Reynolds, S. S. (2016). *Building the future: Big teaming for audacious innovation.* Willistion, VT: Berrett-Koehler Publishers.

Ellis, A. P. J., Bell, B. S., Ployhart, R. E., Hollenbeck, J. R., & Ilgen, D. R. (2005). An evaluation of generic teamwork skills training with action teams: Effects on cognitive and skill-based outcomes. *Personnel Psychology, 58*(3), 641–672. https://doi.org/10.1111/j.1744-6570.2005.00617.x

Gottfredson, L. S. (1997). Mainstream science on intelligence: An editorial with 52 signatories, history, and bibliography. *Intelligence, 24,* 13–23.

Hackman, J. R. (1987). The design of work teams. In J. Lorsch (Ed.), *Handbook of organizational behavior* (pp. 315–342). Englewood Cliffs, NJ: Prentice-Hall.

Hämmelmann, A., & van Dick, R. (2013). Entwickeln im Team – Effekte für den Einzelnen. *Gruppendynamik Und Organisationsberatung, 44*(2), 221–238. https://doi.org/10.1007/s11612-013-0207-1

Hoffman, B. J., Kennedy, C. L., LoPilato, A. C., Monahan, E. L., & Lance, C. E. (2015). A review of the content, criterion-related, and construct-related validity of assessment center exercises. *Journal of Applied Psychology, 100*(4), 1143–1168. https://doi.org/10.1037/a0038707

Hollenbeck, J. R., Beersma, B., & Schouten, M. E. (2012). Beyond team types and taxonomies: A dimensional scaling conceptualization for team description. *Academy of Management Review, 37*(1), 82–106. https://doi.org/10.5465/amr.2010.0181

Horwitz, S. K., & Horwitz, I. B. (2007). The effects of team diversity on team outcomes: A meta-analytic review of team demography. *Journal of Management, 33*(6), 987–1015. https://doi.org/10.1177/0149206307308587

Huffcutt, A. I., Conway, J. M., Roth, P. L., & Stone, N. J. (2001). Identification and meta-analytic assessment of psychological constructs measured in employment interviews. *The Journal of Applied Psychology, 86*(5), 897–913.

Hunter, J. E., & Hunter, R. F. (1984). Validity and utility of alternative predictors of job performance. *Psychological Bulletin, 96*(1), 72–98. https://doi.org/10.1037/0033-2909.96.1.72

Jehn, K. A., & Bezrukova, K. (2010). The faultline activation process and the effects of activated faultlines on coalition formation, conflict, and group outcomes. *Organizational Behavior and Human Decision Processes, 112*(1), 24–42. https://doi.org/10.1016/J.OBHDP.2009.11.008

Jehn, K. A., Northcraft, G. B., & Neale, M. A. (1999). Why differences make a difference: A field study of diversity, conflict, and performance in workgroups. *Administrative Science Quarterly, 44*(4), 741–763. https://doi.org/10.2307/2667054

Johns, G., & Saks, A. M. (2008). *Organizational behaviour: Understanding and managing life at work* (7th ed.). Toronto: Pearson Prentice Hall.

Kearns, P. (2001). *Review of research: Generic skills for the new economy.* Australian National Training Authority And National Centre for Vocational Education Research (Australia): NCVER.

Klein, C. (2009). What do we know about interpersonal skills? A meta-analytic examination of antecedents, outcomes, and the efficacy of training. *Doctoral Dissertation. University of Central Florida.*

Klein, C., DiazGranados, D., Salas, E., Le, H., Burke, C. S., Lyons, R., & Goodwin, G. F. (2009). Does team building work? *Small Group Research, 40*(2), 181–222. https://doi.org/10.1177/1046496408328821

Kluger, A. N., & DeNisi, A. (1996). The effects of feedback interventions on performance: A historical review, a meta-analysis, and a preliminary feedback intervention theory. *Psychological Bulletin, 119*(2), 254–284. https://doi.org/10.1037/0033-2909.119.2.254

Kozlowski, S. W. J., & Bell, B. S. (2013). Work groups and teams in organizations: Review update. In N. Schmitt & S. Highhouse (Eds.), *Handbook of psychology, vol. 12: Industrial and organizational psychology* (2nd ed., pp. 412–469). Hoboken, NJ: Wiley.

Kozlowski, S. W. J., & Ilgen, D. R. (2006). Enhancing the effectiveness of work groups and teams. *Psychological Science in the Public Interest, 7*(3), 77–124. https://doi.org/10.1111/j.1529-1006.2006.00030.x

Kuncel, N. R., & Sackett, P. R. (2014). Resolving the assessment center construct validity problem (as we know it). *Journal of Applied Psychology, 99*(1), 38–47. https://doi.org/10.1037/a0034147

Lacerenza, C. N., Marlow, S. L., Tannenbaum, S. I., & Salas, E. (2018). Team development interventions: Evidence-based approaches for improving teamwork. *American Psychologist, 73*(4), 517–531. https://doi.org/10.1037/amp0000295

Lau, D. C., & Murnighan, J. K. (1998). Demographic diversity and faultlines: The compositional dynamics of organizational groups. *The Academy of Management Review, 23*(2), 325–340. https://doi.org/10.2307/259377

LePine, J. A. (2005). Adaptation of teams in response to unforeseen change: Effects of goal difficulty and team composition in terms of cognitive ability and goal orientation. *Journal of Applied Psychology, 90*(6), 1153–1167. https://doi.org/10.1037/0021-9010.90.6.1153

Levine, J. M., & Moreland, R. L. (1990). Progress in small group research. *Annual Review of Psychology, 41*(1), 585–634. https://doi.org/10.1146/annurev.ps.41.020190.003101

Lim, L. L. K., Laosirihongthong, T., & Chan, C. C. A. (2006). A case study of learning in a Thai manufacturing organization. *Journal of Applied Business Research (JABR), 22*(2), 49–60. https://doi.org/10.19030/jabr.v22i2.1435

Liu, M., Huang, J. L., & Dickson, M. W. (2017). Team assessment and selection. In H. W. Goldstein, E. D. Pulakos, J. Passmore, & C. Semedo (Eds.), *The Wiley Blackwell handbook of the psychology of recruitment, selection and employee retention* (pp. 310–333). Chichester, UK: John Wiley & Sons, Ltd. https://doi.org/10.1002/9781118972472.ch15

Majchrzak, A., Birnbaum, P., & Faraj, S. (2012). Transcending knowledge differences in cross-functional teams. *Organization Science, 23*(4), 951–970. https://doi.org/10.1287/orsc.1110.0677

Mannix, E., & Neale, M. A. (2005). What differences make a difference? *Psychological Science in the Public Interest, 6*(2), 31–55. https://doi.org/10.1111/j.1529-1006.2005.00022.x

Mathieu, J. E., Hollenbeck, J. R., van Knippenberg, D., & Ilgen, D. R. (2017). A century of work teams in the Journal of Applied Psychology. *Journal of Applied Psychology, 102*(3), 452–467. http://dx.doi.org/10.1037/apl0000128

McDaniel, M. A., Whetzel, D. L., Schmidt, F. L., & Maurer, S. D. (1994). The validity of employment interviews: A comprehensive review and meta-analysis. *Journal of Applied Psychology, 79*(4), 599–616. https://doi.org/10.1037/0021-9010.79.4.599

Meyer, B. (2017). Team diversity: A review of the literature. In E. Salas, R. Rico, & J. Passmore (Eds.), *The Wiley Blackwell handbook of the psychology of teamwork and collaborative processes* (pp. 151–175). Chinchester, UK: Wiley-Blackwell.

Morgeson, F. P., & Humphrey, S. E. (2006). The Work Design Questionnaire (WDQ): Developing and validating a comprehensive measure for assessing job design and the nature of work. *Journal of Applied Psychology, 91*(6), 1321–1339. https://doi.org/10.1037/0021-9010.91.6.1321

Morgeson, F. P., Reider, M. H., & Campion, M. A. (2005). Selecting individuals in team settings: The importance of social skills, personality characteristics and teamwork knowledge. *Personnel Psychology, 58*(3), 583–611. https://doi.org/10.1111/j.1744-6570.2005.655.x

Nancarrow, S. A., Smith, T., Ariss, S., & Enderby, P. M. (2015). Qualitative evaluation of the implementation of the Interdisciplinary Management Tool: A reflective tool to enhance interdisciplinary teamwork using structured, facilitated action research for implementation. *Health & Social Care in the Community, 23*(4), 437–448. https://doi.org/10.1111/hsc.12173

TEAM COMPOSITION | 105

O'Neill, T. A. (2019). Individual and Team Performance (ITP) Lab. Retrieved 2019 October 4 from www.itpmetrics.com.

Paoletti, J., Gilberto, J. M., Beier, M. E., & Salas, E. (2020). The role of aging, age diversity, and age heterogeneity within teams. In S. J. Czaja, J. Sharit, & J. B. James (Eds.) *Current and Emerging Trends in Aging and Work* (pp. 319–336). Cham, Switzerland: Springer.

Paris, C. R., Salas, E., & Cannon-Bowers, J. A. (2000). Teamwork in multi-person systems: A review and analysis. *Ergonomics, 43*(8), 1052–1075. https://doi.org/10.1080/00140130050084879

Payne, S. C., Youngcourt, S. S., & Beaubien, J. M. (2007). A meta-analytic examination of the goal orientation nomological net. *Journal of Applied Psychology, 92*(1), 128–150. https://doi.org/10.1037/0021-9010.92.1.128

Porter, C. O. L. H., Webb, J. W., & Gogus, C. I. (2010). When goal orientations collide: Effects of learning and performance orientation on team adaptability in response to workload imbalance. *Journal of Applied Psychology, 95*(5), 935–943. https://doi.org/10.1037/a0019637

Prue, D. M., & Fairbank, J. A. (1981). Performance feedback in organizational behavior management. *Journal of Organizational Behavior Management, 3*(1), 1–16. https://doi.org/10.1300/J075v03n01_01

Rupp, D. E., Hoffman, B. J., Bischof, D., Byham, W., Collins, L., Gibbons, A., ... Thornton, G. (2015). Guidelines and ethical considerations for assessment center operations. *Journal of Management, 41*(4), 1244–1273. https://doi.org/10.1177/0149206314567780

Salas, E., & Cannon-Bowers, J. A. (2001). The science of training: A decade of progress. *Annual Review of Psychology, 52*(1), 471–499. https://doi.org/10.1146/annurev.psych.52.1.471

Salas, E., DiazGranados, D., Klein, C., Burke, C. S., Stagl, K. C., Goodwin, G. F., & Halpin, S. M. (2008). Does team training improve team performance? A meta-analysis. *Human Factors: The Journal of the Human Factors and Ergonomics Society, 50*(6), 903–933. https://doi.org/10.1518/001872008X375009

Salas, E., Rozell, D., Mullen, B., & Driskell, J. E. (1999). The effect of team building on performance. *Small Group Research, 30*(3), 309–329. https://doi.org/10.1177/104649649903000303

Salas, E., Sims, D. E., & Burke, C. S. (2005). Is there a "Big Five" in teamwork? *Small Group Research, 36*(5), 555–599. https://doi.org/10.1177/1046496405277134

Schmidt, F. L., & Hunter, J. (2004). General mental ability in the world of work: Occupational attainment and job performance. *Journal of Personality and Social Psychology, 86*(1), 162–173. https://doi.org/10.1037/0022-3514.86.1.162

Schneid, M., Isidor, R., Li, C., & Kabst, R. (2015). The influence of cultural context on the relationship between gender diversity and team performance: A meta-analysis. *The International Journal of Human Resource Management, 26*(6), 733–756. https://doi.org/10.1080/09585192.2014.957712

Schneid, M., Isidor, R., Steinmetz, H., & Kabst, R. (2016). Age diversity and team outcomes: A quantitative review. *Journal of Managerial Psychology, 31*(1), 2–17. https://doi.org/10.1108/JMP-07-2012-0228

Seidel, V. P., & O'Mahony, S. (2014). Managing the repertoire: Stories, metaphors, prototypes, and concept coherence in product innovation. *Organization Science, 25*(3), 691–712. https://doi.org/10.1287/orsc.2013.0879

Shuffler, M. L., Diazgranados, D., Maynard, M. T., & Salas, E. (2018). Developing, sustaining, and maximizing team effectiveness: An integrative, dynamic perspective of team development interventions. *Academy of Management Annals, 12*(2), 688–724. https://doi.org/10.5465/annals.2016.0045

Smith, T., Cross, E., Booth, A., Ariss, S., Nancarrow, S., Enderby, P., & Blinston, A. (2012). *Interdisciplinary management tool workbook* (2nd ed.). Southhampton: National Institute of Health Research Service Delivery and Organisation Program.

Spearman, C. (1904). General intelligence, objectively determined and measured. *American Journal of Psychology, 15*, 201–293. doi10.2307/1412107

Stahl, G. K., Maznevski, M. L., Voigt, A., & Jonsen, K. (2010). Unraveling the effects of cultural diversity in teams: A meta-analysis of research on multicultural work groups. *Journal of International Business Studies, 41*(4), 690–709. https://doi.org/10.2307/40604760

Stevens, M. J., & Campion, M. A. (1994). The knowledge, skill, and ability requirements for teamwork: Implications for human resource management. *Journal of Management, 20*(2), 503–530. https://doi.org/10.1177/014920639402000210

Stevens, M. J., & Campion, M. A. (1999). Staffing work teams: Development and validation of a selection test for teamwork settings. *Journal of Management, 25*(2), 207–228. https://doi.org/10.1177/014920639902500205

Stewart, G. L. (2006). A meta-analytic review of relationships between team design features and team performance. *Journal of Management, 32*(1), 29–55. https://doi.org/10.1177/0149206305277792

Sundstrom, E., De Meuse, K. P., & Futrell, D. (1990). Work teams: Applications and effectiveness. *American Psychologist, 45*(2), 120–133. https://doi.org/10.1037/0003-066X.45.2.120

Thatcher, S. M. B., & Patel, P. C. (2011). Group faultlines: A review, integration, and guide to future research. *Journal of Management, 38*(4), 969–1009. https://doi.org/10.1177/0149206311426187

Valcea, S., Hamdani, M. R., & Bradley, B. (2019). Weakest link goal orientations and team expertise: Implications for team performance. *Small Group Research, 50*(3), 1–33. https://doi.org/10.1177/1046496418825302

Vandewalle, D. (1997). Development and validation of a work domain goal orientation instrument. *Educational and Psychological Measurement, 57*(6), 995–1015. https://doi.org/10.1177/0013164497057006009

Wageman, R., Hackman, J. R., & Lehman, E. (2005). Team diagnostic survey. *The Journal of Applied Behavioral Science, 41*(4), 373–398. https://doi.org/10.1177/0021886305281984

Weick, K. E., & Roberts, K. H. (1993). Collective mind in organizations: Heedful interrelating on flight decks. *Administrative Science Quarterly, 38*(3), 357. https://doi.org/10.2307/2393372

West, M. A., Hirst, G., Richter, A., & Shipton, H. (2004). Twelve steps to heaven: Successfully managing change through developing innovative teams. *European Journal of Work and Organizational Psychology, 13*(2), 269–299. https://doi.org/10.1080/13594320444000092

Wheelan, S. A. (2009). Group size, group development, and group productivity. *Small Group Research, 40*(2), 247–262. https://doi.org/10.1177/1046496408328703

Wildman, J. L., Thayer, A. L., Rosen, M. A., Salas, E., Mathieu, J. E., & Rayne, S. R. (2012). Task types and team-level attributes. *Human Resource Development Review, 11*(1), 97–129. https://doi.org/10.1177/1534484311417561

Chapter 5

The team does not carry out the tasks in a coordinated manner

A frustrated manager in our exploratory study said, "Why can't they get their act together?" Let's assume that the team's problem with realizing coordinated performance in the action phase is not due to poor team design. In this chapter, the problems with carrying out routine tasks in a coordinated manner are explained by team processes. Effective teamwork requires team members to have a collective understanding of what to do, and how. It is described how the process of building shared meaning develops over time and becomes a knowledge structure that regulates performance. Cognitive, affective and behavioural processes are interlinked, and the chapter shows how these are related to corresponding emergent states that regulate the coordination of work. Our contribution lies in targeting both emergent states and processes that lead to (or constrain) smooth teamwork, and showing how these can be developed through different interventions.

In this chapter, we discuss the situation where the team is in action and carrying out the routine task, yet needs to coordinate its activities in line with task and situational demands to perform effectively. Gersick and Hackman (1990) discussed the significance of habitual routines and meta-routines for team performance. Routines exist when a group performs a functionally similar pattern of behaviour in a given situation without considering alternatives. Meta-routines are to continuously and intentionally discuss habitual routines of both task-work and interpersonal processes. They serve to uncover patterns that impede effectiveness and creativity. Reflexivity is the core of such meta-routines. The quality of habitual routines in the action phase affects meta-routines in the transition phase, and hence adaptation. In Chapter 7, *we will come back to problems with adaptation*: why teams are stuck in habitual routines and fail to adjust their way of working even though change is required. In Chapter 6, we describe problems with interpersonal relations. In these three chapters the focus is on the core of the IMOI model: the team processes.

Coordination means bringing the different elements of a task into a relationship that will ensure efficiency. Different persons' activities are combined and aligned, not only in terms of subtasks in relation to the team's task and shared goal but also in terms of timing. Coordination can be described as a) the combination of disparate team member actions and efforts, and b) temporal and action synchronization when combining team member actions and efforts. Cooperation is the process of working together to the same end. It involves joint efforts and helping each other to a mutual benefit. Coordination is essential within the team. But teams are embedded in a system, and this system requires cooperation and coordination also across borders, i.e. between teams and functions.

We use an authentic case to illustrate the problem of a lack of coordinated performance in the action phase. See the following box.

CASE: TEAM PROCESSES INHIBIT TEAM MEMBERS COMBINING AND MAKING THE BEST USE OF THEIR EMOTIONAL AND COGNITIVE CAPACITIES TO PERFORM AT THE HIGHEST LEVELS

When a top management team (TMT) has problems with collaboration, it can have severe consequences for many. An invited consultant met the CEO of an industrial manufacturer who described her difficulties with her Top Management Team (TMT). The team consisted of eight managers for different functions in the company (managers for the production, technology, maintenance, HR, etc.). The CEO explained that the team was composed of "good and competent people" who took great responsibility for their own departments. But she was dissatisfied with how they worked together as a team. All managers agreed that overall cost efficiency depended on how different functions coordinated different tasks, and how they in the TMT interacted and took decisions to their mutual benefit. After two years of struggling, the TMT had failed to make a significant improvement. The CEO asked the consultant: What is the problem with our teamwork?

---

1 Step 1. Describe the situation

Again we describe the situation and problem from different perspectives to target what the problem is about.

CASE: TEAM PROCESSES INHIBIT TEAM MEMBERS COMBINING AND MAKING THE BEST USE OF THEIR EMOTIONAL AND COGNITIVE CAPACITIES TO PERFORM AT THE HIGHEST LEVELS CONT.

At another meeting the CEO gave a more detailed description of the problem. CEO: "During discussions, we do not look at things from the company's perspective, and managers see things as they concern their department." Managers complained about a lack of coordination between departments and that things were not working in other departments, instead of raising this issue in the team as a *joint* problem. When discussing how to reduce costs, managers had ideas on how costs could be cut in other departments, but not in their own. Managers recognized that decisions should be taken by the team, but wanted the CEO to decide as they could not reach a consensus.

In a second step the consultant met the managers without the CEO present. The managers had different views on the problems with the TMT: "We don't take time to keep track of and manage the TMT's own joint work. We take decisions, and then we do not know if something actually happens." "The meetings have become some sort of competition in who shows the best result in his department." "I think we are a bit afraid of asking one another for advice, and maybe we do not know whom to turn to." "What are the TMT's goals that are different from the CEO's goal for the whole company?" "I am a bit confused about what we should accomplish together as a team." "The meetings are unproductive: we mainly report results and get information from the CEO." "The only way for us to be more effective and cut costs is to integrate our workflows a lot better, and so our task should be to find solutions for that." Someone remarked, "Some of us are not dependent on the others, so what should we integrate and coordinate?"

In a third step the consultant interviewed first-line managers about their expectations of the TMT. The managers had little to say about the TMT, nor had they expectations of what the team should deliver. A typical statement was: "They have meetings, I guess that the CEO has lots of information and they need to follow up results and report."

The consultant raised the issue with the CEO of whether it would be wise also to interview other stakeholders to the TMT, but it was regarded as "too sensitive."

2 Step 2. Identify the core problem(s)

The next step in the problem-solving circle is to systematize the description of the current situation and identify a core problem to tackle. We use the case as an example.

CASE: TEAM PROCESSES INHIBIT TEAM MEMBERS COMBINING AND MAKING THE BEST USE OF THEIR EMOTIONAL AND COGNITIVE CAPACITIES TO PERFORM AT THE HIGHEST LEVELS CONT.

First, all seem to agree that they do not perform well enough. There are signs of problems with team processes that inhibit team members combining their patterns of behaviour and capabilities to achieve the expected end result. There are also leadership issues, and it is plausible that the team design is

> not optimal as there are questions about the interdependence between the managers. There might be a problem with how the organization is structured, how different departments are integrated and the organizational strategy. When the consultant gave feedback to the TMT, it was decided to start working with the team processes. The logic was that the TMT first needs to find a better way of working as a team, before it can take on the task of developing the organization.

Our normative perspective is that teams can accomplish more than merely carrying out the stipulated work. But sometimes that in itself is difficult enough. Acknowledging that the performance may be hindered by situational and contextual aspects, we shall now search for the causes within the team processes.

3 Step 3. Cause analysis

Following is a mindmap of the, according to research, main causes of a lack of coordinated performance in the action phase (Figure 5.1) (first order branches). Second and third order branches are the main predictors of effective teamwork in the action phase, and hence explain differences in team performance, and why coordination sometimes fails. In this chapter we limit the description to causes within the team processes, the mediators between Inputs and Outputs in the IMOI model. This means that other causes might be found in the Inputs (see Chapters 1, 3 and 4). The mindmap can be used as a "research model" when exploring why a specific team has a problem with carrying out its task in the action phase. If so, add relevant input-factors and other specific features of the team to the mindmap. All these potential causes of the team's problem should be explored to find out what needs to be changed. In section 3 we will give further advice on how to diagnose team performance.

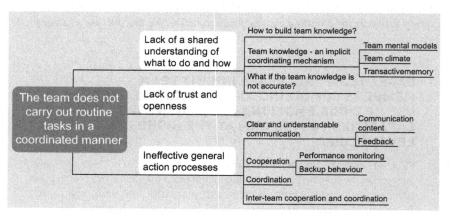

Figure 5.1 Mindmap about main causes of a lack of coordinated performance

In Figure 5.1, the main predictors of effective teamwork in the action phase are 1) team knowledge – emergent states that implicitly regulate activities; 2) affective states such as psychological safety that facilitates learning and teamwork; and 3) activities such as communication, cooperation and coordination. Items 1, 2 and 3 are reciprocally interlinked. Communication regulates activities and is based on team knowledge. It takes communication in a climate of safety and trust to build such team knowledge. Communication is most typically regarded as an explicit means to coordinate individual activities, and it is the foundation for teamwork. Teamwork during the action phase aims to carry out the task. So what patterns of behaviour are key for this to be effective? It is cooperation and coordination.

3.1 Lack of a shared understanding of what to do and how

Research on team performance and effectiveness (Kozlowski & Bell, 2013; Mohammed, Ferzandi, & Hamilton, 2010; Salas, Reyes, & McDaniel, 2018) supports the generally held belief that *effective teamwork requires team members to have a collective understanding of what to do, and how.* How can the seemingly effortless coordination in a soccer game, where one player hits the ball and correctly predicts the positioning and readiness of other players, be understood? It is an implicit coordination that must stem from something, and it is believed to be knowledge. DeChurch and Mesmer-Magnus (2010) define team cognition, or team knowledge, as "an emergent state that refers to the manner in which knowledge important to team functioning is mentally organized, represented, and distributed within the team and allows team members to anticipate and execute actions" (p. 33).

Wildman, Salas, and Scott (2014) conducted a review of 174 empirical studies and found two lines of research in the study of team cognition. In the first approach, team cognition is studied "as relatively stable, emergent knowledge structures that exist within peoples' heads and combine to represent the team" (p. 3). Another line of research has seen cognition as the dynamic processes that occur within the team, and these researchers have studied communication and the processes that we assume yield the emergent states. For our purposes both perspectives are of interest, as the process of building knowledge can be more or less effective, and the knowledge that is built can be of a different quality. We shall start with the processes that enable the team to build knowledge.

3.1.1 How to build team knowledge

What do the team members do when they communicate, learn and build knowledge that enables them to carry out work in a coordinated manner? Van der Vegt and Bunderson (2005 p. 534) describe it as "activities by which team members seek to acquire, share, refine, or combine task-relevant knowledge through interaction with one another". Different reviews of team learning (Decuyper, Dochy, & Van den Bossche, 2010; Edmondson, Dillon, & Roloff, 2007; Van der Haar, Segers, & Jehn, 2013; Wilson, Goodman, & Cronin, 2007) describe in a similar way how teams communicate, learn and build knowledge.

● Team members *share* ideas, thoughts and experiences. Individuals have different perspectives and interpret and understand the environment idiosyncratically.

TEAM DOES NOT ACT IN A COORDINATED MANNER

- *Co-construction of meaning*: a process of developing shared meaning by refining what someone meant, building on, or modifying individuals' ideas and thoughts.
- *Constructive conflict* uncovers diversity in cognition, e.g. differences in opinions, and is a process of negotiation to integrate and overcome differences. Constructive conflicts and co-construction of meaning are closely interlinked, and an open discussion brings about an integrated shared understanding, a team cognition or team knowledge that can later be tested in activities.
- *Team activity*: what was learned is implemented in routines, and by performing the team learns if the routines are adequate.
- *Boundary crossing*: sharing and learning from others outside the team, so-called distal learning, stimulates the sharing of new ideas.
- *Team reflexivity*: "The extent to which team members collectively reflect upon the team's objectives, strategies, and processes as well as their wider objectives" (West, Hirst, Richter, & Shipton, 2004, p. 285). It involves building a new shared meaning.
- *Storage and retrieval*: the way a team saves and stores knowledge and new procedures so that it can later be retrieved, used or further developed.

How a team develops team knowledge will result in different forms and quality of knowledge. Kozlowski and Klein (2000) distinguish between two *forms of emergence of knowledge*: compositional emergence where individuals' thinking is similar and also similar to their manifestation on the team level; and compilation emergence where the team knowledge is different to the individuals'. DeChurch and Mesmer-Magnus (2010) showed in their meta-analysis that the nature of emergence impacts team performance. The effect of knowledge on performance is stronger for compilation emergence than composition emergence. This underlines the importance of making use of all team members' different perspectives and divergent and convergent processes when building knowledge (see Chapter 2).

> Depending on task and team design, different processes will have a different impact on performance for different teams. For a decision-making team like a TMT, it is therefore the cognitive processes that are in focus. DeChurch and Mesmer-Magnus (2010) and Honts, Grossenbacher, Prewett, and Rahael (2012) compared teams that had physical work with teams that had intellectual tasks and found that "intellectual" teams put more emphasis on transition phases, than do teams with physical work. Schippers, Edmondson, and West (2014) find that TMTs must be particularly observant of pitfalls in information sharing. In TMTs there is a tendency to prefer sharing information that is already known to all, and not to share unique information, hence teams tend not to develop and investigate implications of shared information. Further, there is a tendency not to update or modify previous conclusions or current patterns of behaviour. Working in virtual teams limits the everyday and face-to-face communication and signals, and different studies have shown that virtuality is linked to less effective communication (Rico, de la Hera, & Tabernero, 2011).

Team knowledge guides work in the action phase. Different perspectives and heterogeneous task cognition are beneficial when forming a strategy, but research shows that this effect reverses during the implementation phase. When the team is to carry out the task, a homogenous task cognition is more useful (Wang, Sauer & Schryver, 2019). Team knowledge can, over time in the transition phase, be altered and changed through de-construction of meaning and co-construction of meaning, reflexivity and boundary crossing. This process is closely linked to adaptation.

> *To summarize:* The process of building knowledge is to elaborate team members' understanding of the issues at hand. By finding the rationale for different reasoning and identifying conflictual perspectives, it is possible to negotiate and integrate perspectives to build a shared understanding of what to do and how.

CASE: TEAM PROCESSES INHIBIT TEAM MEMBERS COMBINING AND MAKING THE BEST USE OF THEIR EMOTIONAL AND COGNITIVE CAPACITIES TO PERFORM AT THE HIGHEST LEVELS CONT.

In this case, there are signs that they are reluctant to share information and reflections on e.g. how things are running in other departments, and it seems as if the exchange so far has not resulted in a shared understanding of how to work together as a team. In a TMT, members are torn between different interests (their own department's and the team's) that have implications for the process of building shared meaning. Therefore it will be important to clarify their own goals for other team members. The managers reported that this was an issue they needed to discuss further. A work hypothesis could be: The process of building a shared meaning impacts the team's performance and performance outcomes.

3.1.2 Team knowledge – an implicit coordinating mechanism

However, what *kind* of knowledge is important for team performance?

3.1.2.1 Team-mental models

Team members have a mental model of their individual tasks and their environment, and when team members share similar and accurate mental models of the expected outcome, of how to carry out tasks and how to work as a team, *these mental models implicitly regulate performance.* Team-mental models (TMMs) are shared emergent knowledge structures held by team members that enable the team to form accurate explanations and expectations of work, to communicate and to adapt behaviour to task demands and other team members. TMMs guide performance, regulate coordination and enable teams to anticipate what needs to be done, and to form plans for that. Salas et al. (2018) stress that effective coordination is related to the team's engaging in goal setting, as specifying goals reduces ambiguity in coordination by giving the team a shared understanding of their objectives.

Researchers have identified four types of TMMs that are important for regulating team performance:

1. Knowledge about the task, expected results, performance requirements, standards and task-related problems (task-mental model)
2. Knowledge about equipment, tools and resources (equipment-mental model)
3. Knowledge about each other – team composition and resources, team members' preferences, values, habits and KSAs (team-mental model)
4. Knowledge of effective ways of interacting in teams, what ways of interacting function well and are appropriate in this specific team (team-interaction model)

Different TMMs are important to all teams, but play different roles for different kinds of teams. DeChurch and Mesmer-Magnus (2010) showed the task-mental model is vital for teams with a task that is mainly solved through the coordination of the members' actions. Decision-making teams (like TMTs) are to a greater extent mutually dependent on each other's knowledge and complementary perspectives to solve the task. Therefore, a clear picture of the resources in the team and how to interact is central.

3.1.2.2 Team climate

Team climate is defined as "the set of norms, attitudes, and expectations that individuals perceive as operating in a specific context" (Pirola-Merlo, Härtel, Mann, & Hirst, 2002, p. 564). It is a broad concept, and sometimes what is meant is "how it feels to be in this team." The term *team climate* is also used to describe the team's shared understanding of *what should be aimed for*. Then is meant what Kozlowski and Ilgen (2006) call the stakeholders' strategic imperatives to the team. Many organizations describe principles for performance in general. This can be e.g. to economize and try to stop doing things that do not add value for the customer. Such imperatives need to be not only communicated but also interpreted by the team. What does this mean for us in everyday work? The team's understanding of work is *adequate* when it is in line with stakeholders' expectations.

The relationship between team climate and a range of outcomes has long been established (e.g. Schneider & Barbera, 2014; Zohar & Hofmann, 2012). Research shows that a collective climate is related to how work is carried out, as well as to efficiency, at both individual and team level, and to individual learning and well-being (Kozlowski & Ilgen, 2006). Researchers have investigated different types of climate. E.g. a team climate for innovation impacts the team's involvement in change and developmental work as seen in the number and novelty of innovations (Anderson & West, 1998), and also productivity (Patterson et al., 2005). Team-safety climate impacts on how the team follows regulations and safety routines to avoid accidents (Hofmann & Stetzer, 1998). Service climate affects customers' perceptions of service quality (Schneider, Wheeler, & Cox, 1992). Bunderson and Sutcliffe (2003) found that a shared climate of team learning influences team performance.

Further, the *level* of external demands plays a role for team climate. González-Romá, Fortes-Ferreira, and Peiró (2009) tested the role of *team climate strength* for team performance and showed that only a strong climate predicts performance over time. This is supported by Shally, Gilson, and Blum (2009) who found that the more that team members perceive a job requirement for creativity, the more they engage collectively in a creative process.

3.1.2.3 Transactive memory

The team's *awareness* of its knowledge base – the collective understanding of who knows what – is often referred to as *transactive memory*. Team members know whom they can turn to for support, and this provides access to an expanded pool of knowledge. Transactive memory reduces the cognitive load on team members as a member does not need to have in-depth knowledge in all areas, but can rely on others' expertise. Kozlowski and Bell (2013) showed in a review that there is enough empirical evidence to say that transactive memory impacts team performance as it impacts quality and content of information exchange, collaboration and joint decision-making.

3.1.3 What if the team knowledge is not accurate?

So far, the argumentation has been that it is good for teams to have solid team knowledge. But cognitive structures are, apart from the degree of convergence, also distinguished by accuracy. Accuracy mirrors "the true state of the world" (Edwards, Day, Arthur, & Bell, 2006, p. 728). Within social psychology, the notion of *group think* was identified by Janis (1982) when he studied failures in decision-making, and it is the tendency for teams to be more concerned with reaching consensus than with the quality of the decision. This is related to the risk of *social conformity*, when team members do not raise issues or share information that is contrary to what the majority believes. These risks are reduced by constructive conflicts and reflection in the process of building shared meaning. It is easy to give anecdotal examples of when teams have a shared but inadequate TMM, e.g. in a team in a care home for the elderly whose performance seems to be regulated by the goal of spending as little time as possible with the residents, instead investing plenty of time and effort in keeping the kitchen spotlessly clean. The team can claim cleanliness is important. Yet what are the expectations of the main stakeholders – the elderly?

After reviewing the literature, Mohammed et al. (2010) conclude that it is highly convergent mental models, in combination with those that are of high quality, that yield the best performance benefits. If teams are open to stakeholders' demands and learn from others, it is likely that the process of building knowledge will result in shared mental models that are adequate. Team cognition is a growing field in team research as it explains why some teams perform better than others. E.g. in an analysis of 231 correlations cumulated from 25 studies, DeChurch and Mesmer-Magnus (2010) found that team cognition predicted an additional 6.8% of the variance in team-performance outcomes, after effects of behavioural and affective/motivational processes had been controlled.

> *To summarize*: Effective teams integrate individuals' different cognitions and perspectives to build a shared and rational understanding of important aspects of work. This knowledge regulates performance and enables the team members to carry out individual tasks in a coordinated manner. The team builds shared mental models of tasks, equipment, resources and interaction. The team makes use of a transactive memory – the shared collective understanding of who knows what – and uses this knowledge for division and coordination of work. Team climate is the team's understanding of what should be aimed for: it is a concept used to describe values, attitudes shared in the team of how to perform, and goes beyond accomplishing the task. Understanding others' expectations of how the team should perform,

reflecting and refining shared knowledge is to build team knowledge that is shared and adequate. Team knowledge partly explains the team's performance and performance outcomes.

3.2 Lack of trust and openness

Team interdependency will force the different team members to divide tasks, coordinate tasks and cooperate. To do so, they need to communicate. Interpersonal processes are based on interpersonal understanding, acceptance, support, informal interactions, psychological safety, humour, trust and a generally amicable climate where people feel free from pressure and experience positive affect and facilitate teamwork. Notice that climate now is used in a different sense than previously and here means "how it feels to be in this team." Trust affects team members' engagement in building relationships and readiness to support others in an expectancy of mutual benefit. Without trust, team members are reluctant to cooperate.

Amy C Edmondson (1999) defined psychological safety as "a shared belief that the team is safe for interpersonal risk taking" (p. 353). Psychological safety allows group members to freely raise critical issues and put awkward questions without fearing potential threats or embarrassment (Edmondson, 1999), counteracts the tendency of group think and conformity, and supports information sharing and reflexivity. It is part of team members experiencing an amicable climate and has been shown to be of great importance for team performance.

Psychological safety can be assessed in a questionnaire* (Edmondson, 1999) with items like:

Team psychological safety

If you make a mistake on this team, it is often held against you.

Members of this team are able to bring up problems and tough issues.

People on this team sometimes reject others for being different.

It is safe to take a risk on this team.

It is difficult to ask other members of this team for help.

No one on this team would deliberately act in a way that undermines my efforts.

Working with members of this team, my unique skills and talents are valued and utilized.

* 7-point scale from "very inaccurate" to "very accurate."

A systematic review of the research on psychological safety based on 83 empirical studies Newman, Donohue, and Eva (2017) found e.g. substantial evidence that psychological safety positively impacts communication quality and frequency, e.g. as greater reporting of error treatments of patients in hospitals. Individuals who feel safe in their relationships are more likely to raise disagreements and give candid feedback. To openly discuss conflicts and errors, and to ask for help is related to coordination and cooperation (Costa & Anderson, 2011). As well as directly and strongly influencing performance at both individual and team level, psychological safety has been found to impact performance through facilitating learning behaviour patterns (e.g. Brueller & Carmeli, 2011; Ortega, Van den Bossche, Sánchez-Manzanares, Rico, & Gil, 2013). Marlow, Bisbey, Lacerenza, and Salas (2018) in a meta-analysis studied a similar concept, communication openness, by which is meant how comfortable individuals feel talking openly with other members of the team, and showed that it positively related to performance outcomes (ρ = .27).

> ### CASE: TEAM PROCESSES INHIBIT TEAM MEMBERS COMBINING AND MAKING THE BEST USE OF THEIR EMOTIONAL AND COGNITIVE CAPACITIES TO PERFORM AT THE HIGHEST LEVELS CONT.
>
> TMTs have special challenges that we can see in the case. In TMTs, the CEO has the power of hiring, dismissing and rewarding other members, and the team's operations are followed by the entire company, which may affect the climate of safety in the team. Some raised concerns regarding a competitive attitude, and some were reluctant to turn to others for advice. A work hypothesis could be that there is too little safety in the team.

To summarize: An amicable climate is vital for any teamwork. Psychological safety is an affective state that impacts performance, learning and communication. It is a similar concept to communication openness and means that team members feel free to raise issues, including issues that take the team out of their comfort zone, without fearing that this will make others turn against them.

3.3 Ineffective general action processes

In a general sense communication is the process of sending and receiving information between teammates. The findings of a meta-analysis of 142 studies and 9,702 teams showed that communication was positively and significantly related to team performance (ρ = 0.31). The type of team matters, as teams in which team members are familiar with one another and work face-to-face exhibited a stronger relationship between communication and performance outcomes than e.g. virtual teams (Marlow et al., 2018). Breakdowns in communication and misunderstandings have a range of negative outcomes for team performance (Bowers & Cannon-Bowers, 2014). It creates barriers between team members which make it harder to coordinate different activities, team learning diminishes and it is more difficult to adapt to new situations and demands (Chen & Agrawal, 2018).

Some of these general exchanges, for example information sharing and information elaboration, are also characteristics of team-learning processes (Kozlowski & Bell, 2013; Salas, Sims, & Burke, 2005) and coordination (e.g. Kolbe, Künzle, Zala-Mezö, Wacker & Grote, 2009). As learning is closely linked to adaptation, we will come back to what research tells about communication, learning processes and adaptation in Chapter 7. But what characterizes effective communication?

3.3.1 Clear and understandable communication

It is easy to agree that communication should be clear, understandable and avoid jargon. Misunderstandings, e.g. in the exchange of text messages, are often due to the sender meaning one thing and the receiver interpreting it differently. Salas et al. (2005) advocate that closed-loop communication is one of the regulating mechanisms for effective teamwork. Closed-loop communication involves a) the sender initiating a message; b) the receiver receiving the message, interpreting it and acknowledging its receipt; and c) the sender following up to ensure the intended message was received (McIntyre & Salas, 1995). Such a communication pattern should reduce misunderstandings and communication breakdowns.

3.3.1.1 Communication content

Communication quality has a significantly stronger relationship with team-performance outcomes than communication frequency (Marlow et al., 2018). Patrashkova-Volzdoska, McComb, Green, and Compton (2003) showed that the relationship between quantity and performance outcomes is curvilinear, with both excessive and insufficient communications being related to poorer performance outcomes.

Communication quality/content is mainly put into two categories: relational communication and task-oriented communication. One could assume that the latter would have the largest impact on performance outcomes, but a meta-analysis by Marlow et al. (2018) does not support this belief. In a recent study it was found that optimal cognitive benefits were observed in group discussions in which the ratio between task-related and non-task related group arguments was 3 to 1 (Coman et al., 2019). Different communication types show different impacts on team-performance outcomes, and some content types are more important than others. Researchers distinguish between unique information sharing, general information sharing, knowledge sharing and information elaboration. Knowledge sharing and information elaboration show the strongest relations to performance outcomes (Marlow et al., 2018). Notice that these communications are part of the process of sharing, co-construction and constructive conflict which build a shared meaning of work.

3.3.1.2 Feedback

Feedback on performance is often defined as information given by an external source to individuals or teams regarding the quantity or quality of their past performance, allowing the recipient to adjust performance (Daniels, 2000; Prue & Fairbank, 1981). Feedback is essential for learning, can ensure result-orientation and adjusting-behaviour when people move away from set plans, and can promote critical reflection (Bartram & Roe, 2008). Although feedback is often asked for, and feedback is said to boost "the team from the sum of individual performance to the synergy of teamwork and ultimately to team effectiveness" (Salas et al., 2005, p. 576), the empirical results on the effects of feedback are less convincing.

In a review, Balcazar, Hopkins, and Suarez (1985) found that performance feedback given to individuals had consistent effects in 41% of the studies evaluated. Kluger and DeNisi (1996) showed in a review that feedback led to negative results in a third of the investigated studies. A review by Alvero, Bucklin, and Austin (2001) showed that when feedback is combined with other procedures (e.g. training or behavioural consequences) it had consistent effects in 58% of the studies assessed. The source of feedback seems to play a role, and although results are mixed, feedback from a supervisor seems most important. Further, when recipients could compare their performance to a standard, and when verbal information was combined with illustrations like graphs, etc. the effects were higher. Factors such as the source, the timing and frequency of feedback, its reception and acceptance have been discussed when explaining *the disparate results.*

Hinsz, Tindale, and Vollrath (1997) showed that when individuals receive feedback they tend to attribute positive evaluations of performance to their own behaviour, and failures to the situation, while teams given team feedback attributed both success and failure to the team. Gabelica, Bossche, Segers, and Gijselaers (2012) conducted a review of 59 empirical studies of team process- and performance-feedback interventions. Process feedback can be either interpersonal or task oriented. Some main results about *performance feedback* were that no study reported negative results, half of the studies reported positive effects on all the measured outcomes, and half reported positive results on some outcomes and no effects on others. Fewer studies exist on the effects of process feedback. The studies evaluated by Gabelica et al. (2012) showed mixed results, as in some studies processes improved (e.g. strategy development, coordination behaviours or conflicts) and in other studies they did not change. A few studies have shown that *process feedback* reinforces affective emergent states such as cohesion or collective efficacy. A couple of studies have investigated whether process feedback affects performance outcomes, and the results are mixed. But a couple of studies showed positive effects on job satisfaction and performance outcomes like productivity. Positive feedback is generally found to be positively linked to performance and process variables, but negative feedback may enhance motivation.

Although many argue that feedback is a powerful tool to shape processes, strengthen emergent states and enhance performance outcomes, the empirical results are somewhat mixed. The overall picture is that feedback does play a role in enhancing performance in a coordinated manner. Gabelica et al. (2012, p. 140) conclude that intervention effectiveness might be improved if it is "accurate, given in a timely manner, regular, non-threatening, shared, given directly to the team it targets, and when its distribution is fairly equal." Further, feedback in teams with high interdependency that show team trust, and collective efficacy, and feedback combined with other interventions such as goal setting, incentives, reflection upon strategies, seem to further contribute to the effect of feedback.

CASE: TEAM PROCESSES INHIBIT TEAM MEMBERS COMBINING AND MAKING THE BEST USE OF THEIR EMOTIONAL AND COGNITIVE CAPACITIES TO PERFORM AT THE HIGHEST LEVELS CONT.

In this case there are signs of a lack of knowledge sharing and information elaboration. It seems they are withholding information instead of sharing

> such information that could support managers of other departments. Maybe this impedes team performance, but more information is needed to exclude or include communication as a plausible cause of the problem.

To summarize: Communication is the foundation of teamwork as it is the primary manner by which teams share information, cooperate, coordinate and learn. Effective communication is characterized by closed-loop communication. Feedback on process and result can, if given in a thoughtful manner, increase team processes and performance outcomes. All teams communicate, and when solving problems with coordination it is worthwhile to include the hypothesis that communication patterns affect the team's performance.

3.3.2 Cooperation

Wagner (1995) defined *cooperation* as "the wilful contribution of personal efforts to the completion of interdependent jobs" (p. 152). (For the opposite, social loafing, see Chapter 1.) It implies that team members pay attention to what needs to be done, and then do it. But cooperation is about joint efforts, also giving and taking to mutual benefit. To know what needs to be done requires performance monitoring.

3.3.2.1 Performance monitoring

To monitor work processes in relation to goals is what most teams do more or less constantly, and team members' self-monitoring and heeding behaviour (see Chapter 4) aligns individuals' activities with team goals and the situation. Effective teams consist of members who maintain an awareness of team functioning *by also monitoring fellow members' work.* Mutual performance monitoring is to "keep track of fellow team members' work while carrying out their own [...] to ensure that everything is running as expected and [...] to ensure that they are following procedures correctly" (McIntyre & Salas, 1995, p. 23). The reason why mutual performance monitoring is important is that identifying errors or lapses gives information about how things are running, and if this information is used to give feedback and support others with backup behaviour, it affects team performance (Salas et al., 2005). To state the obvious: mutual performance monitoring requires team psychological safety and adequate shared team-mental models.

3.3.2.2 Backup behaviour

Backup behaviour has been defined as "the discretionary provision of resources and task-related effort to another member of one's team that is intended to help that team member obtain the goals as defined by his or her role" (Porter et al., 2003, p. 391). Bowers and Cannon-Bowers (2014) find the empirical evidence for how backup behaviour affects team performance to be mixed. Some studies have demonstrated that backup behaviour by team members is positively related to team performance. Others have shown that backup behaviour may place teams at risk; for example the provision of backup behaviour has been shown to be related to subsequent decreases in effort by the member receiving the help. Therefore, backup behaviour must be carefully considered and be based on an adequate team-mental interaction model. And it takes mutual monitoring of team members' performance to give a helping hand with the right timing. When this is so, backup behaviour is a way of carrying out work in a coordinated manner.

> *To summarize*: Cooperation is the process of working together to the same end. To do so in an effective way requires performance monitoring and backup behaviour.

3.3.3 Coordination

The impact of coordination on effectiveness has received substantial support (LePine, 2003; Rico, et al., 2011). Marks, Zaccaro, and Mathieu (2000, p. 363) describe coordination as "orchestrating the sequence and timing of interdependent actions." Because of differences in tasks (e.g. task complexity and autonomy), team design and situations faced (e.g. time pressure), the demand on team coordination varies widely between teams. Wang, Gao, Li, Song, and Ma (2017) watched videos of training sessions of control-room teams in nuclear power plants to see how they coordinate work during emergencies. The researchers found a surprising 24 basic coordination behaviour patterns. Such a task requires a different coordination and has other implications than coordination of work in a team of professional movers. Larger teams put more demand on team coordination as the dependencies are more complex (Espinosa, Lerch, & Kraut, 2004). A team with pooled or sequential dependencies has a lower demand on coordination than a team with reciprocal dependency. If pooled, it is a question of coordinating the results of individual performance, whereas in reciprocal dependency team members need to coordinate while also carrying out their tasks. Different ways of coordinating may be more or less effective in different teams. One example: Research has found that the coordination of tasks is more complicated in virtual teams than in a "physical" team, and for virtual teams it might be more efficient if coordination decisions such as assigning tasks are not distributed to the team members (De Dreu, 2006).

Effective use of appropriate coordination mechanisms improves team performance (Stachowski, Kaplan, & Waller, 2009). Scholars make a distinction between explicit and implicit coordination mechanisms. We have described communication, an explicit coordination mechanism (for example transferring information), and team knowledge as an implicit coordination mechanism. Team members "know" how things should be coordinated and do not need to communicate. Implicit coordination is smooth as one does not need to take time for meetings, to write schedules or instructions, etc. to coordinate work. But it is only effective if members have shared and accurate TMMs of task and interaction (Kolbe et al., 2009). Teams use both explicit and implicit mechanisms, but the more demand there is on coordination (e.g. in non-routine settings), the more explicit coordination needs to be. When time pressure is high, explicit mechanisms, such as holding meetings or writing reports, tend to be replaced by implicit coordination, which complicates the picture even more (Espinosa et al., 2004).

What kind of explicit coordination *behaviour* do effective teams use? *As it depends on the task and the dependencies*, researchers have taken an interest in what is effective within a specific setting. Kolbe et al. (2009) proposed combining this explicitness dimension with another content-related dimension: information-related (transmission and processing of information) versus action-related coordination (task management between team members). The integrated model of coordination behaviour was tested within anaesthesia teams. Effective coordination through explicit information exchange was e.g. requests for information, providing information, verifying information, acknowledgement, summarizing and note-making. The content was similar to what characterizes closed-loop communication discussed earlier. Explicit coordination of actions was e.g. requesting assistance, giving orders and assigning tasks (e.g. "I'll intubate and you watch the monitor").

CASE: TEAM PROCESSES INHIBIT TEAM MEMBERS COMBINING AND MAKING THE BEST USE OF THEIR EMOTIONAL AND COGNITIVE CAPACITIES TO PERFORM AT THE HIGHEST LEVELS CONT.

We do not know much about how the TMT coordinates, only that this is a problem. To find out one could use the dimensions described earlier. A work hypothesis could be that the TMT has not yet reached a firm shared meaning of what to do, and as a consequence does not know what should be coordinated and how. After this has been made clear, it would be possible to take a closer look at what coordination mechanisms they use. In a decision-taking team like a TMT, the information-related content (transmission and processing of information) is of greater importance than action-related coordination.

3.3.4 Inter-team cooperation and coordination

In the action phase, teams most often need to cooperate with other teams and functions to coordinate tasks in a workflow. Decuyper et al. (2010) identify boundary-crossing as part of, and essential for, both the process of building knowledge and performance. "Teams can neither learn nor work effectively if they cease to share knowledge, competency, opinions or creative ideas across boundaries with the different stakeholders in the learning process" (p. 118). How well the team works with others is a criterion of team effectiveness according to West (2012). By understanding the tasks of other employees and teams, employees get a better understanding of what role they play both in their team and the team's role in the organization (Wageman, Fisher, & Hackman, 2009). Explicit coordination mechanisms may be more efficient than relying on implicit coordination in cross-boundary cooperation (Espinosa et al., 2004). The process of building shared meaning in a workflow is a long and complicated process as teams have different goals and team-mental models.

> *To summarize*: Implicit team coordination is based on team knowledge. Different tasks require different coordination, but any team's explicit coordination can be examined by looking into both information-related (transmission and processing of information) and action-related coordination (task management between team members).

3.4 "Diagnosis" – how to carry out an evaluation of a team's routine-task performance

The main thing when solving problems with teamwork is to target the real causes of the problem. An evaluation of the team's habitual way of working provides this content. Notice that other plausible explanations for a lack of coordinated behaviour exist, such as leadership (see the full IMOI model).

There are different methods of carrying out an evaluation of the team's functioning and different tools that can be used. Methods such as observation by experts of team processes, or using a manager's description, are rarely used. Most often the method for collecting data is verbal or written descriptions of central aspects of team processes. Data can be collected in a team discussion which may be supported by the use of facilitation tools for divergent and convergent processes to ensure full participation and a structured discussion. Team members can privately describe the team's functioning in a more or less structured way, and this may be a better alternative if they feel inhibited about talking freely. A third method could be to use a questionnaire that covers central aspects of the team's functioning. This can be done by using one of the many inventories used for research or available on the market. These cover some, but not all central team processes described earlier. Examples of instruments are the Team Climate Inventory (TCI) (Anderson & West, 1998), Team Diagnostic Survey (Wageman, Hackman & Lehman, 2005) and Group development Questionnaire (Wheelan & Hochberger, 1996, all rights reserved). We recommend evaluating the results and identifying critical issues by looking at mean values and standard deviations. If all team members fill in the questionnaire, it will provide a general overview of the team's perception of its functioning in different dimensions. We give only examples of where other such inventories can be found on the internet. See for example. https://primarycaremeasures.ahrq.gov/team-based-care/ and for explanations see Shoemaker et al., (2014). Another option is the comprehensive version of TCI, Affina Team Performance Inventory (ATPI) (see https://www.affinaod.com/) or Aston Organisation Development (2010). Another option is ITP Metrics (https://www.itpmetrics.com/), where different instruments can be found and used for free. For explanations of how to use peer- and self-evaluations, see Ohland et al. (2012). For some instruments, as the ATPI or GDQ (all rights reserved), it is possible, through expert help, to assess how the team is working and get a comparison of team performance with other relevant teams. General advice is to choose an inventory that has been tested for reliability and validity and to compare what the instrument measures with the mindmap in Figure 5.1.

4 Step 4. Select target dimensions and set goals

Regardless of the method for data collection, the next step is to give feedback and discuss the findings with the team and stakeholders. What are the main causes (the most important dimensions of e.g. team processes) of the problem? Step 4 in the problem-solving circle is to choose dimensions, and this involves ensuring that it is realistic to believe that these can be changed. It is to set goals for how the chosen dimension should be changed (quantitative change). We now go straight to step 5 in the problem-solving circle to find possible solutions to the problem.

5 Step 5. Identify solutions

What kinds of solutions are needed in the coming intervention? In practice, and based on a diagnosis of habitual routines in a specific team, one would look for a solution to implement change in one dimension that causes or impacts the problem (or several dimensions – see step 4). To identify solutions, one should consider a) domain(s) to target and b) inter-dependencies between solutions. *The solution(s) to a problem in one dimension of habitual routines might take solutions also in a different domain* (environmental, organizational or individual) *to be sustainable*. E.g. changing one dimension of habitual work routines, such as coordination mechanisms, might first be possible after decisions in the organization and the team leadership structure is changed. What domains need to be targeted in the intervention and in what order? Table 5.1 shows domains in which solutions to a problem with a lack of coordinated behaviour can be found. The focus in this chapter is on *solutions for enhancing intra-team processes*. But solutions might be needed to change preconditions in other domains that impact team processes, e.g. leadership or HR strategies.

Team processes are interlinked and reciprocally affect one another, and several process dimensions with corresponding solutions might need to be included in the intervention, as a successful result of implementing one solution is dependent on changes in inter-related aspects. One example: A solution aiming at helping a team to better monitor its performance might *be dependent* on adequate TMMs on what to do and how to interact, and a solution to strengthen TMMs should (although it is not directly targeting the chosen dimension) be included in the intervention. What kinds of complementary solutions might be needed due to inter-dependencies between underlying dimensions? It is also possible to argue that a solution will bring change about in one dimension, and this will over time impact other inter-related dimensions. There is no simple answer, but these matters should be considered as it impacts the intervention. Addressing a problem with team coordination would probably involve a bundled

Table 5.1 Domains in which solutions to enhance coordinated performance in the action phase can be found

Choose domain(s) for solutions(s) to enhance routine-task performance			
Prerequisites in the physical environment for enhancing performance	Prerequisites on organizational level for enhancing performance	Solutions on team level for enhancing performance	Prerequisites on individual level to enhance performance
May be relevant as e.g. physical layout might impact communication	HR-support Leadership Team goals Work design Team composition	Shared understanding and team knowledge Trust, psychological safety and an amicable climate Communication, cooperation and coordination	Individual KSAs for task work and teamwork Motivation

TEAM DOES NOT ACT IN A COORDINATED MANNER | 125

solution in different domains and targeting different dimensions to ensure a change in the main dimension identified as the main cause to the problem.

The next step would be to find out what possible solutions exist for changing the chosen dimensions in step 4 to reach the goal set in step 5 in the problem-solving circle, and come to a decision on a single or bundled solution. Although the intervention might include solutions for changes in the organization or environment, or concern individuals, such solutions are beyond the scope of this book.

In the following text we describe solutions, give example of a specific method within this solution and provide some empirical support for the methods' usefulness.

5.1 Develop team mental models

We have found four different solutions for developing team mental models.

1   *Guided self-correction interventions aim* at developing shared understanding of effective approaches for future events. Most often it is done by involving the team in a reflective experience to enable team members to better understand their actions and create lessons for future work. Team members are taught to self-correct, create an open participative climate and establish relevant learning goals (Tannenbaum, Smith-Jentsch, & Behson, 1998). Most interventions are structured team discussions on effectiveness based on an analysis of positive and negative performance in the past. One general solution is *team debriefs*. Debriefs build on active self-learning participants, a self-intention for improvement and learning, and several internal and at least one external sources of information. Debriefs can be carried out as a punctual effort e.g. after a completed project, or as a recurring element of work at e.g. team meetings. Different methods and tools exist, and an example is a structured and facilitated team debrief-method developed by Eddy, Tannenbaum, and Mathieu (2013). In such a debrief a questionnaire is used to measure each team member's perceptions about the team's recent work experiences. Team members answer nine questions adapted to the context. The questions cover team processes, e.g. "We used our meeting time wisely" or "Members of the team were open to ideas and input from other team members." After an analysis of the responses, the team gets customized structured feedback where issues are categorized as being of high, medium or low priority to ensure that teams discuss the most important issues. To get the team to establish forward looking action plans and agreements, the guided debrief also involves asking the team how they will work together to address the identified concerns (Eddy et al., 2013). Meta-analytic results show that debriefing exercises improve performance by up to 25% in comparison with control groups (Tannenbaum & Cerasoli, 2013).

2   *Team building (TB) to develop a shared understanding of goals and task.* TB *aims* at helping the team to define and clarify goals and roles, and to establish open and clear communication and effective decision-making. It is directed towards interpersonal interactions; it is often carried out as informal discussions and has an inherent multi-faceted approach. TB can be facilitated and more or less structured. Shuffler, Diazgranados, Maynard, and Salas (2018) describe the approach to be based on a) a goal-setting model, b) an interpersonal model, c)

a role clarification model and d) a problem-solving model. One cornerstone is goal-setting techniques aiming at forming a shared understanding of specific individual and team goals. Most goal-setting interventions build on goal-setting theory (see e.g. Locke & Latham, 2002) and consist of techniques to guide the team through the process of setting and establishing goals. Best practice in goal-setting interventions is to ensure active participation and allow mistakes; the team should be left to create their own goals, and the process should be guided by an expert (Kramer, Thayer, & Salas, 2013). There are thousands of methods for goal setting in teams and many books such as Biech (2007) describe different such theory-based TB methods. One example is the Paradis and Martin (2012) team-goal-setting programme developed for athletes which can easily be adapted to other contexts. It is based on four principles: selecting team goals, establishing the target for the team goals, reminding team members of the team's goals and evaluation, and providing feedback and re-evaluation for team goal-setting effectiveness. Each principle has a corresponding implementation strategy – how to do it – and these are extensively described and can easily be adapted to different contexts (Paradis & Martin, 2012).

Meta-analysis shows that team-building interventions including goal-setting techniques impact team outcomes, and larger teams benefit more from these activities than smaller teams (Klein et al., 2009). However, the support for team building is mixed; see Chapter 10 for more information why that is so. Team goal-setting training may also be part of different guided self-correction interventions such as team debriefs.

3   *TB for role clarification.* As described earlier role clarification is one of the most important aspects of team building. The techniques aim at reducing confusion about functions and positions and to form a shared understanding of roles in the team. It can be useful in three different situations: job expectation techniques when a new member is introduced to the team or a team is composed, role negotiation techniques when role conflicts exist, and role analysis techniques when high ambiguity in role expectations, or when roles need to be clarified to enhance performance. It is recommended to use a facilitator to ensure that effective feedback is given to the team during the process. A typical procedure in role analysis involves setting goals and ground rules for the discussion and process, using documented divergent and convergent processes to clarify individual roles including relationships to other team members, having discussions on how roles are aligned with team goals, and the documentation of each team member's role and how it supports goal fulfilment. "The Pfeiffer book of successful team-building tools" is a compendium of theory-based interventions that can be useful for practitioners as different methods are described in detail (Biech, 2007). Meta-analyses examining the effectiveness of team-building components show that role clarification is as effective as goal setting for performance, see earlier and Klein et al. (2009).

4   *Team charter.* The procedure of creating a team charter aims at developing preventative measures for minimizing dysfunctional processes and conflicts by building a shared understanding of task work and teamwork. Team charters are documents created by team members through discussions that include agreements on how to carry out task work and teamwork. Norton and Sussman (2009) offer guidance on how to form the content. The procedure

to create a charter typically involves a) clarifying roles, responsibilities, values and mutual expectations; b) finding agreements on coordination mechanisms and how to interact to carry out teamwork; and c) making plans for dealing with performance problems, exchange of positive and constructive feedback and rewards. The discussions include topics such as strengths and weaknesses, preferred work styles, availability in terms of hours and days, sharing of contact information, timing and scheduling issues, backup and feedback mechanisms, when and how to meet, general work styles and decision-making, and how to provide feedback. A facilitator is recommended for structuring the discussion. The different topics are documented in a charter that can be revised over time and used for a reflective discussion on teamwork and performance. Mathieu and Rapp (2009) showed that construction of high quality team charters significantly improves performance, and more so when combined with high-quality performance strategies. Team charters may be part of general team-building interventions and followed up in debriefs.

5.2 Develop team climate

Team climate as the understanding of what to strive for and stakeholders' expectations of team performance and outcomes is closely linked to team mental models. Although we have found no study that shows how the solutions for strengthening and developing team mental models described earlier affect team climate, we would recommend using the reflective discussions part of self-correcting trainings, team building and team charters also when developing team climate.

Collective reflexivity meetings is a solution for developing team climate that has been developed within health care, and these can be adapted to other contexts. An example is an inter-professional learning programme (IPL) for multidisciplinary teams with the aim to develop team climate patient safety and raise awareness of professional roles within clinical teams in British hospital care (Watts, Lindqvist, Pearce, Drachler & Richardson, 2007). Teams meet with a facilitator over a period of eight months identifying areas of practise to be developed, establish learning goals, work between meetings towards achieving these goals and report back on progress at meetings. The method is described and evaluated, and it has been shown to increase team climate (Watts et al., 2007).

5.3 Develop transactive memory

Team training is a broad category, and different training programmes aim at enhancing team-relevant knowledge, skills and attitudes. Team training aiming at developing the consensus of team members' knowledge can target abilities in recognizing, trusting and coordinating specialized knowledge among team members. Team skills training in problem-solving, interpersonal relationships, goal setting and role allocation is recommended by Prichard and Ashleigh (2007). *Cross-training* is a method that aims at teaching each member the duties and responsibilities of his/her teammates and is an appropriate measure when teams are created (Busch & von der Oelsnitz, 2010). Smith-Jentsch, Kraiger, Cannon-Bowers, and Salas (2009) recommend *team simulation experiences accompanied by pre- and post-performance briefings*, especially when new teams are formed or partial turnover has occurred. *After action review* is a training sequence regarded to be an effective tool for updating knowledge about one another in ongoing teamwork (Busch & von der Oelsnitz, 2010). Simple explanations of events only look for external causes to why something happened, while more complex solutions "also look inside participants' heads and this is exactly what transactive memory is about" (p. 116). After action review resembles team debriefs in many ways (discussed earlier). A cross-training programme is often built on three modules: positional clarification (creating transparency about team members' knowledge), position modelling (team members are observed in their natural setting) and positional rotation (experientially based training in which team members perform all or parts of the duties of their teammates). Team skills training programmes have showed positive effects on transactive memory (Prichard & Ashleigh, 2007; Smith-Jentsch et al., 2009).

Collective reflexivity meetings aim at raising awareness and consensus of team members' shared and specialized knowledge. Gómez and Ballard (2011) recommend practitioners to decide on frequency, schedule and develop sites of collective reflexivity based on different action-outcome feedback cycles. We have found no specific description of such methods, but reflexivity is part of all described solutions, and we refer to those and guidelines for team facilitation.

5.4 Develop trust and psychological safety

Team building is used to develop interpersonal relations in general and also trust and psychological safety. One important takeaway from research is that psychological safety does not emerge naturally, and although situations differ, teams benefit from interventions aiming at creating such a state. Google has developed a TB-intervention aiming at creating a culture of trust and safety. It is based on Edmondson's (see e.g. Edmondson & Lei, 2014) and formed on six principles: demonstrate engagement, show understanding, be inclusive in interpersonal settings, be inclusive in decision-making, show confidence and show conviction without appearing inflexible. The method is to run facilitated structured workshops in which teams discuss, watch videos, learn about the subject from research, etc. Google has a website dedicated to a 'collection of practices, research, and ideas from Google and others to help to put people first'. One guide is about teams (retrieved 2019 October 6 from https://rework. withgoogle.com/subjects/teams/). Method description can be found on the website. See the mixed result on TB effectiveness in Chapter 10.

5.5 Develop communication

Team training to develop closed-loop communication can be done in so many ways. Steps 2.0 is an example of a training programme designed to serve as a national standard for team training in health care in the U.S. It is well described on the homepage https://www.ahrq.gov/teamstepps/index.html and explained in King et al., (2008). It is accompanied with instructions to the facilitator and materials, and can be adapted to other settings. The programme is a series of theory-based structured discussions led by a facilitator. The accompanying tool kit follows the principles of effective communication and is used to identify barriers for, and enhancing a closed-loop communication. A meta-analysis of 129 studies has shown the positive impact of training programmes such as TeamStepps on participant learning, training transfer and organizational outcomes (Hughes et al., 2016).

5.6 Develop cooperation

Team building is a general solution for enhancing interpersonal relations and cooperation within a team. See earlier for a description and references to where such methods can be found. Note that the empirical support for TB for enhancing cooperation (mutual performance monitoring and backup behaviour) is mixed and the value can be questioned (see Chapter 10 for more detail).

Team training programmes aiming at enhancing cooperation also most often include measures to train coordination and communication. Different modules or methods within a programme might specifically focus on teaching team members recognizing what team behaviour needs to be monitored, determining how these behaviours can be monitored and developing strategies for team members to assist each other in completing the team's tasks. One example of a training programme is Crew Resource Management (CRM), mainly used within aviation and military, discussed later, and another is Steps 2.0, discussed earlier. In Steps 2.0 the objectives for discussions to enhance e.g. backup behaviour and mutual support are to identify how this affects teams' processes and outcomes, to identify strategies to foster such behaviour, and identify specific tools to facilitate mutual support.

Team training in enhancing team members' mutual exchange of feedback and a feedback friendly culture follows the general principles for effective feedback and we refer to the vast literature (see e.g. Baker, Perreault, Reid, & Blanchard, 2013) and the many methods described in that literature, and to Chapter 10.

5.7 Develop coordination

Team training to develop coordination is often built on Fleishman and Zaccaro's (1992) work on functions important for effective coordination: orientation through information exchange so that team members understand resources and what should be prioritized, resource allocation, timing, sequence, motivation, systems monitoring for error management, and activities so ensure that procedures are followed. One established method for developing cognitive and interpersonal skills, such as communication, cooperation and *coordination* is CRM. CRM training has been defined as a set of "instructional strategies designed to improve teamwork in the cockpit by applying well-tested training tools (e.g., performance measures, exercises, feedback mechanisms) and appropriate training methods (e.g., simulators, lectures, videos) targeted at specific content (i.e., teamwork knowledge, skills, and attitudes)" (Salas et al., 1999, p. 163). From the description it is obvious that it can take many forms. Although initially a training strategy focused on improving crew coordination and performance in aviation, it has been used in different settings and can be adapted for enhancing coordination in high-interdependent teams. A meta-analysis showed that CRM training generally produced positive reactions from trainees, but the impact of training on learning and behavioural changes suggests mixed results (Salas et al., 2006).

> *To summarize:* There are different solutions for enhancing different dimensions of task work and teamwork in action phase, and also solutions (such as some TB solutions and team training programmes) that target several aspects taken together as a whole. Self-correction training such as debriefs, team reflexivity meetings, team building, team charters and different training programmes partly overlap in content, and in tools and methods used. There is

a vast number of different methods and tools, and although there is support that different solutions and specific methods enhance team effectiveness, the support is not fully convincing and it depends on what is done and how it is done (see Chapter 10 where this is discussed further).

CASE: TEAM PROCESSES INHIBIT TEAM MEMBERS COMBINING AND MAKING THE BEST USE OF THEIR EMOTIONAL AND COGNITIVE CAPACITIES TO PERFORM AT THE HIGHEST LEVELS CONT.

What happened in this case? The TMT and the consultant decided to implement an intervention aiming at developing a shared meaning of the TMT's task and goal. The consultant chose a structured team-building solution with practical training inspired by Paradis and Martins's (2012) goal-setting programme. The team got homework after each session and continuous feedback with suggestions of what to develop further. One example of such a task was that each manager documented all tasks and issues that this person encountered during everyday work during a week that he or she found to be an issue that should be handled by the TMT. Some managers took great effort, and some responded only duty-fully and came up with little. This observation was feedback to the TMT in an amicable way without comments on individual differences. Each manager was asked to reflect upon and document driving forces and counterforces for their own engagement in the TMT. At the next session the team first sorted all tasks and issues that should be handled by the TMT. They were given the task to identify criteria for determining if a task/issue was to be managed by an individual manager, by cooperation between individual managers on their level or by the TMT. The simple exercises led to decisions on what tasks/issues did not belong to the TMT; many previous TMT topics were erased from the agenda, and the main tasks/issues for the TMT were clarified. Thereafter it was relatively simple for the TMT to set goals for respective task. One such example was that it was decided that the TMT should ensure that all managers for the production and support-functions should form service level agreements. The results regarding the managers' engagement were used to come up with ideas on how the engagement could be made stronger. The managers were asked to list "What can I myself do about it?" "What can the TMT do?" and "What can the organization do?" The descriptions were thought to be made use of by eliminating hindrances for the engagement, but nothing much happened. It was said that the reason was that it was no longer needed, as the manager now found it more motivating to work as a team. Probably there are more reasons why. One could be the underlying competition between managers that might be a sign of a team conflict.

To summarize: Solving a problem due to a lack of coordinated behaviour in the action phase involves an analysis of potential causes of the problem. In this chapter we have shown that a range of cognitive, affective and behavioural processes can be evaluated to identify core aspects to target when developing the team's effectiveness. We have shown that this probably requires bundled solutions, and that such solutions and valid methods for team development can be found.

Bibliography

Alvero, A. M., Bucklin, B. R., & Austin, J. (2001). An objective review of the effectiveness and essential characteristics of performance feedback in organizational settings (1985–1998). *Journal of Organizational Behavior Management, 21*(1), 3–29. https://doi.org/10.1300/J075v21n01_02

Anderson, N. R., & West, M. A. (1998). Measuring climate for work group innovation: Development and validation of the team climate inventory. *Journal of Organizational Behavior, 19*(3), 235–258. https://doi.org/10.1002/(SICI)1099-1379(199805)19:3<235::AID-JOB837>3.0.CO;2-C.

Aston Organisation Development Ltd (2010). The Aston Team Performance Inventory. Retrieved 2019 October 04 from https://abeyanttraining.files.wordpress.com/2010/09/atpi.pdf

Baker, A., Perreault, D., Reid, A., & Blanchard, C. M. (2013). Feedback and organizations: Feedback is good, feedback-friendly culture is better. *Canadian Psychology/Psychologie Canadienne, 54*(4), 260–268. https://doi.org/10.1037/a0034691

Balcazar, F., Hopkins, B. L., & Suarez, Y. (1985). A critical, objective review of performance feedback. *Journal of Organizational Behavior Management, 7*(3–4), 65–89. https://doi.org/10.1300/J075v07n03_05

Bartram, D., & Roe, R. (2008). Individual and organisational factors in competence acquisition. In W. J. Nijhof & L. F. M. Nieuwenhuis (Eds.), *The learning potential of the workplace* (pp. 71–96). Sense Publishers. Retrieved from https://brill.com/abstract/book/edcoll/9789087903725/BP000006.xml

Biech, E. (Ed.). (2007). *The Pfeiffer book of successful team-building tools: Best of the annuals* (2nd ed.). New York: Pfeiffer.

Bowers, C., & Cannon-Bowers, J. (2014). Cognitive readiness for complex team performance. In H. F. O'Neil, R. S. Perez, & E. L. Baker (Eds.). *Teaching and measuring cognitive readiness.* (pp. 301–323). Boston, MA: Springer US. https://doi.org/10.1007/978-1-4614-7579-8_16

Brueller, D., & Carmeli, A. (2011). Linking capacities of high-quality relationships to team learning and performance in service organizations. *Human Resource Management, 50*(4), 455–477. https://doi.org/10.1002/hrm.20435

Bunderson, J. S., & Sutcliffe, K. A. (2003). Management team learning orientation and business unit performance. *Journal of Applied Psychology, 88*(3), 552–560. https://doi.org/10.1037/0021-9010.88.3.552

Busch, M. W., & von der Oelsnitz, D. (2010). Collective intelligence in teams: Practical approaches to develop transactive memory. *Advances in Intelligent and Soft Computing, 76*, 107–119. https://doi.org/10.1007/978-3-642-14481-3_9

Chen, M.-H., & Agrawal, S. (2018). Exploring student's team behavior through entrepreneurship education: A time-lagged study. *Education + Training, 60*(7/8), 781–799. https://doi.org/10.1108/ET-07-2017-0102

Coman, A. D., Curşeu, P. L., Fodor, O. C., Oţoiu, C., Raţiu, L., Fleştea, A. M., & Bria, M. (2019). Communication and group cognitive complexity. *Small Group Research, 50*(4), 539–568. https://doi.org/10.1177/1046496419853624

Costa, A. C., & Anderson, N. (2011). Measuring trust in teams: Development and validation of a multifaceted measure of formative and reflective indicators of team trust. *European Journal of Work and Organizational Psychology, 20*(1), 119–154. https://doi.org/10.1080/13594320903272083

Daniels, K. (2000). Measures of five aspects of affective well-being at work. *Human Relations, 53*(2), 275–294. https://doi.org/10.1177/a010564

DeChurch, L. A., & Mesmer-Magnus, J. R. (2010). The cognitive underpinnings of effective teamwork: A meta-analysis. *Journal of Applied Psychology, 95*(1), 32–53. https://doi.org/10.1037/a0017328

Decuyper, S., Dochy, F., & Van den Bossche, P. (2010). Grasping the dynamic complexity of team learning: An integrative model or effective team learning in organisations. *Educational Research Review, 5*. https://doi.org/10.1016/j.edurev.2010.02.002

De Dreu, C. K. W. (2006). When too little or too much hurts: Evidence for a curvilinear relationship between task conflict and innovation in teams. *Journal of Management, 32*(1), 83–107. https://doi.org/10.1177/0149206305277795

Eddy, E. R., Tannenbaum, S. I., & Mathieu, J. E. (2013). Helping teams to help themselves: Comparing two team-led debriefing methods. *Personnel Psychology, 66*(4), 975–1008. https://doi.org/10.1111/peps.12041

Edmondson, A. C. (1999). Psychological safety and learning behavior in work teams. *Administrative Science Quarterly, 44*(2), 350–383. https://doi.org/10.2307/2666999

Edmondson, A. C., Dillon, R. J., & Roloff, S. K. (2007). 6 three perspectives on team learning. *The Academy of Management Annals, 1*. https://doi.org/10.1080/078559811

Edmondson, A. C., & Lei, Z. K. (2014). Psychological safety: The history, renaissance, and future of an interpersonal construct. In F. P. Morgeson (Ed.), *Annual review of organizational psychology and organizational behavior* (Vol. 1, pp. 23–43). Palo Alto: Annual Reviews. https://doi.org/10.1146/annurev-orgpsych-031413-091305

Edwards, B. D., Day, E. A., Arthur, W., & Bell, S. T. (2006). Relationships among team ability composition, team mental models, and team performance. *Journal of Applied Psychology, 91*(3), 727–736. https://doi.org/10.1037/0021-9010.91.3.727

Espinosa, J. A., Lerch, F. J., & Kraut, R. E. (2004). Explicit versus implicit coordination mechanisms and task dependencies: One size does not fit all. In E. E. Salas & S. M. Fiore (Eds.), *Team cognition: Understanding the factors the drive process and performance* (pp. 107–129). Washington, DC: American Psychological Association. https://doi.org/10.1037/10690-006

Fleishman, E. A., & Zaccaro, S. J. (1992). Toward a taxonomy of team performance functions. In *Teams: Their training and performance* (pp. 31–56). Westport, CT: Ablex Publishing.

Gabelica, C., Van den Bossche, P., Segers, M., & Gijselaers, W. (2012). Feedback, a powerful lever in teams: A review. *Educational Research Review, 7*(2), 123–144. https://doi.org/10.1016/j.edurev.2011.11.003

Gersick, C. J. G., & Hackman, J. R. (1990). Habitual routines in task-performing groups. *Organizational Behavior and Human Decision Processes, 47*(1), 65–97. https://doi.org/10.1016/0749-5978(90)90047-D

Gómez, L. F., & Ballard, D. I. (2011). Communication for change: Transactive memory systems as dynamic capabilities. *Research in Organizational Change and Development, 19*, 91–115. https://doi.org/10.1108/S0897-3016(2011)0000019006

González-Romá, V., Fortes-Ferreira, L., & Peiró, J. M. (2009). Team climate, climate strength and team performance: A longitudinal study. *Journal of Occupational and Organizational Psychology, 82*(3), 511–536. https://doi.org/10.1348/096317908X370025

Hinsz, V. B., Tindale, R. S., & Vollrath, D. A. (1997). The emerging conceptualization of groups as information processors. *Psychological Bulletin, 121*(1), 43–64. https://doi.org/10.1037/0033-2909.121.1.43

Hofmann, D. A., & Stetzer, A. (1998). The role of safety climate and communication in accident interpretation: Implications for learning from negative events. *Academy of Management Journal, 41*(6), 644–657. https://doi.org/10.2307/256962

Honts, C., Grossenbacher, M., Prewett, M., & Rahael, J. (2012). The importance of team processes for different team types. *Team Performance Management: An International Journal, 18*(5/6), 312–327. https://doi.org/10.1108/13527591211251104

Hughes, A. M., Gregory, M. E., Joseph, D. L., Sonesh, S. C., Marlow, S. L., Lacerenza, C. N., Salas, E. (2016). Saving lives: A meta-analysis of team training in healthcare. *Journal of Applied Psychology, 101*(9), 1266–1304. https://doi.org/10.1037/apl0000120

Janis, I. L. (1982). *Groupthink*. Boston: Houghton Mifflin Company.

King, H., Battles, J., Baker, D., Alonso, A., Salas, E., Webster, J., Salisbury, M. (2008). TeamSTEPPS: Team strategies and tools to enhance performance and patient safety. In *Advances in patient safety: new directions and alternative approaches Volume 3. Performance and tools*. Rockville (MD): Agency for Healthcare Research and Quality (US).

Klein, C., DiazGranados, D., Salas, E., Le, H., Burke, C. S., Lyons, R., & Goodwin, G. F. (2009). Does team building work? *Small Group Research, 40*(2), 181–222. https://doi.org/10.1177/1046496408328821

Kluger, A. N., & DeNisi, A. (1996). The effects of feedback interventions on performance: A historical review, a meta-analysis, and a preliminary feedback intervention theory. *Psychological Bulletin, 119*(2), 254–284. https://doi.org/10.1037/0033-2909.119.2.254

Kolbe, M., Künzle, B., Zala-Mezö, E., Wacker, J., & Grote, G. (2009). Measuring coordination behaviour in anaesthesia teams during induction of general anaesthetics. In R. H. Flin & L. Mitchell (Eds.), *Safer surgery analysing behavior in the operating theatre* (pp. 203–221). Aldershot, UK: Ashgate.

Kozlowski, S. W. J., & Bell, B. S. (2013). Work groups and teams in organizations. In *Handbook of psychology: Industrial and organizational psychology* (Vol. 12, 2nd ed., pp. 412–469). Hoboken, NJ: John Wiley & Sons Inc.

Kozlowski, S. W. J., & Ilgen, D. (2006). Enhancing the effectiveness of work groups and teams. *Psychological Science in the Public Interest, 7*(3), 77–124. https://doi.org/10.1111/j.1529-1006.2006.00030.x

Kozlowski, S. W. J., & Klein, K. J. (2000). A multilevel approach to theory and research in organizations: Contextual, temporal, and emergent processes. In *Multilevel theory, research, and methods in organizations: Foundations, extensions, and new directions* (pp. 3–90). San Francisco, CA: Jossey-Bass.

Kramer, W. S., Thayer, A. L., & Salas, E. (2013). Goal setting in teams. In *New developments in goal setting and task performance* (pp. 287–310). New York, NY: Routledge/Taylor & Francis Group.

LePine, J. A. (2003). Team adaptation and postchange performance: Effects of team composition in terms of members' cognitive ability and personality. *Journal of Applied Psychology, 88*(1), 27–39. https://doi.org/10.1037/0021-9010.88.1.27

Locke, E. A., & Latham, G. P. (2002). Building a practically useful theory of goal setting and task motivation: A 35-year odyssey. *American Psychologist, 57*(9), 705–717. https://doi.org/10.1037/0003-066X.57.9.705

Marks, M. A., Zaccaro, S. J., & Mathieu, J. E. (2000). Performance implications of leader briefings and team-interaction training for team adaptation to novel environments. *Journal of Applied Psychology, 85*(6), 971–986. https://doi.org/10.1037/0021-9010.85.6.971

Marlow, S., Bisbey, T., Lacerenza, C., & Salas, E. (2018). Performance measures for health care teams: A review. *Small Group Research, 49*(3), 306–356. https://doi.org/10.1177/1046496417748196

Mathieu, J. E., & Rapp, T. L. (2009). Laying the foundation for successful team performance trajectories: The roles of team charters and performance strategies. *Journal of Applied Psychology, 94*(1), 90–103. https://doi.org/10.1037/a0013257

McIntyre, M. R., & Salas, E. (1995). Measuring and managing for team performance: Lessons from complex environments. In R. A. Guzzo & E. Salas (Eds.), *Team effectiveness and decision making in organizations* (pp. 9–45). San-Francisco: Jossey-Bass.

Mohammed, S., Ferzandi, L., & Hamilton, K. (2010). Metaphor no more: A 15-year review of the team mental model construct. *Journal of Management, 36*(4), 876–910. https://doi.org/10.1177/0149206309356804

Newman, A., Donohue, R., & Eva, N. (2017). Psychological safety: A systematic review of the literature. *Human Resource Management Review, 27*(3), 521–535. https://doi.org/10.1016/j.hrmr.2017.01.001

Norton, Jr., W. I., & Sussman, L. (2009). Team charters : Theoretical foundations and practical implications for quality and performance. *Quality Management Journal, 16*(1), 7–17. https://doi.org/10.1080/10686967.2009.11918214

Ohland, M. W., Loughry, M. L., Woehr, D. J., Bullard, L. G., Felder, R. M., Finelli, C. J., & Schmucker, D. G. (2012). The Comprehensive Assessment of Team Member Effectiveness: Development of a Behaviorally Anchored Rating Scale for Self- and Peer Evaluation. *Academy of Management Learning & Education, 11*(4), 609–630. https://doi.org/10.5465/amle.2010.0177

Ortega, A., Van den Bossche, P., Sánchez-Manzanares, M., Rico, R., & Gil, F. (2013). The influence of change-oriented leadership and psychological safety on team learning in healthcare teams. *Journal of Business and Psychology, 29*, 311–321. https://doi.org/10.1007/s10869-013-9315-8

Paradis, K. F., & Martin, L. J. (2012). Team building in sport: Linking theory and research to practical application. *Journal of Sport Psychology in Action, 3*(3), 159–170. https://doi.org/10.1080/21520704.2011.653047

Patrashkova-Volzdoska, R. R., McComb, S. A., Green, S. G., & Compton, W. D. (2003). Examining a curvilinear relationship between communication frequency and team performance in cross-functional project teams. *IEEE Transactions on Engineering Management, 50*(3), 262–269. https://doi.org/10.1109/TEM.2003.817298

Patterson, M. G., West, M. A., Shackleton, V. J., Dawson, J. F., Lawthom, R., Maitlis, S., Wallace, A. M. (2005). Validating the organizational climate measure: Links to managerial practices, productivity and innovation. *Journal of Organizational Behavior, 26*(4), 379–408. https://doi.org/10.1002/job.312

Pirola-Merlo, A., Härtel, C., Mann, L., & Hirst, G. (2002). How leaders influence the impact of affective events on team climate and performance in R&D teams. *The Leadership Quarterly, 13*(5), 561–581. https://doi.org/10.1016/S1048-9843(02)00144-3

Porter, C. O. L. H., Hollenbeck, J. R., Ilgen, D. R., Ellis, A. P. J., West, B. J., & Moon, H. (2003). Backing up behaviors in teams: The role of personality and legitimacy of need. *Journal of Applied Psychology, 88*(3), 391–403. https://doi.org/10.1037/0021-9010.88.3.391

Prichard, J. S., & Ashleigh, M. J. (2007). The effects of team-skills training on transactive memory and performance. *Small Group Research, 38*(6), 696–726. https://doi.org/10.1177/1046496407304923

Prue, D. M., & Fairbank, J. A. (1981). Performance feedback in organizational behavior management. *Journal of Organizational Behavior Management, 3*(1), 1–16. https://doi.org/10.1300/J075v03n01_01

Rico, R., de la Hera, C. M. A., & Tabernero, C. (2011). Work team effectiveness: A review of research from the last decade (1999–2009). *Psychology in Spain, 15*. Retrieved from www.psychologyinspain.com/content/full/2011/15006.pdf

Rico, R., Sánchez-Manzanares, M., Gil, F., Alcover, C. M., & Tabernero, C. (2011). Procesos de coordinación en equipos de trabajo. [Team coordination processes.]. *Papeles Del Psicólogo, 32*(1), 59–68.

Salas, E., Prince, C., Bowers, C. A., Stout, R. J., Oser, R. L., & Cannon-Bowers, J. A. (1999). A methodology for enhancing crew resource management training. *Human Factors: The*

Journal of the Human Factors and Ergonomics Society, 41(1), 161–172. https://doi.org/10.1518/001872099779577255

Salas, E., Reyes, D. L., & McDaniel, S. H. (2018). The science of teamwork: Progress, reflections, and the road ahead. *American Psychologist, 73*(4), 593–600. https://doi.org/10.1037/amp0000334

Salas, E., Sims, D. E., & Burke, C. S. (2005). Is there a "Big Five" in teamwork? *Small Group Research, 36*(5), 555–599. https://doi.org/10.1177/1046496405277134

Salas, E., Wilson, K. A., Burke, C. S., Florida, C., Wightman, D. C., & Rucker, F. (2006). Does crew resource management training work? An update, an extension, and some critical needs. *Human Factors, 48*(2), 392–412. https://doi.org/10.1518/001872006777724444

Schippers, M. C., Edmondson, A. C., & West, M. A. (2014). Team reflexivity as an antidote to team information-processing failures. *Small Group Research, 45*(6), 731–769. https://doi.org/10.1177/1046496414553473

Schneider, B., & Barbera, K. M. (Eds.). (2014). *The Oxford handbook of organizational climate and culture.* New York, NY: Oxford University Press. https://doi.org/10.1093/oxfordhb/9780199860715.001.0001

Schneider, B., Wheeler, J. K., & Cox, J. F. (1992). A passion for service: Using content analysis to explicate service climate themes. *Journal of Applied Psychology, 77*(5), 705–716. https://doi.org/10.1037/0021-9010.77.5.705

Shally, C. E., Gilson, L. L., & Blum, T. C. (2009). Interactive effects of growth need strength, work context, and job complexity on self-reported creative performance. *Academy of Management Journal, 52*(3), 489–505. https://doi.org/10.5465/AMJ.2009.41330806

Shoemaker, S J, Fuda, K. K., Parchman, M., Schaefer, J., Levin, J., Hunt, M., & Ricciardi, R. (2014). *Atlas of Instruments to Measure Team-based Primary Care Report.* Rockville, MD. Agency for Healthcare Research and Quality. Retrieved October 4 from https://primarycaremeasures.ahrq.gov/team-based-care/downloads/ccteam/Team-based_Primary_Care_Atlas.pdf

Shuffler, M. L., Diazgranados, D., Maynard, M. T., & Salas, E. (2018). Developing, sustaining, and maximizing team effectiveness: An integrative, dynamic perspective of team development interventions. *Academy of Management Annals, 12*(2), 688–724. https://doi.org/10.5465/annals.2016.0045

Smith-Jentsch, K. A., Kraiger, K., Cannon-Bowers, J. A., & Salas, E. (2009). Do familiar teammates request and accept more backup ? Transactive memory in air traffic control. *Human Factors, 51*(2), 181–192. https://doi.org/10.1177/0018720809335367.

Stachowski, A., Kaplan, S., & Waller, M. (2009). The benefits of flexible team interaction during crises. *The Journal of Applied Psychology, 94.* https://doi.org/10.1037/a0016903

Tannenbaum, S. I., & Cerasoli, C. P. (2013). Do team and individual debriefs enhance performance? A meta-analysis. *Human Factors: The Journal of the Human Factors and Ergonomics Society, 55*(1), 231–245. https://doi.org/10.1177/0018720812448394

Tannenbaum, S. I., Smith-Jentsch, K. A., & Behson, S. J. (1998). Training team leaders to facilitate team learning and performance. In *Making decisions under stress: Implications for individual and team training* (pp. 247–270). Washington, DC: American Psychological Association. https://doi.org/10.1037/10278-009

Van der Haar, S., Segers, M., & Jehn, K. A. (2013). Towards a contextualized model of team learning processes and outcomes. *Educational Research Review, 10,* 1–12. https://doi.org/10.1016/j.edurev.2013.04.001

Van der Vegt, G., & Bunderson, S. (2005). Learning and performance in multidisciplinary teams: The importance of collective team performance. *Academy of Management Journal, 48.* https://doi.org/10.5465/AMJ.2005.17407918

Wageman, R., Hackman, J. R., & Lehman, E. (2005). Team diagnostic survey. *The Journal of Applied Behavioral Science, 41*(4), 373–398. https://doi.org/10.1177/0021886630528198

Wageman, R., Fisher, C. M., & Hackman, J. R. (2009). Leading teams when the time is right. *Organizational Dynamics, 38*(3), 192–203. https://doi.org/10.1016/j.orgdyn.2009.04.004

Wagner, J. A. (1995). Studies of individualism-collectivism: Effects on cooperation in groups. *Academy of Management Journal, 38*(1), 152–173. https://doi.org/10.2307/256731

Wang, D., Gao, Q., Li, Z., Song, F., & Ma, L. (2017). Developing a taxonomy of coordination behaviours in nuclear power plant control rooms during emergencies. *Ergonomics, 60*(12), 1634–1652. https://doi.org/10.1080/00140139.2017.1329941

Wang, S., Sauer, S. J., & Schryver, T. (2019). The benefits of early diverse and late shared task cognition. *Small Group Research, 50*(3), 408–439. https://doi.org/10.1177/1046496419835917

Watts, F., Lindqvist, S., Pearce, S., Drachler, M., & Richardson, B. (2007). Introducing a post-registration interprofessional learning programme for healthcare teams. *Medical Teacher, 29*(5), 443–449. https://doi.org/10.1080/01421590701513706

West, M. A. (2012). *Effective teamwork: Practical lessons from organizational research* (3rd ed.). Oxford: Blackwell.

West, M. A., Hirst, G., Richter, A., & Shipton, H. (2004). Twelve steps to heaven: Successfully managing change through developing innovative teams. *European Journal of Work and Organizational Psychology, 13*(2), 269–299. https://doi.org/10.1080/13594320444000092

Wheelan, S. A., & Hochberger, J. M. (1996). Validation studies of the group development questionnaire. *Small Group Research, 27*(1), 143–170. https://doi.org/10.1177/1046496496271007

Wildman, J. L., Salas, E., & Scott, C. P. R. (2014). Measuring cognition in teams. *Human Factors: The Journal of the Human Factors and Ergonomics Society, 56*(5), 911–941. https://doi.org/10.1177/0018720813515907

Wilson, J. M., Goodman, P. S., & Cronin, M. A. (2007). Group learning. *Academy of Management Review, 32*(4), 1041–1059. https://doi.org/10.5465/amr.2007.26585724

Zohar, D. M., & Hofmann, D. A. (2012). Organizational culture and climate. In *The Oxford handbook of organizational psychology* (Vol. 1, pp. 643–666). New York, NY: Oxford University Press.

Chapter 6

The team does not cooperate adequately due to conflicts and a lack of a positive and amicable climate

This chapter focuses on how to set the stage for a positive and amicable team climate and highlights the affective emergent states: psychological safety, trust and cohesion. Affective states are an important prerequisite for long-term team effectiveness. Conflicts can affect this climate – and so it is important to find a way to prevent and handle them. We will learn that there are different kinds of conflicts depending on the issue: relationship conflicts, task conflicts and process conflicts. Functional conflicts advance, enrich and inspire a team. Dysfunctional conflicts in contrast are destructive and have a negative impact on team output as well as on individual well-being. How can positive interpersonal relationships be ensured? Besides the emergent states just mentioned, specific KSAs for conflict management and the team context affect team climate and the emergence of conflicts. To solve problems, preemptive strategies such as team building and team training can be helpful to enhance affective emergent states and KSAs for teamwork and conflict management. In case of existing dysfunctional conflicts reactive strategies of conflict management are needed to solve them in a constructive way, specifically basing on collectivistic or cooperative processes.

In teams several persons need to cooperate which makes it not surprising that positive interpersonal relationships are very important for successful teamwork. Team climate impacts cognitive processes and influences the team's performance. But working together also means that interpersonal problems can arise and the more dependent we are on each other, the more dynamics exist and the development of conflicts becomes more likely. When talking to people in the practical field, we often hear that conflicts interfere with the work. Some conflicts become even more important than the actual work.

1 Step 1. Describe the current situation

Let us now turn to a concrete case. Chapter 4 already dealt with conflicts in a team – although team composition was focused as an input factor. In this chapter we have not chosen a real life team, but a virtual team as an example. Why? It could be assumed that virtual teams are less affected by conflicts than real life teams because they spend less time together and do not interact physically. But this is not true. As we will learn in this chapter, virtual teams lack important preconditions to prevent conflicts; conflicts can escalate rapidly in the few common interaction phases, and they need platforms to develop a positive team climate and manage interpersonal problems.

CASE: CONFLICT BETWEEN TEAM MEMBERS LEADS TO A HOSTILE ATMOSPHERE AND SUBOPTIMAL STAKEHOLDER SATISFACTION

In a consulting firm, a project team has been set up to advise a company. The team is interdisciplinary and consists of four persons with different expertise: Alan (IT/ Business Intelligence), Rachel (Marketing/Sales), Andrew (Human Resources) and Ella (Controlling). All team members work on different projects at the same time and the team members work in this constellation for this specific consulting contract only. There is no hierarchical structure within the team. In case of difficulties it is Ann's, the company leader's, responsibility to support them. As they live and work in different cities, they are a virtual team.

The overall objective of the project is to diagnose the customer company and to develop proposals for the restructuring of the operational and organizational procedures. In three months' time a project report as well as a presentation must be accomplished.

How do team members coordinate their work? There are online conferences every week to plan the concrete work and to exchange about work status, logged by a team assistant.

The team members were not enthusiastic about the composition of the team; they would have preferred to work together with other colleagues but were given no choice. Still, all of them are used to work in different constellations and have broad experiences in consulting.

The team is progressing according to the project schedule; everybody is bringing in their expertise. However, during the team sessions there are disputes concerning minor details that take up a lot of time. For example, there are long discussions about an adequate form of the transcript of the meeting and the best time of day to communicate.

In the last session, the team needs to decide who will present the results to the customer. Three of the team members would like to present – Ella says that she has the best presentation skills, Andrew would like to deepen his contact with the customer for possible further projects in the field of human resources, and Alan argues that he has invested the most time into this project (which the others deny). At the end of the session all team members shout at each other and they do not come to an agreement – so eventually the leader of the company, Ann, has to decide who will give the presentation.

What about the stakeholders? The contact person of the customer company says that they had expected more, based on their previous experiences with the consulting firm. "I mean they did the minimum of what was needed to be done to fulfil the contract – but not a bit more. And to be honest – it was rather a standard solution, they haven't taken our firm's specifics into account."

THE TEAM DOES NOT COOPERATE ADEQUATELY | 139

> Ann is worried about the situation – first because the team's results are moderately satisfying, but not optimum. And second it is important that organizational members are ready to cooperate with all colleagues in future projects. Ann is wondering what went wrong and how such conflicts can be avoided.

2 Step 2. Identify the core problem

The consequences of the conflict are quite clear: Team members are wasting time of their team sessions on discussions about obviously irrelevant matters – and in the end they do not succeed in deciding about who is taking on an attractive task. Finally, the team's output is not optimal.

But what is the problem? The core problem is that the team is not efficient due to problems with the team's affective states and arising conflicts. We have heard that the team members themselves would have preferred to work with different persons. So one possible problem lies in the team composition (see Chapter 4) – but in this organization the team composition for project teams cannot be adapted, so more possible causes of the problem need to be analyzed.

What is specific for this kind of team? It is a temporary virtual cross-functional team. Such teams are not uncommon, as they are supposed to adapt flexibly to changing demands and environments. A lot of teams in organizations face situations where their members have not worked together before, represent different knowledge domains, are tasked with solving complex problems and have temporary membership (Dougherty, 2001; Edmondson & Nembhard, 2009; Hackman, 2002; Van Der Vegt & Bunderson, 2005).

On top of that, this team is a virtual team. In virtual teams, conflicts are more likely than in teams cooperating face-to-face (see for instance Mannix, Griffith, & Neale, 2002; Mortensen & Hinds, 2001; the meta-analysis of Ortiz de Guinea, Webster, & Staples, 2012; Shin, 2005). Why? Reasons are seen in a lower frequency of communication and common interactions – and consequently less knowledge sharing and opportunities to clarify roles and tasks. So uncertainty about roles and responsibility are more probable in virtual than in face-to-face teams – and can cause process conflicts (as in our case) (Shin, 2005). The lack of direct interaction can also unleash negative forms of communication, such as insults and swearing – probably because there is no direct contact to other persons (Shin, 2005) and so contribute to the escalation of conflicts.

After having stated that the core problem in this case is a lack of positive interpersonal relationships and conflicts in the team, we need to know more about these aspects, e.g. types of conflicts and their implications. Could the conflict have been prevented or better managed? Or – from a different point of view – is the conflict a problem at all, or just a normal kind of communication?

We will again deduce different work hypotheses of what the main factors that caused the problem in this case could be, based on different studies and theoretical approaches (section 3), before we turn towards the selection of target dimensions and goal setting (section 4) and towards ideas for problem solution in section 5.

3 Step 3. Cause analysis: what causes the problem?

Looking back on the Input-Mediator-Outcome-Input (IMOI)-team-effectiveness framework, arising conflicts are a part of the team process. They are impacted by organizational and team contexts as well as by the team member's characteristics. We have seen in Chapter 4 that team composition can be related to conflicts caused by diversity of the team members. We will focus on more relevant factors for the prevention and management of conflicts in the following section. But first we will have a look at different emergent states (see Chapter 1) establishing the framework for conflicts.

Again, the mindmap gives a brief overview of possible causes to the problem (see Figure 6.1). First order branches show possible explanations for problems due to interpersonal issues. For some of them, specific aspects are listed in second order branches. In this section we first describe the theoretical basis of these explanations and then show how they can be assessed to explore problems in specific work-places.

3.1 The climate in the team is not open, trustful and supportive

Cooperation is easier in a positive, friendly, respectful and supportive atmosphere, or in other words in a positive team climate. Team climate is a "set of norms, attitudes, and expectations that individuals perceive to operate in a specific context" (Pirola-Merlo, Härtel, Mann, & Hirst, 2002, p. 564). An integral part of team climate is affective integration: Affective integration is a global attitude toward team members, based on the degree of trust, respect and mutual liking of the team members, that develops over time in teams (Cronin, Bezrukova, Weingart, & Tinsley, 2011). So the concept of affective integration has a focus on interpersonal relationships in the team and is narrower than team climate, which refers to other aspects as well (e.g. innovation climate). Moreover, affective integration supports an effective cooperation, as sharing of information, knowledge and skills is easier in a trustful climate. It prevents that team members

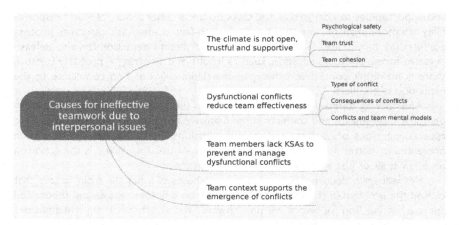

Figure 6.1 Mindmap about reasons why teams do not cooperate adequately due to interpersonal issues

THE TEAM DOES NOT COOPERATE ADEQUATELY

| 141

withdraw from each other in case of controversies, solve conflicts in a constructive and collaborative way without hurting each other (Weingart & Jehn, 2009) – we will later in this chapter go into more details on how conflicts can be managed.

When we talk about conflicts, what do we mean? Is every difference of opinion a conflict? De Dreu, Dierendonck, and Dijkstra (2004) state that a conflict begins "when an individual or group perceives differences and opposition between oneself and another individual or group about interests, beliefs or values that matter to them" (p. 8). So the subjective assessment of differences or oppositions is of importance. And it is possible that some team members are aware of a conflict while others are not.

Before we deepen the subject of conflicts, we will turn to affective processes that are important for affective integration. We refer to three well-researched concepts: psychological safety, trust and cohesion.

3.1.1 Psychological safety

Psychological safety is a concept developed by Edmondson (1999). It is a shared belief of safety in the team to take interpersonal risks in the way of challenging the status quo, questioning habitual routines and usual ways of thinking. To feel safe in a team is an important prerequisite for team reflexivity and better effectiveness. Psychological safety means that critical ideas can be expressed in a team without risking a conflict or other negative personal consequences like being ridiculed or excluded. As we have learned in Chapter 5, a lack of psychological safety inhibits communication and learning. In her studies Edmondson (1999) found strong relationships between team psychological safety and team performance as well as organizational learning (see Chapter 9).

3.1.2 Team trust

Team trust is a shared emergent state that refers to the willingness to accept vulnerability to the actions of other team members – because of positive expectations regarding their intentions and behaviour (De Jong, Dirks, & Gillespie, 2016). Team trust stands for the team members' mutual reliance and confidence – they are not suspicious and do not feel threatened by other team members.

Team trust focusses on aspects other than psychological safety: Trust refers to vulnerability and expectations about favourable behaviours of team mates, whereas psychological safety is more concerned with the belief that team members can feel comfortable communicating their ideas and opinions (Edmondson, 1999; Triplett & Loh, 2018).

Trust is important for team reflexivity and team learning as well. De Jong et al. (2016) found in a meta-analysis that team trust is positively related to team performance ($\rho = .30$). Team trust impacts several more variables on the team level, such as cooperation, information sharing, knowledge creation and satisfaction (Costa & Anderson, 2017).

Beyond that, team trust has shown to help teams handle their conflicts. Jehn and Mannix (2001) conducted a study about favourable conditions for dealing with conflicts: these include open discussion and a high degree of trust and respect. Also, other studies showed that team trust helps to manage conflicts, e.g. as task conflicts can be tolerated and handled without turning into destructive interpersonal conflicts (Rispens, Greer, & Jehn, 2007; Simons & Peterson, 2000).

A problem is that trust can be easier broken than developed – as situations that have a negative impact on trust usually are quite prominent and memorable – e.g. a lack of reliability or the disclosure of sensitive internal information (Elgoibar, Euwema, & Munduate, 2017).

3.1.3 Team cohesion

The forces or components of team cohesion are interpersonal attraction, group pride and task commitment. They all contribute to team performance (Beal, Cohen, Burke, & McLendon, 2003). Cohesion refers to the team members' commitment to the team. It is "the result of all the forces acting on the members to remain in the group" (Festinger, 1950). All these factors are preemptive for dysfunctional team conflicts (see 3.2) – team members who like each other are proud of the team, want the task to be completed and are not interested in risking their cohesion. Conflicts can be regarded as the contrary of cohesion (Kozlowski & Ilgen, 2006). As we have learned in Chapter 4 diversity causing faultlines can be a potential risk for team cohesion (e.g. mixed-gender teams in army teams, Orme & Kehoe, 2019).

Team cohesion is related to several outcomes, like team viability and team member satisfaction and therefore considered as a "key contributor to team effectiveness" (Grossman, Friedman, & Kalra, 2017, p. 248). Team viability is important for future cooperation and continuation of the team, in terms of a "team's capacity for the sustainability and growth required for success in future performance episodes" (Bell & Marentette, 2011, p. 279).

Psychological safety, trust and cohesion are closely connected. Trust is a prerequisite for psychological safety and is correlated significantly to cohesion as bondings and cohesiveness cannot develop in cases of mistrust and suspiciousness (Grossman, 2014).

Jehn et al. (2008) have shown in a study that conflicts have a negative impact on trust, respect and cohesiveness in teams – otherwise effective emergent states impact the likelihood and extent of conflicts – e.g. if team members mistrust each other dissents can easier turn into conflicts than in teams with high mutual trust. The next section is about conflicts as possible causes for problems in teams.

CASE: CONFLICT BETWEEN TEAM MEMBERS LEADS TO A HOSTILE ATMOSPHERE AND SUBOPTIMAL STAKEHOLDER SATISFACTION CONT.

In our case we have a virtual team – does virtuality impact affective processes as team members do not cooperate face-to-face? Psychological safety, trust and cohesion are important for all teams. In virtual teams, it is harder to develop them, as team members do not meet in a physical way and spend little time together. Communication is more complicated, prone to technical disruptions and incomplete – as (parts of) non-verbal information is missing. And distance impedes the building of mutual trust in a team (Costa & Anderson, 2017; Hertel, Konradt, & Voss, 2006; Jarvenpaa & Leidner, 1999). The richness of communication is restricted in virtual interactions – which hinders the development of team cohesion as well (Grossman, 2014). Team members do not see each other working – they do not know the strengths of the others and how they perform. This may also result in mistrust about the workload of the others. Team members not trusting each other won't share information or cooperate – another potential cause for conflicts (Shin, 2005).

THE TEAM DOES NOT COOPERATE ADEQUATELY | 143

> A lack of cohesion is a problem more likely for temporary virtual teams as well (Shin, 2005): Team members do not really feel like belonging to the team and as virtual teams have restricted times of direct team interactions the development of coherence is difficult.
>
> Also, informal interactions, corridor chats, common lunch or a beer after work with talks about hobbies, family and amusing episodes are important for cohesion and trust – and are not (or only very restricted) possible in virtual teams.
>
> Work hypothesis 1 for our case: The conflict has been caused by a lack of psychological safety, mutual trust and cohesion.

3.2 Dysfunctional conflicts reduce team effectiveness

In Chapter 5, we have learned that constructive conflicts support an integrated shared understanding. So obviously, not all conflicts have a negative impact.

Robbins and Judge (2015) differ between functional and dysfunctional conflicts. Functional conflicts are constructive; they support the team's goals and improve its performance by enhancing quality of decisions, creativity and innovation, stimulating interest and curiosity, and fostering an environment of self-evaluation and change. At the same time functional conflicts are a way of dealing with problems and dissolving tensions. Dysfunctional conflicts in contrast hinder team performance and are connected to discontent and distrust of team members, reduced group effectiveness, hindered communication, decreased group cohesiveness and a predominance of conflict behaviour over team and organizational goals. Conflicts do not only impact team efficiency – they can also cause negative effects for the individual health and well-being, such as stress (and release of adrenalin), psychosomatic maladies, headaches, etc. (De Dreu & Weingart, 2003b).

3.2.1 Types of conflicts

There are mainly three categories of team conflicts (de Wit, Greer, & Jehn, 2012; Jehn, 1997):

- Relationship conflict, based on problems of interpersonal connections: Do we disagree about interpersonal issues? Do we have different norms and values?
- Task conflict over content, goals and outcomes of the task being performed: What is our real objective? What are we working for? Why is our work important?
- Process conflict over the way work is to be performed and the logistics of task accomplishment, such as the delegation of tasks, roles and responsibilities: Who is responsible for what? Who is in charge of unattractive tasks? Is the workload fairly distributed?

Other authors differentiate only task from relationship conflicts, classifying process conflict as part of task conflict (Behfar, Mannix, Peterson, & Trochim, 2011).

Hjertø and Kuvaas (2009) have added the dimension of mental state in their 4 IC (intragroup conflict) model. The authors derived from interviews that task conflicts can be emotional as well. In such emotional task conflicts emotion is related to the task, not to other team members. Otherwise, relationship conflicts do not necessarily need to be emotional. When they are dealing with enduring patterns of behaviour in the team, they can be handled in a rational way. The authors postulate that task and relationship conflicts both can be emotional or cognitive. Emotional conflicts are based on the perception that incompatible feelings (approval or avoidance) arise in a team situation. Cognitive conflicts include incompatible perceptions about what is correct or incorrect.

All these categorizations describe different incompatibilities as causes for conflicts. But is it always possible to distinguish clearly between these types of conflicts? Relationship conflicts are often connected with task and process conflicts. So sometimes conflicts that look like task conflicts – as discussions about different views of work content – are originally caused by interpersonal problems. One example: A team member does not really have a problem with the way a colleague works, but all the same criticizes him very often – the real reason is antipathy and dislike. On the other hand – being highly unsatisfied with very differing ideas about work task can also result in a personal antagonism. Choi and Cho (2011) conducted a longitudinal study with project teams. Their results support these connections of conflict types: They found that relationship conflicts can lead to task conflicts as well as task conflicts can turn into relational conflicts. Greer, Jehn, and Mannix (2008) found in another longitudinal study that in particular process conflicts arising soon after team composition have a negative impact and cause more and worse conflicts over time – if the process conflict was not solved by the team and remains active. What does this mean for us? When we are facing symptoms of conflicts in teams, we need to analyze them in a detailed way (see 3.5) to figure out the main causes, as they are not always obvious.

CASE: CONFLICT BETWEEN TEAM MEMBERS LEADS TO A HOSTILE ATMOSPHERE AND SUBOPTIMAL STAKEHOLDER SATISFACTION CONT.

In our case, what type of conflict is it? And how has it developed? There is some evidence that team members do not like each other, or at least do not want to work with each other, and there are disputes over trivialities like the best time for conferring with each other – so a relationship conflict seems to be part of the problem. Furthermore, we see aspects of a process conflict: It is not clear who is in charge of the presentation. We cannot really say what came first and if there is causality – have people started discussing work delegation because they do not like each other? Or has the unclear situation about who in the team is in charge of what caused a generalized dissatisfaction, in turn resulting in quarrels? Or both at the same time?

We have two work hypotheses for the conflict causes:

> Work hypothesis 2: It is a relationship conflict: People have been forced to work together – and they do not like each other. As work is not free time – we can choose our friends but generally not our colleagues – this hypothesis perhaps is not comprehensive. So perhaps it would be

> better to say that team members are not able to handle their antipathy in a way that a good cooperation is possible.
>
> Work hypothesis 3: It is a process conflict: In the debates it became clear that task division (and time needed for the subtasks) were not clear: A process conflict has escalated as a fair task division has not been specified explicitly when the team has started working.
>
> Both work hypotheses are related to specifics of virtual teams – as team members have limited time to interact and do not meet face-to-face, it is harder for them to establish a sound relationship and define tasks, roles and responsibilities.

3.2.2 Consequences of conflicts

What does empirical research contribute to the question of implications of team conflicts? It is assumed that relationship conflicts are usually dysfunctional; conversely, task conflicts can be functional – as long as they are on a low or moderate level. A meta-analysis of de Dreu and Weingart (2003b) does not support the hypothesized positive consequences of task conflicts. The authors analyzed the associations between relationship conflicts and task conflicts on the one hand with team performance and team member satisfaction on the other. What did they find? Both types of conflicts have a similar negative impact on team performance ($\rho = -.23$ resp. $-.22$). Team member satisfaction is even more affected, especially by relationship conflicts ($\rho = -.54$), but task conflicts have a negative effect as well ($\rho = -.32$). So do conflicts have a negative impact in general? Another result of the analysis was that conflicts have stronger negative relations with performance in teams with highly complex tasks than in teams with less complex ones. This makes sense, as complex tasks need more cooperation, common agreements and flexible problem solutions that might be affected by current conflicts.

With regard to the consequences of conflicts there is no consistent state of research: A later meta-analysis by de Wit et al. (2012) on the effects of conflict on group outcomes differentiated between task and process conflicts and showed negative effects for process and relationship conflicts, but not for task conflicts. If task conflicts were not related to relationship conflicts they showed a positive impact on group performance. It makes a difference whether a conflict is based solely on factual differences or personal problems as well. Similar results are reported by Costa, Passos, and Bakker (2015): In their study with research teams they found that relationship conflicts reduce teamwork engagement. They report a positive influence of task conflict on teamwork engagement and team performance. This seems not to be the only factor for functionality or dysfunctionality of task conflicts: O'Neill, Allen, and Hastings (2013) found in a meta-analysis that task conflicts are beneficial in decision-making teams but not in project and production teams. Why is task type of importance? A possible interpretation is that for decisions a discussion of different and perhaps conflicting perspectives is fruitful and results in well-founded decisions (such as non-routine tasks) – whereas for routine team tasks with clearly defined procedures task conflicts are not helpful.

As mentioned earlier, Hjertø and Kuvaas (2017) distinguish between cognitive and emotional conflicts. In a study with 61 working teams from six companies, they researched relationships of different conflict types with team performance and satisfaction (they use a regression analysis as statistical method; the measure for relationship is b). Interestingly, they found differing effects of cognitive and emotional task conflicts: Whereas cognitive task conflicts were negatively related to team performance (b = −.43), emotional tasks conflicts correlated in a positive way with team performance (b = .49). In line with other studies the effects of emotional relationship conflicts on job satisfaction were negative (b = −.38, cognitive relationship conflicts were not part of the study, as no reliable scale exists to measure them). A possible interpretation is that emotions in team conflicts − such as feeling engaged, energized or heated − can be beneficial, if they are not directed to individual team members, but to task concerns.

Psychological safety seems to be another factor for the effects of task conflicts: Bradley, Postlethwaite, Klotz, Hamdani, and Brown (2012) have found in a study on 117 project teams that task conflicts and team performance were positively related only in teams with high psychological safety. This correlation is comprehensible as psychological safety gives team members the chance to freely communicate critical issues and questions (Edmondson, 1999) − which is an important prerequisite for constructive task conflicts. In teams with a low psychological safety, a new idea or the questioning of current routines may be seen as a threat or an affront.

DeChurch et al. (2013) summarize the state of research in a concise way: "The prevailing idea of the past two decades has been that cognitively rooted task conflict should be promoted and affectively laden relational conflict should be avoided" (p. 565). We have learned that it is not as simple as that − task conflicts can also have a negative impact on group performance (De Dreu & Weingart, 2003b) and they are not necessarily cognitive, but can be emotional (Hjertø & Kuvaas, 2017). High performing teams have low or moderate levels of process and relationship conflict as well (Jehn & Mannix, 2001).

3.2.3 Conflicts and team mental models

If conflicts are defined as perceived differences in teams (discussed earlier) − aren't they related to the sharedness of team mental models? Team mental models are emergent states, comprising shared knowledge structures enabling teams to form explanations and expectations of work, to coordinate work, and adapt behaviours to task demands (see Chapter 5). Unfortunately, there are only few studies about this relationship yet. To stimulate research, Hamilton, Shih, Tesler, and Mohammed (2014) have compared the definitions of key categories of conflicts and team mental models (p. 241) and found the following similarities:

- Task-focus in task conflicts and task mental models (knowledge about the task, expected results, performance requirements, standards, task-related problems) and equipment mental models (knowledge about equipment, tools and resources)
- Member-focus in relationship conflicts and team member mental model (knowledge about each other, team composition and resources, team members' preferences, values, habits and KSAs
- Process-focus in process conflicts and team interaction models (knowledge of effective ways of interacting in teams, what ways of interacting functions well and are appropriate in this specific team)

Conflict can influence team mental models – as functional task conflicts can support a shared understanding in the team and dysfunctional conflicts can reduce the sharedness of ideas on how to work. In addition, TMMs can be seen as a protective factor against conflicts – the more sharedness exists the less likely are conflicts. First results of studies show that shared mental models reduce the extent of team conflicts, hence improve team satisfaction (Marques Santos & Margarida Passos, 2013; Santos, Uitdewilligen, & Passos, 2015). The higher satisfaction of teams with SMMs may be explained by the absence of discussions regarding interpersonal relations and work processes, so they can concentrate on task work. This is especially true for process and relationship conflicts – they are more diminished by SMMs than task conflicts (Marques Santos & Margarida Passos, 2013; Santos, Uitdewilligen, & Passos, 2015). A possible explanation might be that task conflicts do not necessarily have a negative impact on team performance (discussed earlier).

3.3 Team members lack KSAs to prevent and manage dysfunctional conflicts

Looking back on Chapter 4 about team composition – a lot of what we have learned about KSAs for teamwork is important to avoid dysfunctional conflicts, build trust and manage constructive conflicts in a way that they do not escalate. We have seen that diversity, especially deep diversity, can cause conflicts. We will not repeat these aspects here, but are there perhaps KSAs that are of specific importance to prevent dysfunctional conflicts – also those caused by deep diversity?

Deutsch (2008) has listed the following competencies and attitudes that are relevant for effective, cooperative problem-solving (instead of fighting in perceived win-lose situations). Team members with these attributes tend to cope with dissents in teams in a way that no dysfunctional effects result from them. These KSAs (derived from "Deutsch's Twelve Commandments of Conflict Resolution") can be seen as a further specification of the interpersonal skills for conflict resolution in the model of Stevens and Campion (1994) and can be used in team composition (selection and recruitment) as well as for personnel development measures:

- Knowledge about conflict types and ability to recognize them
- Awareness of the causes and consequences of violence and ability to manage anger
- Readiness to face conflicts (rather than to avoid them)
- Respect for one's own interests and for the interests of the other team members
- Distinction between interests and positions – team members with different positions can all have the same interest
- Ability to explore the interests of all team members to find out where a consensus is, as well as to identify conflicting interests (as a basis for cooperative problem-solving)
- Skills of active listening, communication and perspective taking
- Knowledge about psychological errors of cognitions such as biases, misjudgements and stereotyped thinking that can influence conflict escalation
- Skills for dealing with difficult conflicts
- Knowledge about and awareness of one's own patterns of behaviour in conflict situations, and readiness to modify them in case of inappropriateness
- Moral values such as justice and care for other team members

> ## CASE: CONFLICT BETWEEN TEAM MEMBERS LEADS TO A HOSTILE ATMOSPHERE AND SUBOPTIMAL STAKEHOLDER SATISFACTION CONT.
>
> Coming back to our case – a possible reason for the emergence of a dysfunctional conflict could also be that team members do not know how to handle dissent in a better way. So work hypothesis 4 states that the team members lack important KSAs enabling them to cooperate and prevent conflicts – irrespective of whether they have sympathies for each other or not. Especially in an organization where everybody has to work in changing and different teams this is an important aspect.

3.4 Team context supports the emergence of conflicts

Conflicts are not solely caused by the "wrong" team members lacking relevant KSAs – the organizational context and team frame conditions are of importance, too. It would not be reasonable to give the sole responsibility for conflicts to individuals – the team members. Unfortunately, there is little research on team context and conflicts, but from case studies we know that a lack of adequate resources can cause interpersonal disputes due to stress and frustration, as well as time pressure. This applies to all kinds of dysfunctional conflicts, like being in a bad mood and feeling under pressure increases the likelihood to interact in an unconstructive way. Disputes over the limited resources can arise – how should the tight budget be spent, who may use the computer at what time, etc.

Another important point is that if there is an uncertainty about quality criteria of the organization – as in what is more important or what has priority – for example productivity, low cost or quality? If teams do not know what is expected of them, this may cause an intra-team conflict and so task and process conflicts can follow (West, 2012). This vagueness can also arise when teams are confronted with different stakeholders and their inconsistent expectations – for example teaching teams are confronted with differing requirements by their leader, children, parents, community, etc.

We now have a closer look at how leadership affects conflicts and their management. As we will see in Chapter 8, it is a leadership task to ensure adequate resources and clarify the team's mission and goals, as ambiguity about what the team is aiming for can cause conflicts. It is important that goals and mission are really shared by all team members. So leaders should support framing (Weingart & Jehn, 2009), meaning to shift in intra-team-communication the focus from "I/me" to "we/us."

Zhang, Cao, and Tjosvold (2011) conducted a study with 108 teams in China. The results indicate that transformational leadership (see Chapter 8) has a positive impact on the use of cooperative ways of conflict management and results in better team performance. Leadership encouraging a cooperative form of conflict management is beneficial for conflict resolution as well as for team performance.

Leadership is associated with conflict culture, defined as "shared norms and associated values and assumptions, that define how conflict should be managed in

THE TEAM DOES NOT COOPERATE ADEQUATELY | 149

organizations and guide organizational members' attitudes and behaviours" (Gelfand, Harrington, & Leslie, 2014, p. 111). Gelfand, Leslie, Keller, and de Dreu (2012) have found in a study that leaders' own conflict management behaviours are related to conflict cultures of their units. They analyzed collaborative, dominating and avoidant conflict cultures in 131 bank branches. In collaborative conflict cultures, conflicts are solved in a common constructive dialogue and by negotiation. In dominating cultures, conflicts are managed in a confrontative and competitive way – so in the end there are winners and losers. In avoidant cultures conflicts are not conducted, but suppressed – conflict parties are passive and agreeable. The results of the study show that leaders' behaviours are associated with the conflict culture in the team, if they manage conflicts in a cooperative or avoidant way – but not for dominant leaders. A possible interpretation of these results is that team leaders affect conflict culture, for example by fostering cooperative behaviour in the team, at least those with a collaborative or an avoidant conflict culture. Dominant leaders perhaps are not seen as positive role models. Moreover, the collaborative conflict culture resulted to be the most beneficial for team effectiveness – as we will also see in the section about solutions.

Team leaders can impact the likelihood of conflicts as well by their rewarding behaviour: Rewards for individual performance encourage a competitive as well as conflicting behaviour, as rivalry is reinforced and individual goals can become more important than the common team goal. If the whole team is rewarded for team performance as well, team members are motivated to cooperate, as they have the same goal: to support each other to achieve the team's goal together (Tjosvold & Tjosvold, 2015).

> ## CASE: CONFLICT BETWEEN TEAM MEMBERS LEADS TO A HOSTILE ATMOSPHERE AND SUBOPTIMAL STAKEHOLDER SATISFACTION CONT.
>
> Transferring this to our case: Has Ann been too passive in her role as leader? Has she supported the team enough, for example by clarifying the roles and tasks of team members and moderating sessions to avoid a waste of time? We have another hypothesis:
>
> > Work hypothesis 5: There is a lack of good leadership supporting the team adequately.

To summarize: Conflicts are interrelated with emergent states of teams, particularly with psychological safety, trust and cohesiveness. Conflicts in teams can be caused by interpersonal problems (relationship conflicts) as well as different ideas about work processes and work task. But beware: These states of conflicts can also occur together or change over time. Relationship and process conflicts have a negative impact on group performance and can be regarded as dysfunctional. Task conflicts can have a positive influence on teamwork and be functional – especially if they are not connected to a relationship conflict, there is a high degree of psychological safety and teams have to make decisions or solve problems. To avoid dysfunctional conflicts, handle constructive conflicts and cooperate in a trustful way adequate KSAs of the team members and a good leadership are of great importance, too.

In the following section we will give examples for methods to profoundly diagnose the causes of a team problem.

3.5 How to diagnose the team's affective state and types of conflicts

In this chapter we have focused on mediators of the IMOI model: the emergent states of team trust, psychological safety and team cohesion and conflicts as team processes. We have seen that these mediators are affected by individual KSAs, leadership and the composition of the team. As KSAs and team leadership are covered in different chapters (4 and 8), we will give examples for the measurement of affective states and conflicts.

How can these be assessed? Usually it is not so easy for team members to talk about such aspects, as they are related to individual emotions and personal needs, especially if there are problems in the team – e.g. if there is a lack of psychological safety team members won't feel free to talk frankly about their problems. Questionnaires that preserve anonymity are often used to find out more about the causes for problems. Again, we recommend choosing tested scales. Exemplary inventories can be found on the web-page of the Agency for Healthcare Research and Quality by the U.S. Department of Health & Human Services (https://primarycaremeasures.ahrq. gov/team-based-care, Shoemaker et al., 2014).

Here are some hints on how to diagnose psychological safety, trust, team cohesion and conflicts.

3.5.1 Psychological safety

In the last chapter it was mentioned how to assess psychological safety: Besides the psychological safety scale by Edmondson (1999), the Team Climate Inventory by Anderson and West (1998) has been recommended. This questionnaire includes a scale on safety as well.

3.5.2 Team trust

An example on how to measure trust in the team is the trust scale by Tseng and Ku (2011). They adapted a version by Jarvenpaa and Leidner (1999). The scale has been developed for research studies. How can results be interpreted? The higher the values, the higher is the extent of trust in a team. Mean results under 3 – the medium response range – indicate low trust in a team.

Trust scale

1   I would be comfortable giving the other team members complete responsibility for the completion of this project.

THE TEAM DOES NOT COOPERATE ADEQUATELY | 151

> 2   I would be comfortable giving the other team members a task or problem which was critical to the project, even if I could not monitor them.
>
> 3   I really wish I had a good way to oversee the work of the other members.
>
> 4   Members of my work group show a great deal of integrity.
>
> 5   I can rely on those with whom I work in this group.
>
> 6   There is a noticeable lack of confidence among my team members.
>
> 7   We are usually considerate of one another's feelings in this work group.
>
> 8   The people in my group are friendly.
>
> 9   Overall, the people in my group are very trustworthy.
>
> Possible responses range from 1 (strongly disagree) to 6 (strongly agree); item 6 needs to be analyzed reverse to the other items.
>
> Box Measures of Trust Scale (Tseng & Ku, 2011)

3.5.3 Team cohesion

The Group Environment Questionnaire (Eys, Carron, Bray, & Brawley, 2007; Whitton & Fletcher, 2014) is a common and validated measure to assess group cohesion – it can be used for work teams as well as for sports teams. It includes scales about integration (sense of team closeness, similarity and bonding as a social unit and around the team task), attractions to the group (social interactions and personal acceptance) and attractions to the task (feelings about personal involvement in relation to shared group goals and productivity). The questionnaire can be downloaded with evaluation forms on the website of the McGill Sport Psychology Laboratory (2019, http://sport psych.mcgill.ca/).

3.5.4 Team conflict

To assess what type of conflict exist in a team, the scales of Hjertø and Kuvaas (2009) can be used. As mentioned earlier they include emotional task conflicts, cognitive task conflicts and emotional relationship conflicts (the fourth scale about cognitive relationship does not meet psychometric standards).

Based on the Intragroup Conflict Scale (Jehn, 1995), another short questionnaire has been developed (Jehn et al., 2008) to assess in a study what type of conflict exists. The scales have been tested with psychometrical methods as well. Higher values indicate conflicts – the theoretical mean per item is 3.5. Please note that the scales measure what types of conflicts occur in the team – but not if they are functional or dysfunctional.

> ## Level of conflict types in teams
>
> ### *Task conflict*
>
> 1   We fought about *work matters*.
>
> 2   We had *task-related* disagreements.

> 3   How much conflict *of ideas* was there in this team?
> 4   How different were members' *viewpoints* on decisions?
> 5   How much did this team have to work through disagreements about varying *opinions*?
> 6   We often disagreed about *work things*.
>
> ### Relationship conflict
>
> 1   How much fighting about *personal* issues was there in this team?
> 2   We disagreed about *non-work* (social or personality) things.
> 3   We fought about *non-work* things.
> 4   Sometimes, people fought over *personal matters*.
>
> ### Process conflict
>
> 1   How much disagreement was there about *delegation issues* within this team?
> 2   We disagreed about the *process* to get the work done.
> 3   To what extent did this team disagree about the *way to do things* in the team?
> 4   How much disagreement was there about *task responsibilities* within this team?
>
> The authors use 7-point scales for possible responses. We suggest 1 (strongly disagree) to 7 (strongly agree) for the statements and 1 (none) to 7 (a lot) for the questions.
>
> Box Scales about the level of conflict types (Jehn et al., 2008)

However, if causes of problems in a team have been discovered – e.g. a lack of team trust or a high conflict level, what can be done? The next step is the search for possible target dimensions and goal setting for interventions.

4 Step 4. Select target dimensions and set goals

As the problem is described and possible factors causing it have been diagnosed, dimensions need to be determined that are to be impacted by interventions. For these dimensions concrete goals should be defined, optimally together with the stakeholders. Specific objectives enable us to take the next step: find the best solutions to reach them.

5 Step 5. Identify solutions

What interventions exist to secure a positive and amicable team climate and prevent conflicts or handle them in a good way? In section 3.2 we have seen that there are functional and dysfunctional conflicts and that moderate conflict levels do not necessarily have negative consequences. So it is not about avoiding team conflicts in general – not even relationship and process conflicts as they are part of team processes. Tjosvold (2008) comments that conflicts are not the problem, but the way they are managed (especially in teams with competitive relationships). But what can be done to manage dysfunctional conflicts and enhance functional conflicts?

In general, there are two strategies to handle conflicts: You can prevent them or you can manage them when they have reached an unacceptable level. Marks, Mathieu, and Zaccaro (2001) indicate preemptive and reactive conflict management strategies. The enhancement of positive affective emergent states can be subsumed under preemptive strategies, as they prevent conflicts as well (see 3.1).

Table 6.1 shows potential domains for solutions. Both – preemptive and reactive strategies – are situated on the team domain. As a lack of appropriate KSAs can cause problems (see 3.3), personnel development is a possible solution on individual domain – and also team composition on the organizational domain – to assure that team members bring the requisites for amicable and constructive cooperation. In 3.4 we have seen that team context may play an important role, too.

If a solution is chosen in the team domain (e.g. an intervention to improve team cohesion), it needs to be considered that perhaps solutions in other domains need to be added. If teams solve conflicts together, it should be ensured that they do not fall under pressure and are given the time needed for conflict management. Or a change of leadership behaviour is needed that supports (and does not undermine) team cohesion.

The next step is to choose the right combination of solutions for the specific situation – based on the results of the diagnosis. In this chapter we will focus on preemptive as well as reactive strategies on the team and the individual domain. More aspects related to the problems described in this chapter are discussed in other chapters: team composition (Chapter 4), development of psychological safety (Chapter 5) and leadership (Chapter 8).

Table 6.1 Domains for designing measures for team climate and conflict management

Choose domain for solution(s) to enhance a positive team climate, prevent and manage conflicts			
Prerequisites in the physical environment	**Prerequisites on organizational level**	**Solutions on team level**	**Solutions on individual level**
Not relevant	To enhance: Leadership Team composition	Preemptive: to enhance affective emergent states (psychological safety, mutual trust and team cohesion) Reactive strategies: to enhance conflict management	Preemptive: To enhance individual KSAs for teamwork and conflict management

5.1 *Preemptive strategies*

5.1.1 Develop mutual trust and team cohesion

Mutual trust and team cohesion are important components of social climate, specifically for affective integration. If problems have been diagnosed for this matter e.g. with the Group Environment Questionnaire (Eys et al., 2007; Whitton & Fletcher, 2014, see also 3.5), teambuilding can be an appropriate intervention to improve team processes. Team-building interventions with focus on mutual trust and cohesion include contents like mutual supportiveness, communication and sharing of feelings (Klein et al., 2009). An example for a method is a team-building activity described by Mendoza (2001). It lasts eight hours and consists of inputs and small group discussions (e.g. about critical trust issues, trust developing behaviours, development of a common language to build trust) as well as experiential activities that require mutual support to handle them (for example to balance across narrow rails, which are installed without touching the ground – to succeed team members need to help and brace each other). In an experimental study, the author could show that the teams that had participated in this intervention reached a significantly higher trust level than a control group (without team building) and another group that took part in team building without experiential activities.

Another intervention was realized at a nursing faculty as a one-day team-building retreat for university teaching staff. It included team challenging activities aiming at more mutual trust and common problem-solving, for instance games to get to know each other better and group problem-solving tasks. Another example is a partner exercise with mouse-traps (and mutual coaching about how to put a hand on the trap without being snapped) with subsequent discussions about trust in the team. The evaluation study showed that after the team building, cohesion had significantly increased (Birx, LaSala, & Wagstaff, 2011).

What about meta-analysis on the effects of team building? Klein et al. (2009) showed a high relationship between team building and affective outcomes ($\rho = .44$). In her doctoral thesis Grossman (2014) conducted a meta-analysis on how team interventions (trainings, buildings and facilitators/tools) impact team cohesion. The result was that team building has the strongest relationship ($d = .7$, d is a measure for the average effect size) with team cohesion.

5.1.2 Develop KSAs for conflict management

In Chapter 4 we have reported that team trainings are a good way to enhance important KSAs. Most of the KSAs that we have highlighted in Chapter 4 are also needed for conflict management, like agreeableness, communicative competences and collectivism. Team regulation skills help avoid process conflicts. Therefore, in this chapter we focus only on KSAs that are specifically important for conflict management (see earlier Deutsch, 2008). Based on their research, Greer et al. (2008) recommend conducting conflict training at the beginning of the team's cooperation to qualify them for conflict solution.

An example on how to develop individual KSAs for conflict management is a short self-guided training for conflict management in virtual teams, developed by Martínez-Moreno, Zornoza, Orengo, and Thompson (2015). The authors evaluated the training with psychology students. The students were grouped into virtual teams of three or four persons. The teams worked on problem-solving tasks (survival situations) that

THE TEAM DOES NOT COOPERATE ADEQUATELY | 155

needed team members to agree upon the right answer. In a session lasting 60–90 minutes team members received constructive and developmental feedback about process and outcome. The process feedback was based on a questionnaire about trust, planning, coordination strategies, written communication strategies and shared information management. In a second step, teams analyzed these feedbacks using guiding questions and discussed their difficulties with an external facilitator. At the end of the session, teams developed three ideas to improve team processes for a second session one week later. The training included a strategy of team debriefs (see Chapter 10). The authors used a control group design and found that the teams that had attended the training used more functional conflict management strategies (e.g. open communication) and less avoiding and dysfunctional strategies than the untrained control group.

5.2 Reactive strategies – solve existing conflicts in a constructive way

5.2.1 Intra-team conflict management

Dysfunctional conflicts need to be solved, as they have a negative impact on team processes and outcomes. Interventions for conflict resolution in teams are subsumed under the term intra-team conflict management. That includes interactions and strategies of team members to reduce or dissolve disagreements (DeChurch, Mesmer-Magnus, & Doty, 2013; Jehn & Mannix, 2001). Before describing a method, a brief explanation of the underlying approach. Different authors use varying terms for conflict management processes, but they are mainly based on the contrast of collectivistic/cooperative and individualistic/competitive strategies (De Dreu & Weingart, 2003a; DeChurch et al., 2013; Tjosvold, 2008).

- Collectivistic/cooperative processes are based on collaborating and openness norms and include open discussions on different issues, concerns and positions. The aim is to find an agreement satisfying everyone as much as possible, via common problem-solving or compromising. Teams with cooperative orientations believe that the whole team can win together – what gives them another motivational turn to get involved in teamwork. Cooperative team members with communication skills enabling them to discuss open-mindedly profit from conflicts as they solve problems, get innovative ideas and learn from each other.
- Individualistic/competitive processes comprise avoiding and competing. Avoiding means not to mention the controversial issues and trying to reduce their significance by ignoring them. Competing means that one conflict party "wins" and dominates the team in the end. This implicates contending or forcing to prevail against the others, using measures as persuasion, threats and bluffs.

A method to solve conflicts in a cooperative manner is "constructive controversy." Constructive controversy is a form of interaction in which contrary views are expressed and discussed openly and respectfully, aiming at agreements acceptable for all and a combination of ideas. It means to "dig into issues, create alternatives, and choose a high-quality solution that solves the problem and strengthens the group" (Tjosvold, 1995, p. 100). An important prerequisite for using it is that the team has cooperative goals and team members do not compete with each other (Guoquan Chen, Tjosvold, Huiqun Zhao, Nan Ning, & Yue Fu, 2011; Tjosvold, 1995; Tjosvold & Ziyou Yu, 2007).

What are concrete strategies of constructive controversy? Tjosvold (1995) names the following:

1. "Establish norms for openness. Everyone is encouraged to express his or her opinions, doubts, uncertainties and hunches. Ideas are not dismissed because they first appear too unusual, impractical or undeveloped. Protect rights: the rights of dissent and free speech reduce fear of retribution for speaking out.
2. Assign opposing views. Coalitions are formed and given opposing positions to present and defend. One person is assigned to take a critical role by attacking the group's current preference.
3. Use the golden rule of controversy. Discuss issues with others as you want them to discuss those issues with you. If you want people to listen to you, listen to them.
4. Consult relevant sources. Articles, books, consultants and experts can provide experience and ideas to help the group decide which course of action is superior. Include diverse people. Independent people with different backgrounds, expertise, opinions, outlooks and organizational positions are likely to disagree.
5. Show personal regard. Criticize ideas rather than attacking an individual's motivation or personality. Avoid insults and implications that challenge another's integrity, intelligence or motives.
6. Combine ideas. Team members avoid "either my way or your way" thinking and try to use as many ideas as possible to create new, useful solutions" (p. 101).

Another concrete method is the virtual conflict resolution system (VNS) aiming at a collaborative win-win process (Shin, 2005). It is an online negotiation system (based on an online chat software) enabling a collaborative negotiation. The principles of this system can be transferred to conflict mediation in other contexts and realized with a consultant virtually or in real life settings. The team members involved in the conflict are called negotiators. The team is passing through four stages:

- Ritual sharing: the negotiators communicate about their interests and values. The aim of this phase is to build rapport and to learn about differing values of the conflict parties. Above that they have to consent to the norms of the system like confidentiality and mutual respect.
- Defining the issues: Now the negotiators are to explain their position or demand – what do they want, what should happen in the team? And conflicts parties are to state explicitly what the reasons for these issues are, for example regarding their needs or interests.
- Reframing and prioritizing issues: How can the problem be described in a way that prioritises and mentions the interests of all conflict parties? Reframing means to express the problem in a way that all negotiators can agree to it. Several issues are part of the reframed problem. Negotiators need to agree about what is the most important one and find an order of priority for all issues.
- Problem-solving and reaching agreement: The last step is to brainstorm about possible solutions (see Chapter 2, convergent and divergent methods) and decide what is the best one for the team, for example based on feasibility or practicability.

THE TEAM DOES NOT COOPERATE ADEQUATELY | 157

DeChurch et al. (2013) found in a meta-analysis that the way of handling conflicts plays a crucial role for a team's performance and well-being. For example, Tekleab, Quigley, and Tesluk (2009) report results of a longitudinal study that indicate that conflict management has a positive impact on team cohesion, performance and satisfaction. Task conflicts – having the potential to advance teams as we have seen earlier – can be handled with active conflict management in a way that they have a positive effect for team performance (DeChurch & Marks, 2001). A meta-analysis by DeChurch et al. (2013) showed positive performance and affective outcomes after collectivistic conflict management and opposite effects for individualistic processes. Alper, Tjosvold, and Law (2000) have found that cooperative conflict resolution has a positive impact on conflict efficacy (a team's trust in its ability to solve conflicts) and group performance whereas a competitive approach has a negative effect on these variables. The same is true for virtual teams; Paul, Seetharaman, Samarah, and Mykytyn (2004) report a positive impact of collaborative conflicts strategies on team performance.

5.2.2 Conflict mediation

Sometimes conflicts can be solved neither by the team alone, nor with support of their team leader. Then it makes sense that a facilitator supports the team. A method to handle conflicts – not only in teams and organizations – is mediation. Mediation is the "involvement in a conflict by a neutral third party, who tries to stimulate parties to jointly search for a win-win solution, while promoting open communication and mutual understanding of underlying interests" (Bollen & Euwema, 2014, p. 482). In a literature review Bollen and Euwema (2014) summarize that participants are satisfied with the mediation procedures and that good conflict solutions are achieved – especially if the mediator is well qualified and the participants have a collaborative orientation. Unfortunately, there is still a need for research on the effects of mediation and promising methods.

Despite all these methods for conflict management, sometimes conflicts have escalated so far that teams cannot go on working together – especially if there have been threats or personal insults (Glasl, 2013). Then teams should be dissolved and recomposed, as team composition can be an intervention as well (see Chapters 4 and 10). But at the same time team members should learn from these experiences, reflect their own share in the conflict and develop better strategies for further cooperation in teams.

> *To summarize*: An amical climate is of high relevance for cooperation in teams. The goal for team development should be to enhance a friendly and supportive climate. Conflicts should not be avoided in general; instead they should be managed in a way that teams can benefit from them. The following suggestions can be made to prevent or solve problems with teams' affective states and dysfunctional conflicts:
>
> - Enhance psychological safety, trust, and cohesiveness in the team
> - Search for team members with KSAs that are fruitful for teamwork – among them good qualifications for conflict management and communication – or let them learn about it
> - Give teams enough time and resources to fulfil their team tasks
> - Clarify expectations toward the team
> - Do not promote competition in the team, e.g. by treating team members differently

THE TEAM DOES NOT COOPERATE ADEQUATELY

- Be attentive for possible areas of conflicts right from the beginning of a team's work and let the team agree on task division and other issues with regard to team processes
- Encourage cooperative conflict management, "constructive controversy," open discussion norms, mutual trust and respect in teams
- Search for conflict solutions beneficial for all team members (win-win) and not for particularistic solutions

CASE: CONFLICT BETWEEN TEAM MEMBERS LEADS TO A HOSTILE ATMOSPHERE AND SUBOPTIMAL STAKEHOLDER SATISFACTION CONT.

What happened in the real case? As the project of the team was nearly finished (and their temporal cooperation as well), Ann intervened and decided that Rachel was to hold the presentation because of her marketing expertise – that should be most relevant for the customer's interest.

Ann took conclusions for the future teamwork in her consulting firm as well and decided to implement preemptive strategies to prevent similar problems. These are related to the affective emergent states and conflict management strategies for all employees. For the development of trust, she realized annual two-day team building activities with external facilitators in a conference venue. As all employees work in different teams at the same time, the team building is for the whole company. To support conflict management she organized an online conflict management training similar to the one described earlier (Martínez-Moreno et al., 2015).

Moreover, she tackled team leadership. She decided to install team leaders in all teams that are in charge of, inter alia, establishing rules for the cooperation and to clarify individual tasks and responsibilities of the team members, to prevent process conflicts. Interventions, which can solve problems when there is a lack of good team leadership, will be discussed in Chapter 8.

Bibliography

Alper, S., Tjosvold, D., & Law, K. S. (2000). Conflict management, efficacy, and performance in organizational teams. *Personnel Psychology*, *53*, 625–642. https://doi.org/10.1111/j.1744-6570.2000.tb00216.x

Anderson, N. R., & West, M. A. (1998). Measuring climate for work group innovation: Development and validation of the team climate inventory. *Journal of Organizational Behavior*, *19*(3), 235–258. https://doi.org/10.1002/(SICI)1099-1379(199805)19:3<235::AID-JOB837>3.0.CO;2-C.

Beal, D. J., Cohen, R. R., Burke, M. J., & McLendon, C. L. (2003). Cohesion and performance in groups: A meta-analytic clarification of construct relations. *Journal of Applied Psychology*, *88*(6), 989–1004. https://doi.org/10.1037/0021-9010.88.6.989

Behfar, K. J., Mannix, E. A., Peterson, R. S., & Trochim, W. M. (2011). Conflict in small groups: The meaning and consequences of process conflict. *Small Group Research*, *42*(2), 127–176. https://doi.org/10.1177/1046496410389194

Bell, S. T., & Marentette, B. J. (2011). Team viability for long-term and ongoing organizational teams. *Organizational Psychology Review, 1*(4), 275–292. https://doi.org/10.1177/2041386611405876

Birx, E., LaSala, K. B., & Wagstaff, M. (2011). Evaluation of a team-building retreat to promote nursing faculty cohesion and job satisfaction. *Journal of Professional Nursing, 27*(3), 174–178. https://doi.org/10.1016/j.profnurs.2010.10.007

Bollen, K., & Euwema, M. (2014). Mediating hierarchical labour conflicts: Dynamics and interventions. In O. B. Ayoko, N. M. Ashkanasy, & K. A. Jehn (Eds.), *Handbook of conflict management research* (pp. 480–492). Cheltenham, UK: Edward Elgar. https://doi.org/10.4337/9781781006948.00041

Bradley, B. H., Postlethwaite, B. E., Klotz, A. C., Hamdani, M. R., & Brown, K. G. (2012). Reaping the benefits of task conflict in teams: The critical role of team psychological safety climate. *Journal of Applied Psychology, 97*(1), 151–158. https://doi.org/10.1037/a0024200

Choi, K., & Cho, B. (2011). Competing hypotheses analyses of the associations between group task conflict and group relationship conflict. *Journal of Organizational Behavior, 32*(8), 1106–1126. https://doi.org/10.1002/job.733

Costa, A. C., & Anderson, N. (2017). Team trust. In E. Salas, R. Rico, & J. Passmore (Eds.), *The Wiley Blackwell Handbook of the Psychology of Team Working and Collaborative Processes* (pp. 393–416). Chichester, UK: John Wiley & Sons, Ltd. https://doi.org/10.1002/9781118909997.ch17

Costa, P. L., Passos, A. M., & Bakker, A. B. (2015). Direct and contextual influence of team conflict on team resources, team work engagement, and team performance. *Negotiation and Conflict Management Research, 8*(4), 211–227. https://doi.org/10.1111/ncmr.12061

Cronin, M. A., Bezrukova, K., Weingart, L. R., & Tinsley, C. H. (2011). Subgroups within a team: The role of cognitive and affective integration. *Journal of Organizational Behavior, 32*(6), 831–849. https://doi.org/10.1002/job.707

DeChurch, L. A., & Marks, M. A. (2001). Maximizing the benefits of task conflict: The role of conflict management. *International Journal of Conflict Management, 12*(1), 4–22. https://doi.org/10.1108/eb022847

DeChurch, L. A., Mesmer-Magnus, J. R., & Doty, D. (2013). Moving beyond relationship and task conflict: Toward a process-state perspective. *Journal of Applied Psychology, 98*(4), 559–578. https://doi.org/10.1037/a0032896

De Dreu, C. K. W., Van Dierendonck, D., & Dijkstra, M. T. M. (2004). Conflict at work and individual well-being. *International Journal of Conflict Management, 15*(1), 6–26. https://doi.org/10.1108/eb022905

De Dreu, C. K. W., & Weingart, L. R. (2003a). A contingency theory of task conflict and performance in groups and organizational teams. In M. A. West, D. Tjosvold, & K. G. Smith (Eds.), *International handbook of organizational teamwork and cooperative working* (pp. 151–166). Chichester, UK: John Wiley & Sons, Ltd. https://doi.org/10.1002/9780470696712.ch8

De Dreu, C. K. W., & Weingart, L. R. (2003b). Task versus relationship conflict, team performance, and team member satisfaction: A meta-analysis. *Journal of Applied Psychology, 88*(4), 741–749. https://doi.org/10.1037/0021-9010.88.4.741

De Jong, B. A., Dirks, K. T., & Gillespie, N. (2016). Trust and team performance: A meta-analysis of main effects, moderators, and covariates. *Journal of Applied Psychology, 101*(8), 1134–1150. https://doi.org/10.1037/apl0000110

Deutsch, M. (2008). Cooperation and conflict: A personal perspective on the history of the social psychological study of conflict resolution. In M. A. West, D. Tjosvold, & K. G. Smith (Eds.), *International handbook of organizational teamwork and cooperative working* (pp. 9–43). Chichester, UK: John Wiley & Sons, Ltd. https://doi.org/10.1002/9780470696712.ch2

de Wit, F. R. C., Greer, L. L., & Jehn, K. A. (2012). The paradox of intragroup conflict: A meta-analysis. *Journal of Applied Psychology, 97*(2), 360–390. https://doi.org/10.1037/a0024844

Dougherty, D. (2001). Reimagining the differentiation and integration of work for sustained product innovation. *Organization Science, 12*(5), 612–631. https://doi.org/10.1287/orsc.12.5.612.10096

Edmondson, A. C. (1999). Psychological safety and learning behavior in work teams. *Administrative Science Quarterly, 44*(2), 350–383. https://doi.org/10.2307/2666999

Edmondson, A. C., & Nembhard, I. M. (2009). Product development and learning in project teams: The challenges are the benefits. *Journal of Product Innovation Management, 26*(2), 123–138. https://doi.org/10.1111/J.1540-5885.2009.00341.X

Elgoibar, P., Euwema, M., & Munduate, L. (2017). *Conflict Management.* In O. Braddick (Ed.), *Oxford Research Encyclopedia of Psychology* (Vol. 1, pp. 1–28). Oxford: Oxford University Press. https://doi.org/10.1093/acrefore/9780190236557.013.5

Eys, M. A., Carron, A. V., Bray, S. R., & Brawley, L. R. (2007). Item wording and internal consistency of a measure of cohesion: The group environment questionnaire. *Journal of Sport & Exercise Psychology, 29*(3), 395–402.

Festinger, L. (1950). Informal social communication. *Psychological Review, 57*(5), 271–282. https://doi.org/10.1037/h0056932

Gelfand, M. J., Harrington, J. R., & Leslie, L. M. (2014). Conflict cultures: A new frontier for conflict management research and practice. In *Handbook of conflict management research* (pp. 109–135). Cheltenham, UK: Edward Elgar Publishing. https://doi.org/10.4337/9781781006948.00015

Gelfand, M. J., Leslie, L. M., Keller, K., & de Dreu, C. (2012). Conflict cultures in organizations: How leaders shape conflict cultures and their organizational-level consequences. *Journal of Applied Psychology, 97*(6), 1131–1147. https://doi.org/10.1037/a0029993

Glasl, F. (2013). *Konfliktmanagement: ein Handbuch für Führungskräfte, Beraterinnen und Berater.* Bern: Haupt.

Greer, L. L., Jehn, K. A., & Mannix, E. A. (2008). Conflict transformation: A longitudinal investigation of the relationships between different types of intragroup conflict and the moderating role of conflict resolution. *Small Group Research, 39*(3), 278–302. https://doi.org/10.1177/1046496408317793

Grossman, R. (2014). How do teams become cohesive? A meta-analysis of cohesion's antecedents. Doctoral Dissertation. University of Central Florida.

Grossman, R., Friedman, S. B., & Kalra, S. (2017). Teamwork processes and emergent states. In E. Salas, R. Rico, & J. Passmore (Eds.), *The Wiley Blackwell handbook of the psychology of team working and collaborative processes* (pp. 243–269). Chichester, UK: John Wiley & Sons, Ltd. https://doi.org/10.1002/9781118909997.ch11

Guoquan Chen, G., Tjosvold, D., Huiqun Zhao, H., Nan Ning, N., & Yue Fu, Y. (2011). Constructive controversy for learning and team effectiveness in China. *Asia Pacific Journal of Human Resources, 49*(1), 88–104. https://doi.org/10.1177/1038411110391708

Hackman, J. R. (2002). *Leading teams: Setting the stage for great performances.* Boston: Harvard Business School Press.

Hamilton, K., Shih, S.-I., Tesler, R., & Mohammed, S. (2014). Team mental models and intragroup conflict. In O. B. Ayoko, N. M. Ashkanasy, & K. A. Jehn (Eds.), *Handbook of conflict management research* (pp. 239–253). Cheltenham, UK: Edward Elgar Publishing. https://doi.org/10.4337/9781781006948.00024

Hertel, G., Konradt, U., & Voss, K. (2006). Competencies for virtual teamwork: Development and validation of a web-based selection tool for members of distributed teams. *European Journal of Work and Organizational Psychology, 15*(4), 477–504. https://doi.org/10.1080/13594320600908187

Hjertø, K. B., & Kuvaas, B. (2009). Development and empirical exploration of an extended model of intra-group conflict. *International Journal of Conflict Management, 20*(1), 4–30. https://doi.org/10.1108/10444060910931585

Hjertø, K. B., & Kuvaas, B. (2017). Burning hearts in conflict. *International Journal of Conflict Management, 28*(1), 50–73. https://doi.org/10.1108/IJCMA-02-2016-0009

Jarvenpaa, S. L., & Leidner, D. E. (1999). Communication and trust in global virtual teams. *Organization Science*, *10*(6), 791–815. https://doi.org/10.1287/orsc.10.6.791

Jehn, K.A. (1995). A multimethod examination of the benefits and detriments of intragroup conflict. *Administrative Science Quarterly*, *40*(2), 256–282. https://doi.org/10.2307/2393638

Jehn, K.A. (1997). A qualitative analysis of conflict types and dimensions in organizational groups. *Administrative Science Quarterly*, *42*(3), 530–557. https://doi.org/10.2307/2393737

Jehn, K.A., Greer, L., Levine, S., & Szulanski, G. (2008). The effects of conflict types, dimensions, and emergent states on group outcomes. *Group Decision and Negotiation*, *17*(6), 465–495. https://doi.org/10.1007/s10726-008-9107-0

Jehn, K.A., & Mannix, E.A. (2001). The dynamic nature of conflict: A longitudinal study of intragroup conflict and group performance. *Academy of Management Journal*, *44*(2), 238–251. https://doi.org/10.5465/3069453

Klein, C., DiazGranados, D., Salas, E., Le, H., Burke, C. S., Lyons, R., & Goodwin, G. F. (2009). Does team building work? *Small Group Research*, *40*(2), 181–222. https://doi.org/10.1177/1046496408328821

Kozlowski, S. W. J., & Ilgen, D. R. (2006). Enhancing the effectiveness of work groups and teams. *Psychological Science in the Public Interest*, *7*(3), 77–124. https://doi.org/10.1111/j.1529-1006.2006.00030.x

Mannix, E., Griffith, T., & Neale, M. (2002). The phenomenology of conflict in virtual work teams. In P. Hinds & S. Kiesler (Eds.), *Distributed work* (pp. 213–233). Cambridge, MA: MIT Press.

Marks, M.A., Mathieu, J. E., & Zaccaro, S. J. (2001). A temporally based framework and taxonomy of team processes. *Academy of Management Review*, *26*(3), 356–376. https://doi.org/10.5465/amr.2001.4845785

Marques Santos, C., & Margarida Passos, A. (2013). Team mental models, relationship conflict and effectiveness over time. *Team Performance Management: An International Journal*, *19*(7/8), 363–385. https://doi.org/10.1108/TPM-01-2013-0003

Martínez-Moreno, E., Zornoza, A., Orengo, V., & Thompson, L. F. (2015). The effects of team self-guided training on conflict management in virtual teams. *Group Decision and Negotiation*, *24*(5), 905–923. https://doi.org/10.1007/s10726-014-9421-7

McGill Sport Psychology Laboratory (2019). Group Environment Questionnaire. Retrieved 2019 October 5 from http://sportpsych.mcgill.ca/pdf/coaching/Group_Environment_Questionnaire%20_GEQ_%20_2_.pdf.

Mendoza, J. G. (2001). Trust and team building: A study comparing traditional and experiential team building methods in relation to trust development. Doctoral Dissertation. University of New Mexico

Mortensen, M., & Hinds, P. J. (2001). Conflict and shared identity in geographically distributed teams. *International Journal of Conflict Management*, *12*(3), 212–238. https://doi.org/10.1108/eb022856

O'Neill, T.A., Allen, N. J., & Hastings, S. E. (2013). Examining the "pros" and "cons" of team conflict: A team-level meta-analysis of task, relationship, and process conflict. *Human Performance*, *26*(3), 236–260. https://doi.org/10.1080/08959285.2013.795573

Orme, G. J., & Kehoe, E. J. (2019). Development of cohesion in mixed-gender recruit training. *Military Medicine*, *1*, 1–6. https://doi.org/10.1093/milmed/usy409

Ortiz de Guinea, A., Webster, J., & Staples, D. S. (2012). A meta-analysis of the consequences of virtualness on team functioning. *Information & Management*, *49*(6), 301–308. https://doi.org/10.1016/J.IM.2012.08.003

Paul, S., Seetharaman, P., Samarah, I., & Mykytyn, P. P. (2004). Impact of heterogeneity and collaborative conflict management style on the performance of synchronous global virtual teams. *Information & Management*, *41*(3), 303–321. https://doi.org/10.1016/S0378-7206(03)00076-4

Pirola-Merlo, A., Härtel, C., Mann, L., & Hirst, G. (2002). How leaders influence the impact of affective events on team climate and performance in R&D teams. *The Leadership Quarterly*, *13*(5), 561–581. https://doi.org/10.1016/S1048-9843(02)00144-3

Rispens, S., Greer, L. L., & Jehn, K. A. (2007). It could be worse: A study on the alleviating role of trust and connectedness in intragroup conflict. *International Journal of Conflict Management, 18*(4), 325–344. https://doi.org/10.1108/10444060710833450

Robbins, S. P., & Judge, T. (2015). *Organizational behavior* (16th ed.). Harlow: Pearson Education Limited.

Santos, C. M., Uitdewilligen, S., & Passos, A. M. (2015). Why is your team more creative than mine? The influence of shared mental models on intra-group conflict, team creativity and effectiveness. *Creativity and Innovation Management, 24*(4), 645–658. https://doi.org/10.1111/caim.12129

Shin, Y. (2005). Conflict resolution in virtual teams. *Organizational Dynamics, 34*(4), 331–345. https://doi.org/10.1016/j.orgdyn.2005.08.002

Shoemaker, S. J., Fuda, K. K., Parchman, M., Schaefer, J., Levin, J., Hunt, M., & Ricciardi, R. (2014). Atlas of Instruments to Measure Team-based Primary Care Report. Rockville, MD. Agency for Healthcare Research and Quality. Retrieved October 4 from https://primarycaremeasures. ahrq.gov/team-based-care/downloads/ccteam/Team-based_Primary_Care_Atlas.pdf

Simons, T. L., & Peterson, R. S. (2000). Task conflict and relationship conflict in top management teams: The pivotal role of intragroup trust. *The Journal of Applied Psychology, 85*(1), 102–111.

Stevens, M. J., & Campion, M. A. (1994). The knowledge, skill, and ability requirements for teamwork: Implications for human resource management. *Journal of Management, 20*(2), 503–530. https://doi.org/10.1177/014920639402000210

Tekleab, A. G., Quigley, N. R., & Tesluk, P. E. (2009). A longitudinal study of team conflict, conflict management, cohesion, and team effectiveness. *Group and Organization Management, 34*(2), 170–205. https://doi.org/10.1177/1059601108331218

Tjosvold, D. (1995). Cooperation theory, constructive controversy and effectiveness: Learning from crisis. In R. A. Guzzo & E. Salas (Eds.), *Team effectiveness and decision making in organizations* (pp. 79–112). San Francisco, CA: Jossey-Bass.

Tjosvold, D. (2008). The conflict-positive organization: It depends upon us. *Journal of Organizational Behavior, 29*(1), 19–28. https://doi.org/10.1002/job.473

Tjosvold, D., & Tjosvold, M. (2015). *Building the team organization: How to open minds, resolve conflict, and ensure cooperation*. London, UK: Palgrave Macmillan. https://doi.org/10.1057/9781137479938

Tjosvold, D., & Ziyou Yu. (2007). Group risk taking. *Group & Organization Management, 32*(6), 653–674. https://doi.org/10.1177/1059601106287110

Triplett, S. M., & Loh, J. M. I. (2018). The moderating role of trust in the relationship between work locus of control and psychological safety in organisational work teams. *Australian Journal of Psychology, 70*(1), 76–84. https://doi.org/10.1111/ajpy.12168

Tseng, H., & Ku, H.-Y. (2011). The relationships between trust, performance, satisfaction, and development progressions among virtual teams. *Quarterly Review of Distance Education, 12*(2), 81–94.

Van Der Vegt, G. S., & Bunderson, J. S. (2005). Learning and performance in multidisciplinary teams: The importance of collective team identification. *Academy of Management Journal, 48*(3), 532–547. https://doi.org/10.5465/amj.2005.17407918

Weingart, L. R., & Jehn, K. A. (2009). Manage intra-team conflict through collaboration. In E. A. Locke (Ed.), *Handbook of principles of organizational behavior* (pp. 327–346). Hoboken, NJ: John Wiley & Sons Inc. https://doi.org/10.1002/9781119206422.ch18

West, M. (2012). *Effective teamwork: Practical lessons from organizational research* (3rd ed.). Oxford: Blackwell.

Whitton, S. M., & Fletcher, R. B. (2014). The group environment questionnaire. *Small Group Research, 45*(1), 68–88. https://doi.org/10.1177/1046496413511121

Zhang, X., Cao, Q., & Tjosvold, D. (2011). Linking transformational leadership and team performance: A conflict management approach. *Journal of Management Studies, 48*(7), 1586–1611. https://doi.org/10.1111/j.1467-6486.2010.00974.x

Chapter 7

The problem with lack of adaptability

In this chapter we explore why some teams are stagnant, caught up in habitual routines that might once have been effective but now impede effectiveness. Changes in the environment or in the system in which the team is embedded put new demands on the team. The team needs to adapt its way of working to be effective but is not successful in doing so. Our contribution is that we integrate previous well-established models of how teams adapt, with new research on what makes teams adapt. Why are some teams better at adapting to novel demands than others? It is a question of the team's capacity to adapt, how well the team performs in the adaptation process, how adequate and developed the team knowledge is and what triggers the adaptation.

Some teams are tone-deaf to expectations from stakeholders outside the team, and never seem to have heard Dylan sing that the times "they are a-changin'." Superficially they appear to be content with being the way they are. They can be stagnant in the meaning of being characterized by a lack of progressive movement, perhaps indifferent to the need for progress. A stagnant team might be good at performing stipulated routine task work. The problem is that it is not so good at handling emergencies, dealing with unpredictable work situations, thinking outside the box, learning new technologies, or being composed and task focused despite dealing with high-demanding tasks and time pressure. Changes in the environment, perhaps due to competition, globalization or new technologies, require flexible responses and if the team does not adjust and alter processes in alignment with these, the organization cannot respond to such changes. One reason for implementing teamwork is that teams are thought to have adaptive advantages over individuals (Mathieu, Maynard, Rapp, & Gilson, 2008). A key characteristic of an effective team is that it adapts its performance processes in response to changes in the external demands from the surrounding system (Salas, Sims, & Burke, 2005). In Chapter 5 it was shown what it takes to work in a coordinated manner, and in this chapter the question is what it takes to realize adaptation.

Team adaptation is to go beyond routine-task performance and proactively or reactively respond to cues that indicate that change is needed, and as a response adjust ways of working, team knowledge or interpersonal relationships. Team members actively do something to change their thinking and working so that they align behaviour with novel demands (Maynard, Kennedy, & Sommer, 2015). By team adaptive performance is meant *how well and accurately the team succeeds in aligning their behaviour with novel demands* (Porter, Webb, & Gogus, 2010). How well a team adapts is shown in results/outcomes. It may result in a qualitative change in team-performance outcomes. *But adaptation is also to recognize deviations and readjust actions accordingly while carrying out routine tasks* although these do not result in a different outcome (Priest, Burke, Munim, & Salas, 2002). Effective routine-task performance, smooth coordination and cooperation are characterized by continuous adaptations. It can be cues that something is not right in the work process, or it can be that adaptation is needed as a team member temporarily cannot perform optimally. *The processes of carrying out the task in a coordinated manner and adaptation to change are interlinked.* Smooth coordination of routine tasks is based on a shared understanding of what to do and how, and such an understanding makes the adjustment of habitual routines to meet new demands easier. The quality of routine action processes will impact how successful the team's performance is in the transfer phase. When a team is facing change, it is engaged both in general action activities and in adaptive processes specific to addressing the change (Maynard et al., 2015).

Depending on what the trigger for change is, it will prompt teams to adjust either task-work or interpersonal relations. *The origin* of the trigger or stimulus (such as a need for change in task-work or interpersonal relations) as well as the *duration* and *severity* of the stimulus will impact the adaptation. The trigger might stem from cues inside the team (an internal stimulus such as the loss of a team member) or from the team's environment (an external stimulus such as a change in tasks or a production crisis). An example will explain what is meant. After months of problems with coordination of tasks, there is a serious conflict between team members A and B that started with a heated discussion in which B aggressively accused A of being a slacker. In response, A accused B of lacking respect and criticized the whole team for not helping out to reduce an imbalanced workload. Two weeks later, A is on sick-leave and B threating to quit. The stimuli for change are internal and severe, and there is a cue that lasts some time. Ideally, the team should (in a transition phase) reflect on what has happened. They could discuss the problem and why it occurred, and come up with a plan to solve the interpersonal problem regarding code of conduct and mutual expectations. What adjustments are needed in how they interact and in the shared understanding of how to cooperate? The outcome of such a transition phase would be whether they succeed in altering their interaction accordingly.

Following, we present a case that illustrates why adaptation is important for the organization, the team and the individual team members. But the case also indicates that this might not be an easy journey.

CASE: TEAM MEMBERS ARE RELUCTANT TO CHANGE HABITUAL ROUTINES AND ADAPT TO NEW MANAGEMENT STRATEGY

The board of a medium-sized company producing floor heating systems had recruited a new manager to lead a conversion of the production. The manager was chosen because he had successfully restructured the entire organization in his previous job and had a reputation of being a transformative leader and delivering results. The strategy was to expand, get business advantages by producing "green" systems which included new products, and also ensuring

THE PROBLEM WITH LACK OF ADAPTABILITY | 165

that all production processes were sustainable for marketing and branding. The company had received substantial support and funding from a national innovation agency to implement the new business strategy. The company made good profits, production ran steadily, the rate of absenteeism was low, and a recent annual survey of work conditions showed that employees in general were satisfied with their workplace. The work plan was to first involve staff and specialists in joint work to describe and analyze all work processes to find out a) how the workflow in the production could be organized according to lean manufacturing principles and b) include staff in the standardization of work processes to reduce non-value adding activities and increase sustainability and c) describe employees' competence profiles to analyze the competence-base in the company for the coming automatized production of more advanced products. Different task forces (specialists and representatives from the shop) worked on these three different projects.

An invited consultant was asked for help as the manager had problems in implementing the strategy and work plan in the organization. Why was it so difficult to get the teams on the shop floor involved in the projects? The manager believed that implementing incremental change must involve the teams and stated that "this process cannot be run solely top-down – it must be a bottom-up process as well. The attitude on the shop floor is as if the change is not for real, that we can work as we always have. But if the teams are not involved in shaping the new production, are not preparing to take on new tasks, we will not succeed and that will affect everyone."

To summarize: Team adaptation is essential for staying in tune with changes in the external environment or in the team. Team adaptation is a process in which team members do something to change their thinking and working so that they align behaviour with novel demands. The outcome of this process is team-adaptive performance, how well and accurately the team aligns behaviour with novel demands, and this should be shown in results/outcomes, for example supervisors' ratings of task-specific criteria such as customer service. Team-adaptive performance is to go beyond routine-task performance and engage in a transition phase. The quality of routine-task performance impacts team-adaptation processes. The novel demand is the motive for change: the stimulus that triggers team adaptation. And stimuli differ in origin, duration and severity. The characteristics of the stimuli will influence what adjustments the team will make, and hence the outcome.

1 Step 1. Describe the current situation

The next step in solving problems would be to describe the situation from different perspectives to get a clearer picture of what the problem is.

CASE: TEAM MEMBERS ARE RELUCTANT TO CHANGE HABITUAL ROUTINES AND ADAPT TO NEW MANAGEMENT STRATEGY CONT.

The consultant interviewed the manager and asked the participants in different focus groups to answer, "How would you describe the teamwork on the shop floor?" and the main results could be documented as follows:

The board (in summary): We have taken the decision to go for a new market, we have a strategy and the manager has a good plan. So far it is running well, we support the manager and follow the process through him. Implementing change has always been hard work, but we have done it before. We expect commitment and people to contribute wherever they are in the company. There is a huge market, and we need to be first.

The manager: "I am content with many things, but I am confused why there is so little energy. I feel like shaking them – to get them out of their comfort zone. But most people in the company really like staying just where they are. The plan is good, we have a fantastic opportunity, but we can't drag people ahead. How do you get rid of the passive attitude? The teams have a great deal of knowledge and we need to make use of that now. Some say it is the culture, but I don't like that explanation. I think, get your finger out and the mindset will follow. How do we change the culture if we don't do anything?"

Three supervisors (in summary): The production is running well. The overall strategy has been communicated, and HR has supported us with presentations that we have used several times. It is not easy to explain what sustainable production is about, and how this is a business advantage. Some are interested, but many laugh about "another good idea from a management consultant." Team meetings, e.g. describing standards and competencies, resulted in little, and teams complained about useless meetings that take up production time. We have switched some members between teams to get new blood into the system, but this resulted in lower productivity and tensions in the teams. We have good cooperation with close-to-production specialists, but they are stressed by the new technology coming in and have too little time in the teams. The main problem is that it is difficult to get the teams on board and engage in the projects. They see no need to change their way of working and are used to getting a lot of credit for their results.

Team leaders (summary): The teams know what to do, and they do it well. Some have good ideas but others react, "Why change a winning concept?" So there has been some irritation. The teams will

THE PROBLEM WITH LACK OF ADAPTABILITY | 167

work fine when it is clear what they should do, but they are not used to this idea of them thinking about what should be done. This is an extra task but no extra pay and some think it is a task for the supervisors. However, some are interested. Specialists have a lot to do, and some want us involved. But it takes time from the production. Each team member has a special role and tasks, and it is difficult for all to discuss how these could be standardized or what competence it takes, as others do not know.

Close-to-production specialists (summary): The idea was that we should coach the teams and they should do a lot of the work in the projects. This is definitely not working. Some are interested, and others want to be in it because they prefer meetings to the production work: They are the real slackers. We want to work with the whole team, but the team leaders complain to the supervisors about loss of production time. Sometimes we work with the team leader in the different tasks in the work plan, and in other teams we mainly do the job and involve someone when needed. It is too early in the change process to involve the teams, as we do not fully know how the production needs to be changed. It is challenging to discuss competence profiles as the climate in the teams sometimes is that one should not show off by describing one's special skills, and it always ends up in a discussion about the remuneration system.

Some team members (summary): We have different tasks that we carry out, and the production is running fine. Nowadays we have some administrative work too, but mainly we work by ourselves at our workstations that are linked in the flow. We don't need to talk much during work as we have a set way of doing things, and it is pre-planned. All work a bit differently, so it is not always easy to take over someone else's station if they are ill. Some want their workstation to be in mint condition, others have it as in their own garage. We cope well and no complaints. Most of us have the same interests, and some are good friends. We don't need much from the team leader, or the supervisor – we are self-managing. If someone thinks it is interesting to work in the projects, why not. It is good that the company develops so that we can have more jobs in this area. Too many meetings and power-points, and lots of talk about AI and new technology, but we are not there yet. We have different backgrounds in the team, and maybe some are ready for it, but we haven't talked about that. We have had changes before: think of when there were no computers, and now we are all used to that.

Union representatives (summary): Our task is to ensure that our members have a good and safe work environment, and that all regulations and rules are followed. We negotiate with the company regarding remuneration systems and salaries. That is what concerns us.

2 Step 2. Identify the core problem

In an authentic case as this, there are different problems such as motivation for change in different stakeholder groups, communication of strategy, leadership, the integration between support functions and the production, organizational culture, individual competence, etc. We use the case to illustrate another important problem: teams may work in a coordinated manner but do not adapt to new demands. Is there enough support for the assumption that there is a fundamental problem with a lack of adaptation? Rosen et al. (2011) developed theoretically based principles to guide the development of an effective team-adaptation measurement system, proposing six guiding principles that capture core features of team adaptation. These can be used to assess a team's adaptation to novel demands. These captures:

a   Bottom-up changes in team performance
b   Top-down changes in strategy that impact team performance
c   A team's recognition of a need for change
d   The team's ability to self-assess
e   What team members are thinking and feeling in a dynamic matter
f   A profile of team adaptation over time

Looking at the case from this perspective, we find credible signs in c, d and e of a lack of adaptation. The other aspects should be explored further.

3 Step 3. Cause analysis

Some researchers regard adaptation as a process, some as a result of specific processes, and others see it as a personality trait or a competence (Baard, Rench, & Kozlowski, 2014). In an attempt to bring some order, Maynard et al. (2015) reviewed the literature on team adaptation between 1998 and 2013 and developed a definitional framework of the concept in line with the IMOI model presented in Chapter 1. They distinguish between a) input factors (the team's starting conditions) on an individual, team and organizational level that form the *team's adaptability*; b) *the team adaptation process* that results in team-adaptive performance; and c) *team-adaptive outcomes*.

Team adaptability is "the capacity of a team to make needed changes in response to a disruption or trigger" (Maynard, Kennedy & Sommer, p. 655), and is identified as a key input to the team-adaptation process to arrive at an outcome. There are few studies that have considered how team-adaptive performance impacts outcomes for the organization (such as innovation or quality) or for the individual (e.g. job

THE PROBLEM WITH LACK OF ADAPTABILITY | 169

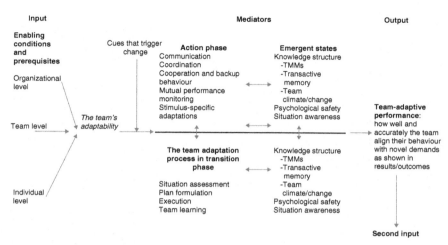

Figure 7.1 Model for the team adaptation process

satisfaction or stress). The focus has been on how adaptation processes affect the team's task-performance effectiveness. Most research has focused on the outcome or the adjustments of routine team processes, and not the adaptive process itself. But there are promising developments with regard to the empirical study of adaptation that we can build on. Christian, Christian, Pearsall, and Long (2017) tested in a meta-analysis how inputs impact processes that result in team-adaptive performance. It is a development of previous dominant models (Maynard et al., 2015; Burke, Stagl, Salas, Pierce, & Kendall, 2006). Our purpose is to explain why teams are stagnant and how to enhance team-adaptive performance, and we have used the model of Christian et al. (2017) as a conceptual model, and include elements from Burke's original model, as in empirical research these have also shown to be of importance. See the model in Figure 7.1.

The model in Figure 7.1 describes a) input features that impact processes and b) the team-adaptation process that enables the team to show adaptive performance. The cues, the triggers for change, impact and moderate the relation between process and outcome. Input factors set the stage for team-adaptive performance as they form the *team's adaptability capacity*. The model includes processes that are part of the transition phase and processes that are part of the action phase. Adaptation processes lead to corresponding emergent cognitive and affective states (i.e. team mental models, transactive memory, team situational awareness, psychological safety). Team adaptation is a process of changing cognitions since what the team does (performance) is formed by and depends on a shared understanding of a) goals, b) tasks, c) how to work and relate and d) behaviour. It is not possible to understand adaptation without taking the demand for change into account – what triggers the adaptation – and this differs from context to context. We will try to sort this out later, and organize the findings on what leads to adaptive performance in line with the mindmap in Figure 7.2.

THE PROBLEM WITH LACK OF ADAPTABILITY

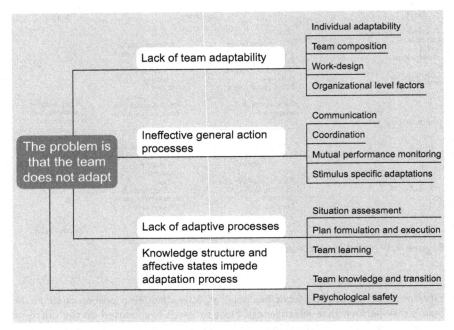

Figure 7.2 Mindmap about causes for team's lack of adaptation

3.1 Lack of team adaptability
Input factors together build team adaptability and are found on three levels. We start with the individual level and highlight some of the many findings.

3.1.1 Individual adaptability
Ployhart and Bliese (2006) defined adaptability as an individual's ability, skill, disposition and/or motivation to change or fit different tasks to social and environmental features. Much of the research builds on Pulakos, Arad, Donovan, and Plamondon (2000) and Pulakos, Dorsey, and White (2006) who identified core individual characteristics linked to adaptability. Some of these were mentioned in Chapter 4 on team composition. Following, we summarize these dispositions and KSAs that together decide how adaptive the individual is.

Individual adaptability is a mix of high scorings in:
- *Cognitive ability.* Cognitive ability predicts performance to a varying degree (correlations of .50 between complex jobs and performance, and .23 for the least complex job) (Hunter & Hunter, 1984). Adaptation is often a complex task.
- *Personality: Emotional stability and openness* predict adaptive performance. Openness describes whether a person is open to new experiences, and emotional stability should increase the individual's ability to cope with the possible negative side of change, e.g. the stress and insecurity it may evoke. *Conscientiousness* and *extraversion* have received some support as predictors as well (Thoms, Pinto, Parente, & Druskat, 2002).

THE PROBLEM WITH LACK OF ADAPTABILITY | 171

- *Team orientation* is linked to member self-ratings of long-term adaptation (Thoms et al., 2002). Burke et al. (2006) argue that individuals who have a general preference for work in teams engage in collective and cooperative behaviour, and accept and give feedback, in contrast to non-collective team members, who tend to disregard input from others.
- *Unique predictors for adaptation.* Change-related self-efficacy, prior experience of adaptation and learning-goals are shown to impact an individual's adaptability (Payne, Youngcourt, & Beaubien, 2007; Porter et al., 2010).
- *KSAs.* Competence in carrying out the routine task is strongly and directly related to adaptive performance (Chen, Thomas, & Wallace, 2005). Self-managerial skills (see Chapter 4) have been shown to impact proficiency, adaptation and proactivity in carrying out individual work (Hauschildt & Konradt, 2012).

The individual's adaptability will impact how they execute their role in the team during the team adaptation process.

3.1.2 Team composition

Different team members and team leaders will differ in adaptability, and the mix will be one aspect of team composition that affects team-adaptation processes. What is the empirical evidence that the mix impacts team-adaptation performance? Team composition with respect to members' *cognitive ability* is positively associated with team-adaptive performance, e.g. a meta-analysis showed a significant positive correlation between cognitive ability and team-adaptation processes (Christian et al., 2017), but less so to team-adaptive performance. Team composition regarding personality dimensions positively impacts team-adaptive performance. LePine (2005, 2003) and Salas et al. (2005) argue with the support of previous research that team orientation may be of even more importance when dealing with change than in routine-task performance as it puts extra demand on collective action. Christian et al. (2017) showed in their meta-analysis that learning-goal orientation positively impacts team processes, but performance-goal orientation did not. However, performance-goal orientation as well as learning-goal orientation both impact team-adaptation outcome. The psychological explanation probably is that some teams are more prone to engage in learning behaviour than others. Teams with challenging tasks and difficult goals and composed of members with a high learning orientation are likely to adapt effectively. A team composed of members high in performance orientation faced with challenging tasks and difficult goals is less likely to adapt (LePine, 2003, 2005). Self-managerial skills have been shown to affect various outcomes on the team level, among them team adaptation(Hauschildt & Konradt, 2012).

CASE: TEAM MEMBERS ARE RELUCTANT TO CHANGE HABITUAL ROUTINES AND ADAPT TO NEW MANAGEMENT STRATEGY CONT.

Transfer to the case. In the case there are descriptions of result-oriented teams, and the close-to-production specialist found that the projects are run more effectively without team participation. There seems to be no consensus on how goals for productivity and learning should be aligned. A work hypothesis could be that the teams' goal orientation impedes team adaptability.

3.1.3 Work design

In Chapter 3 we showed that work-design features either inhibit or facilitate teamwork, and the task is the foundation for a shared mental model of what to do and how. What is especially important for adaptability? Most researchers have focused on autonomy as teams with autonomy may self-design role responsibilities, self-regulate member behaviour, and set goals and direction (Humphrey & Aime, 2014). When a team controls its own functions, it can alter its habitual routines when needed. The research is vast on how autonomy impacts individual performance and team effectiveness, and we conclude in line with Salas et al. (2005) that with little autonomy it is not meaningful for teams to form plans for change, as they cannot implement them fully. It will be half-measures, and the team will be ineffective in completing the adaptation process.

3.1.4 Organizational-level factors

Organizational factors that support routine-task performance are considered important for team adaptation as well. However, when it comes to empirical research on how the organization enhances the team's capacity for adaptability there are few studies. Maynard et al. (2015) recently searched the literature and found little. Nor did we.

Culture and climate seem to play a role, as for example a strong culture and climate favouring innovation might give more cues than a conservative culture. Harrison, McKinnon, Wu, and Chow (2000) showed that culture impacts individuals' propensity to adapt.

Information management. The way organizations manage information is important as this might be a cue that change is needed. This is more important in high-risk environments such as nuclear power plants, hospitals and for disaster response as external cues like disruptions or failures need to be handled promptly by teams (Ren, Kiesler, & Fussell, 2008).

Leadership. Researchers looking into organizational factors have so far mainly focused on the role of leadership. The more dynamic and changing the environment is, the greater the importance of a leadership that informs the team about unexpected and coming changes that they will meet and need to adapt to in the future. The leader's individual adaptive capacity is naturally the basis for being a role model and influencing others to adapt to new situations. Transformative leadership style has been shown to have many advantages for enhancing team effectiveness in general (see Chapter 8). However, Griffin, Parker, and Mason (2010) suggest that vision is unlikely to be sufficient on its own in prompting individual adaptivity and proactivity. Rather leader vision linked to the leader's self-efficacy beliefs and change receptivity build greater openness to change in work roles. Kahol, Vankipuram, Patel, and Smith (2011) studied trauma teams in hospitals and showed that the greater the leader's experience, the more deviations in team processes – and as a consequence the better team-adaptive performance. Organizations increasingly rely on virtual teams. Team dispersion introduces challenges to communication that might impede team performance and adaptation. Transformational leadership has shown to be effective in reducing negative effects of dispersion, but less so for highly dispersed teams (Eisenberg, Post & DiTomaso, 2019). The reason might be that leaders have difficulties in facilitating team communication in highly dispersed teams and that rich elaboration processes are rare. In Chapter 6 the importance of leadership for team outcomes was discussed.

THE PROBLEM WITH LACK OF ADAPTABILITY | 173

> ## CASE: TEAM MEMBERS ARE RELUCTANT TO CHANGE HABITUAL ROUTINES AND ADAPT TO NEW MANAGEMENT STRATEGY CONT.
>
> The teams and some stakeholders see little reason for the teams to get involved: It is as if the new demands and coming changes are of little concern to them yet. Supervisors have presented the strategy but find it difficult to explain it in their own words. The presentations of the vision and the strategy have not made sufficient sense, and it seems as if the manager and supervisors have more work to do explaining the "whys" to themselves, as well as to others. Another issue may be that the motives for team participation are not fully understood, and the idea of participation seems not to be fully accepted by supervisors and close-to-production specialists. A work hypothesis could be that lack of leadership is one cause to the problem.

Leader briefings reflect inputs conveyed to the team about the task environment. The leader gives information and knowledge about the task environment and expected changes in demands from stakeholders, provides knowledge that should help the team to adapt, and *why* the team needs to adapt. It is a form of giving sense to the whys, and we again stress that the motive for doing something will impact the goal for an activity and hence what is done (Randall, Resick, & DeChurch, 2011). Briefings have previously been shown to impact the development of team mental models (Marks, Zaccaro, & Mathieu, 2000). Christian et al. (2017) found support that leader briefings significantly impact team-adaptation processes, but no such direct relation existed to team-adaptive performance. It seems that it is the team processes which impact team-adaptive performance.

> ## CASE: TEAM MEMBERS ARE RELUCTANT TO CHANGE HABITUAL ROUTINES AND ADAPT TO NEW MANAGEMENT STRATEGY CONT.
>
> Although there is much we do not know about the case, it is worthwhile to have work hypotheses that lack of adaptation is due to individual team members' KSAs and attitudes, team composition and the support given by the organization and leadership. There are signs pointing especially towards a problem with attitudes and goal-orientation (not only in the teams), leadership and cross-functional cooperation, but this remains to be explored further.

To summarize: Input factors that impact team adaptation are found on individual, team and organizational levels. Individual characteristics, team composition, autonomy, information management, culture and climate, leadership and leader briefings are essential features of what gives the team the capacity to

174 | THE PROBLEM WITH LACK OF ADAPTABILITY

engage in adaptation processes. Note that the empirical research on how organizational factors impact team-adaptation processes is still in its infancy.

When teams face a change, they engage both in action processes and adaptive processes specific to addressing the change. Each should improve team-adaptive performance. We have made a distinction between task-work and interpersonal relations, and in Chapter 6 it was described how important good interpersonal relations are for team performance. We ask the reader to keep this in mind, as we do not in this chapter describe the importance of interpersonal relations for adaption processes. *Interpersonal relations matter if the team is in action phase or engaged in adapting to novel demands in a transition phase.*

3.2 Ineffective general action processes

Researchers examining the mediating role of team processes on the relationship between inputs and team-adaptability outcomes have focused on communication and coordination (Maynard et al., 2015).

3.2.1 Communication

Research regarding communication and adaptation point in one direction: Clear and accurate exchange of relevant information, as well as closed-loop communication to ensure that what is communicated is correctly received, is perhaps even more crucial when facing change than in routine teamwork. In line with the findings on how important it is that organizations have systems for organizing information, and also that leaders brief the teams, it has been shown that communication within the team strongly affects team-adaptive performance. Teams need to identify changes in the environment and discuss the triggers for change and what it means in terms of changing behaviour (Marks et al., 2000; Resick, Murase, Randall, & DeChurch, 2014). Quality is more important than quantity (Marlow, Lacerenza, Paoletti, Burke, & Salas, 2018). Information elaboration, but not information transfer, impacts team-adaptation performance (Christian et al., 2017). Rich elaboration processes such as the exchange, the analysis and the application of information have a fairly strong impact on team-adaptive performance. By contrast, one-way information transfer, such as sharing information or communicating a request, does not (Resick, et al., 2010).

When examining the role of communication for adaptation in detail, the picture becomes more complicated. A study by Sander, van Doorn, van der Pal, & Zijlstra (2015) showed that even though shared knowledge and efficient communication based on such knowledge are of high value to team performance and success, these characteristics are limited in aiding adaptive team performance *after* unforeseen unique changes that force team members to update their strategies. Moon et al. (2004) reported a negative relationship between communication and coordination and team-adaptive performance after an internal structural change. How can this be understood? The reason might be that the knowledge base of the team is not adequate in the new situation, and hence sharing knowledge built in the previous situation is now not helpful as it is no longer applicable. It takes time to build a new knowledge base for the new situation.

THE PROBLEM WITH LACK OF ADAPTABILITY | 175

> ## CASE: TEAM MEMBERS ARE RELUCTANT TO CHANGE HABITUAL ROUTINES AND ADAPT TO NEW MANAGEMENT STRATEGY CONT.
>
> In this case it seems obvious that something in the communication is not right as the message from the board and CEO is not coming through. Communication should be clear. Ambivalent messages such as on the one hand the teams should participate in different projects, e.g. standardization of work, and on the other that this negatively impacts production, are confusing. Supervisors were not happy with ready-made power-point presentations, and from the description it seems rather like a one-way communication that makes it possible for team members to be passive listeners. Team members' descriptions of communication indicate that information elaboration is lacking. They said they communicate little about task-related matters. A work hypothesis could be that the communication is one cause to the problem with lack of adaptability.

3.2.2 Coordination

Effective coordination improves team performance (see Chapter 5). The alignment of different members' activities and contributions has been shown to be characteristic of adaptation processes. Burtscher, Wacker, Grote, & Manser (2010) studied anaesthesia teams, and when faced with non-routine events those teams with higher levels of task-management activities, such as coordination mechanisms, performed better. Higher-performing teams are better able to shift from routine work to manage critical situations or new tasks since the team's *monitoring* of coordination mechanisms makes it possible to *adapt the coordination mechanisms* when shifting from routine to non-routine performance.

3.2.3 Mutual performance monitoring

Observing one another's actions helps team members ensure that everything is running as expected, to find performance discrepancies and to make efforts to correct them in a timely manner. It enables team members to recognize when others need assistance and to give feedback and suggestions, and it is essential for coordination as it gives others information about their pacing and timing of activities. Mutual performance monitoring is considered a key feature of effective teamwork and team adaptation (Burke et al., 2006).

3.2.4 Stimulus-specific adaptations

Adaptive processes involve behaviour that addresses the change directly. The team members make unique adjustments to their routine patterns of doing things, depending on the type of trigger. E.g. in a restaurant the chefs find that the supplier has not delivered fish, and they tackle this by changing the evening menu. Stimulus-specific actions are the obvious response to a stimulus, and again the severity, duration and origin are important determinants. A meta-analysis (Christian et al., 2017) showed that stimulus-specific actions are highly correlated with team-adaptive performance ($\rho = .41$). The team is more or less used to continuous adaptations.

To summarize: Researchers have so far focused on the role of communication and coordination for team adaptation and showed that these differ between teams that are adaptive and those that are less so. Information elaboration is what makes the difference regarding communication, and coordination is one of the most powerful mechanisms for team-adaptive performance. Mutual performance monitoring helps the team stay on track and is a key feature of both routine and non-routine task work. During action phase the team makes unique adjustments to the habitual way of doing things depending on stimulus indicating something needs to be done differently.

3.3 Lack of adaptive processes

The team is engaged in general action processes, and these will impact the adaptive processes in a transition phase.

3.3.1 Situation assessment

In Chapter 2 it was said that the starting point for solving problems is a more or less thorough analysis of the current situation, and an awareness that something needs to be done to change it for the better. This is also the starting point for adaption processes (Christian et al., 2017; Georganta, 2018; Georganta & Brodbeck, 2018). It is a situational awareness, a perception of environmental elements and events, the comprehension of their meaning and an *assessment* of what in the current situation implies a demand for change. *Team members scan the environment to identify cues indicating that change is needed.* The team needs to form a shared understanding of the team's environment and what needs to be changed, and leader briefings can help the team to this insight.

> ### CASE: TEAM MEMBERS ARE RELUCTANT TO CHANGE HABITUAL ROUTINES AND ADAPT TO NEW MANAGEMENT STRATEGY CONT.
>
> The teams seem to assess the situation only in terms of the routine task work, and this is judged to be running well. The problem seems to be that they scan the situation from only this one perspective, and do not see that things are not running well regarding the implementation of the new strategy in their own team. It seems they need support to accept that scanning the situation is their task, and help in doing so. But do supervisors and team leaders see it as an important issue for the teams? A work hypothesis for further exploration is that lack of assessment of the current situation is one cause to the problem.

3.3.2 Plan formulation and execution

Sometimes it is not so obvious how to adapt routine performance, and the team has to find a plan for what needs to be done to change the current situation towards a desired end point. Team members form a plan by coming up with decisions on what to do, why and how. This also involves clarifying members' roles and responsibilities, environmental constrains and performance expectations, etc. (Burke et al., 2006). It is no surprise that plan formulation has been shown to be an important element in adaptation processes no matter why the team needs to adapt (Christian et al., 2017).

> ### CASE: TEAM MEMBERS ARE RELUCTANT TO CHANGE HABITUAL ROUTINES AND ADAPT TO NEW MANAGEMENT STRATEGY CONT.
>
> Transfer to the case: The strategy and what should be done is communicated, but there seems to be a striking lack of work plans for each team. There was a plan A for example for the standardization of tasks, but this plan was dropped. We do not know why it did not work, but without a plan B or continuing with the plan A, it is difficult to see how the teams could adapt.

3.3.3 Team learning

Learning is closely interlinked to adaptability as both learning and adaptability are essentially about bringing change. Decuyper, Dochy, and Van den Bossche (2010) describe team learning as "a compilation of team-level processes that circularly generate change or improvements for teams, team members, organizations" (p. 128). In Chapter 5 the essence of team learning was explained as a process of building shared meaning and cognitive knowledge structures that guide performance. Team learning has a positive impact on performance (Edmondson, Dillon, & Roloff, 2007; Santos, Uitdewilligen, & Passos, 2015; van Woerkom & Croon, 2009) and effectiveness (Van den Bossche, et al., 2011) in task-routine work. Previous research provides evidence that different aspects of communication and collaboration *across borders* support performance in the action phase, but also knowledge transfer and team learning processes in the transfer phase (Edmondson, 2002; Hirst & Mann, 2004; Sundstrom, McIntyre, Halfhill, & Richards, 2000). Learning from others external to the team (distal learning) about what others do, and getting and giving feedback on work-related issues can provide an impetus for change and increase the diversity of perspectives which is an essential part of team learning (Gersick & Hackman, 1990).

> Although Wong (2004) showed that both local and distal learning impact efficiency and innovativeness, there is a question about how these interact. Results showed that distal learning interacts negatively with local learning and impedes efficiency, and high levels of cohesion promote distal learning but diminish local learning. According to Wong (2004), tensions can arise from simultaneously managing both types of learning.

Team-learning processes enable the team to adapt, but by adapting the team has also learned something new. Learning creates a (relatively) permanent change in the team's collective level of knowledge and skills, and is one of the most important factors for team adaptability (Christian et al., 2017; Tae Young Han & Williams, 2008). Why is that so? Team learning builds new and more adequate knowledge structures that later guide the team's performance in the new situation. Team learning has a positive impact on outcomes such as proactive behaviour and the team's engagement in innovation (Lantz, Hansen, & Antoni, 2015; Lantz Friedrich, Sjöberg, & Friedrich, 2016).

> ### CASE: TEAM MEMBERS ARE RELUCTANT TO CHANGE HABITUAL ROUTINES AND ADAPT TO NEW MANAGEMENT STRATEGY CONT.
>
> Transfer to the case. In this case it is meaningful to hypothesize that problems with assessing the situation, formulating a plan and the learning process of building a shared meaning might explain a substantial part of the problem with a lack of team adaptation.

To summarize: Adaptation processes are situation assessment, stimulus-specific actions, plan formulation and team learning. Team learning is one of the core team processes for team-adaptation performance, as learning enables the team to discover what in the routine performance impedes adapting to novel demands. It enables the team to build more adequate TMMs that can later be tested in a new action phase and over time be adjusted again.

3.4 Knowledge structure and effective states impede adaptation process

Emergent states can be both cognitive and affective, and the team's pre-existing states that guide routine-task performance will affect the adaptation process in the transition phase: Emergent states impact the team-adaptation processes, and vice versa.

3.4.1 Team knowledge and transition

Team-knowledge structures such as team mental models, team climate and transactive memory were described in Chapter 5. Team performance, whether it is routine-task performance or adaptation to new demands, depends on team knowledge as this regulates activities (DeChurch & Mesmer-Magnus, 2010). A number of studies have shown a relationship between a team's cognitive states and its ability to successfully deal with unexpected events (Marks et al., 2000), but the dynamics of these relations are poorly understood (Gevers, Uitdewilligen, & Passos, 2015). Empirical studies have not yet identified what specific knowledge structures are important for which part of the adaptation process. A meta-analysis of Christian et al. (2017) confirmed the role of team knowledge as a mediator between inputs and team-adaptive performance outcomes, as TMMs were moderately related to adaptive performance, and transactive memory was strongly related to adaptive performance. Team cognition is about as important as communication when it comes to impacting team-adaptive performance. Marques-Quinteiro, Ramos-Villagrasa, Passos, and Curral (2015) studied police tactical teams and found that transactive memory moderated the relationship between implicit coordination and adaptive behaviour. These results are fully in line with the review of the literature presented by Maynard et al. (2015). Researchers agree that team-adaptation processes build new shared understanding and knowledge of what needs to be altered in habitual routines to meet novel demands, and hence impact the adaptive-performance outcomes.

THE PROBLEM WITH LACK OF ADAPTABILITY | 179

The adaptation processes refine the existing corresponding emergent cognitive states. But also vice versa: *The more developed, advanced and adequate the existing TMMs and transactive memory are, the easier it should be to integrate new knowledge or use existing knowledge in a new way.* When team members' temporal (pre-existing) team mental models are similar, and accuracy is low, the less they engage in learning behaviour. When accuracy is high, similarity in team members' temporal mental models is not related to team learning. Sharing an inaccurate mental model seems to lead to closed minds (Santos, Passos, & Uitdewilligen, 2016). This is important as it gives a psychological reason for why the quality of temporal (pre-existing) TMMs also forms the team-adaptive performance.

Transactive memory is important for both carrying out a given task and for learning transfer so that the team can go beyond and take on other, perhaps more challenging, tasks (Lewis, Lange, & Gillis, 2005). The team knows its pool of expertise and can use this knowledge to form a plan of what to do and how, and coordinate individual tasks, for example when teams need to adapt after member loss (Siegel, Pearsall, Christian, & Ellis, 2014).

3.4.2 Psychological safety

In Chapter 5 some core affective/motivational emergent states such as psychological safety were discussed in relation to habitual routines for coordination and cooperation. To adapt means to reflect on and question the effectiveness of such habitual routines. Psychological safety and trust are important for team reflexivity and learning, as people tend to act in ways that inhibit learning when they face a potential threat or embarrassment (Edmondson, 1999). It was mentioned earlier that team members shared TMMs, but inaccurate TMMs impede learning. To speak out, questioning habitual ways of thinking, initiating change and being proactive is a potentially risky social behaviour. Not all appreciate changes to the way the team does things. An interesting question is when proactivity is effective or not. Parker, Wang and Liao (2019) identified three factors: 1) ensuring that the proactivity fits the task and strategic environment, 2) more team-oriented forms of proactivity is more positively received by others than I-deals that invoke interpersonal challenges and 3) effective self-regulation is important for fostering the learning and persistence that it takes to reach a result. A recent study showed that team-members were most likely to positively react to and trust another team-member who enacted proactive behaviour if that team-member was high in social skill (Reynolds Kueny, Jundt & Shoss 2019). Again we see a link between individual KSAs and team processes (see the IMOI model in Chapter 1 and multi-level interactions). Psychological safety has been shown to be important for routine, and even more so for non-routine, performance in which learning and creativity is fundamental (Burke et al., 2006; Edmondson, 2003; Edmondson, Winslow, Bohmer, & Pisano, 2003).

CASE: TEAM MEMBERS ARE RELUCTANT TO CHANGE HABITUAL ROUTINES AND ADAPT TO NEW MANAGEMENT STRATEGY CONT.

In this case we would not hesitate to formulate the work hypothesis that it is plausible that the problem with adaptation can be explained by team

180 | THE PROBLEM WITH LACK OF ADAPTABILITY

> knowledge. There are signs indicating that the existing knowledge structures impede the adaptation process. To explore the affective state might also be relevant, as psychological safety is so important for building shared meaning and questioning habitual ways of working and thinking. E.g. HR found it "sensitive" to discuss competence in the teams, and this might be a sign of a lack of openness and safety.

To summarize: Emergent states such as team cognition (team mental models and transactive memory) and affective states such as team psychological safety correspond to adaptation processes and impact team-adaptation performance. The shared understanding of what to do and how, and who knows what is a solid base for altering habitual routines and adapting to new circumstances. Recent research points in the direction that transactive memory plays a large role in explaining why some teams succeed better in adjusting their routine performance to meet novel demands.

3.5 To carry out a diagnosis of the team's adaptation capacity and adaptation processes

We started the chapter by stating that adaptation is about changing cognition and behaviour in alignment with external demands and changes in the environment. The team's capacity to adapt is a "critical long-term characteristic[s] of team effectiveness" (Kozlowski, Gully, Nason, & Smith, 1999, p. 242). Some (Burke et al., 2006) go so far as to cite Darwin who said that it is not the strongest of the species that survives, nor the most intelligent, but rather the one most responsive to change. So how can team adaptation be enhanced? The first step is to carry out an analysis of the core predictors of team adaptation to find out what the reasons could be.

Effective teamwork is characterized by coordinated task work and adaptation to novel demands. Hence most research-based instruments for describing a team's functioning cover essential dimensions that impact adaptation. The instruments presented in Chapter 5 describe how the team functions in core aspects of action phase that impact adaptation processes. As in Chapter 5 on the problem with coordinated task work, we would recommend a data collection with either questionnaires or interviews based on the dimensions described earlier (see the mindmap in Figure 7.1) that are covered in such questionnaires. The items in a questionnaire can easily be adapted to questions in an interview. *When planning the data collection, ensure that the following are covered:*

1 What are the triggers for change? How can they be characterized regarding duration, severity and source? *This is rarely covered in instruments as these are context specific*, and if the triggers are weak this will be a main result in the analysis.
2 How are those factors that build adaptability capacity described? (E.g. team-goal orientation, prerequisites for self-management, leadership and leader briefings.)

THE PROBLEM WITH LACK OF ADAPTABILITY | 181

3   How are core dimensions of the adaptation process described? (E.g. situation assessment, plan formulation and learning processes.) Stimulus-specific actions are context specific and are rarely covered in inventories.
4   How are the corresponding emergent states described? (TMMs, transactive memory and psychological safety).

Georganta (2018) developed and tested a theory-based instrument for description of team adaptivity and team adaptation processes. The Behaviourally Anchored Rating Scales (BARS) assess team behaviour in situation assessment, plan formulation, plan execution and team learning. Team behaviour is described on a five-point scale with behavioural examples for different scale points. The instrument has shown to be reliable and valid; it is well described and can be easily used, see Step 5 below.

4 Step 4. Select target dimensions and set goals

After establishing that a problem with adaptation exists, and a diagnosis of how a team functions in core dimensions that impact adaptive performance, it is possible to select those dimensions that should be addressed in an intervention to enhance adaptation. The next step would be to set goals for such changes in selected dimension(s) and proceed with finding possible solutions that could be used in the intervention.

5 Step 5. Identify solutions

The next step is to select the domain(s) for interventions appropriate for dimension(s) chosen in step 4. Again, *a combination of different solutions in different domains might be needed to* solve *the problem.* The most critical dimensions for a team's adaptation might be found in the organization. Table 7.1 shows domains for main solutions to a problem with adaptation.

Table 7.1 Domains for solutions to a problem with adaptation

Choose domain(s) for solutions(s) to enhance team adaptation to novel demands			
Prerequisites in the physical environment for enhancing team adaptation: Most often not relevant	Prerequisites on organizational level for enhancing team adaptation: Triggers for change Strategy Leadership Information systems HR strategies Decisions about: Team goals Work design Team composition	Solutions on team level to enhance team adaptation: Communication Coordination Mutual performance monitoring Situation assessment Stimulus-specific actions Plan formation Team learning Team knowledge Psychological safety	Prerequisites on individual level to enhance team adaptation: To enhance individual KSAs for teamwork, adaptation and learning-goal orientation

To identify possible solution(s) for bringing change about in the main dimension(s) that most impact the team's adaptation, or that which is most urgent or meaningful to start with, one needs to consider how this main dimension is interrelated to other dimensions in order to find corresponding solutions for those. Addressing a problem with team adaptation would probably involve a bundled solution and solutions in several domains. Again we stress that the adaptation process in the team depends on the organizational context and the triggers for change, and although such may exist in the surrounding system, they need to be communicated to the team.

In this book we limit the scope to solutions on the team level. In Chapters 3, 4, 5 and 6 we have described possible solutions to establish that the team has adaptive capacity (work design and team composition) and carries out work in a coordinated manner in the action phase and that interpersonal relations are satisfactory. The leadership and leader briefings strongly impact team-adaptation processes, and how team leadership can be supported is described in Chapter 8. All these together impact the adaptation. Following, we present possible solutions for implementing change in the dimensions that are specific for adaptation processes. Again we stress that if the stimuli for change are weak, and the need for adaptation is not conveyed to the team, this is the starting point for any intervention regarding team adaptation. We refer to Chapter 3 on how the motives will impact the goals that regulate the activities. We describe solutions targeting crucial processes for adaptation, and we give example of a specific method within this solution and provide some empirical support for the method's usefulness. Important results from our research regarding solutions for developing team adaptation are:

- There is less knowledge about how to develop team adaptation processes than how to develop routine task work.
- Solutions aim at developing the adaptation process as a whole, and address several dimensions at the same time.
- Solutions for developing performance in action phase, if focused on the components of adaptation processes, can be used.

Action phase and transition phase are interlinked; it is difficult to make a distinction between these processes in real life, and to carry out routine work is also to recognize deviations and readjust actions accordingly. Next we describe what solutions and methods we have found targeted at the adaptation process per se.

Team training. Process-oriented training programmes aiming at developing the team's ability to coordinate and act in future scenarios enhance team adaptability (Maynard et al., 2015).

One clearly theory-based, structured and facilitated team training solution developed especially for virtual teams is "Structured on-line team adaptation (STROTA)" (Ellwart, Happ, Gurtner, & Rack, 2015). It addresses a specific problem, information overflow, but the method can easily be applied to different kinds of teams and problems. STROTA's aim is to reduce information overload by improving team mental models. STROTA is a moderated solution to support three stages; individuals' situation assessment, team's situation assessment and plan formulation by means of feedback, individual reflection, moderated team reflection and question-based answering techniques. STROTA supports team members' recognition of the problems and the

THE PROBLEM WITH LACK OF ADAPTABILITY | 183

manifestations of information overload as a starting point for moderated adaptation. Team members discuss in an online meeting the causes and the problems of the perceived information overload as well as the deficits of task and team related cognition. In the final plan formulation, the team decides on strategies for an upcoming action face. STROTA has been evaluated in an experimental setting. The results indicated an improvement of TMM in the subsequent action phase. The STROTA-procedure can be adapted to in real life training and to other settings, but it is necessary to tailor the content of feedback and situation assessment to the specific task and team characteristics.

Team training can incorporate *peer and supervisor feedback* as a method to enhance the team adaptation process. The instrument Behaviourally Anchored Rating Scales, BARS, for describing team adaptation processes (Georganta, 2018) can be used as a team development tool for peer or supervisor feedback, and it can facilitate a better understanding of what constitutes effective team adaptation behaviours. Such specific feedback can encourage the team to improve as a whole. It can help the team to develop team adaptation capacities such as trust and team mental models. BARS can be used for giving feedback to teams regarding situation assessment, plan formulation, plan execution and team learning (Georganta, 2018). Next, one example of team learning behaviour on a 1 to 5-point scale is shown:

BARS: Team learning description on Scale-point 5

The team discovers its own successes.
The team reflects on its own strengths and weaknesses.
Team members discover errors in actions performed.
Team members learn from mistakes and transfer this knowledge to future actions.

Certain strategies, such as reflexivity, help teams to identify cues that should trigger adaptation when faced with changing circumstances. *Guided reflexivity is a method* with the aim to help the team to develop and implement task-adaptive strategies *on their own*. It can be part of most solutions to develop teams, including team training, and can help the team to make sense of and learn from unexpected events (Gurtner, Tschan, Semmer, & Nägele, 2007; Konradt, Schippers, Garbers, & Steenfatt, 2015). Jumping into action is often a team's first response to an emergency or a stressful event, and team training should emphasize in action team reflexivity. In action team reflexivity might slow down the team momentarily, but slowing down enhances mission success and decreases the likelihood of hastily moving in the wrong direction. Regular *simulation training* provides a venue for teams to begin incorporating team reflexivity during action phase.

Guided reflexivity is a method that can be applied rather easily for different teams in different situations and does not require extended task analysis and specific training procedures (Gurtner et al., 2007). Vashdi, Bamberger, and Erez (2013) developed a method for guided reflexivity in hospital care on the basis of a briefing and debriefing-model. Teams are trained to follow protocols during their prebrief (before action) and debrief meetings. An example of content in a debrief protocol is a) what happened during the surgery, b) any problems or complications that arose, c)

184 | THE PROBLEM WITH LACK OF ADAPTABILITY

the degree to which surgical goals were met, d) what prevented the achievement of specific goals and e) what might be done in the future to avoid such complications and to assure a better meeting of the objectives. The method is well described, an evaluation showed that iterative cycles of action and after-action reviews enable teams to successfully manage future events and the method can easily be adapted to other settings (Vashdi et al., 2013).

As we have stated earlier different solutions overlap and can be used for different things, and we recommend the reader to carefully examine what aspects a certain solution or method targets when deciding on a bundled or single solution to be included in the intervention.

> *To summarize:* Team-adaptive performance is a key characteristic of an effective team and is essential for staying in tune with changes in the external environment or in the team. It means going beyond routine-task performance and engaging in a transition phase to assess the situation, make plans and learn how to meet novel demands. The characteristics of the triggers for change influence what adjustments the team will make, the processes and hence the outcome. Task work and interpersonal relations are mutually dependent: Effective routine as well as non-routine task work and good relations go hand in hand. The quality of routine-task performance and pre-existing team knowledge impacts the adaptation processes. How well the team adapts depends on input factors on the individual, team and organizational levels; on team processes both in the action and transition phases; and corresponding emergent cognitive and affective states.

Bibliography

Baard, S. K., Rench, T. A., & Kozlowski, S. W. J. (2014). Performance adaptation. *Journal of Management, 40*(1), 48–99. https://doi.org/10.1177/0149206313488210

Burke, S., Stagl, C. K., Salas, E., Pierce, L., & Kendall, D. (2006). Understanding team adaptation: A conceptual analysis and model. *The Journal of Applied Psychology, 91*. https://doi.org/10.1037/0021-9010.91.6.1189

Burtscher, M. J., Wacker, J., Grote, G., & Manser, T. (2010). Managing nonroutine events in anesthesia: The role of adaptive coordination. *Human Factors, 52*(2), 282–294. https://doi.org/10.1177/0018720809359178

Chen, G., Thomas, B., & Wallace, J. C. (2005). A multilevel examination of the relationships among training outcomes, mediating regulatory processes, and adaptive performance. *Journal of Applied Psychology, 90*(5), 827–841. https://doi.org/10.1037/0021-9010.90.5.827

Christian, J. S., Christian, M. S., Pearsall, M. J., & Long, E. C. (2017). Team adaptation in context: An integrated conceptual model and meta-analytic review. *Organizational Behavior and Human Decision Processes, 140*, 62–89. https://doi.org/10.1016/j.obhdp.2017.01.003

DeChurch, L. A., & Mesmer-Magnus, J. R. (2010). The cognitive underpinnings of effective teamwork: A meta-analysis. *Journal of Applied Psychology, 95*(1), 32–53. https://doi.org/10.1037/a0017328

Decuyper, S., Dochy, F., & Van den Bossche, P. (2010). Grasping the dynamic complexity of team learning: An integrative model for effective team learning in organisations. *Educational Research Review, 5*. https://doi.org/10.1016/j.edurev.2010.02.002

Edmondson, A. C. (1999). Psychological safety and learning behavior in work teams. *Administrative Science Quarterly, 44*(2), 350–383. https://doi.org/10.2307/2666999

Edmondson, A. C. (2002). The local and variegated nature of learning in organizations: A group-level perspective. *Organization Science, 13*(2), 128–146. https://doi.org/10.1287/orsc.13.2.128.530

Edmondson, A. C. (2003). Speaking up in the operating room: How team leaders promote learning in interdisciplinary action teams. *Journal of Management Studies, 40*(6), 1419–1452. https://doi.org/10.1111/1467-6486.00386

Edmondson, A. C., Dillon, R. J., & Roloff, S. K. (2007). 6 three perspectives on team learning. *The Academy of Management Annals, 1*. https://doi.org/10.1080/078559811

Edmondson, A. C., Winslow, A. B., Bohmer, R. M. J., & Pisano, G. P. (2003). Learning how and learning what: Effects of tacit and codified knowledge on performance improvement following technology adoption. *Decision Sciences, 34*(2), 197–224. https://doi.org/10.1111/1540-5915.02316

Eisenberg, J., Post, C., & DiTomaso, N. (2019). Team dispersion and performance: the role of team communication and transformational leadership. *Small Group Research, 50*(3), 348–380. https://doi.org/10.1177/1046496419827376

Ellwart, T., Happ, C., Gurtner, A., & Rack, O. (2015). Managing information overload in virtual teams: Effects of a structured online team adaptation on cognition and performance. *European Journal of Work and Organizational Psychology, 24*(5), 812–826. https://doi.org/10.1080/1359432X.2014.1000873

Georganta, E. (2018). *Team adaptation process: An empirical investigation of its dynamic and complex nature.* Doctoral dissertation. München: LMU München.

Georganta, E., & Brodbeck, F. C. (2018). Capturing the four-phase team adaptation process with behaviorally anchored rating scales (BARS). *European Journal of Psychological Assessment, 1–12.* https://doi.org/10.1027/1015-5759/a000503

Gersick, C. J. G., & Hackman, J. R. (1990). Habitual routines in task-performing groups. *Organizational Behavior and Human Decision Processes, 47*(1), 65–97. https://doi.org/https://doi.org/10.1016/0749-5978(90)90047-D

Gevers, J. M. P., Uitdewilligen, S., & Passos, A. M. (2015). Dynamics of team cognition and team adaptation: Introduction to the special issue. *European Journal of Work and Organizational Psychology, 24*(5), 645–651. https://doi.org/10.1080/1359432X.2015.1065251

Griffin, M., Parker, S., & Mason, C. (2010). Leader vision and the development of adaptive and proactive performance: A longitudinal study. *The Journal of Applied Psychology, 95.* https://doi.org/10.1037/a0017263

Gurtner, A., Tschan, F., Semmer, N. K., & Nägele, C. (2007). Getting groups to develop good strategies: Effects of reflexivity interventions on team process, team performance, and shared mental models. *Organizational Behavior and Human Decision Processes, 102*(2), 127–142. https://doi.org/10.1016/j.obhdp.2006.05.002

Harrison, G. L., McKinnon, J. L., Wu, A., & Chow, C. W. (2000). Cultural influences on adaptation to fluid workgroups and teams. *Journal of International Business Studies, 31*(3), 489–505. https://doi.org/10.1057/palgrave.jibs.8490918

Hauschildt, K., & Konradt, U. (2012). Self-leadership and team members' work role performance. *Journal of Managerial Psychology, 27.* https://doi.org/10.1108/02683941211235409

Hirst, G., & Mann, L. (2004). A model of R&D leadership and team communication: The relationship with project performance. *R and D Management, 34*(2), 147–160. https://doi.org/10.1111/j.1467-9310.2004.00330.x

Humphrey, S. E., & Aime, F. (2014). Team microdynamics: Toward an organizing approach to teamwork. *Academy of Management Annals, 8*(1), 443–503. https://doi.org/10.1080/19416520.2014.904140

Hunter, J. E., & Hunter, R. F. (1984). Validity and utility of alternative predictors of job performance. *Psychological Bulletin, 96*(1), 72–98. https://doi.org/10.1037/0033-2909.96.1.72

Kahol, K., Vankipuram, M., Patel, V. L., & Smith, M. L. (2011). Deviations from protocol in a complex Trauma environment: Errors or innovations? *Journal of Biomedical Informatics, 44*(3), 425–431. https://doi.org/10.1016/j.jbi.2011.04.003

Konradt, U., Schippers, M. C., Garbers, Y., & Steenfatt, C. (2015). Effects of guided reflexivity and team feedback on team performance improvement: The role of team regulatory processes and cognitive emergent states. *European Journal of Work and Organizational Psychology, 24*(5), 777–795. https://doi.org/10.1080/1359432X.2015.1005608

Kozlowski, S. W. J., & Bell, B. S. (2013). Work groups and teams in organizations. In *Handbook of psychology: Industrial and organizational psychology* (Vol. 12, 2nd ed., pp. 412–469). Hoboken, NJ: John Wiley & Sons Inc.

Kozlowski, S. W. J., Gully, S. N., Nason, E. R., & Smith, E. M. (1999). Developing adaptive teams: A theory of compilation and performance across levels and time. In D. R. Ilgen & D. Pulakos (Eds.), *The changing nature of work performance: Implications for staffing, personnel actions, and development* (pp. 240–292). San Francisco: Jossey-Bass.

Lantz, A., Hansen, N., & Antoni, C. (2015). Participative work design in lean production. *Journal of Workplace Learning, 27*(1), 19–33. https://doi.org/10.1108/JWL-03-2014-0026

Lantz Friedrich, A., Sjöberg, A., & Friedrich, P. (2016). Leaned teamwork fattens workplace innovation: The relationship between task complexity, team learning and team proactivity. *European Journal of Work and Organizational Psychology, 25*(4), 561–569. https://doi.org/10.1080/1359432X.2016.1183649

LePine, J. A. (2003). Team adaptation and postchange performance: Effects of team composition in terms of members' cognitive ability and personality. *Journal of Applied Psychology, 88*(1), 27–39. https://doi.org/10.1037/0021-9010.88.1.27

LePine, J. A. (2005). Adaptation of teams in response to unforeseen change: Effects of goal difficulty and team composition in terms of cognitive ability and goal orientation. *Journal of Applied Psychology, 90*(6), 1153–1167. https://doi.org/10.1037/0021-9010.90.6.1153

Lewis, K., Lange, D., & Gillis, L. (2005). Transactive memory systems, learning, and learning transfer. *Organization Science, 16.* https://doi.org/10.1287/orsc.1050.0143

Marks, M. A., Zaccaro, S. J., & Mathieu, J. E. (2000). Performance implications of leader briefings and team-interaction training for team adaptation to novel environments. *Journal of Applied Psychology, 85*(6), 971–986. https://doi.org/10.1037/0021-9010.85.6.971

Marlow, S. L., Lacerenza, C. N., Paoletti, J., Burke, C. S., & Salas, E. (2018). Does team communication represent a one-size-fits-all approach?: A meta-analysis of team communication and performance. *Organizational Behavior and Human Decision Processes, 144*(July 2017), 145–170. https://doi.org/10.1016/j.obhdp.2017.08.001

Marques-Quinteiro, P., Ramos-Villagrasa, P. J., Passos, A., & Curral, L. (2015). Measuring adaptive performance in individuals and teams. *Team Performance Management, 21.* https://doi.org/10.1108/TPM-03-2015-0014

Mathieu, J., Maynard, M. T., Rapp, T., & Gilson, L. (2008). Team effectiveness 1997–2007: A review of recent advancements and a glimpse into the future. *Journal of Management, 34*(3), 410–476. https://doi.org/10.1177/0149206308316061

Maynard, M. T., Kennedy, D. M., & Sommer, S. A. (2015). Team adaptation: A fifteen-year synthesis (1998–2013) and framework for how this literature needs to "adapt" going forward. *European Journal of Work and Organizational Psychology, 24*(5), 652–677. https://doi.org/10.1080/1359432X.2014.1001376

Moon, H., Hollenbeck, J. R., Humphrey, S. E., Ilgen, D. R., West, B., Ellis, A. P. J., & Porter, C. O. L. H. (2004). Asymmetric adaptability: Dynamic team structures as one-way streets. *Academy of Management Journal, 47*(5), 681–695. https://doi.org/10.5465/20159611

Parker, S. K., Wang, Y., & Liao, J. (2019). When is proactivity wise? A review of factors that influence the individual outcomes of proactive behavior. *Annual Review of Organizational*

Psychology and Organizational Behavior, 6(1), 221–248. https://doi.org/10.1146/annurev-orgpsych-012218-015302

Payne, S. C., Youngcourt, S. S., & Beaubien, J. M. (2007). A meta-analytic examination of the goal orientation nomological net. *Journal of Applied Psychology*. Payne, Stephanie C.: Department of Psychology, Texas A&M University, 4235 TAMU, College Station, TX, US, 77843–4235, scp@psyc.tamu.edu: American Psychological Association. https://doi.org/10.1037/0021-9010.92.1.128

Ployhart, R., & Bliese, P. (2006). Individual adaptability (I-ADAPT) theory: Conceptualizing the antecedents, consequences, and measurement of individual differences in adaptability. In *Understanding adaptability: A prerequisite for effective performance within complex environments* (Vol. 6, pp. 3–39). Elsevier. https://doi.org/10.1016/S1479-3601(05)06001-7

Porter, C. O. L. H., Webb, J. W., & Gogus, C. I. (2010). When goal orientations collide: Effects of learning and performance orientation on team adaptability in response to workload imbalance. *Journal of Applied Psychology, 95*(5), 935–943. https://doi.org/10.1037/a0019637

Priest, H. A., Burke, C. S., Munim, D., & Salas, E. (2002). Understanding team adaptability: Initial theoretical and practical considerations. *Proceedings of the Human Factors and Ergonomics Society Annual Meeting, 46*(3), 561–565. https://doi.org/10.1177/154193120204600372

Pulakos, E. D., Arad, S., Donovan, M. A., & Plamondon, K. E. (2000). Adaptability in the workplace: Development of a taxonomy of adaptive performance. *Journal of Applied Psychology, 85*(4), 612–624. https://doi.org/10.1037/0021-9010.85.4.612

Pulakos, E. D, Dorsey, D., & White, S. (2006). Adaptability in the workplace: Selecting an adaptive workforce. In *Understanding adaptability: A prerequisite for effective performance within complex environments* (pp. 41–71). Amsterdam, Netherlands: Elsevier. https://doi.org/10.1016/S1479-3601(05)06002-9

Randall, K. R., Resick, C. J., & DeChurch, L. A. (2011). Building team adaptive capacity: The roles of sensegiving and team composition. *Journal of Applied Psychology, 96*(3), 525–540. https://doi.org/10.5465/amr.1999.2202135

Ren, Y., Kiesler, S., & Fussell, S. R. (2008). Multiple group coordination in complex and dynamic task environments: Interruptions, coping mechanisms, and technology recommendations. *Journal of Management Information Systems, 25*(1), 105–130. https://doi.org/10.2753/MIS0742-1222250105

Resick, C. J., Dickson, M. W., Mitchelson, J. K., Allison, L. K., & Clark, M. A. (2010). Team composition, cognition, and effectiveness: Examining mental model similarity and accuracy. *Group Dynamics, 14*(2), 174–191. https://doi.org/10.1037/a0018444

Resick, C. J., Murase, T., Randall, K. R., & DeChurch, L. A. (2014). Information elaboration and team performance: Examining the psychological origins and environmental contingencies. *Organizational Behavior and Human Decision Processes, 124*(2), 165–176. https://doi.org/10.1016/j.obhdp.2014.03.005

Reynolds Kueny, C. A., Jundt, D. K., & Shoss, M. K. (2019). Initiative in a social context: interpersonal outcomes of interdependent proactive behaviour. *European Journal of Work and Organizational Psychology, 28*(5), 669–681. https://doi.org/10.1080/13594 32X.2019.1634054

Rosen, M. A., Bedwell, W. L., Wildman, J. L., Fritzsche, B. A., Salas, E., & Burke, C. S. (2011). Managing adaptive performance in teams: Guiding principles and behavioral markers for measurement. *Human Resource Management Review, 21*(2), 107–122. https://doi.org/10.1016/j.hrmr.2010.09.003

Salas, E., Sims, D. E., & Burke, C. S. (2005). Is there a "Big Five" in teamwork? *Small Group Research, 36*(5), 555–599. https://doi.org/10.1177/1046496405277134

Sander, P. C., Van Doorn, R. R. A., Van Der Pal, J., & Zijlstra, F. R. H. (2015). Team adaptation to an unforeseen system failure: Limits of the potential aids of shared knowledge and standardized communication aids of shared knowledge and standardized communication.

European Journal of Work and Organizational Psychology, 24(5), 796–811. https://doi.org/10.1 080/1359432X.2015.1006199

Santos, C. M., Passos, A. M., & Uitdewilligen, S. (2016). When shared cognition leads to closed minds: Temporal mental models, team learning, adaptation and performance. *European Management Journal, 34*(3), 258–268. https://doi.org/10.1016/j.emj.2015.11.006

Santos, C. M., Uitdewilligen, S., & Passos, A. M. (2015). A temporal common ground for learning: The moderating effect of shared mental models on the relation between team learning behaviours and performance improvement and performance improvement. *European Journal of Work and Organizational Psychology, 24*(5), 710–725. https://doi.org/10.1080/1359 432X.2015.1049158

Siegel, C., Pearsall, M. J., Christian, M. S., & Ellis, A. P. J. (2014). Exploring the benefits and boundaries of transactive memory systems in adapting to team member loss. *Group Dynamics: Theory, Research, and Practice, 18*(1), 69–86. https://doi.org/10.1037/a0035161

Sundstrom, E., McIntyre, M., Halfhill, T., & Richards, H. (2000). Work groups: From the Hawthorne studies to work teams of the 1990s and beyond. *Group Dynamics: Theory, Research, and Practice, 4*(1), 44–67. https://doi.org/10.1037/1089-2699.4.1.44

Tae Young Han, & Williams, K. J. (2008). Multilevel investigation of adaptive performance. *Group & Organization Management, 33*(6), 657–684. https://doi.org/10.1177/1059601 108326799

Thoms, P., Pinto, J., Parente, D., & Druskat, V. (2002). Adaptation to self-managing work teams. *Small Group Research, 33*. https://doi.org/10.1177/104649640203300101

Van den Bossche, P., Gijselaers, W., Segers, M., Woltjer, G., & Kirschner, P. (2011). Team learning: Building shared mental models. *Instructional Science, 39*(3), 283–301. http://dx.doi. org/10.1007/s11251-010-9128-3

van Woerkom, M., & Croon, M. (2009). The relationships between team learning activities and team performance. *Personnel Review, 38*(5), 560–577. https://doi. org/10.1108/00483480910978054

Vashdi, D. R., Bamberger, P. A., & Erez, M. (2013). Can surgical teams ever learn? The role of coordination, complexity, and transitivity in action team learning. *Academy of Management Journal, 56*(4), 945–971. https://doi.org/10.5465/amj.2010.0501

Wong, S.-S. (2004). Distal and local group learning: Performance trade-offs and tensions. *Organization Science, 15*. https://doi.org/10.1287/orsc.1040.0080

Chapter 8

The teams do not perform well because of a lack of good leadership

After a definition of team leadership, the first emphasis is what team leaders need to do. Basing on the idea of functional leadership – team leaders' main focus is on the team's concrete and actual needs – tasks of team leaders are reported. Team leadership needs to be adaptive: a team in a transition phase requires different support than in the action phase, a team with a lack of mutual trust requires something else than a team that feels overstrained. Besides the "what" (tasks), the "how" of good team leadership is relevant – what are the specific leadership styles or behavioural patterns of leading a team? Main dimensions of leadership behaviour are initiation of structure and consideration. Another topic of this chapter is: Who is leading – and to what extend can teams lead themselves, realizing shared leadership? To solve problems with team leadership interventions mainly focus on leadership development by using methods such as executive coaching, leadership training and multi-source feedback.

It is not the first time we mention leadership in this book – we have seen that it has an impact on many problems of teams focused on in the previous chapters. There are several definitions of leadership and most of them refer to leadership in general. Yukl (2013) argues that the main common ground of most of these definitions is that leaders exert an "intentional influence [...] over other people to guide structure, and facilitate activities and relationships in a group or an organization" (p. 18). The author proposes a more specific definition, integrating a future perspective with regard to the objectives: "Leadership is the process of influencing others to understand and agree about what needs to be done and how to do it, and the process of facilitating individual and collective efforts to accomplish shared objectives" (p. 23).

This is a general definition of leadership, but what is specific for leading teams? Being a leader for several persons working separately, rather than in a team, means to focus on these staff members as different individuals – their working behaviour, strengths and needs. Leading in this sense implies to influence single persons individually. Team leadership includes more: Team leaders need to regard the team as a holistic entity (West, 2012). Although team leadership behaviour is oriented towards individual team members as well, the main focus is on the team as a whole – its resources, processes and interactions. This includes the common task work as well as the enhancement of interpersonal aspects on the team level, such as coherence, integration and psychological safety (see Chapter 6). Unfortunately most of the leadership research concentrates on leadership effects on individuals and the organization – and only a few of them look at how leaders can support teams in carrying out taskwork in a coordinated manner as well as interpersonal processes (DeChurch, Hiller, Murase, Doty, & Salas, 2010).

Supportive and wise leadership affects team processes in a variety of ways, e.g. by establishing direction, input and information from the external context, providing and managing resources, creating work conditions and coaching/transforming team processes. Teams need leadership to be successful – but we have learned as well that teams should have leeway, plan team processes and make their own decisions.

How does leadership impact team effectiveness? In their conceptual framework Zaccaro, Rittman, and Marks (2001) state that different types of team processes are affected by leadership:

- Cognitive processes, like building shared mental models and information processing (see Chapter 5)
- Motivational processes, such as establishing collective or team efficacy (see Chapter 1)
- Affective processes, e.g. handling of conflicts and psychological safety (see Chapter 6)
- Coordination processes, such as timing, resource allocation, systems monitoring and adaptation to new demands (see Chapters 5 and 7)

What team leaders need to do to impact such processes will be subject of this chapter. These processes in turn affect other variables. For example, psychological safety (as well as other affective states) has been studied as a mediator between leadership and team performance outcomes. The review by Newman, Donohue, and Eva (2017) found that supportive leadership behaviours such as leader inclusiveness, support, trustworthiness and behavioural integrity have systematically shown to strongly impact a team's collective perceptions of collective safety, which in turn foster team learning behaviour, team performance, engagement in quality improvement work and reduction of errors amongst team members.

Leadership approaches differ in their main focus on how to bring about effective leadership. Leader-centric approaches look at general characteristics of the leader, such as specific traits, styles and behaviours, that can be applied for all leading contexts, not only team leadership (Shuffler, Burke, Kramer, & Salas, 2012; Yukl, 2013). In contrast, team-centric approaches have a focus on the team. These issues highlight different aspects with regard to the team: its needs as well as leadership functions performed by the whole team (Kozlowski & Bell, 2013; Kozlowski, Mak, & Chao, 2016). These approaches do not describe a specific set of leadership behaviours (Zaccaro et al., 2001) – there are no clear, generalizable rules on how team leaders should behave. Instead, for different constellations and situations appropriate leadership strategies have to be found, considering the specific team situation.

Another prominent approach – the leader-member-exchange (LMX) – focuses on dyadic interactions of the individuals and the leader (Graen & Uhl-Bien, 1995). Although team leaders have individual relationships to team members as well, specific team focused activities, such as the support of team emergent states, are not integrated.

Different approaches concentrate on different aspects – leader, team, dyadic interaction. But that does not mean that they cannot be combined to explain problems with team leadership; they can be regarded as complementary perspectives as well: It may be expedient that team leaders focus on a team's needs (see later for problem causes 3.1), and at the same time specific types of the team leader's behaviour can enhance the team's performance (as we will see in 3.3). Research is integrating different approaches as well, for example there are studies about transformational leadership – a leader-centric approach described later in this chapter – that integrates team-centric perspectives (Kozlowski et al., 2016).

And how can we find out if a leader is effective? Of course one criterion for leadership effectiveness is the performance of the team – good leadership should result in better achievement of team goals, more creativity or improved team decisions. But as we saw earlier there are more indicators for the quality of leadership – such as shared psychological states (e.g. collective efficacy) and processes (e.g. cooperation, van Knippenberg, 2017). Team leadership has shown to be an important factor for facilitating team learning as well (Koeslag-Kreunen, Van den Bossche, Hoven, Van der Klink, & Gijselaers, 2018; Zaccaro, Ely, & Shuffler, 2008).

Before we have a closer look at theoretical and empirical foundations about team leadership, let us start with a concrete case focusing on a team having problems due to team leadership.

1 Step 1. Describe the current situation

CASE: A LACK OF STRONG AND CONSIDERATE LEADERSHIP DEPLETES TEAM MORALE AND REDUCES EFFICIENCY

A production planning team from the automotive industry is responsible for projecting the company's production lines, especially for the planning of elements from the automatic transmission. The team works well together; each engineer is responsible for a specific component, and if necessary they help each other. Teammates exchange experiences, and substitute and support each other mutually.

The team is responsible for quality and logistics planning, in terms of costs, dates and quality. When new product lines are planned, the team is engaged in cross-functional and inter-team collaboration processes. Therefore, team members have good contacts to other teams and hierarchical levels like management and production.

In the past two years, the former team leader often was absent for long periods (sometimes several months) due to a serious illness. As a result, the team often worked in quite an autonomous way. Now the previous team leader has been retired and the team has a new team leader. He has completed several management trainings and has taken up the function of a team leader for the first time. Headquarters management assigned him to develop the team towards more innovation, flexibility and change – to be in line with the enterprise's mission statement.

Half a year later other departments of the firm complain that the quality of the team's output has diminished and that it is not reliable. The innovations have not been achieved. The team often does not meet deadlines. Communication with the team has become more complicated – before they knew what team member to address with what type of question. Now the new leader of the team has decided that he coordinates all team-external communication. But this takes time and very often he cannot give the information needed (and individual team members could).

What is the perspective of the team leader? He thinks that the team does not cooperate with him and does not follow his instructions. In addition, sometimes decisions are made without him and outside the team meetings – although he should have been involved, as he is responsible for the team. One evening he invited the team to his home to create a trustful positive relationship. To present a solution for the problem with the external communication flow he has developed a model – but the team does not accept it. He wonders if it would be best to dissolve the team as in his view they support each other in resisting change and innovation.

In a team meeting the team members agree on the problem in the following statement: "We are a good and responsible team and we have a lot of expertise. Our team-leader is not involved in our work and often gives us advice that is not useful. He is making decisions alone and without asking us, although we are more experienced than he is. He does not know what has been going on here the last years. For example, he did not think of hiring a temporary worker for the peak time in June (as every year), and we could not meet the deadlines. We could work in a better way without him! Sometimes we get important information quite late and only by chance (e.g. during lunch when we meet others by coincidence). At the moment it does not work well, but before, we really did a good job together."

In the next step we try to analyze what the main problem is that needs to be tackled.

2 Step 2. Identify the core problem(s)

There is one point all parties – the team leader, the team and team-externals – agree upon: The team does not perform well since the new team leader has been installed and started to work with the team. The team leader and the team blame each other for being responsible for poor team results. It seems that the team leader is motivated, well qualified after leadership training and, in the management's opinion, trustworthy and competent to lead the team. The team on the other hand has proven to cooperate reliably in times of little support through a leader. The main problem seems to be a misfit between the leader's behaviour and the team's expectations towards him.

In the following section we will develop more specific work hypotheses for the causes of the problem, basing on theory-based research.

3 Step 3. Cause analysis: what are the main causes of problems with team leadership?

Based on the IMOI model, team leadership impacts teamwork in a twofold way:

LACK OF GOOD LEADERSHIP | 193

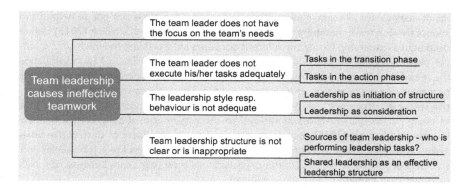

Figure 8.1 Mindmap about why leadership causes ineffective teamwork

- First, it is part of the input, as team leaders have an impact on team composition and frame conditions for teamwork, information and resources. They give direction and define tasks, goals and structure of the team.
- Second, leadership is part of team processes, especially person focused activities like motivation, coaching and supporting, establishing communication in the team, empowerment and consideration.

(Burke, Stagl, Klein, Goodwin, & Halpin, 2006; West, 2012)

In the following, we will cover four aspects. Functions of team leadership that may cause problems (see Figure 8.1): The first aspect is whether and to what extent the team leader considers the specific situation and needs of the team and aligns his/her leadership behaviour corresponding to these requirements (3.1). This main assumption – the focus on the specific team needs – can be considered as basis for the following topics as well: the tasks of a team leader ("the what," 3.2), leadership styles or patterns of behaviour ("the how," 3.3) and the leadership structures ("the who," 3.4).

As for the adequacy of team members, there is a huge discussion about leadership and personality traits. Bono, Shen, and Yoon (2014) refer to a meta-analysis of Judge et al. (2002) about the relationship of the big five personality factors (see Chapter 4) and leadership emergence and effectiveness. It shows that 15%–28% of the variances between leaders can be explained by personality traits. That means that personality has a limited impact on leadership – and more factors need to be considered. In this chapter, we will concentrate on factors that may be impacted using developmental interventions. In the following section, we first describe theoretical and evidence-based findings with regard to these explanations for problems with team leadership and related aspects (see branches in Figure 8.1), before we focus on the question how such problems can be diagnosed in real work-place settings.

3.1 The team leader does not have the focus on the team's needs

Team leadership can be defined from the team perspective – from this point of view, a good leader should satisfy the team's needs and ensure task fulfilment and team maintenance. Not all team leaders have this focus, leadership is not per se helpful and supportive for team members to reach their goals. Schyns and Schilling (2013) define destructive leadership basing on different concepts as "a process in which over a longer period of time the activities, experiences and/or relationships of an individual or the members of a group are repeatedly influenced by their supervisor in a way that is perceived as hostile and/or obstructive" (p. 141). The authors highlight that destructive leadership does not include all ineffective leadership behaviours – there are more as being passive (laisser-faire) or disloyal to the organizational aims. Erickson, Shaw, Murray, and Branch (2015) resume several studies about effects of destructive leadership and report negative consequences on the individual level (e.g. job satisfaction, stress, depression) as well as on the organisational level (e.g. costs because of a high turnover rate, climate of fear, toxic culture).

In contrast, functional leadership implies that a team leader's task is "to do, or get done, whatever is not being adequately handled for group needs" (McGrath, 1964, p. 5; cited by Morgeson, DeRue, & Karam, 2010, p. 8). What is specific for functional leadership? With its main perspective on the team's needs, functional leadership is a team-centric approach (Kozlowski et al., 2016; Morgeson et al., 2010; Shuffler et al., 2012). The focus is not on what a leader should do in general, but what needs to be done with this team at that moment (again: no two teams are the same, and teams as well as their context change and develop).

Within the functional approach, leadership is regarded as a problem-solving process (Burke et al., 2006; Zaccaro et al., 2001), as solutions for (potential) impairments of team processes (regarding task-work as well as interpersonal processes) need to be found. As explained in Chapter 2, problem-solving means – in abbreviated form – to diagnose problems in a thorough way, find and plan adequate solutions, implement them, and evaluate if the problem has been solved. Gathering information inside and outside the team and the structuring of information is important to review if the team is reaching its goals and if it has the resources needed. Above that, processes and developments inside and outside the organization, and in the team have to be monitored. To do so information about these changes needs to be analyzed to find and select possible solutions. It is also important to constantly balance between giving answers and direction and empowering the team and let them be responsible for developing their own processes and taskwork.

As a next step a concrete solution plan needs to be made and realized. To realize the plan leaders act on two dimensions: They manage personnel and material resources (Zaccaro et al., 2001). By solving the problems team effectiveness should be enhanced.

CASE: A LACK OF STRONG AND CONSIDERATE LEADERSHIP DEPLETES TEAM MORALE AND REDUCES EFFICIENCY CONT.

Transferring this to our case we see that the team leader obviously is not effective. One criterion is that the team has not reached the innovations that were expected by the organization. Team members' job satisfaction, another criterion, is low as well. If we adopt the approach of functional leadership, the team leader should make sure that team members can realize their teamwork – by guaranteeing adequate framework conditions and supporting the

> team. The team members mention that they do not have the impression that their leader facilitates their work – in contrast they give examples for obstacles caused by the leader, e.g. information flow. The team leader is not acting as a problem solver either – he does not diagnose the problems in the team and search for adequate solutions; in contrast he is mainly trying to force his ideas of team functioning.
>
> Our first work hypothesis is that the team cannot work effectively because the team leader does not respond to its needs, as for example the possibility to communicate directly with colleagues outside the team.

To summarize: One important approach of team leadership is the functional approach. The idea is that team leaders act as problem solvers to fulfil the teams' needs and ensure that team members can complete their tasks in an effective way.

The next section addresses what exactly team leaders can do to fulfil the team's needs.

3.2 The team leader does not execute his/her tasks adequately

We saw earlier that leadership tasks can be seen as functional, meeting teams' needs. A lack of leadership means that a team is not supported in its work as it should be. But what can a team leader do to make sure that teams have what they need to fulfil their tasks?

There are different categorizations of team leaders' tasks. Hackman's (2002) main point is to create enabling conditions for the team that allow team members to manage their task- and teamwork on their own. Hackman attaches value to the input teams get – the conditions in which the team and the task have been constructed and the support of the organizational context. Above that, giving a clear direction and coaching (as leadership processes) are highlighted. These are main factors for team leaders, as they include the fulfilment of basic team needs. All the same, they do not cover the whole range of what team leaders need to do. Morgeson et al. (2010) have, based on a literature research, found that team leaders usually do even more than establishing enabling conditions, and that the tasks depend on the phase of a team – is it in transition or action phase? We will add Hackman's enabling conditions to Morgeson's leadership functions – into a common model of team leaders' tasks (see Figure 8.2).

But first some explanation about transition and action phase: Teams work in different phases over time (Marks, Mathieu, & Zaccaro, 2001), and they need different support by their leader(s) in these phases. First, there is the transition phase: teams are structuring, evaluating or planning their work and performance to better reach their goals. In this period teams focus primarily on the development or improvement of effective structures and processes, e.g. by making plans for adaptive changes. Second, there is the action phase: teams mainly work on their tasks that are directed at accomplishment of their goals. But beware: This does not mean that teams necessarily

Transition phase	Action phase
- Create a team	- Monitor team
- Design task	- Manage team boundaries
- Define mission	- Challenge team
- Establish expectations and goals	- Perform team task
	- Solve problems
- Structure and plan	- Provide resources
- Train, coach and develop team	- Support social climate
- Sensemaking	- Encourage team self-management
- Provide feedback	

Figure 8.2 Team leadership tasks in transition and action phase
(based on Hackman, 2002, and Morgeson et al., 2010)

go through these phases one after another – very often in a team's transition phase the taskwork needs to be done as well. Therefore, the two phases can overlap. In these two phases, teams have different needs, and similarly different leadership tasks become relevant (see Figure 8.2).

In the following sections, we will focus on how leaders can support teams in transition and in action phase by explaining the corresponding leadership tasks.

3.2.1 Tasks in the transition phase

Let us start with the tasks that are important in the transition phase.

- Create a team: This task integrates team composition (see Chapter 4) or in existing teams, if needed, the replacement of team members. Moreover, a "real" team must be established – team leaders have to ensure that the team has clear boundaries, team members work interdependently and the team is stable (at least for a certain period of time) (see Hackman, 2002, and definition of team, Chapter 3).
- Design task: Team leaders should define a holistic and meaningful task that gives autonomy to team members (Hackman, 2002).
- Define mission: The team needs to know specifically what is expected from them by the organization – an important leadership function is to clarify these expectations and then, based on these demands, define the mission of the team. This mission should be "clear, compelling, challenging, and shared among team members" (Morgeson et al., 2010, p. 13). This compelling direction also serves to enhance compatible knowledge structures guiding team members behaviour (Burke et al., 2006).
- Establish expectations and goals: Based on the mission, the next step is to specify concrete expectations for performance and realistic and challenging team goals.

LACK OF GOOD LEADERSHIP

| 197

Team members should define their own goals as well and clarify what they mean to them. Expectations refer to core norms of conduct about positive and unacceptable behaviour, too (Hackman, 2002).

- Structure and plan: When performance expectations and goals have been set, teamwork needs to be structured and planned in order to reach them. The team needs a common understanding about the optimum process to accomplish these targets, integrated work plans need to be made comprising procedures and methods of task work, distribution of tasks and allocation of responsibilities in the team, as well as timing and schedule planning.
- Train, coach and develop the team: Now it is clear and concrete what the team needs to do in the action phase – but what if there is a lack of qualification or capabilities regarding the realization of this plan whether in the whole team or for single team members? If that is the case training or other measures of personal and team development are needed. Hackman and Wageman (2005) emphasize the importance of expert coaching and describe three different types: motivational coaching to create a common commitment regarding the team and its tasks, consultative coaching to influence performance strategy of a team, and educational coaching that addresses knowledge and skills of team members (Wageman, Fisher, & Hackman, 2009). Another important aspect of coaching is to enhance team members' emotions and affects (interpersonal affect regulation), which in turn has a positive impact on task performance (Holman & Niven, 2019).
- Sensemaking: Changes or disrupting events (e.g. regarding task, team or organizational structure) can have a negative impact on team processes. In such a situation, sensemaking is a relevant leadership task. Sensemaking means to support the team to interpret, understand and reflect the reasons, possible consequences and the sense of the changes (see Chapter 7, leader briefings).
- Provide feedback: Team feedback is important for further development of the team, as it provides an assessment of actual and past interpersonal team processes and performance. Based on this information teams can reflect their task- and teamwork and adapt their behaviour in order to work more effectively, especially when they did not accomplish their goals. Team leaders need to give teams time and space to reflect so they can learn and develop.

This list of tasks does not mean that they need to be fulfilled by team leaders in every transition phase – but only when there is a need for them (see Figure 8.2). Some tasks are very important in the first initial transition phase of a team – as composing the team, defining its mission, and establishing expectations and goals. In the following transition phases sometimes adaptations of these settings are needed, but usually not in every transition phase – and the focus will be more on team reflexivity of the previous action phase.

3.2.2 Tasks in the action phase

What leadership support can become relevant when teams are mainly conducting their taskwork?

- Monitor team: While the team is working actively, it is important to be attentive to team processes and progresses as well as to external aspects like availability of resources. Team leaders should support team members in these monitoring processes if needed.

- Manage team boundaries: Teams are not isolated, but a part of the organization. Managing the connections or boundaries between the team and its organizational context means to keep up and cooperate with other parts of the organization, receive and communicate important information and represent the team's interests. Teams do not always work for themselves; sometimes they share tasks with other teams or organizational units, and this cooperation needs to be coordinated as well. Furthermore, managing team boundaries includes preventing disturbances from outside and ensuring external support if needed. How knowledge sharing between teams enhances organizational learning is the subject of Chapter 9.
- Challenge team: Leadership also means to challenge the team in order to improve the effectiveness, reflect the actual processes and find better ways of working. Ways to challenge teams are for example scrutinizing the actual practice or intellectual stimulation.
- Perform team task: Team leaders can support task performance of the team when needed. This leadership task matters only for external team leaders, as internal leaders, as part of the team, are performing anyway – although internal leaders can also handle subtasks they usually do not perform (see 3.4 about leadership structure).
- Solve problems: This leadership task becomes relevant when problems occur that cannot be solved by the team on its own. This does not mean that the leader should act alone – of course the team's participation and expertise is of great importance to find the best solution and an adequate intervention (see also Chapter 2 about the complete problem-solving cycle). The team's involvement is relevant for team learning and organizational learning as well (see Chapter 9).
- Provide resources: Teams need resources to perform – in the form of information, material, money and personnel. Team leaders need to make sure that these resources are available for the team.
- Support social climate: A good social climate, positive interactions and psychological safety (see Chapters 5, 6 and 7) are prerequisites for good teamwork. What can leaders do to support team climate? They can, for example, show a respectful, validating, warm and concerning communicative behaviour themselves in their leading role.
- Encourage team self-management: This leadership task implies the support and encouragement of teams to act autonomously and manage team processes themselves – for instance to solve occurring problems alone. So this leadership task is more indirect. It consists of empowering teams and giving them the leeway needed to manage themselves. An important way to support teams in their self-management is to coach them (discussed earlier) – instead of giving them instructions.

Morgeson et al. (2010) sum up for each leadership task studies on their importance for the team functioning – but a study integrating these tasks as a whole and taking into account different team contexts has not been conducted yet.

> To summarize: Team leaders need to focus on the team's needs – but there are typical tasks leaders should have in mind. They should make sure that the team

can manage itself as much as possible by establishing enabling conditions, e.g. concerning team composition, clear goals, task design and a support system. In the transition and action phase teams need different support – as their focus is on the development of structures, processes and strategies in transition phases and on performing, monitoring and coordinating in the action phases.

3.3 The leadership style/behaviour is not adequate

We now have ideas of the aims of leadership and specific leadership tasks. But what we have not mentioned yet is "the how" of leading. What do we mean with "the how"? In the organizational literature, we find a lot about different leadership styles, which include different patterns of behaviour. Therefore, in this section we focus on leader-centred approaches. We will see that some of the tasks mentioned earlier are important for some leadership styles, overlaps of "the what" – the tasks – and "the how" – the style of leadership – are inevitable.

The categorization of leadership behaviour into initiation of structure and consideration is a fundamental one. It is based on data collected in the Ohio studies using the Leader Behaviour Description Questionnaire (Hemphill & Coons, 1957). After several data analyses, the two basic dimensions of initiation of structure and consideration were identified. Both dimensions are independent of each other; this means that all combinations of initiation of structure and consideration are possible – both can be on a high or a low degree, or the dimensions are situated on different levels.

In two meta-analyses both dimensions of leadership have been studied (see 3.3.3 for results). Burke et al. (2006) and Ceri-Booms, Curşeu, and Oerlemans (2017) used task- and person-orientation as main categories and allocated different leadership concepts to these categories. Doing so the authors define person- and task-orientation in a broader way, being not merely constituted by consideration and initiating structure. The concepts that the authors subsume under task- and person-orientation in these analyses are different: Some of these concepts are broader leadership styles or behavioural patterns (as transformational and transactional leadership, see definition in the next section). Others are more specific and focused on a certain aspect of leadership behaviour.

In the following sections we will first define these leadership behaviours and then report the results of the meta-analyses about the impact of these leadership behaviours on team effectiveness and team performance.

3.3.1 Leadership as initiation of structure

Initiation of structure (or task-focused leadership) is characterized by a high orientation towards performance and goal attainment. Therefore, emphasis is on structure, organization, clarity of objectives, coordinating and planning mechanisms, as well as on a clear, unambiguous role and task description. Linked to this are measures like target agreements, quality assurance, the accompaniment and control of the work steps and the securing and monitoring of results.

Task-focused leadership comprises the following approaches (Burke et al., 2006; Ceri-Booms et al., 2017):

- Transactional leadership behaviours: This leadership style is based on the idea that taskwork is executed because of an exchange between leaders and employees: Employees work because they get rewards and praise or avoid punishment. In order to realize this exchange, for instance, goal setting and concrete agreements are used.

- Initiating structure behaviour aims at structuring the task and achieving specific team goals by giving the team a unique sense of direction and establishing a structure to follow this direction. So actions of planning, organizing and controlling team processes are main components, as well as fixing clear roles of the team members, assigning tasks and ensuring an adequate flow of information and communication.
- Boundary spanning behaviour means activities outside the team such as cooperating with other teams or organizational instances, negotiating with stakeholders, ensuring resources for the team, networking and gathering information.

3.3.2 Leadership as consideration

Consideration (or person-focused leadership) is characterized by employee orientation and appreciation. This involves good relationships with the employees, respect for a good working atmosphere, support of the team as well as the interest and support of each individual team member. There is a focus on emotions, needs, human relationships and expectations. Consideration includes attitudes and behaviours such as interest, empathy, acceptance, recognition, invitation of participation in team-relevant matters and support.

Person-focused leadership is related to the following approaches (Burke et al., 2006; Ceri-Booms et al., 2017):

- Transformational leadership: The concept of transformational leadership plays a key role in current leadership research; there is a steady increase of publications that address transformational leadership (Felfe, 2006; Kozlowski et al., 2016). It goes back to Max Weber's (1922) concept of charismatic leadership, which refers to political leadership. It was further developed – with different emphases – by House (1976); Bass (1985); and Tichy, Devanna, and Devanna (1986). Key factors are idealized influence, inspirational motivation, intellectual stimulation and individualized consideration – the idea is to lead by establishing visions and motivate team members. The accentuation of transformational leadership also includes the demand for a paradigm shift from more managerial management to leadership, which – mediated by changes in attitudes and values – is supposed to generate higher motivation. Transformational leaders are role models, establish visions for the future and bring in intellectual impulses and new perspectives. Meaningfulness and inspiration are core mechanisms. Furthermore, the employees are supported individually in their development. Transformational leadership is given high relevance especially in the case of organizational changes, as it establishes long-term visions and values, and promotes a team's adaptability (Charbonnier-Voirin, El Akremi, & Vandenberghe, 2010; Groves, 2005; Herold, Fedor, Caldwell, & Liu, 2008). There is criticism of a somewhat indistinct conceptualization (van Knippenberg, 2017) – indeed we will find aspects of this leadership style in the following concepts of leadership behaviour as well.
- Empowering leadership means to enhance autonomy and responsibility of the team members by participation, common decision-making and encouragement

to develop self-management skills. Measures of empowerment are e.g. coaching, feedback and participatory behaviour.

- Consideration refers to leadership behaviours, supporting the quality of relationships and group cohesion by consultation, trust, respect and satisfaction of team members' needs.
- Coaching focused leadership means to support team members in their personal development and learning, also by giving critical feedback and challenging them.
- Emotionally intelligent leadership means that team leaders are able to "perceive, appraise, express, and regulate emotion" (Ceri-Booms et al., 2017, p. 180) and therefor consider team members' emotions in their leadership behaviour.
- Charismatic leadership refers to the personality of the leader, affecting the team members with articulation and impression management skills and working with visions (there is a huge overlap with transformational leadership).
- Motivational leadership includes all behaviours having a positive impact on commitment and willingness to perform – like reward, recognition and support.

3.3.3 Empirical evidence for adequate leadership behaviour

As just mentioned, the author groups Burke et al. (2006) and Ceri-Booms et al. (2017) have conducted meta-analyses on the impact of these leadership behaviours on team effectiveness and team performance. They analyzed task- and person-oriented concepts (with some differences: motivational leadership was researched only in the older analysis, whereas the concepts of emotionally intelligent leadership, coaching focused leadership and charismatic leadership were only part of the later meta-analysis). Both meta-analyses show positive effects of task- and person-focused leadership behaviours on team effectiveness and team performance.

There were also differences in the results: Burke et al. (2006) found that especially boundary spanning and empowerment behaviours showed larger effects on team performance outcomes than other leadership behaviours. And there was a remarkable relationship of empowerment by the leader and team learning in this meta-analysis ($r = .56$).

Furthermore, Burke et al. (2006) found a higher influence of person-focused behaviours ($r = .36$ on perceived team effectiveness and $r = .28$ on team productivity) than of task-focused behaviours ($r = .33$ on perceived team effectiveness and $r = .20$ on team productivity). Ceri-Booms et al. (2017) report similar effects of leadership behaviour oriented towards persons and towards tasks (for subjective team performance both $\rho = .33$, for objective team performance $\rho = .18$ resp. .19). A possible explanation for these differences may be that various teams need distinct forms of leadership behaviour. Perhaps not all teams profit from person-focused leadership to the same extent? In the analysis of Ceri-Booms et al. (2017) different team types were compared. There was a stronger relationship of person-focused leadership and team performance in service and project teams than in action or performing teams consisting of highly qualified experts performing complex tasks. A possible interpretation is that service teams work with customers and person-focused leaders might be role models.

Koeslag-Kreunen et al. (2018) conducted a meta-analysis on the effects of leadership behaviour on team learning. They differentiate between adaptive tasks that are prescribed, structured and contain few new elements (e.g. production or coordination) and developmental tasks that are not prescribed, have few structures and include a lot of new elements (e.g. design or research). The results indicate that person-focused leadership has positive effects on team learning for adaptive and developmental team tasks, whereas task-focused leadership only has a positive impact on teams working on adaptive tasks. Based on these results and on further qualitative analyses, the authors recommend a combination of task- and person-focused team leadership behaviours, depending on the team's temporary needs (e.g. is there a need for trust building or for structuring goals?). This suggestion complies with the functional approach of leadership. Moreover, the authors warn that an extreme task-focus can include an overstructuring of tasks, as too much specification may diminish the leeway of a team and hinder learning processes.

In another meta-analysis Chiaburu, Smith, Wang, and Zimmerman (2014) found that transactional and transformational leadership have similar effects on different proactive and prosocial behaviours and task performance outcomes – however this analysis does not only include leadership of teams but of individuals as well.

In conclusion: There is no empirical evidence that a specific leadership style or behaviour is superior to others. Perhaps it matters more that all leadership tasks are executed in a good way. Another interpretation might be that different situations, circumstances and team types require different leadership behaviours, according to the functional leadership approach. Ceri-Booms et al. (2017) argue that empowering leadership is not necessarily fruitful for all teams and all team situations: For example, if there is a deadline, participative decisions might take too much time and therefore, top-down decisions might be better. In contrast, in situations of organizational change or in transition phase participation (as a key component of empowering leadership) is helpful: Participation has been claimed by many as crucial for increasing acceptance for change and reducing insecurity and resistance (Dunphy & Stace, 1993; von Thiele Schwarz, & Hasson, 2013). The specific task, situation and context of a team have to be considered as well to find the adequate leadership style.

CASE: A LACK OF STRONG AND CONSIDERATE LEADERSHIP DEPLETES TEAM MORALE AND REDUCES EFFICIENCY CONT.

What can we derive for this case? The relation between the team leader and the team is negative, shaped by mistrust and a lack of mutual respect. Some of the decisions taken by the team leader, e.g. rules for communication, were made against the team's will and obviously without the team's participation. The team leader reports that he has tried to create positive relationships by inviting the team to his home. However, a private invitation does not necessarily mean that work-related relations are improved. They are rather shaped by experiences at work – is it possible to trust the leader? Does he value ideas and suggestions, and is he supporting the team?

Work hypothesis 2 refers to a lack of consideration and participation of the team leader's behaviour as cause for the problem.

To summarize: There are several approaches to good leadership. Based on research it makes more sense to use a broad repertory of leadership behaviours – and adapt them to the concrete team situation (or in a functional view to the team's needs) than to realize one specific leadership style in an uniform manner. Both task-oriented and person-focused leadership (and several leadership concepts that can be assigned to these main categories) have shown to have a positive impact on team performance outcomes – it is important to focus structure and goal attainment, as well as consideration and positive relationships.

3.4 Team leadership structure is not clear or inappropriate

Who is leading a team? The question is not as easy to answer as it seems at first sight. Do teams need leaders anyway? We have learned before that teams should make decisions, take responsibility, act autonomously and manage their team processes themselves. Is a team leader with a specific hierarchical position needed? The answer is no, not necessarily – as team members can undertake leadership functions (and need corresponding capabilities, for instance self-management KSAs as interpersonal skills, e.g. goal setting, performance management, planning and task coordination; see Chapter 4). There are also teams with informal leaders, in other words persons who lead, although this function is not part of organization charts. Let us have a more systematic look at how leadership structures may look.

3.4.1 Sources of team leadership – who is performing leadership tasks?

Team leadership structure can be described on two dimensions (Morgeson et al., 2010). The first dimension is called the locus of leadership: Is the team leader inside or outside the team? Is there an internal team leader, such as a team member working on the team task? Or does the team have an external leader, who does not belong to the team? The second dimension is the formality of leadership: Is there a formalized and explicit responsibility for leadership tasks (formal) or is there a person (or more) leading not being formally assigned to do so (informal)? Formal leadership goes together with the traditional approach of vertical leadership – one person is designated to lead the team and is therefore – vertically seen – on a higher level than the team members.

Combining these dimensions, we find four types of leadership. Morgeson et al. (2010) call them the sources of team leadership:

- Internal and formal leaders, who are members of the team, have been formally assigned. They are often labelled as project managers or team leaders.
- External and formal leaders – often called sponsors, coaches, or advisors – have also been formally assigned, but are not part of the team.
- Internal and informal leaders are often found in teams sharing leadership tasks among team members, they "share in fulfilling the leadership role" (van Knippenberg, 2017). In other cases single team members undertake leadership tasks – without being officially assigned to do so: An emergent leader is one team member exercising influence over the whole team. Emergent leadership is an individual phenomenon, whereas shared leadership as a team-centric approach is planned at the team level (Hoch & Dulebohn, 2017).

- External and informal leaders are colleagues outside the team supporting it – often called executive coordinators, team mentors or team champions.

Furthermore, teams can be organized in different kinds of leadership in combination – for example an external advisor and shared leadership inside the team. If we look back at the leadership tasks we see that most of them can be executed in all leadership structures – formal or informal, internal or external. Some functions – such as team composition and ensuring resources – can better be done by formal vertical leaders as they have an official status to do so. Most of them can be shared in the team as well.

It is not sufficient to focus only on formal leaders – the more leeway a team has the more likely and sensible it becomes that they participate in team leadership as well. Burke et al. (2006) argue, based on the results of a meta-analysis, that leadership behaviours matter regardless of leadership structure. In their view it is more important that the leadership behaviours are fulfilled in an adequate way (e.g. with focus on the team members as well as the task, see 3.3.3) than by whom. Nevertheless, in the last decade several studies have been conducted about shared leadership and most of them showed positive effects. In the next section we will have a closer look at shared leadership.

3.4.2 Shared leadership as a specific leadership structure

Several current meta-analyses show that there is a positive relationship between shared leadership and team performance and effectiveness (D'Innocenzo, Mathieu, & Kukenberger, 2016; Nicolaides et al., 2014; Wang, Waldman, & Zhang, 2014) – although the intensity of this relationship is varying. Wang et al. (2014), in their meta-analysis, used team effectiveness as a collective term for different effects: attitudes like job satisfaction and commitment, behavioural processes and emergent states, e.g. cooperation and cohesion, as well as subjective performance (as individual ratings) and objective performance (e.g. productivity). The relatedness of shared leadership was higher with attitudinal outcomes and behavioural processes/emergent states (ρ = .45 resp, .44) as for the performance measures (ρ = .25, resp. .18). And there are more positive correlations: Van Knippenberg (2017) sums up various studies proving the relatedness of shared leadership with trust, consensus, cohesion and innovative behaviour.

For what leadership tasks and styles is shared leadership appropriate? Carter, Mead, Stewart, Nielsen, and Solimeo (2019) found in a meta-analysis positive effects of shared leadership on team performance for different team types, whereas service teams showed the highest values (high-tech teams r = .28, manufacturing teams r = .31, service teams r = .43). Wang et al. (2014) analyzed in their meta-analysis, as well, what tasks exactly teams are sharing, and how these shared leadership tasks matter. To do so they distinguished between traditional leadership and new-genre leadership. Traditional leadership is based on exchanges (transactional leadership, discussed earlier) and the maintenance of the actual state. In contrast, new-genre leaders are oriented toward development and change, for example practicing transformational leadership and empowerment (discussed earlier). The relatedness of shared leadership with team effectiveness in general (attitudes, behaviour/emergent states, subjective and objective performance) is higher when the shared leadership tasks are focused on change and development (new-genre leadership, ρ = .34), than in the case of shared traditional leadership ($\rho = .18$). The authors conclude that it is not so important to share traditional leadership functions, in contrast to "new genre leadership" change orientated tasks, as sharing them is more beneficial for team effectiveness.

What prerequisites are needed for shared leadership? Team confidence seems to be an important factor for these common leadership processes. It includes collective efficacy and potency. Bandura (1997) defines collective efficacy as "a group's shared belief in its conjoint capabilities to organize and execute the courses of action required to produce given levels of attainments" (p. 477). For organizational teams it can be adapted to the belief in the ability to accomplish team tasks. Potency is a broader concept of collective efficacy and goes beyond task-specific abilities; it is generalized across tasks and contexts (Gully, Incalcaterra, Joshi, & Beaubien, 2002).

Team confidence is a precondition for taking on and sharing leadership tasks (Nicolaides et al., 2014; Wang et al., 2014). It should also be mentioned that shared leadership requires specific qualifications. Team members need leadership expertise "to collectively assess situations, collectively clarify direction, collectively monitor performance processes, and collectively maintain team coherence" (Zaccaro, Heinen, & Shuffler, 2009).

But is shared leadership necessarily informal, as Morgeson et al. (2010) argue? We do not think so, and other authors also mention that shared leadership can be realized based on a formal agreement as well (D'Innocenzo et al., 2016). A formal allocation of shared leadership tasks would also make it clear and transparent – for the team members, but for externals, too. In the case of a team member's absence a replacement for his or her leadership tasks can be organized.

CASE: A LACK OF STRONG AND CONSIDERATE LEADERSHIP DEPLETES TEAM MORALE AND REDUCES EFFICIENCY CONT.

The team has a formal team leader, as he is officially assigned to this role. In the past, the team has managed itself quite well. The current team leader wants to undertake leadership tasks that before were completed by the team. The team is not satisfied with this loss of responsibility and scope for autonomous decision-making. There are different ideas about team structure – the team would like to go on sharing leadership tasks whereas the team leader prefers to fulfil them mainly alone.

Work hypothesis 3 is: There is no consensus about the leadership structure and the extent of shared leadership. The team leader assumes he is in charge of all leadership tasks, whereas the team wants to go on sharing team leadership and feels hindered by the leader to overtake leadership tasks and manage themselves.

To summarize: Teams can be led by one or more persons, and these team leaders can be a part of the team (internal) or external leaders. Team leaders can be formal leaders in the sense of assignment to the leadership role or informal leaders. Shared leadership – a collective leadership inside a team – has shown to have a positive impact on team performance and effectiveness as well as on emergent states, such as trust and cohesion, specifically in teams with change oriented and developmental tasks.

3.5 How to assess team leadership

The most common method to assess team leadership is to ask the team about the leader, based on the idea that an external view is more valid and less biased as the self-image. All the same it makes sense to combine these data with the leader's perspective or even more perspectives (see 5.3 for multi-source-feedback as an intervention). If a positive and trustful relationship between team members and team leader exists, a diagnosis can be made in an open group discussion as well. In the next sections examples for the assessment of the problem causes with leadership are described.

3.5.1 To assess if a team leader is focusing a team's needs

The extent to which a team leader corresponds to the needs of his/her team can be diagnosed by first asking the team about expectations towards the leader and then discuss which of them are met by the leader and in what way the team wishes for more support.

A more structured way of assessing if the team leader corresponds to the actual situation of the team is to combine the diagnosis of leadership tasks (see 3.5.2) with a discussion about their actual relevance for the team – this avoids that important aspects of team leadership are not mentioned by the team. A possible instrument is introduced in the next section.

A way to diagnose if a leader is executing destructive leadership and so damaging the team, is the use of the Destructive Leadership Questionnaire (DLQ, Erickson et al., 2015, published in the article). It includes 22 destructive leader behaviours, for example, bullying, exhibiting inconsistent behaviour, making significant decisions without information, communicating ineffectively, over-controlling, and acting in an insular manner. The questionnaire can be completed by the team members or by the leader as a self check.

3.5.2 To assess if the leader executes his/her tasks adequately

To diagnose what leadership tasks are discharged the Team Leadership Questionnaire (Morgeson et al., 2010) can be used. The items of the questionnaire have been published in the article (see publication list) and cover all tasks mentioned in their model (the authors call them functions based on the functional leadership approach, see example in the following box). The authors make them available for future research.

With the instrument, it can be assessed which leadership tasks are executed, to find out if there are problems because specific leadership functions are not fulfilled. The items can be integrated into a questionnaire so team members can indicate for each task if it is fulfilled by the team leader or not (answer scale could be, for example, "task is executed by the leader", "task is partly executed by the leader" and "task is not executed by the leader"). In a discussion of the results with the team and the leader it makes sense as well to reflect on which of these tasks are relevant and helpful to the team right now, and if these tasks are completed or not.

Transition phase leadership functions

Sensemaking

1 Assists the team in interpreting things that happen inside the team
2 Assists the team in interpreting things that happen outside the team
3 Facilitates the team's understanding of events or situations
4 Helps the team interpret internal or external events
5 Helps the team make sense of ambiguous situations

Action phase leadership functions

Challenge team

1 Reconsiders key assumptions in order to determine the appropriate course of action
2 Emphasizes the importance and value of questioning team members
3 Challenges the status quo
4 Suggests new ways of looking at how to complete work
5 Contributes ideas to improve how the team performs its work

Box: Examplary items of Team Leadership Questionnaire
(Morgeson et al., 2010)

3.5.3 To assess leadership style or behaviour

There are a lot of questionnaires to assess leadership styles or behaviours, convergent to the leader-centric approach. It is important that they meet psychometric criteria. Some of them can be found in the internet as documents, while some need to be purchased. A source for leadership survey is the book "Online Instruments, Data Collection, and Electronic Measurements: Organizational Advancements" by Bocarnea, Reynolds, and Baker (2013). This publication contains for example the Leader Behavior Description Questionnaire (LBDQ; Rodriguez, 2013), originally developed by Halpin (1957). This questionnaire can be used to assess the two dimensions of team leadership: the task by initiating structure and the team members by consideration. Team members fill out the questionnaire about their leader, e.g. "S/he finds time to listen to group members" for consideration and "S/he sees to it that the work of the group members is coordinated." for initiating structure.

3.5.4 To assess leadership structure

To diagnose the sharedness of leadership in a team, the "Shared Professional Leadership Inventory for Teams" (SPLIT) by Grille and Kauffeld (2015) has been developed. The questions refer to how a team executes leadership tasks together, e.g. assigning tasks, recognizing good performance, promoting team cohesion, learning from past experiences. The items of the questionnaire are included in the article. Moreover, the Team Leadership Questionnaire (Morgeson et al., 2010) can be used to assess the team leadership structure by adding the question, who is performing the specific tasks – the formal team leader, an informal emergent leader, or is there a sharedness of tasks in the team? This can be done by adding another question for each item with an open answer format about who is fulfilling the task. Then, it can be discussed if this structure is effective or should be adapted.

4 Step 4. Select target dimensions and set goals

At this stage of the process the problem with team leadership as well as its main causes should be quite clear. The next step is to select the dimensions to be targeted by interventions – these dimensions should have a high likelihood to solve the problem and they should be realistically changeable. Afterwards goals for these changes need to be set to have a sound basis for the next step – finding the optimal solutions to reach this goal.

5 Step 5. Identify solutions

Evidence-based studies on solutions for problems with team leadership mostly refer to trainings for leaders to enhance their KSAs (Lacerenza, Reyes, Marlow, Joseph, & Salas, 2017). In addition, we can derive advice from the findings reported earlier – e.g. to make sure that all leadership tasks are executed and that team leaders should focus on both – task fulfilment and personal needs of team members. And we find guidelines or best practices based on different studies, e.g. how to create enabling structures according to Hackman (2002, discussed earlier; Stagl, Salas, & Burke, 2007) or how to cope with problems and improve team processes in science teams (National Research Council, 2015). The main focus for solutions is how to enable team leaders to act in an adequate way.

What are the domains for solutions to enhance team leadership? It depends on the leadership structure – in case of a single team leader, it is a solution on the individual (leader) domain, in case of shared leadership, the solution should be situated in the team domain. Moreover, it is important to ensure appropriate frame conditions, such as defining leadership structure, tasks and goals as well as providing team leaders adequately with information and resources. If problems result because of these factors, solutions on the organizational domain need to be realized (see Table 8.1).

We have to keep in mind that solutions in the area of team leadership possibly have to be combined with solutions on other domains. For example, a more participative leadership style implicates different team processes as well, as team members have more leeway for decisions – so it can make sense to combine an intervention

Table 8.1 Domains for designing measures for team leadership

Choose domain for solution(s) to enhance team leadership			
Prerequisites in the physical environment	**Prerequisites on organizational domain**	**Solutions on team domain**	**Solutions on individual domain**
Not relevant	Frame conditions: • Leadership structure • Leadership tasks • Leadership goals • Information systems • Resources	To enhance KSAs for shared leadership	To enhance KSAs for team leadership

for an individual leader with an intervention on team level, for example team building and work design. Or, in case of shared leadership it is important that adequate frame conditions are created on the organizational domain, e.g. information systems ensuring that all team members are provided with details relevant for leadership.

In section 3, we have learned what team leaders do to support their teams appropriately. But how can team leaders get support for themselves? Hartley and Benington (2010) define leadership development as "activities and experiences that are used to enhance the quality of leadership and leadership potential in individuals, groups, teams, organisations and networks" (p. 112). They do address vertical leaders as well as teams sharing leadership tasks. There are many suggestions on how leaders can develop, that mostly do not refer specifically to team leadership but to organizational leadership in general and – there is still a need for more research about it (DeRue & Myers, 2014). All the same, there is some evidence for the most commonly recommended measures of leadership development: coaching, training and feedback.

5.1 Executive coaching

We learned earlier that coaching is an important task of team leaders – but is it helpful for themselves as well? Leadership or executive coaching refers to the "development or strengthening of managerial competencies amongst executives through intensive dialogue" (Heery & Noon, 2008, p. 56), or a broader definition is that it is based on a helping relationship between a client and a coach with the aim of more effective leadership (Ely, Boyce, Nelson, Zaccaro, Hernez-Broome, & Whyman, 2010; Theeboom, Beersma, & van Vianen, 2014).

Executive coaching is an umbrella term that comprises various forms of support for leaders. The focus can differ between personal issues of the leader (e.g. problems with handling the leading role conflicts, stress) and the leader's handling and managing the processes and performance within the organization (e.g. organizational development). Further, the focus can be short term (e.g. an actual conflict) or long term (e.g. restructuring of the organization or the leader's own carrier development; Berman & Bradt, 2006). Coaching is done by internal or external coaches with different professional background such as psychology, business, human resources, social work and more (De Meuse, Dai, & Lee, 2009). It includes different forms of one-on-one learning targeting behavioural change of the leader (Day, 2000). One-on-one implicates that two persons – the coach and the coachee – participate in the coaching process. It should be mentioned that group coachings exist as well, whereby a coach works with several leaders. The studies mentioned in this section all refer to coaching with a single coachee.

Depending on the coaches academic discipline and specialized direction, coaching processes are based on different theories (e.g. positive psychology, psycho-analysis, systemic approach) and use varying methods (e.g. solution focussed questions to find courses of action, role plays to exercise challenging situations; Greif, Möller, & Scholl, 2018). With this variety – what is common to all coaching processes? Although there is no consensus about key processes of coaching, many coachings include goal setting with the coachee, reflection, feedback, transfer to the workplace and evaluation of the goal attainment (Burt & Talati, 2017; Greif et al., 2018; Jones, Woods, & Guillaume, 2016).

As there is such a variety of methods that are offered as coaching it is even more important to ensure that the methods have been evaluated. For successful coaching three more factors are important: the coach must be professional and well qualified, the coachee should bring motivation and willingness to change behavioural patterns, and the organization needs to provide funding for the coaching as well as time resources for the coachee (Schermuly & Graßmann, 2016).

A method of executive coaching is the strength-based coaching methodology based on the approach of positive psychology. MacKie (2014) evaluated a strength-based coaching intervention comprising six sessions with focus on strength-based interviewing, feedback on strengths in leadership, goal setting and strengths development. The results show that the coaching methodology had a positive impact on the transformational leadership behaviour of the coachees.

Several meta-analyses about leadership coaching (De Meuse et al., 2009; Jones et al., 2016; Theeboom et al., 2014) showed positive effects on different levels like individual performance of the leader, leadership skills, affective outcomes (such as self-efficacy and well-being), coping, work attitudes and goal-directed self-regulation. Burt and Talati (2017) have a critical look at these analyses, as they include studies without randomized samples and only post-intervention measures – and conduct a meta-analysis only on experimental studies. Their results indicate moderate positive effects of executive coaching on well-being, work-related attitude, coping strategies and self-directed goal attainment by the clients.

The studies show that coaching has a positive impact on several aspects of KSAs and leadership performance – but we do not know exactly why, and what type of coaching processes are superior, as the coaching studies that were analyzed hardly disclose how they proceed (Jones et al., 2016).

An exception is a smaller study with 24 participants and a control group by Ladegard and Gjerde (2014): They found that facilitative coaching behaviour – the coach challenges, supports and gives feedback to the coachee – has a positive impact on leader role-efficacy (confidence about their capability to successfully realize the leadership tasks) and trust in subordinates. More well-founded research is needed to learn what coaching processes impact what outputs on individual as well as on team level.

5.2 Leadership training

Team leaders need specific KSAs; we address training as an intervention. Leadership trainings are designed to enhance specific qualifications to execute leadership functions and behaviours adequately (Day, 2000; Lacerenza et al., 2017).

Traditional trainings address team leaders as individuals. An example is the training of adaptability skills by experiential variety (training situations demanding changes of strategies) and strategic information provision (by instructions, performance feedback, cognitive and behavioural guidance) before, during and after training trials (Nelson, Zaccaro, & Herman, 2010). For the field of health care action training, Rosenman, Shandro, Ilgen, Harper, and Fernandez (2014) found in a review that leadership training mostly is a component of general teamwork trainings and focus with varying emphases on transition and action processes, as well as on interpersonal skills facilitating these processes.

To train teams for sharing their leadership it is useful to address them as a group. In her doctoral thesis Allen (2010) developed a work-based action learning shared leadership training programme for teams of nurses. The training consisted of four training sessions. Elements were team action learning projects to implement shared leadership, a cognitive training (e.g. team roles and leadership processes and

LACK OF GOOD LEADERSHIP

| 211

the transfer to their team), an individual and a team coaching, and a final reflection on practice. The training showed a positive impact on team dynamic knowledge, use of shared leadership behaviours and engagement.

A meta-analysis on trainings for team leaders by Lacerenza et al. (2017) based on 335 studies has shown positive effects on four levels (based on Kirkpatrick's (1979) model of training effectiveness):

- Reactions – attitudes towards the training: Are participants satisfied with the training? (δ.63[1], medium effect)
- Learning outcomes related to the acquisition or change of internally based states (affective learning), intellectual or mental-based skills (cognitive) or technical or motor-skills (skill-based learning) (δ.73, medium effect)
- Transfer – realization of learning outcomes at the workplace (δ.82, large effect)
- Results – effects on the organizational level as reduction of costs, better profits and more turnover (δ.72, medium effect)

So there is empirical evidence that leadership trainings impact leadership behaviour as well as the organizational level.

5.3 Multi-source feedback

In the whole book, we have pointed to the relevance of analyzing the current status to plan future actions. The same should apply for team leadership – before developmental measures are implemented it should be assessed what is needed. Multi-source feedback (or 360-degree or multi-rater feedback) is defined as a systematical collection of perceptions of one person from different important perspectives (Day, 2000). The idea is that feedback from several persons with different roles and from different contexts should provide rich, substantial and broad information about a person. Feedback is assessed for example by peers, supervisors, subordinates as well as external stakeholders. The objective is a better self-knowledge as well as self-awareness (Day, 2000).

Hafford-Letchfield and Bourn (2011) have developed a tool for multi-source feedback for managers in social work. Based on leadership and management standards they constructed a questionnaire for the managers themselves, line-management, peers, subordinates, mentors and service users to assess skills in several managerial areas (e.g. personal skills, providing direction to others, facilitating change and achieving results). The results are used to create a learning and development plan together with the line-manager and a mentor. An evaluation with the participants showed a positive impact on their professional development (but it has to be mentioned that the sample was only nine persons).

Multi-source feedback does not have positive effects in general. For instance, in the meta-analysis by Jones et al. (2016) mentioned earlier multisource feedback had – contrary to expectations – a negative impact on coaching outcomes. The authors see as a possible reason that feedback can have a negative impact on the coachee's attention and s/he can be worried about the feedbacks content. For leadership trainings on the other hand Lacerenza et al. (2017) found positive effects of integrated feedback on learning transfer, but not for 360°-feedback. Giving a good and useful feedback is demanding.

Another finding is that feedback alone does not mean change or improvement of leadership behaviour. A possible reason may be that support is helpful in interpreting the data and finding adequate reactions to the feedback, like developing an individual development plan (DeNisi & Kluger, 2000). Many authors propose to link feedback with developmental measures as coaching and mentoring (Day, 2000; Grant, Curtayne, & Burton, 2009; Ladegard & Gjerde, 2014; Smither, London, Flautt, Vargas, & Kucine, 2003; Solansky, 2010; Thach, 2002).

> ## CASE: A LACK OF STRONG AND CONSIDERATE LEADERSHIP DEPLETES TEAM MORALE AND REDUCES EFFICIENCY CONT.
>
> What kind of support could help the team leader in this case? It is interesting that the team leader has passed through leadership trainings, but perhaps they did not fit with the specific needs for this team, e.g. soft skills. As there were severe problems of mistrust and mutual rejection the team leader decided to pass a coaching programme. The lack of consideration – the assumption of work hypothesis 2 – was a relevant starting point for this coaching process. During the coaching, the leader reflected his behaviour and found out that his main focus had been his idea of good team leadership – and not so much the situation and the needs of the team. Another insight was that he had feared to lose his authority if yielding too much to the team's position.
>
> Despite the coaching, the management and the team leader decided that the situation was deadlocked and could not be solved in this constellation, as the team did not trust the leader. In retrospect, they reflected upon their former decision to allocate an unexperienced team leader to a self-confident, experienced and well-coordinated team. They decided together with the team to recruit one of the team members as their leader and supported them with an internal coach in finding a formal solution for shared leadership. The former leader is now leading a team in another company.

> *To summarize*: Solutions for team leadership mainly have a focus on support for the leader. Coachings, trainings and multi-source-feedback are interventions for the improvement of team leader's KSAs – whereas specifically for coaching and multi-source feedback more research-based evidence is needed.

This chapter focused on how team leaders can support their teams to perform in an optimal way. The next chapter will be concerned with the team level, addressing how teams can contribute to organizational learning.

Note

1   The effect size Cohen's δ is a standardized measure that makes it possible to compare effects.

Bibliography

Allen, L. A. (2010). *An evaluation of a shared leadership training program*. Doctoral Dissertation. University of Phoenix.

Bandura, A. (1997). Collective efficacy. In A. Bandura (Ed.), *Self-efficacy: The exercise of control* (pp. 477–525). New York: Freeman.

Bass, B. M. (1985). *Leadership and performance beyond expectations*. New York: Free Press.

Berman, W. H., & Bradt, G. (2006). Executive coaching and consulting: Different strokes for different. *Professional Psychology: Research and Practice*, 37(3), 244–253. https://doi.org/10.1037/0735-7028.37.3.244

Bocarnea, M. C., Reynolds, R. A., & Baker, J. D. (Eds.). (2013). *Online instruments, data collection, and electronic measurements*. Hershey, PA: IGI Global. https://doi.org/10.4018/978-1-4666-2172-5

Bono, J. E., Shen, W., & Yoon, D. (2014). Personality and leadership: Looking back, looking ahead. In D. V. Day (Ed.), *The Oxford Handbook of Leadership and Organizations* (pp. 199–220). New York, NY: Oxford University.

Burke, C. S., Stagl, K. C., Klein, C., Goodwin, G. F., & Halpin, S. M. (2006). What type of leadership behaviors are functional in teams? A meta-analysis. *The Leadership Quarterly*, 17(3), 288–307. https://doi.org/10.1016/J.LEAQUA.2006.02.007

Burt, D., & Talati, Z. (2017). International journal of evidence based coaching and mentoring. *International Journal of Evidence Based Coaching and Mentoring*, 15(2), 17–24. https://doi.org/10.24384/000248

Carter, K. M., Mead, B. A., Stewart, G. L., Nielsen, J. D., & Solimeo, S. L. (2019). Reviewing work team design characteristics across industries: Combining meta-analysis and comprehensive synthesis. *Small Group Research*, 50(1), 138–188. https://doi.org/10.1177/1046496418797431

Ceri-Booms, M., Curşeu, P. L., & Oerlemans, L. A. G. (2017). Task and person-focused leadership behaviors and team performance: A meta-analysis. *Human Resource Management Review*, 27(1), 178–192. https://doi.org/10.1016/J.HRMR.2016.09.010

Charbonnier-Voirin, A., El Akremi, A., & Vandenberghe, C. (2010). A multilevel model of transformational leadership and adaptive performance and the moderating role of climate for innovation. *Group & Organization Management*, 35(6), 699–726. https://doi.org/10.1177/1059601110390833

Chiaburu, D. S., Smith, T. A., Wang, J., & Zimmerman, R. D. (2014). Relative importance of leader influences for subordinates' proactive behaviors, prosocial behaviors, and task performance. *Journal of Personnel Psychology*, 13(2), 70–86. https://doi.org/10.1027/1866-5888/a000105

Day, D. V. (2000). Leadership development: A review in context. *The Leadership Quarterly*, 11(4), 581–613. https://doi.org/10.1016/S1048-9843(00)00061-8

DeChurch, L. A., Hiller, N. J., Murase, T., Doty, D., & Salas, E. (2010). Leadership across levels: Levels of leaders and their levels of impact. *The Leadership Quarterly*, 21(6), 1069–1085. https://doi.org/10.1016/J.LEAQUA.2010.10.009

De Meuse, K. P., Dai, G., & Lee, R. J. (2009). Evaluating the effectiveness of executive coaching: Beyond ROI? *Coaching: An International Journal of Theory, Research and Practice*, 2(2), 117–134. https://doi.org/10.1080/17521880902882413

DeNisi, A. S., & Kluger, A. N. (2000). Feedback effectiveness: Can 360-degree appraisals be improved? *The Academy of Management Executive (1993–2005)*, 14(1), 129–139. https://doi.org/10.2307/4165614

DeRue, D. S., & Myers, C. G. (2014). *Leadership development: A review and agenda for future research*. New York: Oxford University Press. https://doi.org/10.1093/oxfordhb/9780199755615.013.040

D'Innocenzo, L., Mathieu, J. E., & Kukenberger, M. R. (2016). A meta-analysis of different forms of shared leadership–team performance relations. *Journal of Management*, 42(7), 1964–1991. https://doi.org/10.1177/0149206314525205

Dunphy, D., & Stace, D. (1993). The strategic management of corporate change. *Human Relations, 46*(8), 905–920. https://doi.org/10.1177/001872679304600801

Ely, K., Boyce, L. A., Nelson, J. K., Zaccaro, S. J., Hernez-Broome, G., & Whyman, W. (2010). Evaluating leadership coaching: A review and integrated framework. *The Leadership Quarterly, 21*(4), 585–599. https://doi.org/10.1016/J.LEAQUA.2010.06.003

Erickson, A., Shaw, B., Murray, J., & Branch, S. (2015). Destructive leadership: Causes, consequences and countermeasures. *Organizational Dynamics, 44*(4), 266–272. https://doi.org/10.1016/j.orgdyn.2015.09.003

Felfe, J. (2006). Transformationale und charismatische Führung–Stand der Forschung und aktuelle Entwicklungen. *Zeitschrift Für Personalpsychologie, 5*(4), 163–176. https://doi.org/10.1026/1617-6391.5.4.163

Graen, G. B., & Uhl-Bien, M. (1995). Relationship-based approach to leadership: Development of leader-member exchange (LMX) theory of leadership over 25 years: Applying a multi-level multi-domain perspective. *The Leadership Quarterly, 6*(2), 219–247. https://doi.org/10.1016/1048-9843(95)90036-5

Grant, A. M., Curtayne, L., & Burton, G. (2009). Executive coaching enhances goal attainment, resilience and workplace well-being: A randomised controlled study. *The Journal of Positive Psychology, 4*(5), 396–407. https://doi.org/10.1080/17439760902992456

Greif, S., Möller, H., & Scholl, W. (2018). Coachingdefinitionen und -konzepte. In S. Greif, H. Möller, & W. Scholl (Eds.), *Handbuch Schlüsselkonzepte im Coaching* (pp. 1–9). Berlin, Heidelberg: Springer. https://doi.org/10.1007/978-3-662-49483-7_7

Grille, A., & Kauffeld, S. (2015). Development and preliminary validation of the Shared Professional Leadership Inventory for Teams (SPLIT). *Psychology, 6*(1), 75–92. https://doi.org/10.4236/psych.2015.61008

Groves, K. S. (2005). Linking leader skills, follower attitudes, and contextual variables via an integrated model of charismatic leadership. *Journal of Management, 31*(2), 255–277. https://doi.org/10.1177/0149206304271765

Gully, S. M., Incalcaterra, K. A., Joshi, A., & Beaubien, J. M. (2002). A meta-analysis of team-efficacy, potency, and performance: Interdependence and level of analysis as moderators of observed relationships. *Journal of Applied Psychology, 87*(5), 819–832. https://doi.org/10.1037/0021-9010.87.5.819

Hackman, J. R. (2002). *Leading teams: Setting the stage for great performances.* Boston: Harvard Business School Press.

Hackman, J. R., & Wageman, R. (2005). A theory of team coaching. *Academy of Management Review, 30*(2), 269–287. https://doi.org/10.5465/amr.2005.16387885

Hafford-Letchfield, T., & Bourn, D. (2011). "How am I doing?": Advancing management skills through the use of a multi-source feedback tool to enhance work-based learning on a post-qualifying post-graduate leadership and management programme. *Social Work Education, 30*(5), 497–511. https://doi.org/10.1080/02615479.2010.505263

Halpin, A. W. (1957). *Manual for the leader behavior description questionnaire.* Columbus, OH: The Ohio State University, Fisher College of Business.

Hartley, J., & Benington, J. (2010). *Leadership for healthcare.* Bristol: Policy Press.

Heery, E., & Noon, M. (2008). *A dictionary of human resource management.* Oxford: Oxford University Press.

Hemphill, J. K., & Coons, A. E. (1957). Development of the leader behaviour description questionnaire. In R. M. Stogdill & A. E. Coons (Eds.), *Leader behavior: Its description and measurement.* Columbus: Ohio State University, Bureau of Business Research.

Herold, D. M., Fedor, D. B., Caldwell, S., & Liu, Y. (2008). The effects of transformational and change leadership on employees' commitment to a change: A multilevel study. *Journal of Applied Psychology, 93*(2), 346–357. https://doi.org/10.1037/0021-9010.93.2.346

Hoch, J. E., & Dulebohn, J. H. (2017). Team personality composition, emergent leadership and shared leadership in virtual teams: A theoretical framework. *Human Resource Management Review, 27*(4), 678–693. https://doi.org/10.1016/J.HRMR.2016.12.012

Holman, D., & Niven, K. (2019). Does affect-improving interpersonal affect regulation influence others' task performance? The mediating role of positive mood. *European Journal of Work and Organizational Psychology*. DOI: 10.1080/1359432X.2019.1666105

House, R. J. (1976). A 1976 theory of charismatic leadership. In J. G. Hunt & L. L. Larson (Eds.), *Leadership: The cutting edge* (pp. 189–207). Carbondale: Southern Illinois University Press.

Jones, R. J., Woods, S. A., & Guillaume, Y. R. F. (2016). The effectiveness of workplace coaching: A meta-analysis of learning and performance outcomes from coaching. *Journal of Occupational and Organizational Psychology, 89*(2), 249–277. https://doi.org/10.1111/joop.12119

Judge, T. A., Bono, J. E., Ilies, R., & Gerhardt, M. W. (2002). Personality and leadership: A qualitative and quantitative review. *Journal of Applied Psychology, 87*, 765–780.

Kirkpatrick, D. L. (1979). Techniques for evaluating training programs. *Journal of the American Society for Training and Development, 13*, 3–9.

Koeslag-Kreunen, M., Van den Bossche, P., Hoven, M., Van der Klink, M., & Gijselaers, W. (2018). When leadership powers team learning: A meta-analysis. *Small Group Research, 49*(4), 475–513. https://doi.org/10.1177/1046496418764824

Kozlowski, S. W. J., & Bell, B. S. (2013). Work groups and teams in organizations: Review update. In N. Schmitt & S. Highhouse (Eds.), *Handbook of Psychology, vol. 12: Industrial and Organizational Psychology* (2nd ed., pp. 412–469). Hoboken, NJ: Wiley.

Kozlowski, S. W. J., Mak, S., & Chao, G. T. (2016). Team-centric leadership: An integrative review. *Annual Review of Organizational Psychology and Organizational Behavior, 3*(1), 21–54. https://doi.org/10.1146/annurev-orgpsych-041015-062429

Lacerenza, C. N., Reyes, D. L., Marlow, S. L., Joseph, D. L., & Salas, E. (2017). Leadership training design, delivery, and implementation: A meta-analysis. *Journal of Applied Psychology, 102*(12), 1686–1718. https://doi.org/10.1037/apl0000241

Ladegard, G., & Gjerde, S. (2014). Leadership coaching, leader role-efficacy, and trust in subordinates: A mixed methods study assessing leadership coaching as a leadership development tool. *The Leadership Quarterly, 25*(4), 631–646. https://doi.org/10.1016/J.LEAQUA.2014.02.002

MacKie, D. (2014). The effectiveness of strength-based executive coaching in enhancing full range leadership development: A controlled study. *Consulting Psychology Journal: Practice and Research, 66*(2), 118–137. https://doi.org/10.1037/cpb0000005

Marks, M. A., Mathieu, J. E., & Zaccaro, S. J. (2001). A temporally based framework and taxonomy of team processes. *Academy of Management Review, 26*(3), 356–376. https://doi.org/10.5465/amr.2001.4845785

McGrath, J. E. (1964). *Social psychology: A brief introduction.* New York: Holt, Rinehart and Winston.

Morgeson, F. P., DeRue, D. S., & Karam, E. P. (2010). Leadership in teams: A functional approach to understanding leadership structures and processes. *Journal of Management, 36*(1), 5–39. https://doi.org/10.1177/0149206309347376

National Research Council. (2015). *Enhancing the effectiveness of team science.* Washington, DC: National Academies Press. https://doi.org/10.17226/19007

Nelson, J. K., Zaccaro, S. J., & Herman, J. L. (2010). Strategic information provision and experiential variety as tools for developing adaptive leadership skills. *Consulting Psychology Journal: Practice and Research, 62*(2), 131–142. https://doi.org/10.1037/a0019989

Newman, A., Donohue, R., & Eva, N. (2017). Psychological safety: A systematic review of the literature. *Human Resource Management Review, 27*(3), 521–535. https://doi.org/10.1016/j.hrmr.2017.01.001

Nicolaides, V. C., LaPort, K. A., Chen, T. R., Tomassetti, A. J., Weis, E. J., Zaccaro, S. J., & Cortina, J. M. (2014). The shared leadership of teams: A meta-analysis of proximal, distal, and moderating relationships. *The Leadership Quarterly, 25*(5), 923–942. https://doi.org/10.1016/J.LEAQUA.2014.06.006

Rodriguez, R. (2013). Leadership Behavior Description Questionnaire (LBDQ & LBDQ-XII). In *Online instruments, data collection, and electronic measurements* (pp. 97–117). Hershey, PA: IGI Global. https://doi.org/10.4018/978-1-4666-2172-5.ch006

Rosenman, E. D., Shandro, J. R., Ilgen, J. S., Harper, A. L., & Fernandez, R. (2014). Leadership training in health care action teams. *Academic Medicine, 89*(9), 1295–1306. https://doi.org/10.1097/ACM.0000000000000413

Schermuly, C. C., & Graßmann, C. (2016). Erfolgreicher Einsatz von Coaching in der Führungskräfteentwicklung. In J. Felfe & R. van Dick (Eds.), *Handbuch Mitarbeiterführung: Wirtschaftspychologisches Praxiswissen für Fach- und Führungskräfte* (pp. 129–140). Berlin, Heidelberg: Springer. https://doi.org/10.1007/978-3-642-55080-5_41

Schyns, B., & Schilling, J. (2013) How bad are the effects of bad leaders? A meta-analysis of destructive leadership and its outcomes. *The Leadership Quarterly, 24,* 138–158. http://dx.doi.org/10.1016/j.leaqua.2012.09.001

Shuffler, M. L., Burke, C. S., Kramer, W. S., & Salas, E. (2012). *Leading teams: Past, present, and future perspectives.* Oxford: Oxford University Press. https://doi.org/10.1093/oxfordhb/9780195398793.013.0010

Smither, J. W., London, M., Flautt, R., Vargas, Y., & Kucine, I. (2003). Can working with an executive coach improve multisource feedback ratings over time? A quasi-experimental field study. *Personnel Psychology, 56*(1), 23–44. https://doi.org/10.1111/j.1744-6570.2003.tb00142.x

Solansky, S. T. (2010). The evaluation of two key leadership development program components: Leadership skills assessment and leadership mentoring. *The Leadership Quarterly, 21*(4), 675–681. https://doi.org/10.1016/J.LEAQUA.2010.06.009

Stagl, K. C., Salas, E., & Burke, C. S. (2007). Best practices in team leadership: In I.A. Conger & R.E. Riggio (Eds.), *What team leaders do to facilitate team effectiveness. The Practice of Leadership: Developing the Next Generation of Leaders* (pp. 172-197). San Francisco, CA: Jossey and Bass.

Thach, E. C. (2002). The impact of executive coaching and 360 feedback on leadership effectiveness. *Leadership & Organization Development Journal, 23*(4), 205–214. https://doi.org/10.1108/01437730210429070

Theeboom, T., Beersma, B., & van Vianen, A. E. M. (2014). Does coaching work? A meta-analysis on the effects of coaching on individual level outcomes in an organizational context. *The Journal of Positive Psychology, 9*(1), 1–18. https://doi.org/10.1080/17439760.2013.837499

Tichy, N. M., Devanna, M.A., & Devanna, M.A. (1986). *The transformational leader.* New York: Wiley.

van Knippenberg, D. (2017). Team leadership. In E. Salas, R. Rico, & J. Passmore (Eds.), *The Wiley Blackwell handbook of the psychology of team working and collaborative processes* (pp. 345–368). Chichester, UK: John Wiley & Sons, Ltd. https://doi.org/10.1002/9781118909997.ch15

von Thiele Schwarz, U., & Hasson, H. (2013). Alignment for achieving a healthy organization. In G. F. Bauer & G. J. Jenny (Eds.), *Salutogenic organizations and change* (pp. 107–125). Dordrecht: Springer Netherlands. https://doi.org/10.1007/978-94-007-6470-5_7

Wageman, R., Fisher, C. M., & Hackman, J. R. (2009). Leading teams when the time is right. *Organizational Dynamics, 38*(3), 192–203. https://doi.org/10.1016/j.orgdyn.2009.04.004

Wang, D., Waldman, D.A., & Zhang, Z. (2014). A meta-analysis of shared leadership and team effectiveness. *Journal of Applied Psychology, 99*(2), 181–198. https://doi.org/10.1037/a0034531

Weber, M. (1922). *Wirtschaft und Gesellschaft.* Tübingen: Mohr.

West, M. (2012). *Effective teamwork: Practical lessons from organizational research* (3rd ed.). Oxford: Blackwell.

Yukl, G.A. (2013). *Leadership in organizations.* Upper Saddle River: Pearson.

Zaccaro, S. J., Ely, K., & Shuffler, M. (2008). The leader's role in group learning. In V. I. Sessa & M. London (Eds.), *Work group learning: Understanding, improving & assessing how groups learn in organizations* (pp. 15–44). Mahwah, NJ: L. Erlbaum Associates.

Zaccaro, S. J., Heinen, B., & Shuffler, M. (2009). Team leadership and team effectiveness. In E. Salas, G. F. Goodwin, & C. S. Burke (Eds.), *The organizational frontiers series: Team effectiveness in complex organizations: Cross-disciplinary perspectives and approaches* (pp. 83–111). New York, NY: Routledge and Taylor & Francis Group.

Zaccaro, S. J., Rittman, A. L., & Marks, M.A. (2001). Team leadership. *The Leadership Quarterly, 12*(4), 451–483. https://doi.org/10.1016/S1048-9843(01)00093-5

Chapter 9

Teamwork and team learning do not result in organizational learning

Research supports the assumption that teamwork has a positive impact on organizational performance as well as financial outcomes. Teamwork can also contribute to organizational learning that results in changes of organizational structures or processes. In this chapter the focus is on how team learning can be a resource for achieving concrete improvements at organizational level, i.e. in other parts of the organization. Within the organizational learning literature, teamwork is seen as the basis for collective learning that enables organizations to learn. Those with practical experience would say that most teams focus on becoming effective in routine-task performance, and contribute less to change and developmental activities although learning and cross-fertilization of ideas is closely linked to innovation. Our extensive review of the literature resulted in some plausible causes of why teamwork does not result in organizational learning and change. This might help managers and practitioners to decide whether it could be worthwhile to take teamwork to a new and higher level.

In Chapter 7 it was shown that team learning enables the team to adapt to novel demands, and organizations need to adapt to external changes as well. The team is embedded in an organizational context, and team-learning processes can potentially give input to organizational learning (OL), which results in changes in or improvements of organizational structures or processes. OL can be a bottom-up process which improves the organization's ability to respond to internal and external changes, and can result in better work conditions and a more efficient organization. In many team-based organizations the idea of OL is stressed, but in reality, most are content if teams carry out their task in an effective and adaptive way. We regard the team's participation in OL as one of the most important outcomes of teamwork. This chapter is different to the others in two ways: We focus on the interface between teamwork and organization, and the solutions presented are in most cases recommendations and not empirically validated methods. The reason is that research has not yet reported about this kind of method.

1 What is organizational learning?

OL is a collective learning process in which individual and team-based learning are transferred to the organizational level and used to implement change in organizational routines, processes and structures which can later have an effect on individuals and teams (Crossan, Lane, & White, 1999; Schilling & Kluge, 2009). Team learning is a cornerstone in organizational learning (Delarue, Van Hootegem, Procter, & Burridge, 2008). "Team learning is vital because teams, not individuals, are the fundamental learning units in modern organisations. This is where the rubber meets the road; unless teams can learn, the organisation cannot learn" (Senge, 1990, p. 10). The underlying assumption is that individuals are themselves not strong enough to create a basis to support organizational innovation, improvement or change. Team learning and organizational learning research are two separate schools to describe and explain learning at different levels in the organization. There is an increasing awareness that the two approaches can contribute to each other, and that teamwork can be better exploited by this. To provide a more elaborated understanding of how teamwork can contribute to the organization, we first introduce the theory of OL.

1.1 A model for the process of OL

The 4I framework (Crossan et al., 1999; Jones & Macpherson, 2006) is the most frequently used model both to describe the flow of learning from individual to group to organizational level (the feed-forward process) and to describe the result in changes at the organizational level that later affect groups and individuals in the organization (the feedback process). The 4I model consists of different stages/steps described as intuition, interpretation, integration and institutionalization. Intuition is the individual's experiential learning that can be shared with others and gives input to team learning. Interpretation and integration are what in team-learning literature is meant by the process of co-construction of meaning (see team learning in Chapter 7). Integrating can be understood as a process of preparation to take the next step towards the team's contributing with content, (e.g. new practice, adapted knowledge) to the organizational level. By institutionalizing is meant how organizational structures and processes are changed as a result of the upwards learning flow, and these changes later affect groupings and individuals.

1.2 An outward orientation

Engaging in OL requires a team orientation towards changing organizational structures and processes, an output orientation. It means focusing on the intended final product or result for the organization, rather than focusing solely on the results in the team. *Output orientation* means that the team members are aware of what constitutes a successful performance of the task and know what the final product or outcome is, the relative importance of their task for the final product and what criteria will be used for the evaluation of the final product or outcome. Creating this kind of output orientation is a first step and a first specific goal to make the team ready to take part in OL. OL is only possible if individuals, groupings, teams and departments have a clear view of the organization's objectives and understand how they can contribute to goal fulfilment (Jerez-Gomez, Cespedes-Lorente, & Valle-Cabrera, 2005).

1.3 Preconditions and team ability for OL

To create a potential to embed organizational learning into team learning it is necessary to focus both on opportunities and on team ability. Opportunities refer to what teams need from their organizations by way of targets, resources, information, education, feedback, technical and process assistance, etc. to get involved in OL. Team ability highlights what organizations require from teams in respect to team members'

LACK OF ORGANIZATIONAL LEARNING | 219

evolutionary approach to their work. The existence of regular reflection on the team's work and purpose, along with modification of activities and goals to contribute to OL, permeates organizational and communication structures, management styles, leadership and remuneration systems, etc. It is not enough to adapt single aspects to enhance the learning flow. We leave these organizational prerequisites aside as that is beyond the scope of this book, and come back to what was discussed in Chapter 3: The team's possibility to learn is dependent on task (see Chapter 3). It depends on the level of standardization of the activities but also on the degree of specialization (Senaratne & Malewana, 2011). If there is a state of specialization (team members are experts on different tasks), there might be little to learn from others in the team. In standardized work the regular routine is the rule, and such work has a low learning potential. Further, we have shown in Chapters 4, 6 and 7 that differences in individual abilities and teams' internal processes impact team learning.

The creation of a "pro-social atmosphere" in teams supports openness and inter-action with other parts of the organization. This is an important precondition for organization-wide knowledge transfer and for creating an organization-wide energizing behaviour. This is in line with research (Dayaram & Fung, 2014) that showed the importance of external support to the team in reducing insecurity and defensiveness, and making it easier to discuss mistakes and other failures (Edmondson, 1999). A supportive work environment enables employees to believe that they will be fairly treated, and that admitting or calling attention to failure is less likely to be penalized.

In previous chapters we have stressed the importance of triggers for teams adaptation, and something must trigger an interest on the team level to connect to the organizational level and go beyond the stipulated work (Sessa, London, Pingor, Gullu, & Patel, 2011). One motivating trigger can be that team members understand what happens in the company and how their work is related to the overall goal (Hannes, Raes, Vangenechten, Heyvaert, & Dochy, 2013). Another trigger can be that through contact with other teams, functions and leaders, teams find ways to make their work easier (Mueller, 2014). Transformative leadership coupled with pressure on the team to shift goals and roles and look for new ways of interaction triggers learning as well (Sessa et al., 2011). If teams are confident that the organization is willing to absorb practices/knowledge from team learning, this is another trigger for a move towards OL (Hasson, Tafvelin, & von Thiele Schwarz, 2013). Depending on how well the organization is able to make use of the resource that teamwork can be (Barney, 1997), and how effective the team's learning processes are, the team can contribute to a greater or lesser degree to organizational development and change. Organizations need to provide an organizational context that enables teams to coordinate and sustain their organizational learning efforts towards other ongoing developmental processes (Anand, Ward, Tatikonda, & Schilling, 2009). Teams need the full picture of the workflow throughout the organization and what others are doing to bring about change.

> Intellectual capital, knowledge management, organizational learning and learning organization are four theoretical approaches very closely related but also very different in their focus on knowledge and practice. Intellectual capital is defined as representing the "stock" of knowledge (what has been learned in a cognitive sense) that exists in an organization at a particular point in time

> (Bontis, Crossan, & Hulland, 2002). Managing this stock of knowledge is the domain of knowledge management (Nonaka & Takeuchi, 1995). OL broadens this discussion to practice, to behaviours as well as learning, and provides some first steps to understand how the stocks are changed over time by human activities (Bontis et al., 2002). The learning organization approach is prescriptive/normative and describes an ideal form of an organization, while organizational learning is descriptive and explanatory (Tsang, 1997). The OL approach focuses on how collective learning processes unfold in a social system, while the LO approach gives recommendations about what kind of characteristics an organization should fulfil to ensure organizational learning takes place.
>
> Teams and other functions need to join around a common cause in order to exchange ideas and combine knowledge. If the organizational level frames the common cause, then team learning can develop into organizational learning (Barker Scott, 2011). The motive for organizational learning has to be embedded in team learning, and this starts with management's clear vision and message to employees why they should engage in OL. The rationale behind OL, what should be learned, why and how needs to be transparent and communicated.

1.3.1 The OL process should be transparent

Four factors are conducive to OL: environmental uncertainty, the criticality of error, members' professionalism and a committed leadership (Popper & Lipshitz, 1998). It is always the organization which is the reference point in organizational learning. The organization delivers the context and the modus for OL and how to make use of it for change and development. A precondition is a committed leadership and a clear strategy for how individuals and teams are to be engaged in OL to create value for customers and those who are dependent on the organization's services. The OL strategy describes how to establish and monitor the feed-forward flow of learning and the feedback loop. Contextual factors (i.e. supervisors' behaviour, colleagues' behaviour, operating procedures and task structures, and organizational principles and values) impact phases of the learning flow in different ways. These phases can be described as gaining experience, interpreting experience, analyzing experience and disseminating experience (Putz, Schilling, Kluge, & Stangenberg, 2013). The OL process must be understood by all employees and accepted. Organizational efforts to develop a learning-oriented culture through vision statements and top-management actions are not sufficient (Cannon & Edmondson, 2001). Employees need direction and support to understand the process of OL. Communicating strategy is a process of making sense. We give some recommendations for how to establish preconditions for OL:

- First the obvious – the strategy needs to be communicated and different functions and teams need to interpret it and understand what this strategy implies for their goals and activities.
- Cognitive and affective phenomena in the team which are important for team learning need to be recognized and monitored. Examples could be developing TMMs by establishing acceptance of mistakes, allowance of qualified questioning of specialists' proposals or psychological safety.

LACK OF ORGANIZATIONAL LEARNING | 221

- Phenomena important for learning, e.g. the value of experimentation and acceptance of errors during learning, should be an integrated part of how the organizational culture is presented and integrated in organizational principles and values.
- Contextual factors on different levels that impact different phases of the OL processes should be identified so that these can be developed and monitored. Not only the OL process needs to be transparent, but also what impacts the OL process should be known.

1.3.2 A balance between push and pull

Management styles can be classified according to whether they are built on a "push" or "pull" strategy (Denning, 2010; Hagel, Brown, & Davison, 2010). The choice of a "push" or "pull" strategy affects the transitions between individual, team and organizational learning (Renner, Prilla, Cress, & Kimmerle, 2016). From a team perspective this implies on the one hand that teams can push information to other teams and functions, to initiate iterative reflection sessions or the application of insights and solutions on a superior and finally organizational level (Edmondson & Harvey, 2017). On the other hand, the organizational level supports this flow by pulling the learning outcome from the teams upward. But if there is only a pull strategy, the responsibility to make use of the team-learning effort is shifted away from the teams to other parts of the organization. The team should be the owner of the team reflection outcomes; this moves learning towards the organizational level. But this flow needs to be supported by a strong pull from above. The balance between push and pull in management on different levels has an effect on how teams and other functions can contribute to OL. It is difficult to give recommendations on how to balance push and pull, but when forming the management strategy for enhancing OL it might be of use to consider:

- How can "learning highways" (e.g. a web-based platform with a reminder function/prompting), built on both push and pull mechanisms, from the team to other levels in the organization be created and sustained?
- Are teams supported and coached by team leaders and managers to communicate and feed-forward practices and knowledge (supporting push)?
- Are report systems and other steering instruments adapted to support the learning flow between team learning and organizational learning (support pull)?

1.3.3 Select teams for different learning flows

OL consists of different learning flows, and it is not to be understood as a process in which all teams in an organization are part of the same learning process. Different teams and functions can contribute to learning about something specific depending on task, role and the ability to learn what others can make use of (Senaratne & Malewana, 2011). Teams may learn many things, but what they learn might not always necessarily be of interest for organizational learning. Some teams learn little. The structure of the team seems to impact the team's contribution to OL. Project teams, development teams, virtual teams and communities of practice are some examples of teams with different structures, goals and dependencies which research has shown to be efficient in moving team learning to organizational learning. It seems that temporary team solutions are more likely to support OL through team learning than stable teams. This is tricky as the result may be due to the goal for these teams' work being just to change and develop.

All this implies that in a systematic OL process there is a selection of those teams that should be part of a learning process. That is not to say that learning is not of importance for all teams: We have shown its importance for carrying out work in a coordinated manner and adapting to new demands. Over time new topics and problems will usually arise so that most teams can be involved in OL. Further, new teams may be composed of team members from different teams and functions, or team members can work in both a temporary team composed to address a specific issue as well as in their regular team (see Chapter 4). The aspect of team ability highlights the question of what organizations require from teams, e.g. in respect to whether they have an evolutionary (changeable) approach to their own teamwork, whether they regularly reflect on the team's work and purpose, and whether they are used to modifying activities and goals to contribute to OL. The team's ability to be part of OL should be used for the selection of the right team for a specific learning flow. Another selection criterion is whether the outcome of the team's learning is essential for the goal of a specific learning process.

1.4 Organizational learning is not linear

Despite the importance of OL, the empirical research is scarce about the dynamic nature of collective learning processes across the three levels of OL, and how team learning contributes to organizational learning (Campbell & Armstrong, 2013; Matthews, MacCarthy, & Braziotis, 2017). In research there has been a greater interest in the concrete achievements of learning (stocks of knowledge) than in the flows of learning between the levels (Crossan, Maurer, & White, 2011). Especially the mechanisms (Wiewiora, Smidt, & Chang, 2019) that facilitate this flow (Swart & Harcup, 2012), and how the multi-levels of learning interact, are unclear (Doyle, Kelliher, & Harrington, 2016). In our extensive literature we found a longitudinal case study in an international bank which offers a process analysis of the learning flow (see Figure 9.1) (Berends & Lammers, 2010). It will be explained later, but first take a look at the learning flow in the figure.

Figure 9.1 shows the complexity of the learning flow with many discontinuities, where micro-processes of organizational learning are interrupted, delayed or do not progress from level to level. The rows in Figure 9.1 are the four together unfolding processes intuiting (individual level), interpreting, integrating (group level) and institutionalizing on the organizational level. The arrows (with the sun) refer to feed-forward and feedback flows. Lightning interrupted arrows are discontinuities in the learning flow. Arrows with clouds show that both continuity and discontinuity in the learning flow is possible, depending on the aspects in focus. It is a good example of how organizational learning is embedded in activities on the level of individuals, teams and the organization, along a longitudinal timeline, and that some learning flows are interrupted, delayed and stopped. Research shows that the flow does not go as smoothly as it is shown in the theoretical 4I model.

1.5 Balance between learning and task performance

In this chapter we advocate that OL is one strategy for organizations to adapt to changes in the external environment, to improve competitiveness as well as to create more meaningful and motivating work for employees. But there can be an imbalance between learning and exploration and the exploitation of existing knowledge and practices in the organization which affects the efficient use of team-learning outcomes (March, 1991).

	At the end of the episode the director decides for the development of KM. A team for writing a project proposal is selected.	Project priority group ascribes budget. Project management is appointed.	Director demands quick project execution, and discontinuation of KM strategic trajectory
Project-episode	**Project idea is born**	**Project preparations**	**Organizing the project**
Organizational level (Institutionalization)		Local institutionalization of some KM ideas; e.g. creation of communities of knowing within a department	Information technology is chosen as the dominant solution for KM in an IT company		Institutionalization of project management format and procedures		
(Interpretation)	Prior learning experiences from topics related to KM are considered to be of interest (e.g. about best practices)	No widely shared understanding of KM; only local integration	Selective integration of ideas in KM project proposal, focusing on knowledge infrastructure	No feed-forward	Development of an integrated project design, focused on five pilot projects		Delayed kick-off of KM pilots and KM infrastructure development trajectory
					Conflicting schedules between agenda of the project leader and project plan		
Group Level (Integration)	Perspectives of multiple organisational functions	Multiple interpretations of KM are shared in-between managers	Organizational and IT interpretation of writing team and senior management / HRM interpretations of the character of KM remains dominant		KM retreat with employees. Makes it possible to come forward with interpretations of assumptions and problems in five knowledge domains	Discussions in workshops about KM goal and strategy result in a common document 'KM – mapping the terrain'	No feed-forward (reasons not known)	It is decided that the document 'KM – mapping the terrain' is not valid and therefore cannot be used
Individuals Level (Intuition)	Staff manager for 'new developments of a knowledge infrastructure' and other organization members develop entrepreneurial intuitions related to KM and IT			Project manager and project leader learn about KM	Variety of previously uninvolved organizational members intuitions about KM problems and potential solutions		

→ feed back and feed forward flow

→ represent both continuity and discontinuity*

→ discontinuities in learning process or in feed forward and feedback flows

Example: Organizational learning processes in a longitudinal case study of an implementation of knowledge management (KM) in an international bank (3 learning episodes of 5)

*Organizational learning can be simultaneously continuous and discontinuous. It is continuous where any of its constituting processes or connecting flows proceed, and discontinuous where these are blocked.

Figure 9.1 An example of multilevel learning processes
Source: (adapted and developed after Berends & Lammers, 2010)

Exploration is the process of constantly gathering new experience by generating new practices, by searching and generating variation: a process combined with risk taking and experimentation to achieve flexibility and innovation. Exploitation is a process of narrowing, eliminating less satisfying solutions by refining, choosing alternatives and trying to make the best of a given situation. If an organization ventures too far down either route, it can end up in suboptimal forms of learning (e.g. the tendency of an organization to adopt known solutions, the tendency to adopt proven or deployed solutions, and the tendency to adopt solutions which are close to already known solutions). An organization that constantly explores cannot become excellent in task performance, and an organization that only repeats and does not experiment is not successful in innovation.

1.6 Critical incidents and turbulence – motives for OL

Collective learning processes can occur naturally without interventions or external support. Some teams seem eager and able to reflect, engage in new possibilities and implement improvements that serve organizational goals, whereas others do not (Edmondson, 2002). It is important to be aware that there might be a "right" time and occasion for creating interest in a team to bridge TL and OL. Critical incidents, e.g. an accident in the workplace or the unexpected death of a patient in a hospital, as well as turbulent times can be strong motives to prompt managerial actions to connect TL and OL and to embed OL in existing teams' team learning (Friedrich & Hiba, 2016).

> *To summarize*: In team-based organizations the core problem with bottom-up change is most often that the potential for team learning is not taken advantage of. What teams have learned either stays within the team, or team learning is not guided by organizational goals. OL is a bottom-up process (feed-forward) in which learning on the individual level feeds learning on the team level, resulting in new knowledge or practices that are shared with others within the organization and institutionalized as new routines and systems. In a later top-down feedback process, these impact teams and individuals. Not all developments on the team level are important for OL, and the distinction needs to be clear between those which are of internal use and those which are useful for others. The team needs an outward focus, something that triggers the team's learning, and this depends on whether the organization provides such prerequisites and whether there is a demand for the output of the team's learning. If the team takes part in OL, it can not only contribute to organizational change and development, but also in the long run enrich their own work, making it more meaningful and easier to carry out.

Before answering the question why team learning in itself does not contribute to OL, we present an authentic case.

2 Step 1. Describe the current situation

This authentic case is based on a research project in a world-leading construction equipment producer (Lantz Friedrich, Sjöberg, & Friedrich, 2016). The company was striving to work according to the principles of Lean Production Systems (LPS), and one such core principle is that "teamwork is a pillar for innovation." Teamwork should

LACK OF ORGANIZATIONAL LEARNING

result in learning that gives input to organizational learning (see also Netland & Aspelund, 2013). Working and learning in teams should result in continuous improvements to meet customer demands. This was the general idea, but the company struggled with how to put the idea into practice.

CASE: ORGANIZATIONAL LEARNING STRATEGY DOES NOT MAKE USE OF COMPANY-WIDE TEAMWORK

The whole manufacturing process of parts for construction vehicles (assembly, machining, painting, etc.) was team-based. Fifty teams with team leaders carried out the production work. Considerable effort was taken to develop teamwork. Biweekly continuous improvement meetings in teams, in-between teams and with service functions were the platforms for connecting different parts of the organization and for initiating a process of OL. This arrangement was meant to transition team learning into organizational learning. In Figure 9.2 the communication flow is shown.

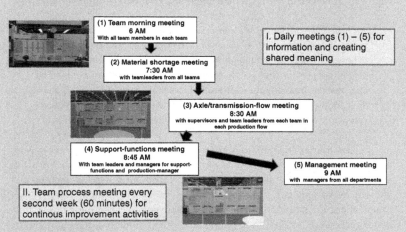

Figure 9.2 An example of OL – platforms for communication and cooperation in and between teams and support functions in a production system

The flow of communication started each morning with a series of meetings on the shop floor (see Figure 9.2). These meetings aimed at sharing information to coordinate the production process, but also to identify problems with e.g. quality, machinery, staffing or product design. Some of the problems were solved by the support functions, but others were handled by the teams during scheduled meetings later on. During a one-hour meeting every second week the teams identified and sometimes found solutions to problems, sometimes asked for cooperation with support functions to be more effective in problem-definition, cause analysis and finding solutions. This was how the process of continuous improvement was organized.

LACK OF ORGANIZATIONAL LEARNING

The production manager had initiated a structure for the developmental process involving different meetings between teams, support functions and flow managers. The idea was that these meetings should focus on production problems with an OL-potential as well as reporting production results. But team members could not transfer ("push") their knowledge and experiences about problems or information about what could be developed in the production process to other functions and departments. This was due to power imbalance, lack of resources (time and methods) and lack of interest from others. The flow of learning was not monitored or evaluated, e.g. how effectively problems were solved, or if support functions used the teams' knowledge and experiences about a reported problem in the production. The meeting arrangement was not motivating the teams to become more active in change and developmental activities and many learning opportunities were lost.

The production manager believed in teamwork and saw its potential for higher productivity, effectiveness and efficiency. She was not satisfied with what was achieved in terms of innovation and continuous improvements.

> We have invested lots in the communication flow, there is plenty of time for meetings, but not much comes out. The teams do not contribute much to how we could develop things, and all developmental activities are handled by support functions – and they don't expect anything else either. No one pushes the teams to contribute. Flow managers and team leaders are happy with productivity outcomes, and first-line managers think there is organizational learning. But subordinates have another perception.

To summarize the situation, representatives of other departments were discontented both with the results of the change and developmental process and with the process itself. Representatives from all functions, including IT and HR, were engaged in various parallel ongoing activities "to do something" about the situation, and this was discussed in many meetings. External experts were brought in to help analyze the situation and they made the following observations:

- Goals defined on the organizational level were not translated to goals on the team level.
- Management predominantly focused on measurable production outcomes.
- The expected direct output of team learning that should contribute to OL was not defined.
- Managers did not support the developing of a shared meaning between support and teams to define what the teams' contribution should be.
- Many team members did not understand why they should engage in tasks conventionally carried out by support functions when they were not getting paid for extra-role activities. (What is in it for us?)

- Responsibilities and roles within a team and between teams and support functions were fixed.
- Support functions prioritized what was important, and when and how to cooperate with teams.
- It was not transparent for the teams (nor anyone else) how the outcome of their learning (e.g. proposed solutions) was captured in organizational processes and by other experts in the organization.
- There was a mass of non-value-adding information (with regard to connecting team and organizational learning) and an inefficient information flow (bureaucratization, unfocused meetings, emphasis on reporting a wide range of measurements of results, report forms, etc.).

The problem-solving process starts with a description of the situation and a definition of the core problem. The list of symptoms helps to decide who the stakeholders are. Choosing stakeholders is not a "democratic" selection in order that every function should be represented in meetings, as in the case. Only those who are directly affected, those who have a direct influence on possible change, and those who are responsible and can make decisions are stakeholders. In this case, those who were involved in discussing and solving the problem often had little to do with it, which impeded the momentum and energy in the problem-solving process.

3 Step 2. Identify the core problem

Production goals were set according to goal-setting theory (Locke & Latham, 2002), and progress was measured in a wide range of dimensions (costs per team, per flow, per department, quality, failures, etc.). There were no goals related to organizational learning. The teams acted on the basis of "do your best." Despite the production manager's vision about and support of teamwork, the core problem in the organizational change and developmental process was that the teams' learning did not contribute to organizational learning.

4 Step 3. Cause analysis

After the presentation of theory for the connection of team learning and organizational learning, we now turn to the empirical evidence of what it takes to make team learning organizational. Due to the scarce empirical research in this area, we have searched for studies not only about teams but also other forms of groupings and loosely tied networks of common interest, such as communities of practice (CoP), virtual teams, project teams, development teams, etc. To summarize what aspects need to be identified for an effective connection of team learning and organizational learning, we conclude following Edmondson (2002):

It's important to identify what kind of modified knowledge/practice is necessary for the organizational level, it's important to identify the individuals and teams who

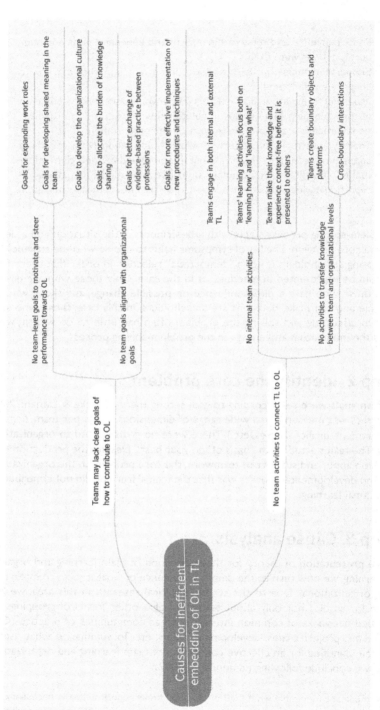

Figure 9.3 Mindmap about causes for inefficient embeddedness of OL in TL

LACK OF ORGANIZATIONAL LEARNING | 229

need the knowledge, it's important to identify the teams which are capable of team learning, it's important to identify the optimum chances for organizational learning, and it needs a process that seamlessly integrates with the way employees already work.

In Figure 9.3 a mindmap summarizes what empirical research has shown to be causes of the problem when team learning does not contribute to organizational learning.

The mindmap in Figure 9.3 shows two main predictors to the problem of the lack of OL: goals for the expected outcome of OL, and activities to embed knowledge created in the team into the organization. The mindmap in Figure 9.3 shows main features that explain why OL is not embedded into TL. First order branches show possible explanations to the problem; second and third order branches show sub-aspects that theory and empirical research tells are important for connecting team learning to OL. It can be used as a practical tool as it provides the reader with an overview of aspects that can be explored one by one to find out if these theoretical explanations cause such a problem in a specific work-place. In the following text we follow this rationale. At the end of this section we give advice in how such a diagnosis of the work design can be carried out.

4.1 Teams that do not contribute to OL may lack clear goals

Goal-setting theory (Locke & Latham, 2002) postulates that goals that are challenging, specific and realistic positively impact performance. It is important to note that goals are not necessarily result-based. Rather goals might blend both results and aspects that refer to changes in behaviour or specific aspects of job performance. As described earlier, the empirical support for goal-setting theory is convincing (Locke & Latham, 2002). It is no surprise that one important factor for understanding the poor bridging of OL and TL is the lack of goals that increase the team's non-routine performance and engagement in OL. We underline the importance of setting learning goals by elaborating on the case.

> **CASE: ORGANIZATIONAL LEARNING STRATEGY DOES NOT MAKE USE OF COMPANY-WIDE TEAMWORK CONT.**
>
> A number of goals for the manufacturing process as a whole were systematically followed up on a daily basis. A number of specific measurement criteria were used (e.g. customer claims, delivery in time, variable and fixed costs, sick leaves, etc.) to follow up goals (production costs, quality, work environment, etc.) for the different teams, production cells and manufacturing flows. There were no goals for team learning or for bridging team learning and organizational learning. What is asked for in a reporting system will indicate what is important. It is a signal that gives direction, and in this case, there are no signals that team-learning outcomes were expected.

Our review of empirical studies showed that those rarely specify the object of the knowledge flow on the team level. The interest has been to find solutions to support the flow of knowledge either by overcoming barriers, or by creating a momentum in developing by enhancing awareness of the value of team knowledge for the whole organization (Erkelens, Hooff, Huysman, & Vlaar, 2015). We describe what research has shown to be team goals that have enabled teams to contribute to OL, but the reader will see that these are examples of what such goals can be. The examples can inspire managers and teams to set identical, similar or other goals depending on the context.

4.1.1 No team-level goals to motivate and steer performance towards OL

> **CASE: ORGANIZATIONAL LEARNING STRATEGY DOES NOT MAKE USE OF COMPANY-WIDE TEAMWORK CONT.**
>
> In the described case-study it was very vague what the added value was for the team by engaging in organizational learning. A working hypothesis for trying to understand why the production manager didn't expect the unsatisfying situation is that both expanded work roles and the development of collective understanding (team mental model) about tasks at the boundary between support-functions and the team is nothing which is "self-propelled", and needs to be introduced and translated into goals at team level. In the mindmap, a distinction is made between goals on the team and the organizational level. We start with the team level.

4.1.1.1 Goals for expanding work roles

To set goals for expanding work roles, e.g. to encourage cross-functional collaboration, can be of value both for the individual and the team. Research within hospitals has shown that individuals' possibilities to improve work processes are often limited by a lack of perspective on the full set of work processes, and a lack of time and resources to implement change. If the organization has set goals with relevance for OL, such as expanded work roles, teams get a wider perspective and can overcome these restrictions (Tucker, Nembhard, & Edmondson, 2007). By carrying out non-routine tasks and expanding their task area, team members develop a broader interest in their work as it becomes more meaningful and motivating (See also job-crafting in Chapter 3).

> **CASE: ORGANIZATIONAL LEARNING STRATEGY DOES NOT MAKE USE OF COMPANY-WIDE TEAMWORK CONT.**
>
> The bi-weekly team meeting to discuss problems and identify change and developmental activities was an opportunity to enlarge work roles to go

beyond the stipulated tasks in the production. The report system, which predominantly targeted the daily production, task descriptions, reward structures and also career paths, did not motivate teams and team members to engage in these meetings or in expanding their roles to encompass external team learning through cooperation with close-to-production specialists. The organizational structure with a clear division between support functions and production teams undermined the possibilities for mutual exchange and teams partaking in the problem-solving process. There was no vision or goal, nor consensus among stakeholders of how teams and support functions should interact and what for. One such goal could have been to expand team members' work roles through blurring the roles between support and production.

4.1.1.2 Goals for developing shared meaning in the team

In Chapter 5 the concept of TMMs and the regulating function of knowledge structures were described. The TMMs are the foundation of how the team will contribute to OL. Interaction, learning and an outward focus enable teams to establish developed and advanced TMMs. To set goals for developing a shared meaning of both the stipulated work and how to embed OL in team learning will help the team to better understand their role and importance for the surrounding system. It can be the understanding of how to learn from mistakes, problems and conflicts in contrast to an implicit shared understanding that these should be ignored or covered up. Cannon and Edmondson (2001) studied 51 teams in a manufacturing company and showed that TMMs about how to respond e.g. to mistakes, problems and conflicts in an organization were shaped in the teams and these affected the organization's ability to learn from failure. The shaping of shared beliefs impacted behaviour more than e.g. persistent vision statements from the management about the teams being part of a learning organization and the importance of learning from mistakes.

The development and refining of existing TMMs can also impact implementation of new technology. A study within British hospitals of the implementation of electronic health record systems showed that the development of TMMs in teams was related to implementation success and boosted user engagement before implementation of the new technology (Takian, Sheikh, & Barber, 2014). The conclusion of studies of virtual teams was that the teams' creation of a shared meaning of what knowledge sharing is about and what it involves is conducive to knowledge sharing in the organization (Kauppila, Rajala, & Jyrämä, 2011). The point is that to develop a shared meaning is for many teams not an explicit goal, and to embed OL in team learning requires TMMs to be adjusted as these regulate the teams' performance in OL.

> *To summarize:* To set goals for developing and changing the team's work roles and goals for developing and refining existing TMMs to facilitate partaking in OL stimulates team interaction and motivation, and is essential if the team itself is to drive the feed-forward process of OL.

4.1.2 No team goals aligned with organizational goals

The expected outcome of OL for the organization can be used to set goals for teams, i.e. we take a top-down perspective to frame potential goals on the team level. A main cause of a lack of organizational change and development is the lack of goals, i.e. organizations do not know how to make use of OL and what should be strived for. When this is the case, goals for teams become vague and the process cannot be properly managed. We have identified four organizational outcomes of OL in empirical research. These can be the starting point for goal setting in organizations that wish to develop and become more adaptive through OL, but do not know what OL should result in. Again, there might be other outcomes of OL, but this is what empirical research has shown are concrete results of OL.

CASE: ORGANIZATIONAL LEARNING STRATEGY DOES NOT MAKE USE OF COMPANY-WIDE TEAMWORK CONT.

In the case it is meant that the team should contribute to better effectiveness of the production and to different kinds of developmental work but without indicating what the resulting outcome of this should be on the organisational level. A working hypothesis is that team learning is mainly handled very introvertedly (how can the team become better?) and the potential contributions to the organizational level have not come to use as this has not been conveyed as a goal to the team.

4.1.2.1 Goals for more effective implementation of new procedures and technique

Team learning explains long-time success in adoption and implementation of new medical procedures (Spânu & Băban, 2013). A study in hospital intensive-care units showed that project teams had the role of being an organizational change agent, and supported the successful implementation of new practices (Tucker et al., 2007). As described earlier, the development of TMMs about procedures prior to deployment contributed to the smooth implementation of an electronic health record system in hospitals (Takian et al., 2014).

4.1.2.2 Goals to develop the organizational culture

Company-wide shared beliefs are part of the organizational culture. Culture is the way we do things, and how to deal with errors and mistakes is one of many cultural aspects. In a study team interventions were used to enhance the team's process of building shared meaning of how to handle mistakes and failures (Cannon & Edmondson, 2001). The team's learning and development of TMMs (see Chapter 5) had later a positive influence on company-wide shared beliefs, e.g. about what consequences to expect when telling about errors, mistakes or problems. It can change the culture of error management to learn from errors instead of taking all efforts to avoid them. This is important as it supports experiential learning, taking charge and helping

LACK OF ORGANIZATIONAL LEARNING | 233

overcome employees' reluctance to deal with unusual or unexpected situations in which the aftermath might show that they took the wrong decision or actions.

4.1.2.3 Goals to allocate the burden of knowledge sharing

Team learning contributes to knowledge transfer and experimentation and recreation of knowledge in the overall organization (Dayaram & Fung, 2014) and to more knowledge sharing (Mueller, 2014). An important aspect of team learning is the enhancement of internal knowledge sharing across organizational borders and boundaries by the reallocation of the knowledge-sharing burden (Kauppila et al., 2011). What is meant is that if the knowledge transfer relies on single experts this eventually becomes a burden for them in an OL process. Imagine the number of meetings and encounters. If there is internal team learning, all individuals or at least several team members are able to contribute to others and they can all be involved in the transfer process. Distributing the burden of contributing to others' learning is supposed to increase the motivation to transfer knowledge.

4.1.2.4 Goals for better exchange of evidence-based practice between professions

The facilitation of professional development through the exchange of evidence-based practice between different professions in hospitals (nurses, medical doctors) can eliminate so-called practice silos. Differences in status and hierarchical position between professions can be barriers to networking and knowledge sharing, and especially so for low-status employees who might be reluctant to engage in collective learning behaviour (Spânu & Băban, 2013). To offer space and a network for knowledge sharing and developmental work creates value for the organization, and it increases employees' awareness of how their knowledge can be valuable in the whole organization (Dayaram & Fung, 2014). Research has shown that when health care professionals used social media and created virtual communities to share domain-specific knowledge this resulted in more effective cooperation, problem-solving and improvement of patient care (Rolls, Hansen, Jackson, & Elliott, 2016). As mentioned in Chapter 1, teamwork contributes to higher performance in health organizations by reducing errors and improving the quality of patient care (Woods & West, 2014).

> To summarize: Teams are motivated by goals, and goals steer behaviour. Explicit expected outcomes for both the team and for the organization are necessary to trigger the organizational learning process. The outcome on the team level is to be understood as a lever, and a resource, to achieving goals for the overall organization. Such team goals can be to expand work roles and build a new shared meaning of work. Although OL is defined as a knowledge flow between individual, group and organizational levels, research shows that the outcome of team learning at the team level is more about creating resources to be able to modify or expand knowledge in other parts of the organization than the stock of knowledge itself. Outcomes at the organizational level that can be goals for OL are for example a more effective process of implementation of new technology or procedures, changes in specific cultural aspects, allocating the burden of knowledge sharing and goals for sharing expertise between functions and groups of professionals.

4.2 No team activities to connect TL to OL?

> ### CASE: ORGANIZATIONAL LEARNING STRATEGY DOES NOT MAKE USE OF COMPANY-WIDE TEAMWORK CONT.
>
> Despite the massive flow of information from teams upwards in the organization in terms of reporting of daily production results, deviations and problems, this did not stimulate cooperation and cross-boundary activities between the team and other functions. The team leader represented the team in the meetings and so could learn more, but feedback loops back to the team were not part of the formalized communication and reporting system. The teams reported their observations of problems but were rarely involved in what happened next. There were no other activities in which experiences and knowledge from the team were pushed forward in the feed-forward process of OL. What was learned in the team that could be important for solving problems stayed in the team.

4.2.1 No internal team activities

> ### CASE: ORGANIZATIONAL LEARNING STRATEGY DOES NOT MAKE USE OF COMPANY-WIDE TEAMWORK CONT.
>
> In the case, team activities focused mostly on securing a smooth production process and, to some degree, to reflect continuous improvements. A working hypothesis for the insufficient connection to the team's work with the goals of the organization is that team members didn't have any platforms for external team learning (together with other people outside the team), and didn't know how to learn from others, as much as they didn't know how to dis-embed their own experiences, practice and knowledge from their context to make it usable for others. Teams do three things within the team to connect team learning and organizational learning. They might be doing more, but this is what research has so far identified as crucial activities.

4.2.1.1 Teams engage in both internal and external TL

Teams who are successful in connecting team learning and organizational learning learn in two ways. OL researchers refer to internal team-learning activities (see Chapters 5 and 7) and external team-learning activities such as learning how and what others do, or asking for information and feedback from stakeholders (Edmondson, 1999). Both internal and external team-learning activities mediate the relationship between individual learning and organizational learning (Dayaram & Fung, 2014; Mukherjee, Lapré, & Van Wassenhove, 1998). To allow teams to be a part of the OL-process it is not enough that they learn how to improve their own teamwork, they also need to be able to learn from others.

4.2.1.2 Teams learning activities focus both on "learning how" and "learning what"

In a study of external and internal learning processes within improvement project teams in hospitals two different types of learning activities were identified that were found to be crucial where OL was embedded in team learning (Tucker et al., 2007). Teams engaged in learning activities such as identifying current best practices and understanding the underlying concept. The latter is necessary when adopting a practice developed elsewhere in the team's practice in a different context. "Learning what" obviously depends on what the team's task is. The teams in the intensive-care unit distributed scientific articles, took part in conferences, made site visits to other hospitals and wrote pamphlets to describe potentially better practices. To "learn how" to carry out the new practices they created opportunity for staff feedback before implementation, ensured solicitation of ideas from staff, had educative sessions, performed dry runs, etc. The study showed that learning what (finding practices) and how to carry out practices in a psychologically safe climate enabled teams to connect team learning and organizational learning. "Learn-how helps to find ways to make new practices work in a specific context, and psychological safety makes willingness to engage in this disruptive process possible" (Tucker et al., 2007, p. 904f).

4.2.1.3 Teams make their knowledge and experience context-free before it is presented to others

In a team, knowledge is developed within a certain social and physical context (Johns, 2006). Teams who are successful in "pollinating" others with knowledge developed in the team are actively making preparations for the transfer to others (Erkelens et al., 2015). Dis-embedding knowledge from characteristics typical for the local context is one way to make this knowledge meaningful and actionable in a different context. It is a way to make it appealing and increase others' motivation to try it out.

4.2.2 No activities to transfer knowledge between team and organizational level

In the 4I model OL occurs as knowledge and practices developed in teams are forwarded in their original form and what was learned in the team, e.g. a best practice, is institutionalized on the organizational level as a new standard, routine or structure that later determines how something is done in the whole organization (Crossan et al., 1999). Others argue that organizational learning is instead about applying and using knowledge developed in the team in a different context (Erkelens et al., 2015). The key is then to support the learning flow by making use of the existing borders between the team and other teams and functions. Next we describe how the creation of boundary objects and boundary activities supports the learning flow (Impedovo & Manuti, 2016).

4.2.2.1 Teams create boundary objects and platforms

Teams create platforms or a communal space to meet others outside the team to un-bed and re-contextualise, adapt, recreate and transfer knowledge to other parts of the organization (Kauppila et al., 2011). Transferring knowledge and practice to others is a complex task, and it has been shown that teams create so-called boundary objects to make the knowledge sharing easier. Examples of boundary objects are repositories, standardized forms (Star & Griesemer, 1989), models and established processes (Wenger & Snyder, 2000). Recently technical solutions (like social media) have been introduced as possible platforms. A common technique mentioned is "lessons learned" (Carrillo, 2005; Schindler & Eppler, 2003). It can also be a document similar to a team charter describing how the exchange should take place, or a picture or description of the workflow throughout the organization, so all involved see how they in different ways are interdependent. Such a simple picture enables functions to visualize the transfer of knowledge in order to make the workflow more efficient. The point is that all parties need to find these objects helpful to support the flow between teams and others and use them as a complement to meetings and dialogue. Boundary objects are necessary to establish a learning transfer inside the teams to prepare for the step of moving the learning flow towards the organizational level. Knowledge/practice developed at team and/or individual level has to be "transferred" in a way so it is usable at the organizational level, and for this reason boundary objects are required. Teams need to take part in the development of tools and practice that are agreed and shared across team and organizational levels, and which satisfy the requirements of each of them (Benn, Edwards, & Angus-Leppan, 2013, p. 187).

4.2.2.2 Cross-boundary interactions

Moving learning from individual insight into embedded change in organizational practice or routines requires a process of transfer to qualitatively change what was learned by individuals and teams (Benn et al., 2013). We have stressed that OL is different from simply transferring what was learned in one unit to another. That can be done without learning from others, e.g. if a manager explains that a new routine has been put in place and should be followed. To de-contextualise, adapt and re-embed knowledge in a new context takes cross-boundary interactions. One example: Experts who work in a team in a multi-national company transfer knowledge about work practices to an expert team in a company in a different country, but the knowledge is not usable before it has been altered to suit this new context. The process to adapt the knowledge is critical for OL but in the literature is only vaguely described. There is very little empirical research about these cross-boundary interactions that bring about organizational change. The process is described in similar terms as for team learning (see Chapter 7 regarding interpreting, constructive conflicts, co-construction of meaning and reflection). It is plausible that cross-boundary learning is essentially comparable to the process of team learning. As long as it is clear which cross-boundary collaborations are necessary for the transfer process, cross-boundary activities can take many forms (Impedovo & Manuti, 2016). It can be encounters (e.g. visits, discussions) that provide exposure to a practice, or even intermediaries who have the role of transferring expertise. Widespread technical solutions such as "frequently asked questions/FAQ" can be used to transfer knowledge as well. For example: A team of engineers who develop products learns from users in the organization what problems they encounter.

> *To summarize*: There is only limited research about activities in teams to embed organizational learning into team learning. The distinctions between internal

and external team learning, and between learn-what and learn-how activities is a step in the right direction. It is also clear that teams need to prepare actively to take a step towards the organizational level of organizational learning. To use knowledge developed on the team level to change practices in different units in the organization requires a social process of negotiating and building shared meaning between teams and other functions. Teams can get feedback about how useful their way of working or their results are for others, and they can learn how to better contribute to others' learning. Some essential activities for OL are:

Within the team

- Internal and external learning processes
- Learning what and learning how
- Making knowledge and practices free of context

Between teams and other functions in the organization

- Creating platforms and boundary objects
- Cross-boundary interactions and collaborations

4.3 How to carry out a diagnosis of how a team contributes to OL

The third step in the problem-solving circle to solve a problem where there is a lack of down-up driven change and development is to diagnose the team's way of working with OL. Causes of why a team is disengaged might be found in input, processes and outputs in the IMOI model. An absence of secondary input (feedback) is also a possible cause (see the IMOI model in Chapter 1). As said, much of the OL research is not empirical, and hence few tools for diagnosis exist although the need for such has been discussed for many years now (Moilanen, 2005). As the team's contribution to OL depends on organizational structure and processes, the existing tools also diagnose or describe the organizational level. The most used tool for diagnosing problems with OL is the "Dimensions of Learning Organization Query." The DLOQ (Marsick, 2013) was developed in the '90s, and has been found valid for measuring organizational learning. It is a questionnaire measuring seven dimensions with different items answered on a scale of 1–6. The dimensions to describe the team's engagement in OL are the extent the team creates continuous learning opportunities and promotes inquiry and dialogue. Dimensions that describe the organization's support for OL are the extent of encouragement of collaboration and team learning, established systems to capture and share learning, empowering people toward a collective vision, connecting the organization to its environment and providing strategic leadership for learning.

The 4I model has been used as a framework for data collection, and these original research methods, "Strategic Learning Assessment Map" (SLAM), can be used to diagnose a team as well (Bontis et al., 2002). In Table 9.1 some items are shown. The questionnaire measures OL activities with five subscales that address individual learning, group or team learning, OL, feed-forward learning and feedback learning, and are in line with the IMOI model (Mainert, Niepel, Lans, & Greiff, 2018). The questions can be used as a guide both for reflection about the state of the art, as well as a diagnosis. Questions answered negatively indicate what target dimensions need to be developed.

LACK OF ORGANIZATIONAL LEARNING

Table 9.1 Questions for diagnosing the embeddedness of OL into TL (adapted from Bontis et al., 2002, p. 462)

Focus areas for the evaluation of team's contribution to OL	Questions to the team about the actual situation
Feed-forward learning flow: Has TL an influence on the organizational level? *Focus: whether and how individual learning feeds forward into team learning and learning at the organizational level*	Are lessons learned by one group actively shared with others? Do individuals/teams have an input into the organization's strategy? Are results from the team used to improve products, services and processes? Are recommendations by teams adopted by the organization? Are we "reinventing the wheel"? (reversed)
Feedback learning flow: Does the organizational level support TL? *Focus: whether and how the learning that is embedded in the organization (e.g. systems, structure, strategy) affects individual and group learning*	Do policies and procedures aid individual work? Are company goals communicated throughout the organization? Do company files and databases provide the information necessary for a team's work? Are team decisions supported by the organization?
Evaluate the potentials of the individual-level learning stocks. *Focus: analyze individual competence, capability and motivation to undertake the required tasks to embed OL into TL*	Are team members able to break out of traditional mindsets to see things in new and different ways? Do team members have a clear sense of direction in their work? Are team members aware of the critical issues that affect their work? Do team members create many new insights?
Evaluate the potentials of the group-level learning stocks. *Focus: analyze group dynamics and the development of shared understanding from the perspective of embedding OL in TL*	Do we have effective conflict resolution when working in teams? Are different points of view encouraged in teamwork? Are teams prepared to rethink decisions when presented with new information? Do we seek to understand everyone's point of view in meetings? Do teams have the right people involved in addressing the issues? Are the competent teams involved in addressing the issues?
Evaluate the potentials of the organizational-level learning stocks. *Focus: analyze the alignment between the non-human storehouses of learning, including systems, structure, strategy, procedures and culture, given the competitive environment*	Do we have a strategy that positions us well for the future? Does the organizational structure support the team's strategic direction? Can the organization's culture be characterized as innovative? Does the organizational structure allow the team to work effectively? Do our operational procedures allow us to work efficiently?

The use of the DLOQ and/or SLAM will help to identify in what areas the teams and the organization need to develop to enhance OL. Such data collection is only descriptive, and the analysis can only result in showing weaknesses and strengths in the specific workplace. We now turn to the difficult part: What solutions exist to solve a problem with organizational change and development due to a lack of OL? Research

LACK OF ORGANIZATIONAL LEARNING | 239

is scarce, and most of what is presented in the literature as solutions has not been tested for validity. We present what we have found.

5 Step 4. Select target dimensions and set goals

The target dimensions can be found on the individual, team and organizational level, and all three levels need to be addressed in a practical case. Why is that so? It becomes obvious when reviewing the literature on organizational learning (Leufvén, Vitrakoti, Bergström, Ashish, & Målqvist, 2015), and results from DLOQ and SLAM, that various dimensions (target areas, see Table 9.1) and domains need to be considered simultaneously and in an integrated manner. There is no benefit if a team is developed to engage in both internal and external learning, to create boundary objects, etc., if others in the organization are not actively interacting and seeking to learn from the team. Nothing will happen. It is the flow of learning that needs to be addressed. Depending on what the diagnosis indicates, target dimensions can be chosen and explicit goals can be set for how these should be developed. One example from a nursery school regarding the target dimension "external learning activities": Once a month each team should visit another team to see how they deal with a critical situation, and in their work adapt the procedure to their own team's context.

6 Step 5. Identify solutions

Systems theory conceives learning organizations as comprising interdependent building blocks at the individual, group, organizational and global levels. The idea is that the dimensions and propensities detected at various levels necessarily combine, interact and co-evolve to shape a learning organization. The main implication here is that the visible progress detected in one or more dimensions needs to be complemented with equal progress in other dimensions to foster a complete effective learning cycle and obtain the overall capabilities of an advanced learning system. The contribution here is to choose from solutions in the team domain, and we refer to the literature in Organizational Development (OD) of how the organizational domain can be addressed. Individual team members' dispositions and KSAs to develop and use their teamwork for more than the stipulated task have been discussed in Chapters 4 and 7. In Table 9.2 different domains for developing OL are shown.

Table 9.2 Domains for developing teamwork for OL

Choose domain for developing teamwork for OL			
Prerequisites in the physical environment for enhancing OL	**Prerequisites on organizational level for enhancing OL**	**Solutions on team level for enhancing OL**	**Prerequisites on individual level to enhance OL**
Not relevant	OL-focused management-style	Specify goals on team level for the contribution to OL	Enhance individual KSAs for embedding OL into TL
	Choose appropriate team for OL	Specify internal and external team-learning activities	
	Transparent learning flow		

LACK OF ORGANIZATIONAL LEARNING

Theories of organizational learning are typically weak at spelling out specific processes or actions that constitute the learning process (Engeström, 2009). Few interventions are described. It is not possible from existing accounts to describe exactly how a learning organization is created (Watkins & O'Neil, 2013). A view of the learning organization as an unattainable ideal (Garad & Gold, 2019) may discourage efforts to identify solutions that transform an organization's culture to promote learning and change, yet this is the work that needs to be undertaken. Organizations need to embrace the idea of identifying evidence-based practices that enable an organization to learn more effectively rather than relying on prescriptions or simple steps to become a learning organization.

The empirical research shows that there are three main causes for a problem when a team does not embed OL in team learning (or the opposite, three success factors): goals, activities and prerequisites (see 1.3) for the team to contribute to others.

6.1 Specify goals on the team level for their contribution to OL

Teams need to know with what and how they can contribute to others through developing their own work. OL requires some autonomy so that the team can develop their work and influence goals, and these goals need to be important if the team is to become engaged.

6.1.1 Set specific goals for the kind of practice and knowledge with which the team can contribute to OL

Earlier in the chapter we showed that teams successfully partaking in OL processes had goals for the kind of knowledge or practices with which they are able to contribute to others. Examples of such goals were efficient implementation of company-wide technical and organizational solutions (Takian et al., 2014); the development of a company-wide shared belief system to give guidance on how to cope with unexpected situations (Rolls et al., 2016); expansion of knowledge sharing by reducing the individual burden for this activity (Kauppila et al., 2011); and specific organizational outcomes, such as higher quality of patient care in hospitals (Rolls et al., 2016).

We give some recommendations about how to set goals for teams to contribute to OL. Most of the propositions are inspired by empirical research in companies where employees had to deal with turbulent situations (Friedrich & Hiba, 2016).

- Managers and team need to reflect upon and clarify how the outcomes on the organizational level depend on team learning (e.g., *teams and managers must know if teams have experience from and competence in managing extraordinary situations. It helps stakeholders outside the team to be assured that they, together with this team, without losing too much time, can handle turbulent situations*).
- Clarify what kind of knowledge on the organizational level can be developed through the team's learning (e.g., *managers have to explain that other stakeholders in the organization will learn that the team has developed a meta-competence which helps to distinguish very quickly between normal and extraordinary situations, and to act accordingly*).

LACK OF ORGANIZATIONAL LEARNING | 241

- Reflect upon and clarify what the outcome for team learning should be (*Managers and team members need to know, for example, that one possible result could be that a team learns to leave a prevalent action-path, so that the willingness to change behaviour and actions from normal to turbulent situations is increasing, and by this, qualified decisions can also be made in extraordinary situations*).
- Discuss and explain "what is in it for the team" by embedding OL into team learning (*e.g., can managers explain that the team in the framework of its own preconditions is able to be active in managing extraordinary situations, and by this they are not forced into a passive waiting position, to see if any action is going to develop (or not) in the organization*).
- Set goals for concrete learning outcomes on the team level. What should be learned? (*e.g., the manager can explain that the team should develop qualifications, so that the team members are able to communicate with each other in a way they develop a shared understanding to plan and decide together what kind of activities are necessary in a turbulent situation*).
- Motivate the team to see the potential that is created in OL for more meaningful work, a more developed shared meaning as the foundation for effective teamwork, meaningful relations and a social climate that supports learning (*e.g., the manager can explain, as the team has learned to handle unexpected situations, that this can, on one side, mean more difficult tasks to perform but on the other side a much more interesting job content and a better cohesion among team-members*).

CASE: ORGANIZATIONAL LEARNING STRATEGY DOES NOT MAKE USE OF COMPANY-WIDE TEAMWORK CONT.

In this case there were two main reasons why the teams had no specified learning goals. Support functions to the production teams did not see what team members could contribute to their work. Most team members did not see why they should perform tasks that they considered others were paid to carry out. "We have support functions to support us, don't we?" The company decided to implement a new lean-principle, so-called end-to-end alignment which meant that all functions that in some way contributed to or were dependent on a task or process should be involved in any related change and developmental activities or problem-solving.

6.1.2 Set goals referring to changes of the team mental models (TMMs)

The team's belief system or knowledge structure in terms of their shared meaning, the TMMs, and their understanding of team climate (see Chapter 5) regulate performance in all respects, including internal and external learning processes. Depending on the situation, a change in one or more of those cognitive patterns might be necessary to involve the team in OL and this means setting goals for how the mindset should be changed. Team-level interventions can be used to promote organizational outcomes by shaping *organization members' beliefs* (Cannon & Edmondson, 2001). In Chapters 5 and 7 some specific interventions to develop the shared meaning of work were described. In Chapter 8 it was shown how team leaders can influence a team's collective shared understanding of their work and objectives.

- Help team members to understand that in order for individual learning activities to form coherent collective action, individual learning has to be guided by the expected team output *(e.g. is it necessary to convey to the team that the preparedness to change between normal and turbulent situations has its base in the activities and competences of the team; individual interests of members of the team are subordinated).*
- Create understanding in the team for how OL is created by their process of embedding OL into team learning *(e.g. is it necessary to convey to the team members that they are in an interactive relation with the surrounding external environment. The own organisation should not be seen as a protection/safety net, but as a permeable and mediating unit to make it possible to manage external changes together).*

6.1.3 Think and act "organizationally" from the beginning

It is not unusual that OL is understood as a stepwise process in which first the individual learns, then the team and lastly the organization. But learning on the individual and team level cannot contribute to overall learning and change if it is not guided from the start by the organizational outcome. "The reference to the organization is the frame and reason/motive for the individual learning. The member of an organization learns so to say from the beginning organizational" (Schreyögg, 1999, p. 535). If there are no goals for OL from the beginning to guide a team's learning goals, it cannot be expected that internal and external learning will contribute to OL.

- Make sure from the beginning that a team's learning goals are related to OL
- Clarify how overall organizational goals guide the learning goals of the team
- Plan for how and when to communicate overall goals

CASE: ORGANIZATIONAL LEARNING STRATEGY DOES NOT MAKE USE OF COMPANY-WIDE TEAMWORK CONT.

The lack of a clear OL-strategy for change and development had several consequences. There was no monitoring of the process or analysis of causes as to why team learning did not result in OL. To compensate for a systematic process, different functions did initiate projects to make the production flow more efficient, and HR initiated projects for team development in areas they deemed important. All these many ongoing projects concerned work on the shop floor but a) were not aligned; b) were initiated and run top-down; c) as already said, did not make use of the teams' unique knowledge and experiences; and d) it was difficult to keep track of the many parallel ongoing projects. All this resulted in confusion and frustration about what should be prioritized in the teams as many experts put demands on activities at the same time, and there was a lack of motivation to transfer learning outcomes upwards and sideways to others.

LACK OF ORGANIZATIONAL LEARNING | 243

To design OL is to set goals both for results and learning. Our experience is that there are rarely understandable and concrete goals for learning. As a consequence, the learning process is not monitored, nor is it evaluated.

6.2 Specify internal and external team-learning activities

Some things need to be done if teams are to learn organizational. We show the relevance of specific activities by referring to the case.

> ### CASE: ORGANIZATIONAL LEARNING STRATEGY DOES NOT MAKE USE OF COMPANY-WIDE TEAMWORK CONT.
>
> The structure for the learning flow was meant to be organized through the various daily meetings between team leaders, managers and support functions (see Figure 9.2). Many other meetings took place also, e.g. team leaders, managers and support functions had internal meetings, as well as spontaneous meetings between e.g. support functions and managers. Different projects to enhance the production demanded various contacts and meetings between functions. A lot of activities were carried out, but these did not result in the team being engaged in the OL-process. The transfer of knowledge was not managed or monitored. The case illustrates that the activities need to be of a certain kind if the teams are to become motivated to contribute to others with their experience and knowledge. The top management had decided the form and activities for the OL process, but from that perspective the numerous meetings were not effective.

Next we describe some activities to stimulate the teams' motivation to engage in OL.

6.2.1 Teams need to engage in both internal and external team learning to contribute to OL

Internal team learning (divergent and convergent processes for sharing experiences and knowledge, interpreting and building a shared understanding in the team) and distal learning (learning from others) are interrelated. Distal learning activities can be inviting stakeholders to discuss a team's performance and performance outcomes, or study visits, etc. Managers need to support and help organize such activities. We give some advice on how internal and external learning can be supported.

- Provide team training to enhance team competencies in e.g. problem-solving and not only individual training programmes for individual KSAs. Collective learning in a team stems from interaction, and training programmes should increase the team's competence in making use of the learning potential in this interaction.
- Make use of team debriefing to detect important areas for learning.
- Use facilitation techniques to encourage all team members to express their ideas and take part in joint reflection.

- Establish a pro-social atmosphere in teams and throughout the organization. The work to change these cultural aspects may well start within teams.
- Teams and team members should be encouraged to communicate and challenge each other's notions within the team, and to reach out to others outside the team and ask for input and feedback.
- Ask for the team's conclusions about the input and feedback received from the outside.
- Shift focus on meetings from information exchange to reflection about work and outcomes.
- Plan activities for distal learning.
- The agenda for regular meetings can include "lessons learned."
- The result of activities for external and internal learning should be documented and discussed.

6.2.2 Develop learning activities so that teams learn from others what to do and how to do it

A critical factor for team learning is whether there are opportunities for the team to become familiar with new practices in other parts of the organization or externally. Most often activities are oriented towards learning what to do, and less on learning how to do it. Learn-how activities are important for organizational change as learn-how knowledge helps the team to modify practices to fit their own context. Learning how provides opportunities for experimenting with new practices and hence has a role in shaping organization-wide practices (Tucker et al., 2007). We give some general recommendations for how to combine learning what and learning how.

- Training and vocational development of teams could include instructional methods to teach teams and their team leaders ways to learn the "how" from others. That could be training in e.g. how to arrange encounters with stakeholders to receive and take care of their feedback; how to encourage and present innovative ideas; clarifying a team's role, responsibilities and learning potential in pilot projects.
- Training and vocational development of teams should include instructional methods to teach teams approaches to learn "what" from others. This can be to find learning experiences, e.g. the idea of distributing articles to staff, a team's participation in conferences or going for site visits to other workplaces. But it is equally important to help the team identify their learning needs, what they should learn so that e.g. on a visit to a different workplace the team knows what to look for and what questions to put.
- Possible choices for the combination of learning activities (what and how) during a team's lifecycle need to be transparent. Learning activities need to be labelled (e.g. by managers, HR, team leaders) as to whether they belong to the category of learn-what or of learn-how.

6.2.3 Create boundary objects to facilitate the learning flow

We give an example of how the abstract concept of boundary objects can be of help in developing OL.

LACK OF ORGANIZATIONAL LEARNING | 245

CASE: ORGANIZATIONAL LEARNING STRATEGY DOES NOT MAKE USE OF COMPANY-WIDE TEAMWORK CONT.

For most involved, the reason for the new lean-principle "end-to-end align-ment" to enhance OL was easy to understand. But how to put it into prac-tice? The team leader and representatives from all functions decided to create what in the OL literature would be called a boundary object. They met on several occasions around a whiteboard to map the different pro-cesses related to production. One process was for example logistics and another was material flow. The idea with this "boundary object" was to align the different functions by gaining insights into each other's problems and processes, and to become aware of potentials for knowledge and informa-tion exchange. These meetings sometimes became heated, as when during mapping-out processes questions about who was responsible for what needed to be discussed, and especially who was responsible for solving dif-ferent problems and when. Someone said, "We kick ball with the problem, we pass it to someone else to get rid of it." Should support functions be responsible for finding solutions, or did responsibility lie with the teams involved in the problem-solving process? The end result after long discus-sions was a consensus of what the "end-to-end" alignment implied in prac-tice. The different maps were visualized and discussed within the teams to increase motivation to be active in the OL process by seeing in what flows their experience and knowledge were useful. The simple mapping out of dif-ferent processes made management realize the importance of integration between teams and support functions in order to get efficient flows for both production and learning.

Here are some recommendations for how to help teams contribute to OL in their meeting with other parts of the organization:

- Elaborate in the team with regard to specific learning-transfer content what boundary objects would make the transfer process easier. E.g. when a practice was to be shared with others, would a video demonstration help? If a team of architects has a problem with the safety of a construction, and needs to transfer knowledge about safety issues to the construction firm, maybe a joint watching of a film showing how a fire develops might enable both parties to learn from one another.
- Reflect whether in the team the preferred objects are meaningful and of help for others in their context.
- Find out if the team and others concerned have a similar view on the usefulness of boundary objects.
- The development and implementation of chosen boundary objects may well be done in cross-functional cooperation to ensure that these will later be used.

6.2.4 Boundary activities to move team learning into OL

A linear and stable process in embedding organizational learning into team learning cannot be expected. Cross-functional learning is as complicated as team learning (see Chapter 7). So what can be done to make it easier?

- Managers need to help those involved to understand that difficulties in cross-functional cooperation, stops and breakdowns are normal in the process of change and developmental processes.
- Teams might need support to handle the "groan zone" when difficulties in cross-functional learning and cooperation occur.
- Those involved need to reflect on causes of problems in the cross-functional learning process and plan for activities to restart or sustain organizational learning after a breakdown in the flow.
- Teams need a transition phase to prepare for becoming engaged in OL. This involves building a shared meaning of issues of relevance such as how a practice or knowledge about something can be made usable for others by de-contextualizing it before sharing it. An example of this is to un-embed knowledge, beliefs and shared meaning from their local context, to be able to re-contextualize those in a new practice (e.g. in another team or another department).
- Create platforms for discussions and cross-functional learning to find out how a practice or knowledge can be made of use in a different context (re-contextualization).

> *To summarize:* There exist no empirically tested or validated interventions for developing organizational learning. We have derived what can be done from the normative literature and our own experience, and we have given some recommendations about what could be done. Certain prerequisites need to be put in place. Management should provide a clear and communicated strategy so organizational goals can be embedded in a team's learning. The team's learning pushes the flow of transfer of learning outwards and upwards in the organization, but demands on and expectations of outcomes of learning from above pull the flow and give extra momentum. Not all teams take part in all different flows of learning, and teams should be selected according to their ability to learn and transfer knowledge. Certain activities need to be carried out to enhance the learning flow. The team needs to set specific goals for the learning outcome and build an expanded shared meaning of work to let the organizational perspective guide internal and external learning processes. The team needs to adapt what others have learned to make it useful in its own context, and to do this the team needs to learn both what the others do and how they do it. Both what and how might need to be changed to fit the team's work. Cooperation and collective learning are facilitated by boundary objects that visualize, describe or collect experiences that can clarify why and how different teams and functions should learn from one another. No learning process is smooth and easy, and disturbances and frustration are more easily handled if the learning flow is facilitated and monitored.

Bibliography

Anand, G., Ward, P. T., Tatikonda, M. V., & Schilling, D. A. (2009). Dynamic capabilities through continuous improvement infrastructure. *Journal of Operations Management, 27*(6), 444–461. https://doi.org/10.1016/j.jom.2009.02.002

Barker Scott, B. (2011). *Organizational learning: A literature review.* Discussion Paper No. 2.

Barney, J. B. (1997). *Gaining and sustaining competitive advantage.* Reading, MA: Addison-Wesley.

Benn, S., Edwards, M., & Angus-Leppan, T. (2013). Organizational learning and the sustainability community of practice: The role of boundary objects. *Organization and Environment, 26*(2), 184–202. https://doi.org/10.1177/1086026613489559

Berends, H., & Lammers, I. (2010). Explaining discontinuity in organizational learning: A process analysis. *Organization Studies, 31*(8), 1045–1068. https://doi.org/10.1177/0170840610376140

Bontis, N., Crossan, M. M., & Hulland, J. (2002). Managing an organizational learning system by aligning stocks and flows. *Journal of Management Studies, 39*(4), 437–469. https://doi.org/10.1111/1467-6486.t01-1-00299

Campbell, T. T., & Armstrong, S. J. (2013). A longitudinal study of individual and organisational learning. *The Learning Organization, 20*(3), 240–258. https://doi.org/10.1108/09696471311328479

Cannon, M. D., & Edmondson, A. C. (2001). Confronting failure: Antecedents and consequences of shared beliefs about failure in organisational work groups. *Journal of Organisational Behaviour, 22*(2), 161–177. https://doi.org/10.1002/job.85

Carrillo, P. (2005). Lessons learned practices in the engineering, procurement and construction sector. *Engineering, Construction and Architectural Management, 12*(3), 236–250. https://doi.org/10.1108/09699980510600107

Crossan, M. M., Lane, H. W., & White, R. E. (1999). An organizational learning framework: From intuition to institution. *The Academy of Management Review, 24*(3), 522–537. https://doi.org/10.5465/amr.1999.2202135

Crossan, M. M., Maurer, C. C., & White, R. E. (2011). Reflections on the 2009 AMR Decade Award: Do we have a theory of organizational learning? *Academy of Management Review, 36*(3), 446–460. https://doi.org/10.5465/amr.2010.0544

Dayaram, K., & Fung, L. (2014). Organizational learning in the Philippines: How do team and individual learning contribute? *Asia Pacific Journal of Human Resources, 52*(4), 420–442. https://doi.org/http://dx.doi.org/10.1111/1744-7941.12039

Delarue, A., Van Hootegem, G., Procter, S., & Burridge, M. (2008). Teamworking and organizational performance: A review of survey-based research. *International Journal of Management Reviews, 10*(2), 127–148. https://doi.org/10.1111/j.1468-2370.2007.00227.x

Denning, S. (2010). Rethinking the organization: Leadership for game-changing innovation. *Strategy & Leadership, 38*(5), 13–19. https://doi.org/10.1108/10878571011072039

Doyle, L., Kelliher, F., & Harrington, D. (2016). How multi-levels of individual and team learning interact in a public healthcare organisation: A conceptual framework. *Action Learning: Research and Practice, 13*(1), 10–22. https://doi.org/10.1080/14767333.2015.1122574

Edmondson, A. C. (1999). Psychological safety and learning behavior in work teams. *Administrative Science Quarterly, 44*(2), 350–383. https://doi.org/10.2307/2666999

Edmondson, A. C. (2002). The local and variegated nature of learning in organizations: A group-level perspective. *Organization Science, 13*(2), 128–146. https://doi.org/10.1287/orsc.13.2.128.530

Edmondson, A. C., & Harvey, J.-F. (2017). Cross-boundary teaming for innovation: Integrating research on teams and knowledge in organizations. *Human Resource Management Review.* https://doi.org/https://doi.org/10.1016/j.hrmr.2017.03.002

Engeström, Y. (2009). Expansive learning: Toward an activivity-theoretical reconceptualization. Retrieved 2019 September 30 from http://pagi.wikidot.com/engestrom-expansive-learning

Erkelens, R., Hooff, B., Huysman, M., & Vlaar, P. (2015). Learning from locally embedded knowledge: Facilitating organizational learning in geographically dispersed settings. *Global Strategy Journal, 5*(2), 177–197. https://doi.org/10.1002/gsj.1092

Friedrich, P., & Hiba, J. C. (2016). Learning to cope with turbulent situations: A study of owner-managers in Argentine SMEs. In K. North & G. Varvakis (Eds.), *Competitive Strategies for small and medium enterprises increasing crisis resilience, agility and innovation in Turbulent Times* (pp. 153–180). Heidelberg: Springer International Publishing.

Garad, A., & Gold, J. (2019). The learning-driven organization: toward an integrative model for organizational learning. *Industrial and Commercial Training, 51*(6), 329–341. https://doi.org/10.1108/ICT-10-2018-0090

Hagel, J., Brown, J. S., & Davison, L. (2010). *The power of pull: How small moves, smartly made, can set big things in motion.* New York: Basic Books.

Hannes, K., Raes, E., Vangenechten, K., Heyvaert, M., & Dochy, F. (2013). Experiences from employees with team learning in a vocational learning or work setting: A systematic review of qualitative evidence. *Educational Research Review, 10*, 116–132. https://doi.org/10.1016/j.edurev.2013.10.002

Hasson, H., Tafvelin, S., & von Thiele Schwarz, U. (2013). Comparing employees and managers' perceptions of organizational learning, health, and work performance. *Advances in Developing Human Resources, 15*(2), 163–176. https://doi.org/http://dx.doi.org/10.1177/1523422313475996

Impedovo, M. A., & Manuti, A. (2016). Boundary objects as connectors between communities of practices in the organizational context. *Development and Learning in Organizations: An International Journal, 30*(2), 7–10. https://doi.org/10.1108/DLO-07-2015-0065

Jerez-Gomez, P., Cespedes-Lorente, J., & Valle-Cabrera, R. (2005). Organizational learning capability: A proposal of measurement. *Journal of Business Research, 58*(6), 715–725. https://doi.org/10.1016/j.jbusres.2003.11.002

Johns, G. (2006). The essential impact of context on organizational behavior. *The Academy of Management Review, 31*(2), 386–408. https://doi.org/10.2307/20159208

Jones, O., & Macpherson, A. (2006). Inter-organizational learning and strategic renewal in SMEs: Extending the 4I framework. *Long Range Planning, 39*(2), 155–175. https://doi.org/https://doi.org/10.1016/j.lrp.2005.02.012

Kauppila, O.-P., Rajala, R., & Jyrämä, A. (2011). Knowledge sharing through virtual teams across borders and boundaries. *Management Learning, 42*(4), 395–418. https://doi.org/10.1177/1350507610389685

Lantz Friedrich, A., Sjöberg, A., & Friedrich, P. (2016). Leaned teamwork fattens workplace innovation: The relationship between task complexity, team learning and team proactivity. *European Journal of Work and Organizational Psychology, 25*(4), 561–569. https://doi.org/10.1080/1359432X.2016.1183649

Leufvén, M., Vitrakoti, R., Bergström, A., Ashish, K. C., & Målqvist, M. (2015). Dimensions of Learning Organizations Questionnaire (DLOQ) in a low-resource health care setting in Nepal. *Health Research Policy and Systems, 13*, 6. https://doi.org/10.1186/1478-4505-13-6

Locke, E. A., & Latham, G. P. (2002). Building a practically useful theory of goal setting and task motivation: A 35-year odyssey. *American Psychologist, 57*(9), 705–717. https://doi.org/10.1037/0003-066X.57.9.705

Mainert, J., Niepel, C., Lans, T., & Greiff, S. (2018). How employees perceive organizational learning: Construct validation of the 25-item short form of the strategic learning assessment map (SF-SLAM). *Journal of Knowledge Management, 22*(1), 57–75. https://doi.org/10.1108/JKM-11-2016-0494

March, J. G. (1991). Exploration and exploitation in organizational learning. *Organization Science, 2*(1), 71–87. https://doi.org/10.1287/orsc.2.1.71

Marsick, V. J. (2013). The Dimensions of a Learning Organization Questionnaire (DLOQ) Introduction to the special issue examining DLOQ use over a decade. *Advances in Developing Human Resources, 15*(2), 127–132. https://doi.org/10.1177/15234223 13475984

Matthews, R. L., MacCarthy, B. L., & Braziotis, C. (2017). Organisational learning in SMEs: A process improvement perspective. *International Journal of Operations & Production Management, 37*(7), 970–1006. https://doi.org/10.1108/IJOPM-09-2015-0580

Moilanen, R. (2005). Diagnosing and measuring learning organizations. *The Learning Organization, 12*(1), 71–89. https://doi.org/10.1108/09696470510574278

Mueller, J. (2014). A specific knowledge culture: Cultural antecedents for knowledge sharing between project teams. *European Management Journal, 32*(2), 190–202. https://doi.org/ http://dx.doi.org/10.1016/j.emj.2013.05.006

Mukherjee, A. S., Lapré, M. A., & Van Wassenhove, L. N. (1998). Knowledge driven quality improvement. *Management Science, 44*(11-part-2), S35–S49. https://doi.org/10.1287/ mnsc.44.11.S35

Netland, T. H., & Aspelund, A. (2013). Company-specific production systems and competitive advantage: A resource-based view on the Volvo production system. *International Journal of Operations & Production Management, 33*(11/12), 1511–1531. https://doi.org/10.1108/ IJOPM-07-2010-0171

Nonaka, I., & Takeuchi, H. (1995). *The knowledge-creating company: How Japanese companies create the dynamics of innovation.* New York: Oxford University Press.

Popper, M., & Lipshitz, R. (1998). Organizational learning mechanisms: A structural and cultural approach to organizational learning. *Journal of Applied Behavioral Science, 34*(2), 161–179. https://doi.org/10.1177/0021886398342003

Putz, D., Schilling, J., Kluge, A., & Stangenberg, C. (2013). Measuring organizational learning from errors: Development and validation of an integrated model and questionnaire. *Management Learning, 44*(5), 511–536. https://doi.org/10.1177/1350507612444391

Renner, B., Prilla, M., Cress, U., & Kimmerle, J. (2016). Effects of prompting in reflective learning tools: Findings from experimental field, lab, and online studies. *Frontiers in Psychology, 7,* 820. https://doi.org/10.3389/fpsyg.2016.00820

Rolls, K., Hansen, M., Jackson, D., & Elliott, D. (2016). How health care professionals use social media to create virtual communities: An integrative review. *Journal of Medical Internet Research, 18*(6), 19. https://doi.org/10.2196/jmir.5312

Schilling, J., & Kluge, A. (2009). Barriers to organizational learning: An integration of theory and research. *International Journal of Management Reviews, 11*(3), 337–360. https://doi. org/10.1111/j.1468-2370.2008.00242.x

Schindler, M., & Eppler, M. J. (2003). Harvesting project knowledge: A review of project learning methods and success factors. *International Journal of Project Management, 21*(3), 219–228. https://doi.org/https://doi.org/10.1016/S0263-7863(02)00096-0

Schreyögg, G. (1999). *Organisation: Grundlagen moderner Organisationsgestaltung mit Fallstudien.* Wiesbaden: Gabler Verlag.

Senaratne, S., & Malewana, C. (2011). Linking individual, team and organizational learning in construction project team settings. *Architectural Engineering and Design Management, 7*(1), 50–63. https://doi.org/10.3763/aedm.2010.0133

Senge, P. M. (1990). *The fifth discipline: The art and practice of the learning organization.* New York: Doubleday/Currency.

Sessa, V. I., London, M., Pingor, C., Gullu, B., & Patel, J. (2011). Adaptive, generative, and transformative learning in project teams. *Team Performance Management: An International Journal, 17*(3/4), 146–167. https://doi.org/10.1108/13527591111143691

Spânu, F. D., & Băban, A. S. (2013). A review of empirical studies investigating antecedents and consequences of collective learning behaviors in hospitals. *Psihologia Resurselor Umane Revista Asociației de Psihologie Industrială Și Organizațională, 11*(1), 65–82.

Star, S. L., & Griesemer, J. R. (1989). Institutional ecology, "translations" and boundary objects: Amateurs and professionals in Berkeley's Museum of vertebrate zoology, 1907–39. *Social Studies of Science, 19*(3), 387–420. https://doi.org/10.1177/030631289019003001

Swart, J., & Harcup, J. (2012). "If I learn do we learn?": The link between executive coaching and organizational learning. *Management Learning, 44*(4), 337–354. https://doi.org/10.1177/1350507612447916

Takian, A., Sheikh, A., & Barber, N. (2014). Organizational learning in the implementation and adoption of national electronic health records: Case studies of two hospitals participating in the National Programme for Information Technology in England. *Health Informatics Journal, 20*(3), 199–212. https://doi.org/10.1177/1460458213493196

Tsang, E. W. K. (1997). Organizational learning and the learning organization: A dichotomy between descriptive and prescriptive research. *Human Relations, 50*(1), 73–89. https://doi.org/10.1177/001872679705000104

Tucker, A. L., Nembhard, I. M., & Edmondson, A. C. (2007). Implementing new practices: An empirical study of organizational learning in hospital intensive care units. *Management Science, 53*(6), 894–907. https://doi.org/10.1287/mnsc.1060.0692

Watkins, K. E., & O'Neil, J. (2013). The Dimensions of the Learning Organization Questionnaire (the DLOQ) a nontechnical manual. *Advances in Developing Human Resources, 15*(2), 133–147. https://doi.org/10.1177/1523422313475854

Wenger, E. C., & Snyder, W. M. (2000). Communities of practice: The organizational frontier. *Harvard Business Review, 78*(1), 139–145.

Wiewiora, A., Smidt, M., & Chang, A. (2019). The 'how' of multilevel learning dynamics: A systematic literature review exploring how mechanisms bridge learning between individuals, teams/projects and the organization. *European Management Review, 16*(1), 93–115. https://doi.org/10.1111/emre.12179

Woods, S. A., & West, M. A. (2014). *The psychology of work and organizations.* Andover, UK: South Western Cengage Learning.

Chapter 10

Requirement specification of systematic team interventions

Providing team interventions to the many team-based organizations is a lucrative market, but much of what is learned during different interventions is not transferred to daily work, nor does it increase performance outcomes. Evaluations often tell if the participants liked the intervention programme and found it engaging, but rarely how it affected team effectiveness in the long run. In line with Chapter 9, we underline the importance of a systematic approach to team development interventions by following the steps in the problem-solving circle. As we have seen in previous chapters, there is a variety of dimensions which can be targeted to develop team effectiveness and there are different types of interventions. In this chapter we go into depth and describe the elements of an intervention and what is known about the evidence of different interventions. Our main contribution is that we specify certain issues that need to be handled and decisions that need to be taken in each step in the problem-solving process. These can be used either as an essential part of the requirement specification of the intervention during acquisition of consulting services to develop teamwork, or as a guide for experts, consultants, HR, leaders and teams when solving problems with or enhancing teamwork. Our focus is on the final steps in the problem-solving circle, how to bring about change and how to make the intervention sustainable.

In this chapter we address a perhaps not very common yet essential problem with teamwork: Team development interventions (TDI) are ineffective due to a lack of ordering expertise and to poor quality. A team intervention is any action by professionals (or the team) designed to bring about change in a team. There is a jungle of tools and instructional methods for team-development interventions on the market: a jungle in which many consultants have become lost. We draw a map of this "jungle" to help the reader's orientation – from the starting point when something in the situation indicates that there is a need for change, to when the problem is solved. It can be used as:

- A requirement specification of what consultants and experts should deliver, i.e. a manual for the acquisition of a TDI
- A guideline for how to form and carry out TDIs

In the previous chapters we have followed the steps in the problem-solving circle (PSC) up to step 5 (identify solution), and ended by concluding that we can only give examples of how to solve the problem discussed as the causes of the problem, the needs and what should be achieved, etc. all depend on the context. We repeat: No two teams are alike. This leaves the reader somewhat empty-handed because if a practical problem exists, something needs to be done, and it is the final steps in the problem-solving circle that bring about change. We now focus on how to identify a solution (step 5), plan the intervention (step 6), implement (step 7), and evaluate the process and results (step 8). We solve the dilemma of "everything depends on the context" on the one hand and the need for advice on "how to do it" on the other by compiling a list of requirement specifications for a systematic TDI. We do so by specifying questions, and the answers to these questions will be a sound rationale for the TDI strategy, implementation and evaluation.

Why is this important? It is a problem if organizations lack competence in specifying what they need so that they can put demands on suppliers of services and evaluate different consultants' offers. Second, it is a problem if organizations spend resources on TDIs that do not work, if consultants sell products off the shelf, if some TDIs are built on good practice and research and many are not, and if there is a gap between the team's needs and many consultants' offers. There is a tendency to focus more on tools and instructional methods than on how the problem can be understood and explained, and scientifically derived, evidence-based TDIs are too often lumped with more haphazard "feel good" TDIs. Third, a strong and informed demand on consultants will in the long run raise the quality of TDIs on the market. This is relevant regardless of whether teams, managers and HR seek support from internal or external experts or work on their own.

1 What is team-development intervention?

1.1 Systematic team-development intervention and the problem-solving circle

Throughout the book we have advocated that solving problems with teamwork and supporting team performance should be done systematically in line with the problem-solving circle presented in Chapter 2. *Systematic team-development intervention = all the steps in the problem-solving circle.* Sound interventions begin with an analysis of the current situation and by identifying the needs for change, and there are several steps and much work to be done before it is time to find a solution and form a plan of how to solve the problem. TDI is "a systematic activity aimed at improving requisite team competencies, processes and overall effectiveness" (Lacerenza, Marlow, Tannenbaum, & Salas, 2018, p. 518). TDIs can serve a vital role in improving team effectiveness if they are designed and implemented using evidence-based practices and principles derived from research (Shuffler, Diazgranados, Maynard, & Salas, 2018). TDIs are solutions *based on solid theoretical notions about team performance and team effectiveness* to create an opportunity for learning, and to maintain and enhance team performance under different conditions. Much of the up-to-date literature on TDIs is influenced by Salas and Cannon-Bowers' (1997) early work in the '90s in which they described that TDIs have a specific content and are made up of tools for diagnosing, assessing and remediating team performance and (often, but not always) instructional methods for delivery that create the opportunity for learning.[1]

The description of TDIs as a combination of content, tools and instructional methods stems from team-training interventions. The content of e.g. a team-training intervention is to enhance knowledge, skills and attitudes. Within team training, different tools are used to enhance KSAs. Such tools can be team-task analyses to find out what tasks are performed and task demands; performance measurement to assess team members' level of competence and learning progress; and task simulation and feedback as a tool for remediating performance. Instructional methods can be grouped as information-based (e.g. lectures, computer-based instructions), demonstration-based (e.g. video, observing the required behaviour) or practice-based (one does something, e.g. role-play). While not all interventions, e.g. task design, need to include instructional methods, they may. One can e.g. present the results of a task analysis to team members to explain why the task design is to be changed.

The combination of content, tools and instructional methods yields different interventions. It is sometimes difficult to make clear distinctions between tools for remediating team performance and instructional methods for delivery as how the intervention is implemented depends on the delivery methods (e.g. is guided reflexivity a tool or a method?). One could argue that it is a tool that can be "delivered" in a lecture in which the value of reflexivity is taught, and it can be a practice in the form of a reflective discussion. We refrain from going into such details, as when reviewing the literature on TDIs often we could not sort out if authors were describing a tool, a method or a combination of tool and method.

Within each broad category of TDIs (e.g. team building) there are different interventions for how to implement change depending on the combination of content, tools and (for most) instructional methods. As we demonstrated earlier, different TDIs can be used for the same purpose and the same objective. For example team building, team debriefs and team training can all develop a shared meaning of work. TDIs can overlap, e.g. elements of team building can be part of team training and the reverse. Earlier it was stated that team training can be based on task analyses, i.e. including task analysis as a tool for diagnosis. But task analysis can also be an intervention in itself. The same tools and instructional methods can be used for different contents. E.g. monitoring performance or feedback can be a part of team training to develop coordination, and it can also be used for developing backup behaviour. In addition, TDI is not necessarily a single programme or intervention, but can be a combination of different TDIs to bring about sustainable change.

Interventions that involve team members should be founded on principles for creating conditions that foster engagement and learning. An example of such a principle is that there should be an acceptance of errors, as otherwise experiential learning is inhibited. The intervention needs to be guided by principles that help the trainee to understand, organize and assimilate the learning objective.

Systematic work is the key: "We start with our most important advice: Be systematic" (Salas & Cannon-Bowers, 2001). *We equate systematic TDIs with the problem-solving circle (PSC)*, and this is fully in line with how systematic TDIs are described in research (see tools for diagnosing and assessing team performance as well as remediating performance earlier). E.g. Salas and Cannon-Bowers (1997) argued that diagnosis is a critical part of team training; it is the basis for remediation, linking skill deficiencies to training objectives and strategies. In an intervention, different tools are used in different steps in the problem-solving circle. Tools for identifying the team's needs and assessing team performance are used in step 3 – cause analysis.

Although systematic TDIs are based on all the steps in the problem-solving circle, in the literature and in everyday language the term TDI often refers only to a certain solution to bring about change such as team training or team building. TDIs are described as the actions taken at team level to alter the performance trajectories of teams (Shuffler et al., 2018). What is meant is the solution to solve the problem, what is done to alter the performance trajectories and how it is done: the tools and instructional methods for remediation of teamwork and task work. The actions taken to implement change, the intervention, depend on the problem and what should be targeted, i.e. how-to-do and what-to-do cannot be separated.

1.2 TDI can be a primary or secondary type of intervention

A TDI is initiated to improve performance, to restore capacity or to help new teams to achieve a high performance as fast as possible. There are a number of reasons why teamwork development is important, and in the book, we have shown that one reason is to deal with problems such as:

- The motives for a team-based organization, the goals for team outcomes are unclear, and guidelines to the team on how to work and what to achieve are vague.
- The team structure is not optimal.
- Team processes are not optimal for carrying out routine work.
- There are misunderstandings and conflicts between team members.
- Team leadership is insufficiently supportive.
- The team is stagnant and has difficulty adapting to new situations and demands.
- The team does not contribute to the overall organization's learning and change.

TDI is then a secondary (reactive) intervention (see Chapter 2), but TDI can also be a pre-emptive primary intervention to minimize the risk of problems occurring or to support the team becoming even more effective. Comelli (2003) give some examples:

- A new team is composed or a team is restructured.
- Tools, instructional methods, guidelines, etc. are used to support teamwork.
- The team is striving to be the best.
- Team development is seen as essential for developing inter-team collaboration and organizational efficiency.

In the final chapter we will discuss TDI from a time perspective, and what TDIs might best serve the team in the long term.

1.3 What team-development intervention is not

TDI can be an effective means, but it depends on how it is done (Salas, 2015). The often lucrative nature of team-development consulting has also resulted in many popular activities that are not actually effective and *often not theoretically based*. The assumptions are often simplistic, sometimes false and do not consider the complexity of the context or that the team's situation may require a team-specific TDI strategy. TDI is not an off-the-shelf set of exercises that can be applied to any team situation (Salas & Cannon-Bowers, 1997). It is not simply an event in which team members or a group of individuals go to engage in *non-task-related* exercises and goals (e.g. rock climbing). Such exercises may have merit for other reasons – they might be fun or a break from daily work – but they are not consistent with the conceptualization of a TDI. In short: If something is called a TDI but consists of a method or a set of activities

SYSTEMATIC TEAM INTERVENTIONS | 255

that is said to be useful for any team, is not based on a needs analysis, is not systematically done through all the steps in the problem-solving circle, then it is not a TDI. This is important as only systematic TDIs work.

To summarize: Four elements are necessary for effective TDIs:

1 Content (cause analysis, diagnosing and assessing team performance by using different tools to identify target dimensions and objective)
2 Tools for *remediating* team performance
3 Instructional methods for delivery that create the opportunity for learning
4 An approach or mechanisms that should be used to facilitate the acquisition of the specified TDI objectives, i.e. conditions that foster engagement or learning

The TDIs we are discussing differ from off-the-shelf products on the market by being theory-based, systematically carried out by following all the steps in the problem-solving circle and by being customized to meet team needs within a specific context and situation. They can be used to solve problems, or as a means to support and develop teamwork as part of ongoing change and developmental activities.

2 Forming the TDI content through PSC steps 1–4: demand specification of what should be done

We first describe *the content* of TDIs by summarizing steps 1–4 in the PSC. These steps have been described in detail in previous chapters. We now come to the central issue in this chapter – how to choose a solution – the team interventions for remediation of team performance, to implement change and to solve a specific team's problem.

To describe the current situation from different perspectives (PSC step 1) is to identify what needs to be changed as a starting point for identifying the core problem (PSC step 2). The right fit between the problem, team characteristics, team context and the intervention is more important for the result than how the intervention is carried out (Buljac-Samardzic, Dekker-van Doorn, van Wijngaarden, & van Wijk, 2010). The intervention for remediating the team's performance, e.g. team training, and how the training is carried out can be excellent but if it does not address the team's needs, it is ineffective. A valid analysis of the "right" problem to be solved is probably the most important aspect in a systematic TDI. It is here the TDI can go astray.

To describe the current situation is also to investigate the organization's readiness for change, and if the required resources are in place (including a supportive organizational context; basic tangible resources such as staffing, space and time; as well as psychological resources in the form of an amicable climate, civility and mutual respect). Front-line leaders need to be on-board, and all involved should have the right expectations of what can be achieved. These preconditions provide a fertile ground for effective teamwork and can be seen as a baseline level of resources for team development (Miller, Kim, Silverman, & Bauer, 2018).

Step 3 in the PSC, based on theory about team development and effectiveness and a needs analysis, is to find out what is causing the problem. Before an intervention can be planned, a thorough theory-based *needs analysis* must be carried out to diagnose and assess the team's functioning in relevant aspects. In line with many others, we stress that the specific circumstances of a team should be diagnosed by using valid, theory-derived tools to measure team performance in relevant aspects of the problem. We have given examples of tools for assessing and describing target dimensions in previous chapters. The cause analysis uncovers the specific elements, the target dimensions that the TDI should focus on (step 4), e.g. the KSAs, mutual-performance monitoring and coordination mechanisms that should be enhanced if the team is to coordinate tasks more effectively.

We summarize the findings presented in previous chapters on causes of frequent problems with teamwork and integrate those in Buljac-Samardzic et al.'s (2010) summary of the literature in Figure 10.1. These can be seen as the possible causes of problems with teamwork, or aspects that can be enhanced to support teamwork, i.e. what should be assessed and diagnosed.

The IMOI model was described in Chapters 1 and 7, and we will come back to the second Input in Chapter 11. Figure 10.1 shows how inputs on different levels are interlinked, form the team's adaptability, and impact mediators (team processes and emergent states). Over time team processes become emergent states, and these will regulate future processes. As described in Chapter 7, action and transition phases are related. Inputs impact outputs on different levels through team processes and emergent states. The second Input is the lessons learned from a work cycle, and may trigger change and development (through team adaptation or interventions). All dimensions shown in Figure 10.1 are of importance for the long-term development of teams. Dimensions on team-level are the possible targets for TDIs (e.g. work design, team training, team composition, etc.). Tools for assessing and diagnosing core aspects of the team's performance are used to get information about what the team's needs for development are, i.e. the basis for selecting target dimensions (PSC step 4).

We have emphasized that dimensions closely related to the target dimension should be included in the TDI. *Diagnosis and assessment of individual and team proficiency in target dimensions precede remediation of performance.* The needs analysis uncovers the specific dimensions that the TDI should focus on. Some refer to these elements as attitudinal, behavioural and cognitive "competencies" and are defined by Cannon-Bowers, Tannenbaum, Salas, and Volpe (1995) as: 1) the requisite knowledge, principles and concepts underlying the team's effective task performance; 2) the repertoire of required skills and behaviours necessary to perform the team task effectively; and 3) the appropriate attitudes on the part of team members (about themselves and the team) that foster effective team performance (p. 336). *Depending on the needs analysis,* the TDI might develop attitudes such as team orientation, behaviour as coordination, backup, conflict resolution and cognition as shared mental models. The point is that the TDI should consider the fact that what people feel, think and do go together, and in interaction affect team performance. The cause analysis will tell which are most important, a choice has to be made, and goals for the development of target dimensions need to be set (PSC step 5). It is essential to ensure that stakeholders' expectations of team performance align with the goals of the TDI, and goals for the team need to be aligned with the organizational goal.

We have covered the content of the intervention under PSC steps 1–4 by identifying the needs for change and what should be changed by identifying target dimensions derived from theory and context. Goals need to be set for target dimensions (PSC 4), and these are the overall objectives of the TDI. The content of the TDI is now

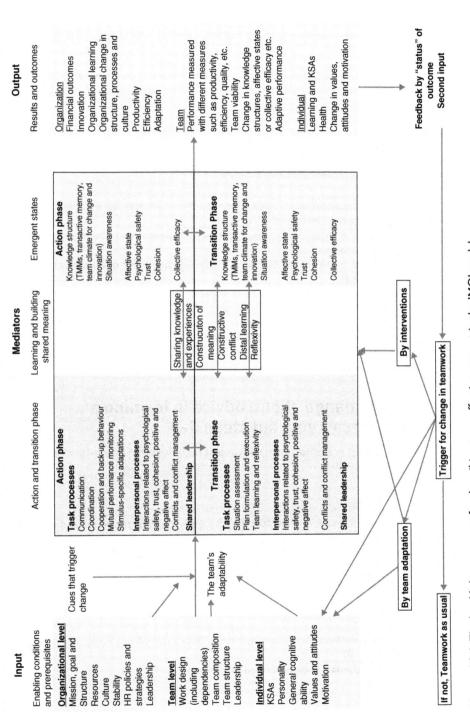

Figure 10.1 The book's key concepts for describing team effectiveness put in the IMOI model

set: what should be developed or changed and why, i.e. what kind of team intervention is needed?

> *To summarize:* Our recommendation is that the considerations and decisions in steps 1–4 are explicitly described and documented in a rationale for the TDI. *Without a rationale, the intervention is built on sand.*

The following points can be part of the requirement specification to consultants, experts and HR in the procurement of services or the rationale provided by those who deliver the TDI. Our bullet points for ensuring that the steps in the PSC are taken to determine content and objectives are:

- Is the current situation thoroughly described from different stakeholders' perspectives so that the needs analysis is valid?
- Is there consensus regarding the main problems/challenges and what needs to be developed and changed?
- Is the analysis of causes of the problems/challenges/needs for development solid and theory-based?
- Can the chosen target dimensions be changed?
- Is the assessment and diagnosis of the team's functioning and performance carried out thoroughly and *with valid tools*?
- What were the results of the needs analysis?
- Are the goals for how target dimensions should be changed made explicit and in line with goal-setting theory?

3 Bringing change about: advice in forming a rationale for carrying out steps 5–9

The team is embedded in a context, and this context might impact the team-development intervention.

3.1 Identify solutions in different domains

The next step is to identify in what domains change is needed to develop the target dimensions within the team domain (PSC step 5), i.e. if solutions are needed to implement change in the organization, the environment or within the individual domain as well as solutions for implementing change in the team. Theoretically there are four possible domains within an organization for the development of teams:

- Individual domain (not described in the book apart from how to compose teams, Chapter 4)
- Organizational domain (not described in the book, apart from leadership structure in Chapter 8)
- Environmental domain (not described in the book)
- Team domain

We have argued that although the focus for team development obviously is the team, changes might be needed within other domains in order to bring about sustainable

SYSTEMATIC TEAM INTERVENTIONS | 259

change. The reason is twofold: Aspects within different domains are interrelated and changes might be needed in other domains as these are prerequisites for a change in the team. E.g. a change in coordination might only be possible if the physical layout in the workplace is changed. An increase of learning processes might put demands on more complex tasks with greater autonomy, i.e. changes in work design and work organization.

If there are doubts about the organization's readiness for change, preconditions, support and resources for the TDI, these obviously need to be dealt with and would involve work on the organizational level. *Team members need to be motivated for, and engaged in, the TDI and the organization needs to provide opportunities in everyday work to do what will be learned during the intervention.* If the organization and managers do not support the TDI and its objectives, stakeholders are not committed and the signals to the team are unclear, team members will most likely find the TDI meaningless. The team needs to be prepared and know what the TDI is all about and recognize the needs for development. It is common sense that the organization needs to support team development, but research on TDIs has shown that it is rare to include means for change on the organizational level. For instance, a review of interventions in health care to improve team effectiveness showed that only eight out of 48 interventions were considered organizational, while 32 were considered team-training interventions and eight were implementation of tools or instruments that teams used independently and not part of a systematic TDI, e.g. checklists, goal sheets (Buljac-Samardzic et al., 2010). A meta-analysis of studies aimed at identifying whether teamworking is related to organizational effectiveness showed that teamworking had a small but significant relationship with organizational performance and staff attitudes. *Teamworking had a stronger relationship to performance outcomes when accompanied by complementary Human Resource Management measures* (Richter, Dawson, & West, 2011).

A conclusion is that an analysis of relevant aspects on environmental, organizational and individual levels is part of a systematic TDI and that solutions often need to be found for developing relevant aspects in these other domains.

3.2 Identify solutions for implementing change in the team

The next steps are about how to enact change and achieve the goals. Salas (2015) presents five pillars for effective team training, and these are equally valid for all TDIs:

1   Ensure the need for teamwork behaviours and TDIs
2   Create a positive, safe and non-critical climate for the intervention
3   Design the TDI for maximum accessibility, usability and learnability
4   Evaluate whether the TDI meets the practice needs
5   Create a system for sustaining teamwork behaviour in the organization

The first and most critical pillar is making sure that there is a need for teamwork and teamwork behaviour. We have devoted a full chapter to this topic (Chapter 3). We have described how a climate of trust and psychological safety affect learning processes (2) in Chapter 5. We now address (3): designing the tools in the TDI for remediating performance: At one point an initial decision needs to be taken on what kind of TDI is most suitable for the development of a specific team, and the second question will be how to design the chosen TDI (step 6). Later we come back to the remaining pillars, *how* to sustain what was achieved during the intervention (pillar 5) and *how* to carry out the intervention (PSC step 7). We will describe the remaining pillar, evaluation (step 8 in the PSC) at the end of this chapter.

What to do and how to do it are closely related. For a successful TDI it is necessary to decide about tools and, when relevant (as in most TDIs it is), the instructional methods for delivery of an intervention (Shuffler, DiazGranados, & Salas, 2011).

The TDI is dependent on what is likely to work well for a specific team in a specific context, but transferable criteria exist that can help choosing and designing the TDI for maximum accessibility, usability and learnability.

3.2.1 Describe the empirical evidence for the link between target dimension and tools for remediating team performance in target dimension

The first criterion for choosing a TDI strategy for solving the problem should be that there is empirical research showing a link between the TDI strategy and the target dimension.

In Table 10.1 we present a definition, the aim, the relevant target dimensions and the timing of different TDIs. The table summarizes what conventionally is meant by different TDIs (Shuffler et al., 2018), but this is not clear-cut. E.g. some prefer to use the term team training instead of team building. Within the team-training category, different team-training interventions are grouped. Some regard Team Task Analysis (TTA), Team Work Design (TWD) and Team Performance Monitoring (TPM) as essential tools to be used within other TDIs, e.g. TTA can be used as a tool to assess what KSAs are needed to form a Team Training intervention (TT). It is impossible to present a complete list of examples of strategies – there are thousands of them (different combinations of content, tools and instructional methods). *The point is that the table shows what should be described in a TDI strategy rationale.* Obviously, it is the provider of the TDI, the expert or consultant who should describe the empirical evidence of the link between target dimension and TDI strategy – not the organization that is seeking help. But the buyer would do well to put this as a requirement specification to the provider.

Table 10.1 shows the link between different TDIs and target dimensions in general terms. *The description of the intervention, its purpose, target dimensions and timing should be made explicit in any TDI rationale.*

3.2.1.1 What evidence exists that the chosen TDI strategy works?

In most cases there are several different TDIs that could be used to bring about change in the target dimensions (Weaver, Dy, & Rosen, 2014). Is there evidence that one kind of TDI is more successful than others? Evidence can be based both on empirical research and best practice. *The second criterion* for choosing a TDI should be evidence that it works.

3.2.1.1.1 What do we know about evidence regarding TDIs?

Before we show some results regarding evidence, we will discuss several important issues concerning what this evidence is worth.

Extensive resources have been devoted for several decades to developing TDIs, and a solid base of evidence of their usefulness is emerging. Within this research we rely on meta-analyses, systematic reviews of previous studies and reviews of best practice. Questions can be posed regarding 1) the overall effectiveness of

Table 16.1 A description of team interventions, aim, target dimensions and timing of interventions *(Continued)*

Intervention	Definition	Aim	Target dimensions (theoretical base)	Timing for use

Team Work Design (focus INPUT)	The specification and structuring of team tasks, goals and roles	→ To design meaningful and motivating tasks and a work design that is suitable for teamwork
		→ To connect task work and teamwork
			→ Goals
			→ Task characteristics
			  a motivational characteristics such as autonomy, significance, completeness, feedback from task, complexity, specialization and variation
			  b Social characteristics such as task interdependence and relations outside the team
			→ Roles
				→ Provide enabling conditions for teamwork at the beginning of the team's lifecycle
				→ A recurring process over the lifecycle of a team

Team Task Analysis (TTA) (focus INPUT) **TTA is part of Work Design**	An intervention to identify task demands on work behaviours, associated with KSAs	→ To identify KSAs associated with task demands for selection of team members and to identify training needs	→ Task demands such as complexity (demand on problem-solving and planning), task criticality, frequency and overall importance for team performance	→ Provide enabling conditions for teamwork at the beginning of the team's lifecycle → A recurring process over the lifecycle of a team
Team Composition (focus INPUT)	An intervention to select or remove individuals for a team, based on individual attributes relevant to task performance and teamwork	→ To enable the team to make use of team members' capabilities in an optimal way → Ensure that the team has the full complement of knowledge and skills to achieve the team's purpose	*Individual level* → Personality → KSAs → Attitudes and motivation → General cognitive ability *Team level* → Diversity → Team size (decision on organizational level) → Team structure and task (decision on organizational level)	→ Provide enabling conditions for effective teamwork at the beginning of a team's lifecycle → A recurring process over the lifecycle of a team
Team Charters (focus INPUT)	An intervention in which team members create an agreement focusing on clarifying team direction, goals, work processes, boundaries and mutual expectations on teamwork (often a document)	→ To develop a shared understanding of teamwork by eliminating misunderstandings and clarifying how the team should function	→ Mission and goals → Operating guidelines → Behavioural norms → Performance management processes → Shared leadership tasks	→ At the beginning of a team's lifecycle → A recurring process over the lifecycle of a team, such as after an evaluated performance cycle

(Continued)

Table 10.1 (Continued)

Intervention	Definition	Aim	Target dimensions (theoretical base)	Timing for use
Performance Monitoring & Assessment (focus PROCESS)	An intervention to assess the degree to which teams are achieving goals	→ To provide the team with periodic updates of their performance status → To support result-orientation → To provide information about if operating procedures are adequate and everything is running as expected → To ensure that procedures are followed correctly	Targets individual and team performance processes Evaluation depends on goals such as: → Organizational outcome (contribution to organizational learning, change and development, costs, etc.) → Team performance outcome → Team affective outcome (team viability – willingness to work together in the future, team satisfaction, team member trust) → Individual outcomes (learning, satisfaction, stress, etc.)	→ A recurring process
Team Debriefs/guided self-correction / reflective discussions (focus OUTCOME)	Interventions that encourage reflection and self-discovery. Teams are asked to reflect on a recent past event or performance cycle by asking a series of questions and discuss lessons learned.	→ To help the team identify opportunities for improvement → To develop the heuristics (the way of solving problems by finding solutions) to be used in the task and teamwork → Change of knowledge structures (such as TMMs) → Reduce decision time	→ Team knowledge structures → Team affective emergent states → Individual values, attitudes, motivation and KSAs	→ Can be a recurring process → After a critical period of performance and when development is most needed
Team Building (Focus: MULTIFACETED*)	An intervention to enhance social relations and define roles within teams by promoting goal setting, providing interpersonal relationship management, role clarification, and improving problem-solving techniques	→ To improve interpersonal relations and affective climate → Clarifying procedures, work roles and goals to enhance performance and results	→ Goal setting: setting objectives for individual and team goals → Interpersonal goals: increasing teamwork processes and forming an amicable team climate → Role clarification: increasing communication about work roles → Problem-solving: encouraging team members to participate in problem-solving tasks and enhance problem-solving skills	→ Can be a recurring process → After a critical period of performance and when development is most needed → Conflict management

Intervention	Definition	Aims	Target dimensions	Timing
Team Training (TT) (focus: MULTIFACETED)	An intervention to train all sorts of KSAs and develop team members' understanding of team relevant knowledge, skills and attitudes necessary for effective individual task work and teamwork	→ To train team members so that they obtain the required KSAs for individual task work and teamwork → To develop shared understanding of the overall function of each team member's roll/duties → To improve knowledge structure → To improve coordination and adaptation	→ KSAs to perform teamwork → KSAs to perform individual tasks → Team regulation processes (i.e. coordination mechanisms and communication)	→ At the beginning of a team's lifecycle → When training programmes have the strongest impact on team's development over time
Team Coaching (focus: MULTIFACETED)	An intervention in which a helping relationship between a coach and a team is established	→ The direct interaction between coach and team is intended to enable members to make coordinated and task-appropriate use of their collective resources and enhance effectiveness → Enhance reflexivity → To support teams to implement skills developed in other interventions and make use of lessons learned	The target dimensions depend on the team's needs and goals. Target dimensions can be e.g.: – Team self-management – Shared leadership – Team regulation – Cognitive processes and emergent states – Affective processes and emergent states – Behavioural processes	→ Can be a recurring process → After a critical period of performance and when development is most needed → Conflict management → After a training programme to ensure transfer of knowledge to daily work
Team Leadership training (focus: MULTIFACETED)	Interventions to enhance leader's effectiveness Interventions to enhance shared leadership	→ Strengthen focus on team needs → Training leaders to fulfil those needs by using an effective leadership style and engaging in particular behaviours to fulfil team needs → Establishing an adequate team structure → Prepare team members to share leadership responsibilities and tasks	The target dimensions depend on team needs and goals in action and transition phase. Target dimensions can be: – Leadership tasks – Leader behaviour – Leadership style – Role clarification and leadership task allocation within the team and between team and team leader	→ At the beginning of a team's lifecycle → When a team leader is recruited → Can be a recurring process → After a critical period of performance and when development is most needed

*Multifaceted: Intervention addresses factors from more than one IMOI dimension.

team development interventions, 2) intra-organizational validity (i.e. would the TDI achieve similar, better or worse outcomes in other units in the same organization?), and 3) inter-organizational validity (i.e. would similar, better or worse outcomes be achieved using the TDI in other organizations?). Answering these questions requires an advanced research design and, as we will see, there are limitations in the research that meta-analyses and reviews build on.

It sounds impressive when results from meta-analyses are presented, but one should keep in mind that the evidence depends on how many studies were included in the study (e.g. meta-analyses on the effect of team debriefs are based on only a few studies) and the quality of the studies included. If the meta-analyses or reviews are built on studies with a weak design and methodology, this will affect the validity of the conclusions.

A number of guidelines have been developed for assessing the level of empirical evidence, i.e. quality of a study. One example is the "Grading of Recommendations Assessment, Development and Evaluation scale (GRADE)." The GRADE system gives a general rating of the level of evidence. The GRADE rating scale has four levels of quality of evidence: (A) high, (B) moderate, (C) low and (D) very low (Guyatt et al., 2008).

This grading system has been used to evaluate the studies behind conclusions on TDI effectiveness. The majority of studies on TDI effectiveness had a low quality of evidence (C). The studies most often have a design with a pre- and post-measurement of target dimensions, no control group, data that were collected with one method only and often subjective ratings such as questionnaires, and such a design does not make causal inferences possible. Relatively little statistical evidence directly related to the effectiveness of the interventions was found (Buljac-Samardzic et al., 2010). Within the research community there is growing consensus that the strong pressure to publish, plus the tendency to publish mainly positive results, impact what is known about the state of the art. We rarely read about studies that show what was done did not have any impact on team effectiveness, and the chosen research designs rarely make it possible to draw conclusions on intra- or inter-organizational validity.

Another common problem for many evaluations of TDIs is that they address mostly the outcome (team-performance effectiveness and other outcomes) but rarely measure what changed in the team processes and emergent states (Shuffler et al., 2018). We often know that something worked, but we do not know *why* it worked. One example: Meta-analytic findings (based on few studies) have shown that team debriefs increase team-performance outcomes. But during a debrief, teams discuss many things and reflect upon prior experiences. What was it in the team debrief that brought change about? An issue related to this is that in many studies it is difficult to tell what specific target dimension(s) the TDI addressed, and if different interrelated dimensions were included.

Some interventions grouped as team building and team training have been developed over decades, and much more is known about the effectiveness of these than of interventions such as team debriefs and team coaching. It seems as if team training has become more popular, and team building less so, and maybe that is because in the early years many team-building strategies included team training, and nowadays the distinction is clearer.

Further, as we have described, sometimes task analysis is used as a tool for diagnosing. In other instances team-performance monitoring is used as a tool for monitoring the implementation, and is part of team building and team training. When several TDIs are part of an intervention then it's difficult to know what causes the result.

There are also some concerns regarding specific TDIs such as team-leadership interventions and coaching. It is often difficult to tell whether the intervention is about leadership in general or team leadership in which coaching is part of leadership.

All TDIs need to be adapted to a specific team's needs and context to be successful, and a meta-analysis cannot tell how well this was done.

Keeping in mind the limitations described, we turn to what is known from empirical research about the effectiveness of TDIs.

3.2.1.2 What is known from research on TDIs' effectiveness?

The ultimate goal of TDIs is to contribute to beneficial changes for the business/ organization and most meta-analyses of evidence for different TDIs are inspired by Kirkpatrick's (1996) evaluation criteria (reaction, learning, transfer and results). Meta-analytic findings suggest that TDIs *can* improve team effectiveness across proximal outcomes, e.g. *learning* (impact on participants' knowledge, self-efficacy and attitudes) and *transfer* to the workplace (performance as changes in behaviour, affective processes or emergent states). Distal outcomes as *results* are found on the organizational level, e.g. patient safety, reduction in patient deaths and quality indicators such as reduced length of patient stay, or cost savings within health care (e.g. Hughes et al., 2016; Salas, Nichols, & Driskell, 2007). Interventions (i.e. those in which team members are partaking) will also cause a *reaction*, e.g. the team members liked or found the intervention engaging and useful. Reactions can impact outcomes as participants with a positive reaction are more likely to retain what they have learned and use it at work. We first discuss what is known about the impact of TDIs on different levels. The second issue is then what is known about the evidence of the impact of different TDIs on target dimensions.

Since teamwork and coordination of work are essential in health care and hospital settings, many studies have been conducted within this context. Most studies are based on team training, but also team building has been evaluated.

A meta-analysis (mainly on team training studies) showed that most interventions could report improvements in proximal outcomes such as development of teamwork skills, but only a few studies reported effects on team performance or team leadership. Some studies reported improvements of outcomes on the organizational level (e.g. staff retention, reduced absence, decreasing turnover time and length of patient stay in hospital care). It is noteworthy that the majority of studies reported effects on the team level, some also on the individual level and only about 10% on the organizational level. There was only one study reporting changes on all three levels (Buljac-Samardzic et al., 2010). Other meta-analytic studies come to similar results. E.g. a study of team training in health care showed that out of 26 studies studying effects *on one or several* levels, ten (out of ten) reported positive findings in reactions, five (out of seven) studies found significant changes in learning, and 12 (out of 16) significant changes in performance and ten (out of 13) on an organizational level (Weaver et al., 2014). The field is developing, and a recent meta-analysis of 129 studies of health care team training synthesized the evidence of health care team training *using all four criteria*. The results showed that team training in health care has an impact on all the earlier-mentioned criteria, further the analyses showed that with a sequential model of team training where training affects the results via learning, this leads to transfer which increases results (Hughes et al., 2016). Several meta-analyses and a review conclude that there are effects of team training (mainly studies in health care) on learning, team performance and organizational outcomes (Buljac-Samardzic et al., 2010; Cunningham, Ward, De Brún, & McAuliffe, 2018; Körner et al., 2015; McEwan, Ruissen, Eys, Zumbo, & Beauchamp, 2017; Weaver et al., 2014). Different meta-analyses differ regarding the effect sizes, but most show low to medium-sized effects.

A meta-analysis of studies on team-building interventions showed less convincing results, and only a few studies considered outcomes on the organizational level. In general participants' reactions were positive, but only one out of 25 studies showed a significant increase in learning, and the results were mixed regarding transfer to work, i.e. changes in team performance and functioning (Miller et al., 2018).

To draw conclusions on the effects of TDIs is complicated as different TDI strategies within one group of TDIs (e.g. team training) focus on different problems and heterogeneous dimensions are targeted. Studies measured different outcomes, and the target dimensions to be changed by the interventions were not comparable or not clearly defined: all of which makes it difficult to compare the findings and synthesize the results of different studies. Most studies have been conducted within health care. Several authors raise concerns regarding the quality of evidence, that negative results are not reported and very few studies include a control condition (discussed earlier). Most studies presented results with a low level of evidence (Buljac-Samardzic et al., 2010). Studies measuring the result of the intervention on all four levels (reaction, learning, transfer to workplace and outcome on organizational level) are rare, and many do not consider if the intervention resulted in changes in team performance at work, and also outcomes on the organizational level. Further, we know little about whether TDIs other than team training result in changes on all four levels. Whereas all this is based on scientific studies, consider the results of the many interventions that are carried out without proper evaluation of the results. In our experience most evaluations are based on little more than participants' reactions: Did they like it and find it engaging? Yes, in many cases. But did it change anything? Later in this chapter we will give some advice on how to form the intervention so that it is worth investing in.

3.2.1.3 Do different TDIs bring about change?

We now discuss what is known about whether different TDIs bring about change without considering if they affect all four levels, and we include all TDIs although we have not found meta-analytic studies of all.

Team Task Analysis (TTA) is a TDI that often is the starting point for other TDIs, and we have not found any studies examining the effect of a TTA as an intervention on team effectiveness. This does not mean that the task does not impact team performance – here it is the intervention that is of interest.

Team Work Design (TWD) as an intervention has not been investigated regarding its impact on team effectiveness (Shuffler et al., 2018). Again, TWD impacts team performance and outcomes, but we do not know about the results of a TWD intervention.

Team Charters (TC) quality has been investigated, but the research on the impact of team charters is very limited. Some found no relation between team-charter quality and team performance over time (Mathieu & Rapp, 2009), but more recent research has shown a small significant relation between team conscientiousness and team-charter quality (Courtright, McCormick, Mistry, & Wang, 2017). The study implies that teams low on conscientiousness, i.e. those which would benefit the most from a good charter, also have difficulties in creating them.

Team Performance Monitoring & Assessment (TTM) is, as mentioned earlier, often used as a tool in e.g. team training and TTM can also be used to develop more specialized and customized team training (Kash, Cheon, Halzack, & Miller, 2018). Little is known about its impact on team performance or effectiveness as a TDI in its own right. Perhaps the literature in the domain of performance management in general could shed light on the subject.

Team debriefs (TD) have been used as a TDI for some decades. Although not many studies exist, there is growing evidence that TDs impact team performance (Tannenbaum & Cerasoli, 2013) and result in safer care within health care settings.

Team Building (TB) has been used for many years, and while meta-analyses have shown that TB has a positive effect on cognitive, affective and behavioural processes and emergent states, no significant effects have been demonstrated on team-performance outcomes. Goal setting and role clarification have been shown to be the most effective parts of TB (Klein et al., 2009; Lacerenza, Reyes, Marlow, Joseph, & Salas, 2017). One could argue in line with Hughes et al. (2016) that learning should result in results, but for TB no such evidence so far exists.

Team Training (TT) is the TDI about which most is known. It is safe to draw the conclusion that it is a well-evidenced TDI, and that it improves learning, transfer and results (Rosen et al., 2018; Salas, Cooke, & Rosen, 2008; Shuffler et al., 2018). Notice that TTA, TWD, TTM are often part of a systematic TT, and as described earlier a bundled approach may produce the greatest impact.

Team Coaching (TC) is one of the TDIs that little is known about when it comes to the evaluation of its impact on team effectiveness. A recent meta-analyses could not find any scientific evaluations (Shuffler et al., 2018) and nor could we.

Team Leadership (TL) as a TDI to enhance team leadership has been investigated in many studies, often as part of a broader TDI. A meta-analysis of as many as 335 evaluation studies of TL provided substantial evidence that TL is effective and impacts not only leader learning, transfer to leadership behaviour performed on the job, and overall leader performance but also increases subordinates' and organizational outcomes (Lacerenza et al., 2017).

Throughout the book we have given examples of different TDI strategies and we have given support of the evidence by sometimes referring to single studies. We hope we have clarified that earlier we were discussing what is known about the evidence of the impact of different TDIs on team effectiveness rather than whether the target dimensions that they address affect team performance and team-performance outcomes. This is a different matter but could of course impact the results indirectly. Maybe leadership is more important for performance than rules for code of conduct and how to carry out the work (targeted e.g. in team charters), and that is maybe also why an increase of good leadership impacts more on performance outcomes than a high-quality charter. But that is a different story.

3.2.2 Is the good-practice approach an alternative or complementary to relying on research?

One approach for choosing interventions is that meta-analyses have shown that they work. Another way could be to rely on best practices in a specific context. A good practice (e.g. a process, a routine or a method) is a solution that has generally been accepted as superior to other alternatives, or it is a standard way of doing things. Most often good practices have not been validated by strict scientific criteria, but have worked well according to experts or those involved. Best-practice reports from e.g. health care indicate that TDIs have positive effects on different parts in the IMOI-model (Körner et al., 2015). The advantage with the best-practice approach is that the intervention is embedded in a specific context (e.g. health care) and if it is a good-practice report, it is possible to learn about different aspects of the context which have been conducive to the success of the intervention. Knowing what works in a specific context and learning from what others have done can inspire managers and teams that it might be worthwhile to invest in developing teamwork.

3.3 What are the mechanisms that enable teams to develop through TDIs?

A TDI should both bring change about and give momentum to further development, and it can be carried out at a certain time-point, or over time, and in a specific context. We have shown that some TDIs only have a limited or unclear effect on teamwork. There is a flaw in the research on the effectiveness of TDIs. There has been a reliance on measuring the effectiveness of e.g. team-building interventions with process measures. Improvements in processes cannot always be linked to improvements in team performance, and although there might be an improvement in team performance it is not clear what kind of team processes were involved. Often evaluations of TDIs are carried out as a pre- and post-measurement to tell whether the TDI worked or not. But why it has or has not remains unclear, thus giving no input to organizational learning. Common to all intervention studies *is the difficulty in answering the question "What are the underpinning processes that make an intervention* work?" (Hewitt, Sims, & Harris, 2014). What is it within the team and the context that causes team members and the team as a whole to enact the behaviour that promotes positive outcomes? An understanding of these factors can contribute to designing more effective TDIs since how to enable and how to sustain outcomes of TDIs remains a challenge (Cunningham et al., 2018). Understanding the underlying processes that make an intervention work is necessary as TDIs and long-term support for teams also need to target these mechanisms. The mechanisms become visible over time when the team's progress is monitored, and information about the mechanisms can be used to alter both the content and how the interventions are carried out. A mechanism is an element of the reasoning or the reactions of the individual team members and the entire team that make the intervention work (Lacouture, Breton, Guichard, & Ridde, 2015). Mechanisms are the team members understanding, for example, why they should change behaviour, and reactions such as active participation, having ownership over the change process, a sense of shared accountability and responsibility and confidence – all of which will impact the TDIs' outcome.

Too often interventions have no precise target and that is like throwing a stone into a pond and letting the waves hit the bank to see what and whether something happens. But also when there is a precise target dimension (e.g. role and goal clarification) and the TDI is well-designed, the results can be limited. Experience shows that when different teams in an organization are supported with the same TDI it will work in some teams yet not in others. Researchers investigating organizational interventions by the so-called realist evaluation strategy (Pawson & Tilley, 2013) suggest that this is best understood by investigating the configuration of context, mechanisms and output

(Nielsen & Miraglia, 2017). The approach includes three themes: 1) understanding the mechanisms through which an intervention achieves outcomes; 2) understanding the contextual conditions necessary for triggering these mechanisms and 3) understanding outcome patterns (Greenhalgh et al., 2015). Factors in the context may enable certain mechanisms to trigger the intended outcomes, and there is always an interaction between context and mechanisms – and it is this interaction that creates the intervention's outcome. We stress the importance of the support from leaders and a learning organizational culture as contextual characteristics will impact whether the TDI works or not.

The mechanisms can change over the duration of the intervention, and although they cannot be observed, they are real and may interact with each other and can be linked in negative or positive feedback loops, i.e. one mechanism informs the other. They can be on an individual level (e.g. motivation or readiness for change) or on a team level (e.g. shared understanding of the intervention). An example: One or two unmotivated team members can over time make the whole team passive and unengaged. There is a process behind the intervention that will impact the outcome. There are examples of interventions that contributed to the opposite of the intended result, so obviously something other than the expected was triggered. We have stressed that a TDI should include instructional strategies that enable the team to engage and learn from the TDI. The context triggers mechanisms that result in outcomes (see Table 10.2), and in a review a number of mechanisms were identified that make TDIs work within hospital settings (Cunningham et al., 2018).

TDIs have intended and unintended consequences for the teamwork. The TDI is expected to trigger a chain of changes. An important factor in this process is how the team members interpret and act upon the intervention strategy, how the resources on offer (through the intervention) permeate into the reasoning of team participants, and if the contextual conditions enable, facilitate or diminish the intervention (Cunningham et al., 2018). Because of the variations in context and mechanisms, there may be different outcomes for the same TDI.

We have shown throughout the book that there is solid evidence that contextual aspects impact team performance and team-performance outcomes (see IMOI and earlier discussion). We have argued that a process perspective is not enough when enhancing team effectiveness. There is growing evidence that the context also impacts whether a TDI will work and be sustainable. This is also a further strong argument for why consultants should not sell products off the shelf.

Table 10.2 An example of a CMO configuration (adapted from Cunningham, et al 2018, p.6)

Context: if there is	Mechanism: this enacts	Outcome: and results in
Leadership support and alignment of team goals and organizational goals	Motivates, empowers and engages staff and creates a sense of team efficacy and a shared sense of responsibility and accountability	Team pride, camaraderie, connectedness with the broader system, implementation of intervention and sustainability of the intervention

3.4 Advice on designing a TDI

Earlier we gave advice on how to choose a specific TDI. We now turn to some advice regarding the designing of a TDI.

3.4.1 Use multiple tools to implement change in interlinked target dimensions

We have shown that a number of solutions might be needed as change is required within different domains to solve the team's problem or to enhance team effectiveness. Further, that dimensions that are closely interrelated to the target dimensions should be included (see PSC step 5 earlier). Meta-analysis about the effectiveness of team training shows that bundled TDI strategies give better results (McEwan et al., 2017). With regard to improving team-performance outcomes, there were significant effects when one or several dimensions of teamwork (preparation, execution, reflection or interpersonal dynamics) were targeted. Regarding improving teamwork behaviours, significant effects only existed when two or more dimensions were targeted. The practical implication is that if the purpose of a TDI is e.g. to develop a team's communication, greater effects may be derived by targeting not merely communication, but also by incorporating interventions that target other dimensions of teamwork. These might be setting goals and making action plans for how communication will be improved, and enhancing reflection to adjust action plans if necessary.

3.4.2 Use multiple instructional strategies

Whether people have different learning styles is debated, and when using instructional methods the use of multiple instructional strategies (information, demonstration and practice) is more likely to be effective, also for the additional reason that different learning strategies appeal to different learning styles (Franzoni, Assar, Defude, & Rojas, 2008). That debate is beyond the scope of this book, and here it is enough to say that using instructional strategies involving both passive and active learning has been shown not only to be more effective but also more engaging and fun. The combination of a presentation (e.g. a lecture), a demonstration (e.g. a video) and opportunities for team members to practise is more likely to result in long-term retention of learning than a single instructional strategy. Information helps the team members to learn about the content, i.e. what coordination means; watching a demonstration induces social learning; action-based learning by practising what should be performed during daily work. Such a combination is likely to result in long-term retention of learning.

3.4.3 Provide feedback during the learning experience – but be cautious

Providing feedback during the learning experience makes the TDI more effective, *if given right*. We have in a previous chapter summarized how feedback should be given: accurately and task specific; given to both individuals and the team as a whole in a timely manner during and after mission completion; focusing on both task-work and interpersonal processes, etc. Feedback based on different sources, both subjective evaluations and objective measures, enhances the learning potential. However, a meta-analysis showed that feedback was negatively related to performance and results when used in team training of teams within health care (Hughes et al., 2016). It might depend on who provides the feedback – if the power distance is big, e.g. between a senior staff member giving feedback to a junior member, it can have the reverse effect. Kluger and DeNisi (1996) discussed that feedback can decrease performance if attention is drawn to the self instead of the task. One could argue that in certain TDIs, such as e.g. team composition or task design, feedback is not relevant, and this might be so if it is done prior to implementing teamwork. But if changes are done for an existing team, the team needs feedback in order to understand the motives for change and to make use of the new solution.

3.3.4 Choose tools high on work environment-, task- and psychological fidelity

The overall aim of a TDI is that what is being learned should transfer to daily work. The analysis of the current situation, cause analysis and the choice of target dimensions show what the team needs to cope with in its work environment. It might be time stress, uncertainty or conflicting task demands. This implies that tools used in the intervention, e.g. simulation for practise of coordination, should be high on psychological fidelity, i.e. replicate the psychological demands in the team's ordinary work. Examples and learning materials must be conceptualized to the work context. This is far more important than replicating the physical workplace (Kozlowski & Deshon, 2004).

3.4.5 Create the system for learning transfer, maintenance and sustainability

Transfer to everyday work is critical for obvious reasons. The conditions that enable transfer and sustainability are most often organizational factors such as leaders' continual feedback on team performance, encouragement of discussions of what was learned and how it can be used, and a supportive climate for teamwork. Things in an organization change over time, and teams might need support to adapt what was learned to new circumstances. As described earlier, if stakeholders and leaders are not supportive and invested in team development and the TDI strategy, it is likely that the TDI will have little impact on team performance (Weaver et al., 2010).

> *To summarize*: It has become evident that changes in the environmental, organizational or individual domain might be needed if a TDI is to succeed. Earlier we were concerned with whether TDIs are useful for enhancing different target dimensions and achieving different outcomes. We have shown that the general empirical support for the effectiveness of different kinds of TDIs is not impressive. Different TDIs have been shown to be of value, but not very much is known of how different TDIs affect performance outcomes on different levels. A TDI should bring about change in learning, transfer to the workplace and performance outcomes (results), and participants should find the TDI meaningful, but so far there is only evidence that team training brings change about on all four levels. The evidence of the impact of different TDIs on team effectiveness is very mixed. Little is known about this as little research exists. We have raised several issues regarding the quality of the evidence, as many studies are not rigorously conducted.

There is substantial evidence for the effectiveness of team training, leadership training and team building depending of their focus; there is growing evidence for the effectiveness of team debriefs; there is some support for team-charter interventions. Little is known about task analysis, teamwork design, and team performance monitoring and assessment as TDIs are carried out separately, but these are sometimes used in a bundled solution or as part of a systematic TDI. Too little is known about team coaching as a separate TDI to draw conclusions about its value.

We have concluded that it is more meaningful to evaluate different TDIs as the combination of content, tools and strategies, than discussing the value of different kinds of TDIs in general since these differ a lot within one category. *Whether a TDI succeeds depends on the rationale and how it is done.* A "one-size-fits-all" approach will not work – in line with our criticism regarding programmes sold off the shelf. People and settings differ. Important criteria for choosing solutions and TDIs for bringing about change are:

- Are needs for change in domains other than the team level identified?
- If needs for change in other domains exist, are there solutions to bring that change about?
- Are dimensions on the team level that are closely interdependent on the main target dimensions included in the TDI?
- Provide evidence that the tools and instructional methods in the chosen intervention are likely to change target dimensions and result in specific measurable performance outcomes on the individual, team and organizational level
- Consider if multiple tools should be used to enhance target and interlinked dimensions
- Use different instructional methods to create more effective learning, including practising what was learned
- Provide diagnostic feedback during the TDI on both task-work and interpersonal processes
- Design the tools so that they are high on psychological fidelity to everyday work
- Ensure opportunities for learning transfer and sustainability by establishing how effective teamwork should be reinforced at work
- Decide how the evaluation should be carried out

4 To plan (PSC 6) and carry out the TDI (PSC 7)

Forming a plan for how the intervention should be carried out, the practicalities, and creating the setting is dependent on the context: what will work well for this specific team, for the coaches/experts who are to implement the TDI and in this specific setting. The planning can be guided by principles that are transferable between contexts and applicable to different kinds of TDIs. The plan should consider accessibility (if it is available to all who need to take part), usability (if it is designed and carried out at a level that all participants can understand) and learnability (if it helps performing what is being learned). It should be based on an approach to facilitate the acquisition of the specified TDI objectives. We pin-point some issues that should be considered during the planning and execution of the TDI (Lacerenza et al., 2018; Salas, 2015; Weaver, Rosen, Salas, Baum & King, 2010). Content, tools and instructional strategies have implications for what to do: what and how should go hand in hand.

SYSTEMATIC TEAM INTERVENTIONS | 273

- The basis of teamwork is that team members are dependent on each other. This means that whatever is done during a TDI, it should reflect the task interdependencies.
- Task-work and interpersonal processes should not be divorced.
- Set team-specific goals and, when relevant, individual goals depending on diagnosis, needs analysis and team assessment.
- Make an inventory of the resources needed and the time for the TDI.
- Ensure that there are enough resources and time for both the TDI and team members' transfer of what was learned between sessions.
- Team structure impacts the execution of a TDI. If e.g. team members belong to different teams, transferable competencies should be trained at the individual level. If a team needs certain competencies to carry out a specific task, all team members should take part in the TDI to enhance TMMs.
- The TDI is more effective if it is carried out over time and with spaced sessions rather than one massive intensive session. Research has found that spaced sessions lead to better transfer of what is learned; one does not get overwhelmed, and one can practise and explore in everyday work between sessions.
- Provide opportunities to practise what was learned between sessions.
- Provide opportunities for assessment of and feedback on practice between sessions.
- If it is a TDI that needs space and time to meet, choose a location that supports learning and accessibility. There is little research on how the location impacts TDI effectiveness, but there is some support for TDIs carried out at the workplace or in the organization being more effective, better able to facilitate on-the-job training experiences and being less costly than off-work locations. Further, employees with families or obligations outside work will have greater opportunities to take part.
- Facilitators or trainers obviously need to be trained for their task, including assessment and process evaluation.
- Foster a friendly, accepting climate characterized by psychological trust, set the rules for how to interact and give peer feedback.
- Document and follow up plans and agreements.
- Evaluate and monitor processes and performance.

5 Evaluation (PSC 8)

In our experience most of the evaluations of results of TDIs are carried out as subjective descriptions of team members' reactions, generally their opinion of the programme and how engaging it was. In many cases the evaluation is done in the last session, and that was it. Such an evaluation says nothing about the learning transfer: if the team members use what was learned on the job; if the TDI increased outcomes such as team-performance effectiveness e.g. in productivity and quality; or increased outcomes on the individual level, e.g. absenteeism; on the organizational level, e.g. input to organizational learning. Ideally the evaluation of results should encompass reactions, learning, i.e. any increase in competencies, transfer and performance outcomes.

We have described that the TDI needs to be monitored and evaluated during the process. Here the transfer phase should definitely be included in the TDI strategy, i.e. monitoring and evaluating how what was learned is used in everyday work should be part of the process evaluation. Monitoring the implementation of the strategy makes it possible to alter things that do not work and strengthen parts that need to work better.

Evaluation can be carried out in different ways, and the quality depends on the design of the evaluation and the methods. Evaluations can be done using methods such as subjective measurements, e.g. questionnaires, and experts can assess and evaluate processes and results; these can be complemented by objective measurements of e.g. productivity or errors. In observation Behaviourally Anchored Rating Scales (BARS) can be used, and we have described these in earlier chapters. Triangulating methods is advisable as all methods have different strengths and weaknesses. In our experience, consultants are often not keen on carrying through an extensive evaluation. This may sometimes be because it is difficult to convince the organization it is worth the time and cost, and sometimes because consultants do not want to take the risk of showing the results. If the TDI evaluation results in positive evaluations of the TDI programme, that does not mean that it impacts behaviour. The result depends greatly on what happens after a TDI programme is finished, and the organization is in most cases responsible for that. Our viewpoint is that if the organization is not interested in carrying out an evaluation after a transfer phase, maybe it is not committed enough to developing teamwork through TDIs.

6 End the TDI (step 9 in the PSC)

Although a systematic TDI involves a lot of work in many steps, the work is not infinite. We have said before, any task's completeness, even a TDI's, is the whole chain from setting goals, planning, execution, evaluation of results and feedback. We quote the Bible to describe the essence of completeness: "And God saw everything that he had made and, behold, it was very good" (Book of Genesis, Chapter 1, verse 31). Being proud of what was accomplished is important, although maybe not all was achieved and not all was considered that ideally should have been part of the TDI.

> To summarize: The process of implementing TDIs includes respect for both scientific evidence regarding effective strategies and for experiential knowledge of what is likely to work in a particular context, supported by continuous monitoring, adjustment and adaptation.

Note

1   "Team development intervention (e.g. team composition, team training) are a culmination of tools used for training (e.g. simulation, feedback, adaptive training), methods used for delivery (e.g. information, demonstration, practice) and content (e.g. competencies, knowledge skills attitudes, abilities) created with a specific training objective (e.g. improve attitudes, change in behaviour) in mind" (DiazGranados, Shuffler, Wingate, & Salas, 2017, p. 4).

Bibliography

Buljac-Samardzic, M., Dekker-van Doorn, C. M., van Wijngaarden, J. D. H., & van Wijk, K. P. (2010). Interventions to improve team effectiveness: A systematic review. *Health Policy, 94*(3), 183–195. https://doi.org/https://doi.org/10.1016/j.healthpol.2009.09.015

Cannon-Bowers, J. A., Tannenbaum, S. I., Salas, E., & Volpe, C. E. (1995). Defining team competencies and establishing team training requirements. In R. Guzzo, E. Salas, & Associates (Eds.), *Team effectiveness and decision making in organizations* (pp. 333–380). San Francisco: Jossey-Bass.

Comelli, G. (2003). Anlässe und Ziele von Teamentwicklungsprozessen. In S. Stumpf & A. Thomas (Eds.), *Teamarbeit und Teamentwicklung* (pp. 169–189). Göttingen: Hogrefe Verlag.

Courtright, S. H., McCormick, B. W., Mistry, S., & Wang, J. (2017). Quality charters or quality members? A control theory perspective on team charters and team performance. *Journal of Applied Psychology, 102*(10), 1462–1470. https://doi.org/10.1037/apl0000229

Cunningham, U., Ward, M. E., De Brún, A., & McAuliffe, E. (2018). Team interventions in acute hospital contexts: A systematic search of the literature using realist synthesis. *BMC Health Services Research, 18*(1), 536. https://doi.org/10.1186/s12913-018-3331-3

DiazGranados, D., Shuffler, M. L., Wingate, J. A., & Salas, E. (2017, March 17). Team development interventions. In *The Wiley Blackwell handbook of the psychology of team working and collaborative processes.* https://doi.org/doi:10.1002/9781118909997.ch24

Franzoni, A. L., Assar, S., Defude, B., & Rojas, J. (2008). Student learning styles adaptation method based on teaching strategies and electronic media. In *2008 Eighth IEEE International Conference on Advanced Learning Technologies* (pp. 778–782). IEEE. https://doi.org/10.1109/ICALT.2008.149

Greenhalgh, T., Wong, G., Jagosh, J., Greenhalgh, J., Manzano, A., Westhorp, G., & Pawson, R. (2015). Protocol-the RAMESES II study: Developing guidance and reporting standards for realist evaluation. *BMJ Open, 5*(8). https://doi.org/10.1136/bmjopen-2015-008567

Guyatt, G. H., Oxman, A. D., Vist, G. E., Kunz, R., Falck-Ytter, Y., Alonso-Coello, P., & Schünemann, H. J. (2008). GRADE: An emerging consensus on rating quality of evidence and strength of recommendations. *BMJ, 336*(7650), 924–926. https://doi.org/10.1136/bmj.39489.470347.AD

Hewitt, G., Sims, S., & Harris, R. (2014). Using realist synthesis to understand the mechanisms of interprofessional teamwork in health and social care. *Journal of Interprofessional Care, 28*(6), 501–506. https://doi.org/10.3109/13561820.2014.939744

Hughes, A. M., Gregory, M. E., Joseph, D. L., Sonesh, S. C., Marlow, S. L., Lacerenza, C. N., Salas, E. (2016). Saving lives: A meta-analysis of team training in healthcare. *Journal of Applied Psychology, 101*(9), 1266–1304. https://doi.org/10.1037/apl0000120

Kash, B. A., Cheon, O., Halzack, N. M., & Miller, T. R. (2018). Measuring team effectiveness in the health care setting: An inventory of survey tools. *Health Services Insights, 11*, 1178632918796230–1178632918796230. https://doi.org/10.1177/1178632918796230

Kirkpatrick, D. L. (1996). Great ideas revisited: Revisiting Kirkpatrick's four-level model. *Training & Development, 50*, 54–59.

Klein, C., DiazGranados, D., Salas, E., Le, H., Burke, C. S., Lyons, R., & Goodwin, G. F. (2009). Does team building work? *Small Group Research, 40*(2), 181–222. https://doi.org/10.1177/1046496408328821

Kluger, A. N., & DeNisi, A. (1996). The effects of feedback interventions on performance: A historical review, a meta-analysis, and a preliminary feedback intervention theory. *Psychological Bulletin, 119*(2), 254–284. https://doi.org/10.1037/0033-2909.119.2.254

Körner, M., Becker, S., Zimmermann, L., Müller, C., Luzay, L., Plewnia, A., Rundel, M. (2015). *Entwicklung und Evaluation eines Konzeptes zur patientenorientierten Teamentwicklung in Rehabilittionskliniken (PATENT).* Retrieved November 5 2019 from http://www.forschung-patientenorientierung.de/files/abschlussbericht_final.pdf

Kozlowski, S., & Deshon, R. P. (2004). A psychological fidelity approach to simulation-based training: Theory, research, and principles. In E. Salas, L. R. Elliott, S. G. Schflett, & M. D. Coovert (Eds.), *Scaled worlds: Development, validation, and applications* (pp. 75–99). Burlington, VT: Ashgate Publishing.

Lacerenza, C. N., Marlow, S. L., Tannenbaum, S. I., & Salas, E. (2018). Team development interventions: Evidence-based approaches for improving teamwork. *American Psychologist, 73*(4), 517–531. https://doi.org/10.1037/amp0000295

Lacerenza, C. N., Reyes, D. L., Marlow, S. L., Joseph, D. L., & Salas, E. (2017). Leadership training design, delivery, and implementation: A meta-analysis. *Journal of Applied Psychology, 102*(12), 1686–1718. https://doi.org/10.1037/apl0000241

Lacouture, A., Breton, E., Guichard, A., & Ridde, V. (2015). The concept of mechanism from a realist approach: A scoping revie to facilitate its operationalization in public health program evaluation. *Implementation Science, 10*(1), 153. https://doi.org/10.1186/s13012-015-0345-7

Mathieu, J. E., & Rapp, T. L. (2009). Laying the foundation for successful team performance trajectories: The roles of team charters and performance strategies. *Journal of Applied Psychology, 94*(1), 90–103. https://doi.org/10.1037/a0013257

McEwan, D., Ruissen, G. R., Eys, M. A., Zumbo, B. D., & Beauchamp, M. R. (2017). The effectiveness of teamwork training on teamwork behaviors and team performance: A systematic review and meta-analysis of controlled interventions. *PLoS One, 12*(1), e0169604. https://doi.org/10.1371/journal.pone.0169604

Miller, C. J., Kim, B., Silverman, A., & Bauer, M. S. (2018). A systematic review of team-building interventions in non-acute healthcare settings. *BMC Health Services Research, 18*(1), 146. https://doi.org/10.1186/s12913-018-2961-9

Nielsen, K., & Miraglia, M. (2017). What works for whom in which circumstances? On the need to move beyond the "what works?" question in organizational intervention research. *Human Relations, 70*(1), 40–62. https://doi.org/10.1177/0018726716670226

Pawson, R., & Tilley, N. (2013). An introduction to scientific realist evaluation. In *Evaluation for the 21st century: A handbook.* https://doi.org/10.4135/9781483348896

Richter, A. W., Dawson, J. F., & West, M. A. (2011). The effectiveness of teams in organizations: A meta-analysis. *The International Journal of Human Resource Management, 22*(13), 2749–2769. https://doi.org/10.1080/09585192.2011.573971

Rosen, M. A., DiazGranados, D., Dietz, A. S., Benishek, L. E., Thompson, D., Pronovost, P. J., & Weaver, S. J. (2018). Teamwork in healthcare: Key discoveries enabling safer, high-quality care. *American Psychologist, 73*(4), 433–450.

Salas, E. (2015). Team training essentials: A research-based guide In L. Benishek, C. Coultas, A. Dietz, R. Grossman, E. Lazzara, & J. Oglesby (Eds.), *Team training essentials: A research-based guide.* New York, NY: Routledge/Taylor & Francis Group.

Salas, E., & Cannon-Bowers, J. A. (1997). Methods, tools, and strategies for team training. In *Training for a rapidly changing workplace: Applications of psychological research* (pp. 249–279). Washington, DC: American Psychological Association. https://doi.org/10.1037/10260-010

Salas, E., & Cannon-Bowers, J. A. (2001). The science of training: A decade of progress. *Annual Review of Psychology, 52*(1), 471–499. https://doi.org/10.1146/annurev.psych.52.1.471

Salas, E., Cooke, N. J., & Rosen, M. A. (2008). On teams, teamwork, and team performance: Discoveries and developments. *Human Factors, 50*(3), 540–547. https://doi.org/10.1518/001872008X288457

Salas, E., Nichols, D. R., & Driskell, J. E. (2007). Testing three team training strategies in intact teams. *Small Group Research, 38*(4), 471–488. https://doi.org/10.1177/1046496407304332

Shuffler, M. L., Diazgranados, D., Maynard, M. T., & Salas, E. (2018). Developing, sustaining, and maximizing team effectiveness: An integrative, dynamic perspective of team development interventions. *Academy of Management Annals, 12*(2), 688–724. https://doi.org/10.5465/annals.2016.0045

Shuffler, M. L., DiazGranados, D., & Salas, E. (2011). There's a science for that: Team development interventions in organizations. *Current Directions in Psychological Science, 20*(6), 365–372. https://doi.org/10.1177/0963721411422054

Tannenbaum, S. I., & Cerasoli, C. P. (2013). Do team and individual debriefs enhance performance? A meta-analysis. *Human Factors: The Journal of the Human Factors and Ergonomics Society, 55*(1), 231–245. https://doi.org/10.1177/0018720812448394

Weaver, S. J., Dy, S. M., & Rosen, M. A. (2014). Team-training in healthcare: A narrative synthesis of the literature. *BMJ Quality & Safety, 23*(5), 359 LP–372. Retrieved from http://qualitysafety.bmj.com/content/23/5/359.abstract

Weaver, S. J., Lyons, R., Diazgranados, D., Rosen, M., Salas, E., Oglesby, J., King, H. B. (2010). The anatomy of health care team training and the state of practice: A critical review. *Academic Medicine, 85*(11), 1746–1760. Retrieved from https://doi.org/10.1097/ACM.0b013e3181f2e907No Title

Weaver, S. J., Rosen, M. A., Salas, E., Baum, K. D., & King, H. B. (2010). Integrating the science of team training: Guidelines for continuing education. *Journal of Continuing Education in the Health Professions, 30*(4), 208–220. https://doi.org/10.1002/chp.20085

Chapter 11

Effective teams over time

In this final chapter we discuss and compare different models of team development over time and explain our rationale for choosing the IMOI model to describe team effectiveness. Teams develop over time and we go into some depth to describe how teams make use of the second I in the IMOI, TDIs and systematic monitoring of output and behaviour to increase effectiveness over time. We show how behavioural markers can be of practical use when team members, team leaders, supervisors or consultants explore the second I to gain insight into what needs to be developed to increase effectiveness. What was learned during a performance cycle can be used to form TDIs and to monitor teamwork in the next performance cycle. Based on the research presented in this book and on our own experience, we conclude by presenting our three take-home messages for how to enhance team effectiveness in practice.

In the previous chapters the idea of development and change over time has been an important aspect. The whole book is based on the idea of intended change to improve team effectiveness by using the problem-solving cycle and applying team-development interventions (see Chapters 2 and 10). Different concepts of change have been mentioned, e.g. team learning, the shift between transition and action phase, or adaption caused by external changes, etc. The theoretical basis of this book is the IMOI model. Different models exist and they stem from different research traditions and have been developed for different purposes. In this section we want to show which other models exist and make our reasons for choosing the IMOI model transparent. To do so, we first outline the criteria for a model that is suitable to describe change and development in *work* teams, before we describe and compare the most important developmental models and present our reasons why, for the purposes of this book, we found the IMOI model to be more useful than other models.

1 Team development over time: different models of how teams develop

We found the following criteria useful for comparing models. For a different purpose than ours, other criteria could be used.

The model should meet the following requirements:

- Appropriate complexity: Teams change and develop – these processes can be intended or unintended and may result in positive as well as negative consequences. Raes, Kyndt, Decuyper, Van den Bossche and Dochy (2015) describe

EFFECTIVE TEAMS OVER TIME | 279

team development as complex and chaotic – as many organizations operate in a fluid, dynamic and complex environment. Teams can develop in very different ways, and sometimes problems arise. So the model should be complex with regard to the magnitude of variables and their interactions that can cause problems in teams and trigger team development. Moreover, it should be flexible enough to explain different paths teams take.

- Explanation of team-development interventions and their effects: our book is about problem-solving in work teams, and we have highlighted solutions that involve realizing team-development interventions (see Chapter 10). Therefore we need a model that can explain such intended developments, based on reflection and planned change.
- Generalizability: The model should be valid for all kinds of work teams in their diversity. Team composition is often not stable, and individuals belong to several teams at the same time (Bell & Kozlowski, 2012; Wildman et al., 2012). So the model needs to be suitable for all constellations. It needs to be generalizable to differing team goals, work tasks, life spans, contextual factors, etc.
- Empirical evidence: The model should be validated in several well-funded studies.

There is a lot of literature about how groups develop. Chidambaram and Bostrom (1997) analyzed models of team development and found two main categories that are still useful: sequential models that define phases or stages teams pass through in a certain order, and non-sequential models that focus on factors that cause development processes and do not assume a predetermined sequence of specific stages. Mannix and Jehn (2004) have outlined that specifically team-performance models like the IPO model are relevant as they link temporal processes to team performance. Therefore we will focus on the IMOI model as a further development of the IPO model (see Chapter 1), and we will explain why later.

Despite their differences, all team-development models stress the relevance of time and dynamic processes. In the following section, we will first briefly summarize the most important sequential models before coming back to the IMOI model as a non-sequential model.

1.1 Sequential models – team development as systematic changes over time

Some authors argue that there are specified patterns of phases all teams go through. Several models describe a sequential development of teams consisting of different stages. In this section we will briefly describe the most widely discussed stage models.

1.1.1 Tuckman's model of team development

The most famous stage model was developed by Tuckman (Tuckman & Jensen, 1977; Tuckmann, 1965). It says that all teams pass through four stages. Each stage refers to interpersonal team structure and to the kind of task performance

> forming involves testing and orientation for the group structure and the task; storming includes intra-group conflict and emotional response to the task demands; norming includes the development of group cohesion and the open

discussion of the elements of the task; and performing involves the development of functional roles and the development of task insights.

(Mannix & Jehn 2004, p.14)

In their later publication, Tuckman and Jensen (1977) added a fifth stage – adjourning, which refers to the time when a team is dissolved. The model is based on a literature review of group studies, therapeutic and training groups.

Kozlowski and Bell (2013) have analyzed several stage models of group development and come to the conclusion that most of them "are remarkably parallel with respect to the descriptive stages" (p. 426). Almost all of the authors of the following models refer explicitly to Tuckman's model, so we will mainly point out what additional aspects they emphasize.

1.1.2 Wheelan's integrated model of group development

Wheelan's (2005b, 2005a) integrated model of group development is based on Tuckman's model and includes five phases (analogue to his model). Compared to Tuckman, she adds the idea that teams not only pass through these stages but also gain maturity during these phases by working together. The phases are:

1   Dependency: Team members have safety concerns, are dependent on their leaders and make efforts connected to the group.
2   Counter-dependency and fight: Individuals try to gain more independency and argue about their goals and procedures. In doing so (and solving the conflicts), they develop common aims, procedures and values. Mutual trust, commitment, motivation for cooperation as well as an open and task-oriented communication is established.
3   Trust and structure: Team members are now able to negotiate more maturely about their roles, work structure and procedures, and to strengthen their mutual relationship.
4   Work and productivity: The team is focused on goal achievement and works intensively and effectively.
5   Adjourning: The team is dissolved for various reasons. It may have completed its task or lost its viability, or the organization might be restructured, etc.

Mature teams can be described as cohesive groups with common goals and clear communication processes that use their resources in an optimal way and participate in leadership. Wheelan mentions that not all groups pass through these phases in a predictable way as some do not reach maturity or regress to an earlier stage.

Wheelan assumes that these stages are connected to specific communication patterns and has developed instruments – Group Development Observation System (GDOS) and Group Development Questionnaire (GDQ) – to assess the developmental stage of a team (Wheelan & Hochberger, 1996; Wheelan, Verdi, & McKeage, 1994). Using these instruments in several groups, different developmental patterns of communication indicating the phases have been found (Wheelan, Davidson, & Tilin, 2003; Wheelan & Kaeser, 1997; Wheelan & Mckeage, 1993). Other studies confirmed a relationship between team members' individual perceptions of the developmental stage and team productivity (Wheelan, 2009; Wheelan, Murphy, Tsumura, & Kline, 1998).

EFFECTIVE TEAMS OVER TIME | 281

1.1.3 Worchel's model of cyclical stages

Both of those models assume that teams develop in a linear way and are finally dissolved. Worchel (1994) and Worchel, Coutant-Sassic, and Grossmann (1991), by contrast, assume that teams pass through several repeating cycles of stages. These cycles can also be interrupted, or teams can – as in Wheelan's model – fall back to earlier stages.

Integration and disintegration in the team are the main characteristics of this model. In the first stage – discontent – team members feel alienated. Some of them have withdrawn and act in a passive way instead of participating. A precipitating event like an open conflict evokes the development to the next stage – group identity. Members define their team and its boundaries and act in a conforming way. In the following stage – group productivity – the group is mainly oriented towards goal achievement. This is ensued by the next stage – individuation. Team members pay more attention to their individual needs and contributions. In the last stage – decay – the team disintegrates: Members compete and conflict with each other.

1.1.4 Gersick's punctuated equilibrium model

Gersick's punctuated equilibrium model (Gersick, 1988, 1991) focuses on teams with temporal deadlines and assumes that they dramatically reorganize their roles and proceedings at about the midpoint of their existence because they need to focus on meeting their deadline. She describes team development as the result of choices about boundaries, norms and methods made by the team. The model can be regarded as a two-stage model (although not all authors do, see Chidambaram & Bostrom, 1997). First the establishment of norms and inertia, and second – due to time pressure – reorganization to accomplish the task on time and intensification of activity. The model has been developed based on research with project teams and has a strong focus on task performance processes, so some authors regard it more as a model for task progress than for team development (Okhuysen & Waller, 2002).

1.1.5 Morgan, Salas and Glickman's TEAM-model

The TEAM-model (Team Evolution and Maturation) by Morgan, Salas, and Glickman (1993) integrates the ideas of two quite different models: Tuckman's model of team development and Gersick's punctuated equilibrium model. After Tuckman's first four phases, the team is in a reforming phase of re-evaluating their efforts to the demands and transformation (analogue to Gersick's model), before it enters a second performance stage. The model proposes two alternative paths through the stages of the model in terms of different maturation of task-work and teamwork skills. So teams can develop mainly in regard to task-related KSAs or teamwork-related KSAs (see Chapter 4) – an overlap of these maturation processes at the final stages of skilled performance is most suitable for team efficacy. In which stage a team starts depends on its experience, as well as on task and contextual characteristics. In the case of negative performance, a team can go back to an earlier stage to readjust team processes. The TEAM-model focuses on the skills of team members – not surprisingly, the authors recommend their model as a framework for the development and evaluation of trainings and other team-development interventions that enhance qualifications.

> *To summarize*: the models have in common that they all describe different stages of groups. All models highlight that teams are not static; they develop and have

changing needs, focuses and problems that need to be addressed in the different stages. The models differ in several ways. Some propose a strict sequence of stages (Tuckman, Gersick), while others describe the development in a more flexible way (Wheelan, Worchel, Morgan). In their description of stages, some models focus mainly on a specific aspect of team development (Gersick on task processing and Morgan on skills). In most of the models, interpersonal group processes inside the team such as conflict, integration, building cohesion and trust are of main relevance. Gersick emphasizes that active choices of team members trigger development.

1.2 IMOI model as a complex non-sequential team-performance model to describe team development

Team development can also be described using team-performance models, as they imply the passage of time but do not assume a predetermined sequence of stages (Mannix & Jehn, 2004). In the first chapter, such a team-performance model, the IPO model by McGrath (1964) was mentioned. The idea of this model is quite simple: Inputs on the individual, team and organizational levels impact processes, defined as interactions on the team level. These processes cause the outcomes. As discussed in Chapter 1, the IPO model cannot adequately describe complex and dynamic team development. Moreover, it does not cover the mediation aspect (including emergent states, see Chapter 1). Therefore we refer here only to the IMOI model (Ilgen, Hollenbeck, Johnson, & Jundt, 2005). IMOI stands for Input-Mediator-Output-Input model – so team development is seen as a cycle of relations between inputs, mediators, outcomes and (second) inputs (see next section for more types of development).

As the IMOI model has been broadly described in the first chapter, we limit ourselves here to the aspects related to team development.

Team development can happen in a linear, an episodic and/or a cyclical way. The IMOI model integrates such differing developmental paths (Bell & Kozlowski, 2012). Linear means simple cause-effect relationships. Episodic refers to specific sequences in a team, e.g. transition and action phases in teams (Marks, Mathieu, & Zaccaro, 2001). Cyclical includes a circular process with a feedback loop, i.e. the second I, comprising the lessons learned from the former performance cycle. (This will be explained in more detail later in this chapter.) Team learning is an example of cyclical development. After reviewing the literature, Knapp (2010) advocates that the essence of team learning can be described as a collective thought process, combined with reflexivity (metacognition and critical reflection). Metacognition allows teams to understand their own belief systems that affect the action phase, interpersonal processes and the transition phase. In the team-learning literature, the transition phase of reflexivity, de-construction and re-construction of the team cognition in order to enhance future work, will impact both form and content of developed team knowledge. So in a cyclical process, team learning enables the team to build collective meaning and form emergent states. These states guide future teamwork in the action phase. In the following transition phase, experiences in the action phase are evaluated and reflected, and so team learning can change team cognitions, which then again impact the team's next action phase.

Teams are integrated in a multilevel system. At a minimum the levels are organization (or team context), team and individual – but more levels are possible, e.g.

different domains of an organization, subteams in a team with different professional background, etc. The IMOI integrates three levels that interact: one, individual members form the team as a collective unit; two, at the same time the team is a context for the individuals that possibly supports them or limits their leeway; three, the organizational level supplies resources and also puts demands on the team and on individual team members. All levels are connected.

An example of multilevel interrelations is that interactions in a team are impacted by technology (organizational level) and emergent team phenomena (such as trust and cohesion). These can affect the way the team uses technology in the future (Bell & Kozlowski, 2012). But there are even more factors that are part of the interaction, e.g. individual skills for the use of technology and for cooperation (see Chapter 4). Psychological safety as an emergent state in turn originates from individual characteristics, e.g. as individual feelings of safety (Kozlowski & Klein, 2000), and is then again influenced by the organizational context factors such as team design, e.g. high task interdependence in terms of shared rewards, work design and leadership as well (Newman, Donohue, & Eva, 2017; Sanner & Bunderson, 2013).

Adaptation is an example of multilevel phenomena. It exists on the individual level, team level and organizational level; hence theoretically there are interaction effects between these levels (see Chapter 7).

Mediation between inputs and outputs is based on emergent phenomena. One main difference between the IPO and IMOI model is that the term "process" is insufficient to describe what factors mediate between inputs and outputs, especially as emergent states are not mentioned. Mediation explains "why certain inputs affect team effectiveness" (Ilgen et al., 2005, p. 519). The same inputs may result in very different outcomes depending on mediators.

Mediators include team processes and emergent states. Team processes are team behaviours and interactions (the actions of the team members), whereas team-emergent states are characteristics of the whole team, including common attitudes, cognitions and values. They are dynamic and impacted by the team context, processes and outcomes (Marks et al., 2001; Mathieu, Gallagher, Domingo, & Klock, 2019). (See also earlier examples of multilevel interactions.) An example: Team cohesion is an emergent state, and it is important for conflict management (see Chapter 6). A team with high cohesion can achieve better outcomes than a team with low cohesion (e.g. because teamwork is impaired by dysfunctional conflicts), although both teams have the same input.

Emergent states result from individual characteristics of the team members that over time turn into collective qualities of the team. Bell and Kozlowski (2012) describe two ways of how emergence develops: Composition is based on linear and convergent processes. That means the content does not change – e.g. a team of trustful individual team members builds team trust on the collective level. Compilation is more complex: Due to team members' diversity, the collective level is more than just a summary of the individual characteristics. An example is that team trust may be impacted by just one team member who impedes trust building by spreading rumours.

1.3 Comparison between the models

We now compare sequential and non-sequential models in the respects mentioned earlier.

1.3.1 Appropriate complexity

A main criticism of the Tuckman model (which, as already mentioned, is the basis for most stage models) is that the model focuses strongly on personal relationships and less on organizational context (for example, organizational socialization of team members), on work-task specifics and their implications for the team, as well as on different levels of team processes (Kozlowski & Bell, 2013). This is not true for all stage models: the TEAM-model of Morgan et al. integrates the organizational level, and Wheelan (2005a) refers to the organizational level having an impact on group processes as well.

The IMOI includes both personal relationship variables as well as context characteristics. It is detailed enough to capture temporal dynamics of intended and unintended team development triggered by several interacting factors on different levels (individual, team and organization). The model integrates processes and emergent states that mediate between inputs and outcomes. By including emergent states, it also explains how individual factors change into team characteristics, e.g. how individual trust of team members develops into team trust and team cohesion.

Emergent states such as team trust, integration and cohesion, as well as team processes such as conflicts, are also part of most stage models (with the exception of Gersick's punctuated equilibrium model). Wheelan's model in particular includes detailed descriptions of developmental processes. All stage models are based on the idea that teams develop in a predictable and systematic sequential way – although the extent of determination varies. But all in all their flexibility in describing differing ways of team development is restricted in comparison to the IMOI model, as e.g. the impact of multilevel interactions on development are not part of the models.

1.3.2 Explanation of team-development interventions and their effects

Stage models propose specific needs of teams in different stages – so team development should be in line with the current stage of a team. For instance, Spielberger (2016) gives examples of which team-building activities are appropriate in each of the stages of the Tuckman model. Wheelan and Burchill (1999) describe how to derive team-development activities based on the results of an assessment with the GDQ (discussed earlier). Morgan et al. (1993) see the TEAM-model as a starting point for the development of trainings.

The IMOI model is more complex – and does not give indications per se for solutions based on a stage or the time a team is cooperating. A thorough assessment of the concrete situation is essential before solutions can be found. The IMOI is a broad basis for diagnoses and possible solutions.

The IMOI model includes a second I, comprising the lessons learned from the former performance cycle. So this feedback loop explains *the intended development of teams, based on feedback and possibly on team-development interventions*. Looking at the stage models, the only model that refers explicitly to former experience as a driver for development is Morgan et al.'s TEAM-model. Worchel has developed a cyclical stage model, but these cycles focus mainly on group-dynamic aspects (such as alienation after competition and conflict at the last stage of the circle: There is no feedback loop about "lessons learned" based on experiences with teamwork). Wheelan describes how teams develop and mature, and this implies that previous experiences impact the development, but the concept is not an explicit part of the model.

1.3.3 Generalizability

The models of Gersick and of Morgan (who integrates Gersick's model) explicitly refer to teams with deadlines only. The stage models mentioned earlier mostly do not integrate context (except Morgan et al., and to some extent Wheelan, discussed earlier). Beyond that, sequential-stage models assume that teams have time to develop and reach their full productivity in a later phase. But many teams need to cooperate in a functional and effective way at once.

The IMOI model can describe developments of all organizational teams in their particularity and diversity. This is contradictory to the idea of a simple pattern of process that is valid for all work teams. Most stage models can be used to describe different types of groupings, e.g. Tuckman's model was developed on research on therapy groups. The IMOI model is developed for teams in a system and context.

1.3.4 Empirical evidence

The research on stage models has a focus on group processes, like minority influence, group homogeneity, social identity and social loafing (Worchel, Grossman, & Coutant, 1994; Worchel, Rothgerber, & Day, 2011; Worchel, Rothgerber, Day, Hart, & Butemeyer, 1998); on patterns of communication indicating different phases (Wheelan et al., 2003; Wheelan & Kaeser, 1997; Wheelan & Mckeage, 1993); and on team members' individual perceptions of the developmental stage and team productivity (Wheelan, 2009; Wheelan et al., 1998).

The IMOI model is supported by empirical evidence, as are some (though not all) of the stage models.

How the different parts of the IMOI interact is shown in the meta-analysis of Lepine, Piccolo, Jackson, Mathieu, & Methot (2008). The results indicate that different types of team processes are linked with each other over time and correlate with emergent states like cohesion and potency (mediators) as well as with team performance (outcome). But the input is also important: The relationship between processes and performance has been shown to be stronger in teams with higher task interdependence and more team members. A meta-analysis on the relationship between team design and effectiveness showed that several team-design variables/team-performance effects were notably larger than or similar to other meta-analytic effects observed for team processes (Bell, 2007). Mathieu and colleagues (Mathieu, Hollenbeck, van Knippenberg, & Ilgen, 2017; Mathieu et al., 2019) report several meta-analyses that show correlations between team compositional and structural features, mediators and outcomes. The authors conclude that, in general, research has shown that team processes and emergent states as mediators connect team composition and context factors with outcomes on the team and individual level.

Another characteristic of the IMOI is that it integrates multilevel interaction and phenomena. Several studies show relations between different levels, e.g. between team cohesion and individual satisfaction (Picazo, Gamero, Zornoza, & Peiró, 2015), individual creative self-efficacy/creativity and shared knowledge (Richter, Hirst, van Knippenberg, & Baer, 2012) as well as individual project learning and team creativity/team external cooperation (Parboteeah, Hoegl, & Muethel, 2015). Earlier it was mentioned that adaptation is a phenomenon that exists on individual, team and organizational levels. In contrast to stage models, the IMOI model can be used for multilevel analysis. Few such studies exist although many researchers stress the importance of such studies in explaining how much of the total effect (for example of adaptation on productivity) can be explained by the individual, team and organization and the interaction between these levels. Without taking this into account, it is easy to come to the false conclusion that the whole effect is due e.g. to team adaptation.

> *To summarize*: For the purposes of our book based on the problem-solving cycle, the IMOI has the following advantages: It is complex enough to map very different constellations teams may be in, and it is a good basis for an adequate diagnosis as well as an exploration of the right domains for solutions. Solutions can be found in different domains, and changes in different domains might be needed as these interact. The model integrates what drives team-developmental processes (with the second I).

Most of the stage models regard teams as infants that grow up. In reality, teams are composed and recomposed. Major criticisms are the lack of empirical evidence for most of them; the uncertainty about their generalizability for all types of organizational teams; and the predominant neglect of contextual factors, work-task specifics and their implications (Chidambaram & Bostrom, 1997; Kozlowski & Bell, 2013).

Further, we consider that models predefining a certain development are not adequate to describe the variety of possibilities of team development. Moreover, there is more empirical evidence for the IMOI model than for the stage models (although more research is still needed) that captures the complexity and convertibility of teams, e.g. regarding dynamic and contextual features and multilevel perspectives (Mathieu et al., 2019; Ramos-Villagrasa, Marques-Quinteiro, Navarro, & Rico, 2018).

2 Team development through the feedback loop, TDIs and systematic monitoring

Earlier we described the importance of the "second" I, also called feedback, for team development. A team develops and may become more effective by itself by making use of the second I, by TDIs and by systematic monitoring of the mechanisms that enable and give momentum to the developmental process, as well as the mechanisms that hinder the developmental process. We now go into some depth to describe how, through the feedback loop and interventions, teams develop over time.

2.1 How the second I drives team development

As shown earlier, the second input is the conclusions drawn from the outcomes of a performance cycle – the take-home messages which generate a cyclical causal feedback loop (Ilgen et al., 2005). By feedback is meant the process in which parts of the output of a system are returned to their inputs in order to regulate further output. It can be feedback on inputs (e.g. a person has shown to lack teamwork skills), on performance processes as well as on performance outcomes. The feedback (second I) can be the motive for changing the inputs (first I) that will feed another performance cycle for the team. It can also trigger change in team processes and emergent states. Providing individuals and teams with feedback about their performance can in itself be an effective intervention in any learning process and achievement. Individuals and teams need feedback to improve their strategies, to gain deeper understanding of their task and how to better regulate and monitor their work (Hattie & Timperley, 2007). In a review Gabelica, Bossche, Segers, & Gijselaers (2012) integrated findings from 59 empirical studies investigating the effects of feedback in teams in educational and professional settings. They hypothesized that beyond the most extensively considered dependent variable "team performance," feedback also seems to be an agent through which central team processes and emergent states may be developed and strengthened. Research suggests that prompting feedback processing at an early stage of collaborative work through relevant interventions has the power to help teams benefit from their past experiences and improve performance. But as mentioned several times, the use of feedback depends on how it is given and received, and the results of the effectiveness of feedback to individuals and teams are mixed.

Teams can actively seek feedback (situation awareness) and ask for feedback from the surrounding system. In the action phase team members can provide one another with feedback through mutual performance monitoring, and in the transition-phase can explore the second I. To make use of the learning potential in the second I, the team must actively process this feedback by stepping back from their team activity, and in a transition-phase reflect, draw conclusions, build plans and ultimately put them into action. Chapter 7 shows a model of how teams work differently in the action and transition phases to learn and develop (Marks et al., 2001). It is only the combination of team performance feedback and reflexivity that leads to performance change (Gabelica, den Bossche, Maeyer, Segers, & Gijselaers, 2014).

2.2 TDIs in a time perspective

Some teams have the ability to reflect, make use of the second I, learn and develop whereas others do not. These who do not, as well as those who do, might develop further with the support of TDIs. Some teams need a TDI to learn to reflect, e.g. a team debrief, and others might use a team debrief to accelerate the processes of making use of what the team members have already concluded from the feedback on outcomes. The second input is one starting point for carrying out a TDI. TDIs can also be used to establish teamwork in a pre-process such as a team charter, e.g. to select team members and compose the team, or an early intervention when the team is first established and making plans for how to work. TDIs can contribute to the re-shaping of existing inputs, of mediators/processes and of outcomes during the process, e.g. team training to learn and practice how to communicate better. TDIs can also create qualitatively new inputs, mediators/processes and outcomes, such as a structured team building to expand existing goals to include that of organizational learning.

The first concern is to fit content (target dimensions and goals) and solution together. In Figure 10.1 in Chapter 10 it was shown how the second I form development and TDIs, and also ten different TDIs in relation to target dimensions were presented. When planning a TDI to develop an existing team, it first has to be asked which elements need to be targeted with the help of the second I to enhance effectiveness through development. For example, if a team needs assistance to overcome emotional reactions to feedback on poor performance, coaching and/or team building could be suitable. If the second I show that the team has to manage performance pressure, interventions that provide support via leadership and/or work-design options may be optimal. This underscores the need for a customized rather than a blanket approach to the implementation of interventions (Quigley, Collins, Gibson, & Parker, 2018). As described in earlier chapters, part of this customization of TDIs is also likely to be contingent on the team's context, e.g. the kind of organization and task (Bresman & Zellmer-Bruhn, 2013). If a team has a complex task that puts demands on advanced problem-solving, and if decisions have major consequences, this involves autonomy and the team will be composed of highly skilled individuals. An intervention for such a team, e.g. team building for role clarification, must be formed to meet the team's cognitive capacity.

Interventions focus on certain target dimensions such as inputs (team composition, team charters, teamwork design, etc.), team processes (team training and team building, etc.) or processes as well as outcomes (team coaching, team leadership, team debriefs, etc.) and influence the whole subsequent performance cycle. The outcome is targeted through the team's making use of the second I, as this will impact the next performance cycle. An outcome showing poor quality, e.g. in patient care, can indirectly be targeted by team training in coordination. It can be directly targeted by an intervention such as directive leadership and performance monitoring. When selecting an intervention, one should be clear about whether a direct and/or indirect impact on inputs, processes/mediators and outputs is expected, otherwise the proposed TDI doesn't make sense (Shuffler, Diazgranados, Maynard, & Salas, 2018).

The second concern when planning TDIs is at what time point in the team's performance cycle it should be implemented. Everyone agrees on the complexity of teamwork, and researchers are advised to "embrace the complexity" of team dynamics (Mathieu, Maynard, Rapp, & Gilson, 2008, p. 461), but little is known about how teams change and develop over time through TDIs (Mathieu et al., 2017). Some researchers discuss patterns of team performance over time to incorporate the temporal dimension of team performance, and suggest that different interventions will be needed along the way, depending on the team's performance pattern (Quigley et al., 2018). See e.g. the contributions of researchers from the stage-model tradition (such as Wheelan's earlier) that describe these different performance patterns.

The point at which it is carried out during a performance cycle will impact the effectiveness of the TDI and the performance patterns in the subsequent performance episode. *It can be a reactive measure or a measure to put the team on the right trajectory from the start.* As has been said many times now, a diagnosis and a needs analysis precede any meaningful TDI. But it is also necessary to understand which trajectory characterizes the team, and this will help to choose relevant interventions. There might be patterns over performance cycles in how the team's performance changes over time that show *when* a positive momentum is created or sustained. This pattern provides information on when a TDI is best carried out to create momentum and have maximum effect. One example: Consider the problems with the digitalization of systems within public organizations and authorities – problems that, according to many in the production, ultimately take even more time for administrative work and reduce the time for value-creating work. A team might be in the groan zone after having had several meetings with the administrative support function aimed at transferring their experience and knowledge so that they adapt their way of interacting with the teams in the production and lessen their own workload. The team is about to declare this an impossible mission and so give up. But a team debrief might help the team find a different strategy for how to interact with support functions – and knowing what to do creates momentum.

How effective a TDI is, due to timing and the team's performance episodes, can also be discussed from the perspective of whether it is implemented to change existing inputs, mediators or outputs, or whether it is implemented to create the right inputs from the start so that a positive performance pattern can develop. In Figure 11.1 we present two examples of how different TDIs can be used to develop I, M, O at different time points for teams with different trajectories.

Figure 11.1. should be read top-down. In the figure the development of two teams is shown over time. Team 1 received a bundled TDI at the pre-process of establishing teamwork, and is later supported by only two TDIs. (We remind the reader that team design and work design are also TDIs.) Team 2 is supported by a range of TDIs as the second I at different time points after a performance cycle indicated that support is needed to alter performance patterns. The right conditions were not established at the beginning of the team's life-span. The figure illustrates that the timing of interventions plays a role for the team's development, and for how much support the team will need. It is our experience that if the contextual and situational prerequisites at the beginning (the first I) are unsuitable for effective teamwork, no matter what TDIs are carried out later, team performance will not result in the expected outcomes. Even if better prerequisites are later put in place, patterns and mindsets have developed that later are very difficult to change, and some perhaps still cannot be expected to be developed, e.g. due to work design. If the task lacks learning potential, it will affect team cognition and outcomes. Pseudo-teamwork is not easily developed into teamwork (see Chapters 1 and 3).

3 How to monitor team development

After a TDI, attention should be given to evaluation and maintenance of the outcome. If not, there is a risk that the impacts of TDIs as a momentum for further development are overlooked (Salas, Reyes, & Woods, 2018). We described in Chapter 10 that considerable work needs to be done to make use of what was gained by the TDI after it is carried out. One way to do this is to monitor the output which is supposed to be affected by the intervention. Often the output is defined on a level distant to the one the intervention is focusing on. It takes time before an intervention on the team level has changed an attitude, behaviour, team knowledge or conditions for teamwork so that an intervention in the next performance cycle can measure an outcome. In the complex world of an organization it is also very difficult to detangle all mediating processes and mechanisms which have an effect on the outcome. As described previously, such an approach does not tell what it was that brought change about. What is the real-time evidence that the team develops, i.e. what are the observable changes in team behaviour that contribute to improved team performance? *This is important both during a TDI and after a TDI is carried out, as well as in general.* During an intervention such information might initiate necessary adaptions of the TDI to make it work. After a TDI it tells about what was learned and whether this has been transferred to the workplace. All teams need to reflect upon their processes. We suggest the use of behavioural markers in the process of selecting TDIs, monitoring processes during the TDI and the task-work process as well as interpersonal relations in everyday work. No matter if the team is supported by TDIs or not, and by adequate leadership,

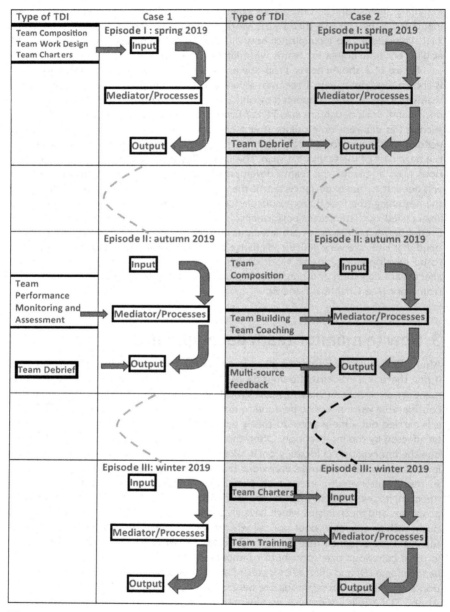

Figure 11.1 Examples of the role of interventions for teamwork development
Source: (adapted from Shuffler & Carter, 2018)

monitoring of the development is crucial to keeping a positive momentum. This is of interest for management, team leaders, teams and team members.

An understanding of the specific behaviours associated with effective team performance can help to better diagnose teams' problems, develop appropriate TDIs and be the foundation for systematic monitoring of team processes. We give a short recap of what these processes are before we suggest how these can be observed.

We have described that specific behaviour functions a) to regulate the team's performance and b) to keep the team together. Regulation occurs before and in preparation for task performance, during the action phase and after completing the task in the transition phase. It is first the process of defining mission, setting goals and formulating action plans. Execution of team tasks includes actions that correspond to members' communication, coordination and cooperation with each other, such as mutual performance monitoring and backup behaviour. Teamwork behaviours that occur after completing the team task (i.e. reflection in the transition phase) include reviewing important situations and conducting appraisals of the team's performance and prerequisites (e.g. internal team resources, broader environmental conditions), solving problems that are hindering goal attainment, and making adjustments to the team's strategy and work plan, etc. The team members assess whether their actions have moved them closer towards accomplishing the expected results and what modifications are required to facilitate future success. In addition to these three dimensions related to task work, a fourth dimension of teamwork is the behaviour that keeps the team together (i.e. maintenance). These activities are linked to the interpersonal relations and their dynamics, and include managing interpersonal conflict between members, social support and actions taken to build an amicable climate, etc. The KSAs of individual team members are essential, but so too are the KSAs of the team as a whole for team performance.

Behavioural markers are "statements that serve as indicators or the presence or absence of the associated construct (*e.g. coordination, goal specification*)" (Rosen et al., 2011, p. 114). In previous chapters we have described that behavioural markers can be used to diagnose the team as these identify behavioural strengths and weaknesses, and the team's needs for targeted team development. The ultimate goal for a TDI is that the team should become more effective. We suggest the use of behavioural markers to observe changes in team processes when monitoring whether interventions are resulting in any changes of team behaviour. They can be used to monitor all four dimensions of teamwork described earlier. However, interpersonal dynamics is not yet part of this approach.

Team adaptation is an essential characteristic of an effective team and is closely linked to effective coordination. The need for adaptation is stronger for teams in dynamic environments. Effective teams assess the current situation, and notice and respond to relevant stimuli in the work environment to accomplish the shared goal. They are adept at behaving in similar, but not identical, ways that fit to different situations during routine work. The team rapidly adapts its way of working when faced with new demands and non-routine situations, and has a repertoire of adaptations that enable the team to meet demands in non-routine situations appropriately (Gorman, Grimm, & Dunbar, 2018). So far empirical studies have not assessed team adaptation directly. There is a lack of an appropriate method for capturing the team adaptation process (Maynard & Kennedy, 2016). Rosen et al. (2011) have introduced behavioural markers that could serve as the foundation for developing such a measurement. Following the recommendations provided by Rosen et al. (2011), Georganta (2018) developed BARS (Behaviourally Anchored Rating Scales) for the team adaptation that include both effective and ineffective behaviour, thus enabling the assessment of the entire spectrum of the team-adaptation process.

Researchers have summarized 22 behavioural markers for behaviours before and during preparation of teamwork, during execution and after completion (Rosen et al., 2011). Later we give a few examples of these BARS and recommend those concerned with team effectiveness to consider if such BARS can be of practical use. In our experience such concrete examples of what to strive for during everyday work help teams and team leaders to understand and build a shared understanding of what effective teamwork is about.

Table 11.1 shows some examples of how behavioural markers could be used a) to select TDIs for solving a problem and b) to monitor the development of team behaviour. For full descriptions, see Rosen et al. (2011, p. 115f) and Rosen & Dietz (2017). Notice that these behavioural markers can easily be adapted and put into practical use for monitoring ongoing task work and as a basis for reflection in the transition phase.

Behavioural markers help practitioners to identify specific behavioural strengths and weaknesses of teams, to facilitate team adaptation and to develop TDIs to enhance team effectiveness. Feedback and reflection with the support of behavioural markers will provide input to forming the second I. The BARS can be implemented as a team-development tool for feedback. The BARS can be used to provide peer and/or team leader/supervisor feedback directed at specific behaviours. This developmental feedback can facilitate a better understanding of what constitutes effective and less effective team coordination and adaptation behaviour, thus encouraging the team to improve as a whole. It can help the team to develop other team capacities related to team adaptation, such as trust and shared mental (Burke, Stagl, Salas, Pierce, & Kendall, 2006).

4 Our take-home messages

In the IMOI model there is substantial support for the constructs, and the relations between the constructs, to explain team coordination and team-adaptive performance. But there are many things that need to be researched further in order to provide practitioners with knowledge about how to solve problems with teamwork. We have e.g. highlighted the importance of the mechanisms that make TDIs work in Chapter 10. In the book we have presented models for examples of how teams adapt, and some of the many models presented in the literature of how different constructs interact and impact team effectiveness. The problem is that there are, as mentioned earlier, few empirical studies that take the full complexity of teamwork into account. Single tests of models are not enough, and sometimes there is evidence for the constructs in the model but not for the model as a whole. We give an example: a recent doctoral dissertation (Georganta, 2018) tested Burke et al.'s (2006) original adaptive cycle. Georganta found support for that situation assessment, plan formulation and execution and impact adaptation, but team learning was not related to post-change

EFFECTIVE TEAMS OVER TIME | 293

Table 11.1 Examples of behavioural markers for the selection and monitoring of TDIs (source and adapted from Rosen et al. (2011, p. 115f) and Rosen and Dietz (2017, p. 488)

Problem to be solved	Is there a potential in selected TDIs to develop behaviour?	Use of behavioural markers to select TDI and to monitor team behaviour
Need to develop the ability to anticipate other team members' needs (includes shift of workload) through accurate knowledge about their responsibilities. Backup/ supportive behaviour	Team Building Team Charters Team Learning	For backup (plan execution) • Do team members proactively step in to assist fellow team members when needed? • Do team members proactively provide feedback to fellow team members to facilitate self-correction? • Do team members redistribute workload to underused team members? • Do team members communicate the need for assistance? • Do team members identify unbalanced workload situations?
Need to develop intra-team feedback; provision of information about team or individual performance either before, during or after a performance cycle	Team Training Team Charters Team Debriefs	Intra-team feedback (team learning) • Do team members seek information and feedback from other team members about past performance? • Does the team develop and integrate lessons learned from past performance? • Does the team articulate information to correct deficient performance during a performance episode? • Do team members provide constructive and specific comments to other team members?
Need to improve the exchange of information among team members emphasizing appropriate content, form, structure and timing	Team Building Team Training Team Coaching	Team communication (situation assessment) • Does the team clearly communicate problem definitions? • Does the team follow up to ensure that messages are received and understood? • Does the team acknowledge messages when they are sent? • Does the team cross check information with the sender to ensure that the message meaning is understood? • Does the team articulate the "big picture" to one another as appropriate? • Does the team proactively pass on information without being asked?

team performance. This implies that the theoretical suggestion of Burke et al. (2006) of the completion of the overall four-phase process (situation assessment, plan formation, plan execution and learning) for team adaptation may not be correct. There are myriads of factors that explain why some teams perform better in routine tasks and adapt better to new demands. Time is important, but we know little about how time impacts development. Kennedy and Maynard (2017) ask for more research from a temporal perspective to explain when the team adapts across its lifecycle (adaptation timing), how long the team takes to adapt (adaptation duration), the recurrent need to adapt (adaptation frequency), and if and how this leads to positive adaptive performance. We, too, have searched the databases in vain for empirical research on how time for engaging in teamwork affects adaptive performance. We still argue that although much is not known, it is far better to use the knowledge there is than invent something. All can fall into the trap when incompetence is not recognized, as one is too incompetent to see one's limitations (see the Dunning-Kruger effect). *Our first take-home message is: Whatever you do to support a team, it should be based on theory.* Not everything is known, but very much is. It is our experience that far too often, well-meaning support to teams is based on subjective perceptions and the use of anecdotal evidence to prove assumptions.

Theoretically, adaptation processes depend not only on time for the adaptation processes themselves; it also takes time to form the interpersonal relationships to build trust, efficacy and a cooperative climate. All elements in the processes and refining of team cognition *may* take time from the routine-task performance. Sometimes it is possible to reflect and talk, engage in adaptive performance and other change and developmental activities, and simultaneously perform routine tasks, and sometimes it is not. Teams differ from one another, but for all teams the issue of how much time, and how this time should be spent, is a feature that might impact the team's coordination and adaptation, the outcomes and the second I. Teamwork in itself takes time, and not all managers and team members embrace this fact. We do not say that this should mean meetings or extra events, but with no or little time for reflexivity and transfer phases many teams cannot be expected to be adaptive and contribute to the expected outcomes. Further, we have shown that interventions are either more or less effective depending on whether they are carried out over time or as single events, and different TDIs can be needed at different time points. *Our second take-home message is: Invest in time and support over time.* That is different from the many one-day interventions that teams are supposed to develop from.

Throughout the book we have shown how the context impacts the team's performance and how it sets the frame for what outputs can be reached. *Our third take-home message is: Provide adequate prerequisites, a good enough context, otherwise do not expect teamwork.* And if there is no expectation of teamwork – why invest in it? This is very different from the often dominant focus on intra-team processes. We have shown that there is substantial support for the assumption that contextual aspects have equal or greater impact on team-performance effectiveness than team processes. Often the team is encouraged or supported in different ways including TDIs to develop their teamwork and interpersonal processes. But if the context simply remains the way it is, not much will happen.

Bibliography

Bell, B. S., & Kozlowski, S. W. J. (2012). Three conceptual themes for future research on teams. *Industrial and Organizational Psychology, 5*(1), 45–48. https://doi. org/10.1111/j.1754-9434.2011.01403.x

Bell, S. T. (2007). Deep-level composition variables as predictors of team performance: A meta-analysis. *Journal of Applied Psychology, 92*(3), 595–615. https://doi.org/10.1037/0021-9010.92.3.595

Bresman, H., & Zellmer-Bruhn, M. (2013). The structural context of team learning: Effects of organizational and team structure on internal and external learning. *Organization Science, 24.* https://doi.org/10.1287/orsc.1120.0783

Burke, S., Stagl, K., Salas, E., Pierce, L., & Kendall, D. (2006). Understanding team adaptation: A conceptual analysis and model. *The Journal of Applied Psychology, 91.* https://doi.org/10.1037/0021-9010.91.6.1189

Chidambaram, L., & Bostrom, R. (1997). Group development (I): A review and synthesis of development models. *Group Decision and Negotiation, 6*(2), 159–187. https://doi.org/10.1023/A:1008603328241

Gabelica, C., Bossche, P. Van den, Segers, M., & Gijselaers, W. (2012). Feedback, a powerful lever in teams: A review. *Educational Research Review, 7*(2), 123–144. https://doi.org/10.1016/j.edurev.2011.11.003

Gabelica, C., den Bossche, P. Van, Maeyer, S. De, Segers, M., & Gijselaers, W. (2014). The effect of team feedback and guided reflexivity on team performance change. *Learning and Instruction, 34,* 86–96. https://doi.org/https://doi.org/10.1016/j.learninstruc.2014.09.001

Georganta, E. (2018). *Team adaptation process: An empirical investigation of its dynamic and complex nature.* Doctoral dissertation. München. LMU München.

Gersick, C. J. G. (1988). Time and transition in work teams: Toward a new model of group development. *Academy of Management Journal, 31*(1), 9–41. https://doi.org/10.5465/256496

Gersick, C. J. G. (1991). Revolutionary change theories: A multilevel exploration of the punctuated equilibrium paradigm. *The Academy of Management Review, 16*(1), 10–36. https://doi.org/10.2307/258605

Gorman, J., Grimm, D., & A. Dunbar, T. A. (2018). Defining and measuring team effectiveness in dynamic environments and implications for team ITS: What matters (pp. 55–74). https://doi.org/10.1108/S1534-085620180000019007

Hattie, J., & Timperley, H. (2007). The power of feedback. *Review of Educational Research, 77*(1), 81–112. https://doi.org/10.3102/003465430298487

Ilgen, D. R., Hollenbeck, J. R., Johnson, M., & Jundt, D. (2005). Teams in organizations: From Input-Process-Output Models to IMOI Models. *Annual Review of Psychology, 56*(1), 517–543. https://doi.org/10.1146/annurev.psych.56.091103.070250

Kennedy, D. M., & Maynard, M. T. (2017). It is about time: Temporal considerations of team adaptation. In E. Salas, W. Brandon Vessey, & L. Landon, Blackwell (Eds.), *Team Dynamics Over Time (Research on Managing Groups and Teams, Volume 18)* (pp. 29–49). Emerald Publishing Limited. https://doi.org/doi:10.1108/S1534-085620160000018002

Knapp, R. (2010). Collective (Team) Learning Process Models: A conceptual review. *Human Resource Development Review, 9*(3), 285–299. https://doi.org/10.1177/1534484310371449

Kozlowski, S. W. J., & Bell, B. S. (2013). Work groups and teams in organizations: Review update. In N. Schmitt & S. Highhouse (Eds.), *Handbook of psychology, vol. 12: Industrial and organizational psychology* (2nd ed., pp. 412–469). Hoboken, NJ: Wiley.

Kozlowski, S. W. J., & Klein, K. J. (2000). A multilevel approach to theory and research in organizations: Contextual, temporal, and emergent processes. In *Multilevel theory, research, and methods in organizations: Foundations, extensions, and new directions* (pp. 3–90). San Francisco, CA: Jossey-Bass.

Lepine, J. A., Piccolo, R., Jackson, C., Mathieu, J., & Methot, J. (2008). A meta-analysis of teamwork processes: Tests of a multidimensional model and relationships with team effectiveness criteria. *Personnel Psychology, 61.* https://doi.org/10.1111/j.1744-6570.2008.00114.x

Mannix, E., & Jehn, K. A. (2004). Let's norm and storm, but not right now: Integrating models of group development and performance. In S. Blount (Ed.), *Time in Groups* (Research on

Managing Groups and Teams, Vol. 6, pp. 11–37). Bingley: Emerald Group Publishing Limited. https://doi.org/doi:10.1016/S1534-0856(03)06002-X

Marks, M. A., Mathieu, J. E., & Zaccaro, S. J. (2001). A temporally based framework and taxonomy of team processes. *Academy of Management Review, 26*(3), 356–376. https://doi.org/10.5465/amr.2001.4845785

Mathieu, J. E., Gallagher, P. T., Domingo, M. A., & Klock, E. A. (2019). Embracing complexity: Reviewing the past decade of team effectiveness research. *Annual Review of Organizational Psychology and Organizational Behavior, 6*(1), 17–46. https://doi.org/10.1146/annurev-orgpsych-012218-015106

Mathieu, J. E., Hollenbeck, J. R., van Knippenberg, D., & Ilgen, D. R. (2017). A century of work teams in the Journal of Applied Psychology. *Journal of Applied Psychology, 102*(3), 452–467. https://doi.org/10.1037/apl0000128

Mathieu, J., Maynard, M. T., Rapp, T., & Gilson, L. (2008). Team effectiveness 1997–2007: A review of recent advancements and a glimpse into the future. *Journal of Management, 34*(3), 410–476. https://doi.org/10.1177/0149206308316061

Maynard, M. T., & Kennedy, D. M. (2016). Team adaptation and resilience: What do we know and what can be applied to long-duration isolated, confined, and extreme contexts, (NASA/TM-2016-21859).

McGrath, J. E. (1964). *Social psychology: A brief introduction.* New York: Holt, Rinehart and Winston.

Morgan, B. B., Salas, E., & Glickman, A. S. (1993). An analysis of team evolution and maturation. *The Journal of General Psychology, 120*(3), 277–291. https://doi.org/10.1080/00221309.1993.9711148

Newman, A., Donohue, R., & Eva, N. (2017). Psychological safety: A systematic review of the literature. *Human Resource Management Review, 27*(3), 521–535. https://doi.org/10.1016/j.hrmr.2017.01.001

Okhuysen, G. A., & Waller, M. J. (2002). Focusing on midpoint transitions: An analysis of boundary conditions. *Academy of Management Journal, 45*(5), 1056–1065. https://doi.org/10.5465/3069330

Parboteeah, K. P., Hoegl, M., & Muethel, M. (2015). Team characteristics and employees' individual learning: A cross-level investigation. *European Management Journal, 33*(4), 287–295. https://doi.org/10.1016/J.EMJ.2015.02.004

Picazo, C., Gamero, N., Zornoza, A., & Peiró, J. M. (2015). Testing relations between group cohesion and satisfaction in project teams: A cross-level and cross-lagged approach. *European Journal of Work and Organizational Psychology, 24*(2), 297–307. https://doi.org/10.1080/1359432X.2014.894979

Quigley, N. R., Collins, C. G., Gibson, C. B., & Parker, S. K. (2018). Team performance archetypes: Toward a new conceptualization of team performance over time. *Group & Organization Management, 43*(5), 787–824. https://doi.org/10.1177/1059601118794344

Raes, E., Kyndt, E., Decuyper, S., Van den Bossche, P., & Dochy, F. (2015). An exploratory study of group development and team learning. *Human Resource Development Quarterly, 26*(1), 5–30. https://doi.org/10.1002/hrdq.21201

Ramos-Villagrasa, P. J., Marques-Quinteiro, P., Navarro, J., & Rico, R. (2018). Teams as complex adaptive systems: Reviewing 17 years of research. *Small Group Research, 49*(2), 135–176. https://doi.org/10.1177/1046496417713849

Richter, A. W., Hirst, G., van Knippenberg, D., & Baer, M. (2012). Creative self-efficacy and individual creativity in team contexts: Cross-level interactions with team informational resources. *Journal of Applied Psychology, 97*(6), 1282–1290. https://doi.org/10.1037/a0029359

Rosen, M. A., Bedwell, W. L., Wildman, J. L., Fritzsche, B. A., Salas, E., & Burke, C. S. (2011). Managing adaptive performance in teams: Guiding principles and behavioral markers for measurement. *Human Resource Management Review, 21*(2), 107–122. https://doi.org/10.1016/j.hrmr.2010.09.003

Rosen, M. A., & Dietz, A. S. (2017). Team performance measurement. In E. Salas, R. Rico, & J. Passmore (Eds.), *The Wiley Blackwell handbook of the psychology of team working and collaborative processes* (pp. 481–502). New York: John Wiley & Sons Ltd.

Salas, E., Reyes, D. L., & Woods, A. L. (2018). *Team Training in Organizations* (Vol. 1). https://doi.org/10.1093/oxfordhb/9780190263362.013.38

Sanner, B., & Bunderson, J. S. (2013). Psychological safety, learning, and performance: A comparison of direct and contingent effects. *Academy of Management Proceedings, 2013*(1), 10198. https://doi.org/10.5465/ambpp.2013.10198abstract

Shuffler, M. L., & Carter, D. (2018). Teamwork situated in multiteam systems: Key lessons learned and future opportunities. *American Psychologist, 73.* https://doi.org/10.1037/amp0000322

Shuffler, M. L., Diazgranados, D., Maynard, M. T., & Salas, E. (2018). Developing, sustaining, and maximizing team effectiveness: An integrative, dynamic perspective of team development interventions. *Academy of Management Annals, 12*(2), 688–724. https://doi.org/10.5465/annals.2016.0045

Spielberger, T. (2016). *Maßnahmen zum Outdoor-Teambuilding.* Wiesbaden: Springer Fachmedien Wiesbaden. https://doi.org/10.1007/978-3-658-12299-7

Tuckmann, B. W. (1965). Developmental sequence in small groups. *Psychological Bulletin, 63*(6), 384–399. https://doi.org/10.1037/h0022100

Tuckman, B. W., & Jensen, M. A. C. (1977). Stages of small-group development revisited. *Group & Organization Studies, 2*(4), 419–427. https://doi.org/10.1177/105960117700200404

Wheelan, S. A. (2005a). *Group processes: A developmental perspective.* Boston: Allyn and Bacon.

Wheelan, S. A. (2005b). *The handbook of group research and practice.* Thousand Oaks, CA: SAGE Publications.

Wheelan, S. A. (2009). Group size, group development, and group productivity. *Small Group Research, 40*(2), 247–262. https://doi.org/10.1177/1046496408328703

Wheelan, S. A., & Burchill, C. (1999). Take teamwork to new heights. *Nursing Management (Springhouse), 30*(4), 28–31. https://doi.org/10.1097/00006247-199904000-00009

Wheelan, S. A., Davidson, B., & Tilin, F. (2003). Group development across time. *Small Group Research, 34*(2), 223–245. https://doi.org/10.1177/1046496403251608

Wheelan, S. A., & Hochberger, J. M. (1996). Validation studies of the group development questionnaire. *Small Group Research, 27*(1), 143–170. https://doi.org/10.1177/1046496496271007

Wheelan, S. A., & Kaeser, R. M. (1997). The influence of task type and designated leaders on developmental patterns in groups. *Small Group Research, 28*(1), 94–121. https://doi.org/10.1177/1046496497281004

Wheelan, S. A., & Mckeage, R. L. (1993). Developmental patterns in small and large groups. *Small Group Research, 24*(1), 60–83. https://doi.org/10.1177/1046496493241005

Wheelan, S. A., Murphy, D., Tsumura, E., & Kline, S. F. (1998). Member perceptions of internal group dynamics and productivity. *Small Group Research, 29*(3), 371–393. https://doi.org/10.1177/1046496498293005

Wheelan, S. A., Verdi, A., & McKeage, R. (1994). *The group development observation system: Origins and applications.* Philadelphia: GDQ Associates.

Wildman, J. L., Thayer, A. L., Rosen, M. A., Salas, E., Mathieu, J. E., & Rayne, S. R. (2012). Task types and team-level attributes. *Human Resource Development Review, 11*(1), 97–129. https://doi.org/10.1177/1534484311417561

Worchel, S. (1994). You can go home again: Returning group research to the group context with an eye on developmental issues. *Small Group Research, 25*(2), 205–223. https://doi.org/10.1177/1046496494252004

Worchel, S., Coutant-Sassic, D., & Grossmann, M. (1991). A developmental approach to group dynamics: A model and illustrative research.–PsycNET. In S. Worchel, W. Wood, & J. A.

Simpson (Eds.), *Group process and productivity* (pp. 181–202). Thousand Oaks, CA: Sage Publications, Inc.

Worchel, S., Grossman, M., & Coutant, D. (1994). Minority influence in the group context: How group factors affect when the minority will be influential. In *Minority influence* (pp. 97–114). Chicago, IL: Nelson-Hall Publishers.

Worchel, S., Rothgerber, H., & Day, E.A. (2011). Social loafing and group development: When "I" comes last. *Current Research in Social Psychology, 17.*

Worchel, S., Rothgerber, H., Day, E.A., Hart, D., & Butemeyer, J. (1998). Social identity and individual productivity within groups. *The British Journal of Social Psychology, 37*(4), 389–413. https://doi.org/10.1111/j.2044-8309.1998.tb01181.x

Index

Note: page numbers in *italic* indicate a figure and page numbers in **bold** indicate a table on the corresponding page.

absenteeism 10, 13, *14*, 58, 60
action phase: leadership functions 207; team knowledge 111, 113; workflow 122
activity theory 53
adaptability: communication for 174; defined 168; effective team 84; individual 170; lack of 168, *169*, *170*; novel demands 163; team process *169*; valued behaviour 57
adaptation: domains for solution **181**; plan formulation 176; processes 178, *179*; starting point 176; stimulus specific 175; target dimensions 181; timing, duration, frequency 294
affect: adaptive performance 294; autonomy, positive 59; behaviour, performance 83; belief systems 282; decisions, functions, teams 33, 41; different factors 36, 49; features of work, individual, team 50; feedback, performance 60, 98; with HR practices, outcomes 10; other outcomes 13, 15; outcomes of team's functioning 9; performance 40, 53; sense of belonging 4; skill variety, performance 62; TDI's, performance 266, 271; team cognition 289; team effectiveness 283; team learning, outcomes 18; team participation 61; timing will 43; training, results 265; unfavorable team composition 94; well-functioning teamwork 11; work design 48, 51, 57
Allen, L.A. 210
Allen, N.J. 145
Alper, S. 157
Alvero, A.M. 119
analysis: cause 36, 37, 79; theoretical 36
Arad, S. 170
Ashleigh, M.J. 127
assessment 176
assessment centre 96

attitudes: autonomy linked to 58; deep-level diversity 88; good 96; heedful interrelating 83; implications of related to performance 55; job satisfaction 64, 204; leadership consideration 200; and motivation 49, **261**; negative, towards diversity 88–9; personal 14; relevant for effective problem solving 147; TDI might develop 256, **263**; team climate 114–115, 140; team members, composition 17, 79, 256; team processes 283; team training to acquire 98, 127; work-design features impact 65; work related 10, 49, 62, 210
Austin, J. 119
authority differentiation 90, 92
autonomy: definition 58; impacts innovation 59; job satisfaction 58; positive performance 58; stress 65; work characteristic 50

backup behaviour: defined 120; team building 129
Bacon, N. 10
Baker, J.D. 207
Balcazar, F. 118
Ballard, D.I. 128
Bandura, A. 205
Bass, B.M. 200
Beal, D.J. 11
Beaubien, J.M. 10, 85
Bedwell, W.L. 168, 292
behaviour: adaptability 57; Behaviourally Anchored Rating Scales (BARS) 181, 183, 292; effective team performance 291; four constructs 12; goals steer 233; lack of coordinated 123; markers, monitor TDI's **293**; modelling training 98; motivation impacts 40; and performance 16, 57;

proactive 13; social 97; work 57; work design impacts 65

Behaviourally Anchored Rating Scale (BARS) 274

Bell, B.S 18, 115, 280, 284

Bell, S.T. 63

Benington, J. 209

Biech, E. 126

Bisbey, T. 117

Bliese, P. 170

Blyton, P. 10

Bocarnea, M.C. 207

Bollen, K. 157

Bono, J.E. 193

Bontis, N. 238

boundary: activities 246; objects 236

boundedness 4

Bourn, D. 211

Bowers, C. 120

Bradley, J.C. 96

Branch, S. 194

Bransford, J.D. 32

Bucklin, B.R. 119

building shared meaning: company-wide shared beliefs 232, 237; constructive conflicts 115; team learning 177–178; transition phase for OL 246; what the problem/goal is 32–33, 64, 68, 111, 113; in a workflow 122

Buljac-Samardzic, M 255

Bunderson, J.S. 114

Burchill, C. 284

Burke, C.S. 2, 16, 118, 154, 169, 171, 292

Burke, M.J. 11

Burke, S. 199, 201, 204

Burridge, M. 10, 12, 13, 14

Burt, D. 210

Burtscher, M.J. 175

Campion, M.A. 147

Cannon-Bowers, J.A. 2, 120, 252–253, 256

Cao, Q. 148

Carter, K.M. 204

cause analysis: assess performance 253; conflict 140; hypotheses 79; IMOI team effectiveness 140; leadership 192, 193; mindmap, lack of learning 228; organizational learning 227, 228; problem solving 36; producer of an effect 37; the "right" problem 255; team adaptability 168; uncoordinated team 110

Ceri-Booms, M. 199, 201, 202

Chan, C.C.A. 85

change: adaptive processes 164; agent 232; bottom-up/top-down 168, 224; communication 174; organizational structure 219; proactive effectiveness 179; readiness for 259, 269

Che-Ha, N. 85

Chiaburu, D.S. 202

Cho, B. 144

Choi, K. 144

Chow, C.W. 172

Christian, J.S. 85, 169, 171, 173, 178

Christian, M.S. 85, 96, 169, 171, 173, 178

closed-loop communication: develop team training 128; effective teamwork 118

close-to-production 166, 171

cognitive ability: barriers 37–8; individual and team 61, 84; team-adaptive performance 171

Cohen, R.R. 11

cohesion: The Group Environment Questionnaire 151; impacts performance 11

collective efficacy 205

collective regulation: of activities 55; routine tasks don't need 61

collectivism: KSA's for conflict management 154; team need over individual 85, 86; values, motivational orientations **82**

collectivists 86

common problems **22–23**

communication: clear 118, 174; closed-loop 118, 174; leader briefings 173; openness, elaboration 117, 174–175; performance feedback 97; relational 118; safety, psychological 116, 117; task interdependence 64; task-oriented 118; team performance 117; within teams 174; trust, openness 116–17; yield emergent state 111

competencies 90, 256

conflict management: needs intervention 157; online training 158; positive impact, team cohesion 157, 283; preemptive and reactive strategies **153**, 153–157; transformational leadership and 148–149

conflicts: consequences 145; constructive 112, 115, 143, 146–147, 150; constructive controversy 155; cultures 149; dysfunctional 141, 143–144, 147, 153; emotional 145; functional 87; health/

INDEX

well-being 143; 4 IC model 143; Intragroup
  Conflict Scale 151; intra-team conflict
  management 155; leadership affects 148;
  mediation 157; mental models 146; open
  discussion 141; organizational context
  148; process 143–145; relationship 139,
  143–147, 151–152; role 63; task 145–147,
  157; types of 143
conscientiousness 170
consensus: group think 115, 116; no 53; with
  stakeholders 35; team training 127
consultants 33, 252
convergent tools: facilitate decision-making
  32, 68, 123; knowledge building 113
Cooke, N.J. 16
cooperation: defined 120; team training
  129; team trust 116–117; working
  together 107
coordination: defined 107, *110*; explicit/
  implicit 121–2; impact on effectiveness 121;
  monitor and adapt 175; related to goal
  setting 113; team training for 129
core problems: conflict, identify 139;
  dysfunctional team, identify 108; lack
  of adaptability, identify 168; leader,
  identify 192; little teamwork, identify
  52–53; organizational learning, identify
  227; symptom/problem 34–35; team
  composition, identify 78–79
Costa, P.L. 145
Côté, S. 11
Coutant-Sassic, D. 281
Crant, J.M. 12
Crew Resource Management (CRM) 129
critical incidents 224
Crossan, M.M. 217, 218, 220, 222, 235
cross-boundary: collaboration 64;
  cooperation 122; interactions 236–237;
  objects 235
cross training 127–128
culture: to adapt processes 173; conflict
  148–149; each organization has 16;
  feedback friendly 129; impacts individual
  172; learning oriented 220; organizational
  168, 232, 240, 269; team effectiveness
  studied in different 17; toxic 194
Curşeu, P.L. 199
Curral, L. 178

Darwin 180
Dawson, J.F. 10

debriefs: self-correction training 129; team
  training 43, 125
DeChurch, L.A. 5, 111, 112, 114, 115, 146, 157
decision-making: dependent on knowledge,
  perspectives 114; team participation 90; in
  teams 15; tools 32
Decuyper, S. 122, 177
de Dreu, C.K. 141, 145, 149
Dekker-van-Doorn, C.M. 256
Delarue, A. 10, 12, 13, 14
DeNisi, A. 118, 271
DeRue, D.S. 195, 203, 205, 284
Destructive Leadership Questionnaire
  (DLQ) 206
Deutsch, M. 147
Deutsch's Twelve Commandments of
  Conflict Resolution 147
Devanna, M.A. 200
de Wit, F.R.C. 145
diagnose: critical for team training 253;
  embeddedness of OL to TL **238**; model,
  what to 68; routine-task performance
  123; team 36; team adaptive capacity 180;
  team cohesion 151; team conflict 151;
  team process with OL 237; team's affective
  state 150; team structure 92; team trust
  150–151
Diazgranados, D. 125, 154
Dierendonck, D. 141
Dijkstra, M.T.M. 141
Dimensions of Learning Organization Query
  (DLOQ) 237
D'Innocenzo, L. 11
divergent: perspectives 33, 34; processes 112;
  tools, brainstorming 32, 68, 123
diversity: appropriate 79; assessing 91–92;
  deep-level 88; faultlines 88; heterogeneity
  86–7; perspectives 177; surface 87–8; task
  related 87; The Team Diagnostic Survey 92
Dochy, F. 122, 177, 278
Donohue, R. 116, 190
Donovan, M.A. 170
Dorsey, D. 170
D'Zurilla, T.J. 30

Eddy, E.R. 125
Edmondson, A.C. 116, 141
Edwards, B.D. 96
effectiveness model *20*
Ellis, A.P. 174
embed OL 231

emergent states: mental models 146; predictors of effective teamwork 110; processes become 5; processes yield 18; team-adaption process 178; team learning forms 282; team members collective 11
emotional intelligence 1
empirical evidence 285–286
employee: commitment 10; turnover 7, 10
Erickson, A. 194
Euwema, M. 157
evaluation: diagnosis routine-task 123; methods 273–274; PSC 273
evidence-based 260–268; exchange between professions 233; practices, identify 240; TDI's 251–252
executive coaching 209–210
expectations: clear/explicit 15; performance 17; public's 30; stakeholders 33, 68, 114; of team performance 17, 115; team results 65

facilitator: conflict resolution 157; external 155; role clarification 126–7; team training 127
Fay, D. 10
feasibility study 43
feedback: 360-degree 211; intervention/training 97; loop 286; multi-rater 211; multi-source-feedback 212; performance 118–119; performance improvement 119; process 119; process/result 60; reduces role ambiguity, anxiety 63; team 197
feedback loops 19, 234
feed-forward 218, 220, 222, 231, 234
Fernandez, R. 210
Ferzandi, L. 115
Fleishman, E.A. 129
Fortes-Ferreira, L. 114
Fritzsche, B.A. 168, 292
Fuda, K.K. 123

Gabelica, C. 119, 287
Gao, Q. 121
Gelfand, M.J. 149
Georganta, E. 181, 292
Gersick, C.J. 107
Gijselaers, W. 119, 201, 287
Gilson, L.L. 9
Gjerde, S. 210
Glassop, L.I. 10
Glickman, A.S. 281

goal-setting: altered 70; clarity 56; effective coordination 113; expand work roles 230; impact behaviour/motivation 40; organizational strategy 56; shared understanding 126, 231; S.M.A.R.T. 70; summary 57; target dimensions 39; team goals/work design 67; theory 39; unclear 67
Gómez, L.F. 128
González-Romá, V. 114
Goodwin, G.F. 16, 154
Grading of Recommendations Assessment, Development, and Evaluation scale (GRADE) 264
Green, S.G. 118
Greer, L.L. 141, 144, 154
Gregory, M.E. 267
Griffin, M. 172
Grille, A. 207
Grossenbacher, M. 112
Grossman, M. 281
Grossman, R. 154
Grote, G. 121, 175
Group Development Observation System (GDOS) 280
Groups Development Questionnaire (GDQ) 280
group think 115–116
Guillaume, Y.R.F. 211
Gully, S.M. 11

Hacker, W. 55
Hackman, J.R. 107, 195
Hafford-Letchfield, T. 211
Hamilton, K. 115, 146
Harper, A.L. 210
Harrison, G.L. 172
Hartley, J. 209
Hastings, S.E. 145
Hawthorne studies 9
heterogeneity 86–7
heterogeneous perspectives 33
Hinsz, V.B. 119
Hjertø, K.B. 143, 151
Hoffman, B.J. 96
Hollenbeck, J.R. 17, 50, 174
Holman, D. 49
Honts, C. 112
Hopkins, B. 118
House, R.J. 200
Hoven, M. 201

INDEX

| 303

HR policies **257**
Hughes, A.M. 267
Humphrey, S.E. 48, 57, 63, 174
Hunt, M. 123

Ilgen, D.R. 5, 16, 17, 50, 114, 174
Ilgen, J.S. 210
implementation 31, 34–44, 46, 51, 73
Incalcaterra, K.A. 10
incompetence 294
Individual and Team Performance (ITP) 91
individual regulation: need to align with
others 53, 55, 56; routine tasks 61
information management 172
initiative 55
innovation: climate 140; complexity, team
learning 61, 66; culture and climate impact
172; exploration 223, 224, **257**; functional
conflicts improve 143; little autonomy
48, 59; organizational 218; task related
diversity 87; team learning 177; team
proactivity 12; teamwork outcome 9
Input-Mediator-Outcome-Input (IMOI model)
20; cause within team processes, mediators
110; feedback loop 45; interactions
18; interactions between elements 18;
mediators 20, 110, *169*; model 17; second
input 286; team development cycle 282;
team effectiveness IMOI model **257**
Input-Process-Outcome (IPO) 17, 139
instructional strategies 270
intellectual capital 219
interdependent 3, 63
Interdisciplinary Management Tool (IMT) 99
interlinked: symptoms/problems 35–36; team
processes 124
interpersonal: issues, team performance
97–98, 107, 128, 129, 137; issues diversity
140; mindmap, issues *140*; relationships,
affective processes 140; relationships,
conflicts dysfunctional 145
inter-professional learning programme
(IPL) 127
interventions: analysis prior 67; cause 43–44;
definition, tables **261–263**; different
domains 70, **70**; end 73; evaluate 44–45,
73, 99, 289; guided self-correction 125;
implement 43, 73; Interdisciplinary
Management Tool (IMT) 99; mutually
dependent **72**; reactive 24, 254;

targeted 42, 288; TDI, systematic 253;
team composition 157; team level 242;
teamwork development *290*
intrinsic motivation 10
inventory, research: Affina Team Performance
Inventory (ATPI) 123; Aston Organisation
Development (2010) 123; ITP Metrics 123;
Team Climate Inventory (TCI) 123, 150

Janis, I.L. 115
Jarvenpaa, S.L. 150
Jehn, K.A. 141, 144, 154
job crafting 50, 56–57
job satisfaction: autonomy improves 58;
relates to task complexity 61
Johnson, M. 17
Jones, R.J. 211
Joseph, D.L. 211, 265
Joshi, A. 10
Judge, T. 143
Jundt, D. 17

Kahol, K. 172
Karam, E.P. 195, 203, 205, 284
Kauffeld, S. 207
Keller, K. 149
Kennedy, C.L 96
Kennedy, D.M. 5, 168, 172, 178, 294
Kirkpatrick, D.L. 265
Klein, C. 154
Kluger, A.N. 118, 271
Knapp, R. 282
Knippenberg, D. 204
knowledge management: cross-boundary
learning 236; de-contextualize, adapt 236;
dis-embedding knowledge 235; knowledge
transfer 233, 236; managing intellectual
capital 219; push, pull 221
knowledge structure: existing, impede
adaptation process 180; model for team
adaptation process **169**; team learning
builds 177
Koeslag-Kreunen, M. 201
Kohn, M.L. 50
Kolbe, M. 121
Konradt, U. 6
Kozlowski, S.W.J. 5, 16, 18, 115, 280, 284
Kravitz, D. **15**
KSA (Knowledge, Skills, and Abilities): assess
team members' 81, 96; coaching 210;

for conflict management 154; individual competence 170; interpersonal 83; lack of appropriate 153; needed by team 81; self-management 83; team members lack 147; work design determines 48

Ku, H. 150

Kukenberger, M.R. 11

Künzle, B. 121

Kuvaas, B. 143, 151

Kyndt, E. 278

Lacerenza, C.N. 117, 211, 218, 267

Ladegard, G. 210

Lance, C.E. 96

Liao, J. 179

Laosirihongthong, T. 85

Law, K. 157

Le, J. 154

Leader Behaviour Description Questionnaire 199

leadership: assess 206; behaviour, misfit 192, 193, 194; consideration 193, 199–201; defined 189; Destructive Leadership Questionnaire (DLQ) 206; development 195, 210–212; effectiveness 191; executive coaching 209; formal/informal 205, 208; functional 194; initiation of structure 199; internal/external 203; lacking 22, 195; Leader Behaviour Description Questionnaire 199; leader-member-exchange (LMX) 190; measure 208; mindmap, ineffective 193; not clear 203; person-focused 200; psychological safety 190; shared 204, 205; Shared Professional Leadership Inventory for Teams (SPLIT) 207; style 172, 190; task-focused 199; team leaders' tasks 196; training 210; transactional 199; transformational 148, 172, 199, 200, 201, 210

Lean Production Systems (LPS) 224

learning: activities 244; distal 177, 243; flows 221; goal orientation 85; internal, external activities 243; internal team 243; multilevel 223; new practices 232, 235; task performance 222

learning highways 221

learning organization see organizational learning (OL)

Leidner, D.E. 150

LePine, J.A. 171

Leslie, L.M. 149

Levin, J. 123

Li, Z. 121

Lieberman, M.D. 1

Lim, L.L. 85

Long, E.C. 85, 169, 171, 173, 178

LoPilato, A.C. 96

Lyons, R. 154

MacKie, D. 210

Makker, A.B. 145

Mannix, E.A. 141, 144, 154

Manser, T. 175

Marks, M.A. 5, 121, 153, 190

Marlow, S.L. 117, 206, 211, 218, 267

Marques-Quinteiro, P. 178

Martin, B. 15

Martin, L.J. 126, 130

Martínez-Moreno, E. 154

Maslow, A.H. 1

Mason, C. 172

Mathieu, J.E. 5, 9, 11, 121, 125, 127, 153

Maurer, S.D. 96

Mavonda, F.T. 85

Maximilien, M. 14

Maynard, M.T. 5, 125, 168, 172, 178, 294

McComb, S.A. 118

McDaniel, M.A. 96

McDaniel, S.H. 4, 113

McEwan, D. 266

McGrath, J.E. 17, 282

McKinnon, J.L. 172

McLendon, C.L. 11

Mead, B.A. 204

mechanisms 268–269, 286, 289, 292

mental barriers: impede problem-solving 37–38; knowledge sharing 233; support knowledge flow 230

mental model: convergent 115; four solutions 125–127

Mesmer-Magnus, J.R. 5, 111, 112, 114, 115, 146, 157

Models: IMOI, stage: definition 17, 282; diagnosis of processes 237; inputs 256; mediators 18, 20, 110, 169, 258, 283, 285, 287, 289; model, team adaption process 169; outputs 110, 237, 256, 257; second 1, lessons learned 19, 20, 45, 169, 237, 256, 257, 282, 284; used for multilevel analysis 285

Mohammed, S. 115, 146

Mohd-Said, S. 85

INDEX

| 305

Monahan, E.L. 96
Moon, H. 174
morale 212
Morgan, B.B. 282
Morgeson, F.P. 49, 57, 63, 195, 203, 205, 284
motivation: definition 1, 10; determines
objectives 53; extrinsic 10; intrinsic 10, 58,
59, 60; misguided 38
Murray, J. 194
mutual performance monitoring: action
phase, feedback 287; in execution of
team tasks 291; key feature of effective
teamwork 20, 175, 257; model for
team adaption process 169; mutual
backup, support 80, 120–1; TB enhance
cooperation 129
Mykytyn, P.P. 157

Nahrgang, J.D. 63
negotiators 156
Newman, A. 116, 190
Nezu, A.M. 30
Nielsen, J.D. 204
Norton, Jr. W.I. 126

Oerlemans, L.A. 199
O'Neill, T.A. 145
Online Instruments, Data Collection, and
Electronic Measurements: Organizational
Advancements 207
Orenga, V. 154
Organ, D.W. 13
organizational: change and development
2, 12, 13, 30, 219, 232; communication
225; competence 33; context 14, 19,
140; culture and climate 172; decision
team goals 68; Dimensions of Learning
Organization Query (DLOQ) 237; goals/
develop culture 232; leadership 172;
learning (OL) 217–224, 223; objectives
16; outcomes 242, 265; Strategic Learning
Assessment Map (SLAM) 237; strategy/
structure 33, 48; TMMs 232
Organizational citizenship behaviours
(OCB) 13
organizational learning (OL): critical incidents,
motives for 224; definition 217; embed
into team learning 218; intellectual capital,
knowledge management 219; learning-
oriented culture 220; not linear process,
feed-forward, feedback 222, 223; team

structure affects 221; teamwork learning
leads to 225
organizational outcomes 12, 13
orientation: learning goal 171; performance
goal 171
Otte, K. 6

Paradis, K.F. 126, 130
Parchman, M. 123
Parker, S.K. 50, 172, 179
Passos, A. 178
Passos, A.M. 145
Patel, V.L. 172
Patrashkova-Volzdoska, R.R. 118
Patterson, M. 10
Paul, S. 157
Payne, S.C. 85
Pearsall, M.J. 85, 169, 171, 173, 178
Peiró, J.M. 114
performance: chain 13, 14; criteria 17; defined
16; feedback 97–98, 119; function of
group size 14; monitoring 120, 175; not
coordinated 110; psychological safety 116;
team adaptive 175; TMM's guide 113
performance chain 13, 14
persistence 11
personality: agreeableness, conscientiousness
81, 82, 100, 154; emotional stability 82,
170; extraversion, openness 82, 170
personnel selection 91, 112
Plamondon, K.E. 170
plan formulation: action phase IMOI model
257; BARS give feedback 183; STROTA
supports 182; team forms, adaptation
processes 176, 178, 181, 292
Ployhart, R. 170
Porter, C.O.L.H 174
preference for teamwork: collectivism 100;
definition 85
prerequisites 95
Prewett, M. 112
Prichard, J.S. 127
priority 35–36
problem solving: defined 30; employee
involvement 33; evidence based 30, 36;
mental barriers 37–38; process 32–33;
symptoms 35–36; top management 32
problem-solving circle (PSC) 24, 109;
systematic TDIs 253
problem solving cycle: involved members 32,
34, 45, 46

INDEX

process see building shared meaning:
collectivistic/cooperative 155; exploitation
224; IMOI 237; individualistic/competitive
155; innovation 13; interlinked 164;
learning 243; OL 218
Proctor, S. 10, 12, 13, 14
productivity 9, 12
pseudo-teams 3, **23**
psychological safety: affect learning processes
259; climate 235; correlation to conflicts
146, 149, 157; develop trust, team building
128, 141, 142; emergent state 111, 149,
150, 179, 180, 283; facilitate learning/
teamwork 111; important for team
reflexivity, routine 179; leadership handling
190; model for team adaptation process
169; one of the mediators of IMOI 150,
153; team, impacts performance, learning,
communication 116, 117, 120, **124**
Pulakos, E.D. 170
push and pull 221

quality management 2
quantitative change 123
questionnaire 180, 211, 237, 264;
Destructive Leader 206; diagnose
team 92; Group Development 123,
280; Group Environment 151, 154;
Leader Behaviour Description 199;
psychological safety assessed 116;
Team Leadership 207; Team Work
Competency Test (TWCT) 91; Work
Design Questionnaire (WDC) 68, 92
Quigley, N.R. 15

Raes, E. 278
Rahael, J. 112
Ramos-Villagrasa, P.J. 178
Rapp, T.L. 127
REBA 69
reflexivity: consensus of team 128; core of
meta routines 107; guided 183; process 6;
reflect, evaluate team 3; team climate 127;
trust for team 141
regulation: collective 3, 18, 53, 55, 61;
individual 53,
Reilly, G. 11
remediation 254, 255
requirement specification 251–274
retention 13
Reyes, D.L. 4, 113

Reynolds, R.A. 207
Ricciardi, R. 123
Richter, A.W. 10
Rittman, A.L. 190
Robbins, S.P. 143
Roberts, K.H. 83
role clarification 126
Rosen, M.A. 16, 168, 292
Rosenman, E.D. 210
routines: habitual 107; meta-routines 107

Saavedra, R. 11
safety, psychological: communication
openness 116–117; routine/non-routine
performance 179; task conflicts 146; team
performance 141; team reflexivity 179
Salas, E. 2, 14, 16, 111, 113, 117, 118, 125, 154,
169, 172, 211, 218, 252, 253, 256, 260, 267,
281, 292
Samarah, I. 161
Sander, P.C. 174
Schaefer, J. 123
Schippers, M.C. 6
Schmidt, F.L. 96
Schooler, C. 50
Schyns and Schilling (2013) 194
Scott, C.P.R. 111
second input 19, *20, 169*, 256, 282, 286–287
Seetharaman, P. 157
Segers, M. 119, 287
self-managerial 171
self-regulation 83
Shally, Gilson, and Blum (2009) 114
Shandro, J.R. 210
Shared Professional Leadership Inventory for
Teams (SPLIT) 207
Shaw, B. 194
Shen, W. 193
Shih, S. 146
Shipton, H 10
Shoemaker, S.J. 123
Shuffler, M.L. 125
Sims, D.E. 118, 171
Situational judgment test (SJTs) 96
situation assessment: current situation,
different perspectives 46; IMOI model,
team effectiveness 257; problem solving,
adaptation processes 176, 178, 181;
STROTA, feedback 182–183
skill differentiation 92
S.M.A.R.T. 70

INDEX | 307

Smith, M.L. 172
Smith, T.A. 202
social conformity 115
social loafing 14, 15, **15**, 120
Solimeo, S.L. 204
solutions: adaptability 181; brainstorm 156; criteria, TDIs 41, 272; domain **124**, **153, 208**, 258; domain interaction 40; implement change 259; for intervention 124; intra-team processes 124; leadership 208; organizational learning 239; problem solving 40, 41; problem solving process 32–33; team composition 94; team debriefs 43; work design 70
Sommerr, S.A. 5, 168, 172, 178
Sonesh, S.C. 267
Song, F. 121
stage models: focus on group processes 285; specific team needs 284; team compose and recompose 286
Stajkovic, A. 11
stakeholder: analysis 33; expectations 67–68; shared understanding 49
Steenfatt, C. 6
Stein, B.S. 32
Stevens, M.J. 147
Stewart, G.L. 63, 204
Strategic Learning Assessment Map (SLAM) 237
strategies: constructive controversy 156; preemptive 153–154; reactive 153, 155
stress 65
structured employment interview 96
Structured on-line team adaptation (STROTA) 182
Suarez, Y. 118
Sussman, L. 126
sustainability 271
Sutcliffe, K.A. 114
Sy, T. 11
synergies 77

Talati, Z. 210
Tannenbaum, S.I. 125, 218, 256
target dimensions: coordinated manner 123; description **261–263**; interventions 288; lack of leadership 208; little teamwork 69; organizational learning 239; problem solving 38; team composition 94
task: autonomy 58; complexity 61, 85; demands 16; identity, completeness 60;

initiative 55; interdependence 3, 63, 65, 66; interpersonal processes 5; interrelated 65; performance 57–58; routine/non-routine 49, 55–56, 59–60, 61, 67–68, 230; routinization 61; significance 59; skill variety, specialization 62; standardization 49; variety 59
TBS 69
team see team adaptation; team climate; team knowledge: charter 126–127; composition 17, 78–101, 79, **94–95**, 139, 171; context 19; definition 3; design 19; diagnosis 36; disengaged 237; effectiveness 16, 17, 20, 84, 143; efficacy 11; evaluation 123, 273; feedback 197; four characteristics of 3; goals 38–40, 56–57, 67–70; interactions 12; interdependence 115; interventions **261–263**; members 17, 19; momentum 291; multilevel system 282–283; persistence 11; personality 81, **82**; proactivity 12; processes 5, 16, 17, 124; resources 114; size 80, 89–90, 92, 97, 126; structure 90, 92; temporal stability 90, 93; training 98, 100, 127, 182; well performing 86
team adaptation: adaptability 84; analysis core predictors 180; causal analysis 168; effective teamwork 5; mindmap *170*; multi-level 18; performance process 163; problem solutions **181**; process model *169*; routines 107; team composition 171; team effectiveness 20–1, 291; trigger response 168
Team Building (TM): best outcomes 99; evaluate 265; goal setting 267; hire the right person 95–96, 99; interpersonal relations 128; interventions 266; relation with team cohesion 154; role clarification 267; shared understanding, goals 125; Team Charters (TC) 266; Team Task Analysis (TTA) 266; Team Work Design (TWD) 266; trust/psychological safety 128
team climate: affective integration 140; defined 114; develop 127; psychological safety 116
team cohesion: affect performance 9, 11; boundedness 4; develop mutual trust and 154; The Group Environment Questionnaire 151; key contributor, effectiveness 142; team viability 12, 142
team composition: build the right team 97–98; defined 79; faultlines 88; model,

effective teamwork 17; not effective 86; not team players 80; problems due to their 78–79, *80*, 90–91, 94, **94–95**; structure and task 90, 92; support problem teams 99; team size 92; well performing 86

team development: comparison of models 283–286; evaluation 289; feedback loop 286; Gersick model 281; IMOI model 282; interventions *290*; models 278–283; monitor 289; Morgan, Salas and Glickman 281; TEAM-model (Team Evolution and Maturation) 281; Tuckman's model 280; Wheelan's model 280; Worchel's model 281

Team Development Interventions (TDIs): CMO configuration **269**; context 254; criteria 272; defined 252, **261–263**; designing 270–272; effectiveness 265; effective timing 289; evaluation 273–274; four elements 255; GRADE evaluate 264; markers, monitor TDI's **293**; needs analysis 255; outcomes **269**; problem-solving circle 252; provide feedback 270; PSC steps used 255, 272; rationale 258; reflect, debrief 287; the "right" problem 255; team building 253, 260, 264, 266, 267; Team Charters (TC) 266; Team Coaching 267; team composition 271; team debriefs 267; Team Leadership (TL) 267; Team Performance Monitoring & Assessment (TTM) 267; Team Task Analysis (TTA) 266; Team Training (TT) 267; Team Work Design (TWD) 266; teamwork solutions 41; theory based vs off-the-shelf 255

Team Diagnostic Survey 92

team intervention *see* Team Development Intervention

team knowledge: cognition 178; emergent states 111; how to build 111–113; inaccurate 116; mediator 178; mental models 178; shared 115; transferring knowledge 236

Team Leadership Questionnaire 207

team learning: activities 235–237, 243; adaptability 177; boundary activities 246; bring about change 177; cross-boundary 236; Cross-functional learning 246; cycles 19; debriefs 43, 125, 129; FAQ 236; goal setting 69; impact 18–19; impacts change development 12; internal and external 234, 243; self-correction training 129; task

coordination 123; tools to facilitate 32–33; trust 141

Team-mental models (TMM): contribute to OL 231; four types 114; integrate new knowledge 179; organizational culture 232; set goals 241–242

team orientation: broader than collectivism 85; OL requires 218; TDI might involve 256

TeamStepps 128

team training 98, 100, 128–129, 182–183

team trust: affect team 18; build 5; climate not trustful 140–141; conflicts interrelated 149; develop and psychological safety 128; lack of 116–117; shared emergent state 141

team viability: definition 12; important for cooperation/continuation 142

teamwork: adaptable 6, 21, 57, 84; competencies 83; coordinated 4–6; core processes 17; defined 4; domains for OL **239**; higher performance 233; lack of coordinated performance *110*; little 48, 53, *54*; most common problems **22**; positive effects 14; set goals OL 240–242; shared objectives 4; social interaction 3, 9, 15, 17; as task work 21; team players 80

Team Work Competency Test (TWCT) 91

Teamwork Development Interventions *290*

team worker: feedback 60; personality traits 79–80, **82**; virtual 19, 112, 117, 137

teamwork outcomes: clear explicit 15; customer satisfaction 9; empirical research 12–13, 36, 38, 41; job satisfaction 9; negative 14–15; no consensus 53; organizational safety 9; reduction of costs 9; survey positive **7–8**

Tekleab, A.G. 157

temporal stability 90, 93

Tesler, R. 146

Tesluk, P.E. 15

theoretical analysis 36

Thompson, L.F. 154

Tichy, N.M. 200

Tindale, R.S. 119

Tjosvold, D. 148, 153, 156, 157

Top Management Team (TMT) 107–110, 112, 113

training: cross training 127–8; simulation 183

transactive memory 115, 127–128, 178–181

transitional phase: analysis 6; goal clarification 6; planning 6; routines affect 107; teams shift 5–6

INDEX

| 309

trust: building 5; climate not trustful 140–141; lack of 116–117; measure 150–151; not cooperative 116; shared emergent state 141; team knowledge builds 111
Tseng, H. 150
Tuckman, B.W. 280
turnover 7, 10

Ulich, E. 10

values: collectivist 88; "Deutsch's Twelve Commandments of Conflict Resolution" 147; motivational orientations 81, 85; organization 16
Van den Bossche, P. 119, 122, 177, 201, 278, 287
Van den Broeck, A. 49
Van der Klink, M. 201
Van Der Pal, J. 174
Van Doorn, R.R.A. 174
Van Hootegem, G. 10, 12, 13, 14
Vankipuram, M. 172
Van Rooy, D.L. 13
van Wijk, K.P. 256
van Wijngaarden, J.D.H. 256
Vera 69
Virtual Conflict Resolution System (VNS) 156
virtual teams: communication challenges 172; conflict 137; conflict management 154; less effective communication 112; temporary 142
Viswesvaran, C. 13
vocational development 244
Vollrath, D.A. 119
Volpe, C.E. 256

Wacker, J. 121, 175
Wagner, J.A. 120
Waldman, D.A. 204
Wang, D. 121, 204

Wang, J. 202
Wang, Y. 179
WDQ 69
Weaver, S.J. 260, 265, 266, 271, 272
Weber, M. 200
Weber, W.G. 10
Weick, K.E. 83
Weingart, L.R. 145
West, B. 174
West, M.A. 10, 122
Western Electric Company 9
Wheelan, S.A. 280, 284
Whetzel, D.L. 96
White, S. 170
Whitman, D.S. 13
Wildman, J.L. 111, 168, 192
Woods, S.A. 211
Worchel, S. 281, 284
work design: affects performance 50; autonomy 172; contextual features 57; diagnose 68; impacts individual/team 57; mindmap/team effectiveness 54; REBA 69
Work Design Questionnaire (WDQ) 92
workflow: shared meaning 122; throughout 219
work phases 5–6
work role 50, 230
Wu, A. 172

Yoon, D. 193
Youngcourt, S.S. 85
Yukl, G.A. 189

Zaccaro, S.J. 5, 121, 125, 129, 153, 190
Zala-Mezö, E. 121
Zhang, X. 148
Zhang, Z. 204
Zijlstra, F.R.H. 174
Zimmerman, R.D. 202
Zornoza, A. 154

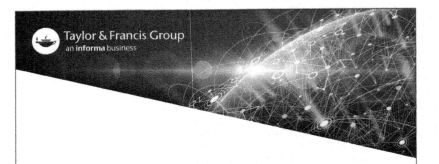